enVisionmath 2.0

SCOTT FORESMAN · ADDISON WESLEY

Volume 2 Topics 8–16

Authors

Randall I. Charles
Professor Emeritus
Department of Mathematics
San Jose State University
San Jose, California

Jennifer Bay-Williams
Professor of Mathematics
Education
College of Education and Human
Development
University of Louisville
Louisville, Kentucky

Robert Q. Berry, III
Associate Professor of
Mathematics Education
Department of Curriculum,
Instruction and Special Education
University of Virginia
Charlottesville, Virginia

Janet H. Caldwell
Professor of Mathematics
Rowan University
Glassboro, New Jersey

Zachary Champagne
Assistant in Research
Florida Center for Research in
Science, Technology, Engineering,
and Mathematics (FCR-STEM)
Jacksonville, Florida

Juanita Copley
Professor Emerita, College of
Education
University of Houston
Houston, Texas

Warren Crown
Professor Emeritus of Mathematics
Education
Graduate School of Education
Rutgers University
New Brunswick, New Jersey

Francis (Skip) Fennell
L. Stanley Bowlsbey Professor
of Education and Graduate and
Professional Studies
McDaniel College
Westminster, Maryland

Karen Karp
Professor of Mathematics
Education
Department of Early Childhood
and Elementary Education
University of Louisville
Louisville, Kentucky

Stuart J. Murphy
Visual Learning Specialist
Boston, Massachusetts

Jane F. Schielack
Professor of Mathematics
Associate Dean for Assessment
and Pre K-12 Education,
College of Science
Texas A&M University
College Station, Texas

Jennifer M. Suh
Associate Professor for
Mathematics Education
George Mason University
Fairfax, Virginia

Jonathan A. Wray
Mathematics Instructional
Facilitator
Howard County Public Schools
Ellicott City, Maryland

PEARSON

Glenview, Illinois   Boston, Massachusetts   Chandler, Arizona   Hoboken, New Jersey

Mathematicians

Roger Howe
Professor of Mathematics
Yale University
New Haven, Connecticut

Gary Lippman
Professor of Mathematics
and Computer Science
California State University,
East Bay
Hayward, California

ELL Consultants

Janice R. Corona
Independent Education
Consultant
Dallas, Texas

Jim Cummins
Professor
The University of Toronto
Toronto, Canada

Reviewers

Debbie Crisco
Math Coach
Beebe Public Schools
Beebe, Arkansas

Kathleen A. Cuff
Teacher
Kings Park Central School District
Kings Park, New York

Erika Doyle
Math and Science Coordinator
Richland School District
Richland, Washington

Susan Jarvis
Math and Science Curriculum
Coordinator
Ocean Springs Schools
Ocean Springs, Mississippi

ISBN-13:   978-0-328-88716-3
ISBN-10:   0-328-88716-1

PEARSON

8 18

Digital Resources

You'll be using these digital resources throughout the year!

Go to PearsonRealize.com

 MP
Math Practices Animations to play anytime

 Learn
Visual Learning Animation **Plus** with animation, interaction, and math tools

 Practice Buddy
Online Personalized Practice for each lesson

Assessment
Quick Check for each lesson

Games
Math Games to help you learn

ACTIVe-book
Student Edition online for showing your work

 Solve
Solve & Share problems plus math tools

 Glossary
Animated Glossary in English and Spanish

 Tools
Math Tools to help you understand

 Help
Another Look Homework Video for extra help

 eText
Student Edition online

 **realize** Everything you need for math anytime, anywhere

KEY

- Operations and Algebra
- Numbers and Computation
- Measurement and Data
- Geometry

Digital Resources at PearsonRealize.com

And remember your eText is available at PearsonRealize.com!

Contents

TOPICS

TOPIC 8 Use Strategies and Properties to Add and Subtract

Properties, such as the Commutative Property, can help you to add and subtract.

$$57 + 35 = 35 + 57$$

TOPIC 9 Fluently Add and Subtract within 1,000

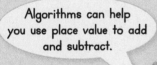

Algorithms can help you use place value to add and subtract.

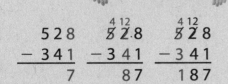

$$\begin{array}{r} 5\,2\,8 \\ -\ 3\,4\,1 \\ \hline 7 \end{array} \qquad \begin{array}{r} {}^{4\ 12}\\ \cancel{5}\,\cancel{2}\,8 \\ -\ 3\,4\,1 \\ \hline 8\,7 \end{array} \qquad \begin{array}{r} {}^{4\ 12}\\ \cancel{5}\,\cancel{2}\,8 \\ -\ 3\,4\,1 \\ \hline 1\,8\,7 \end{array}$$

TOPIC 10 Multiply by Multiples of 10

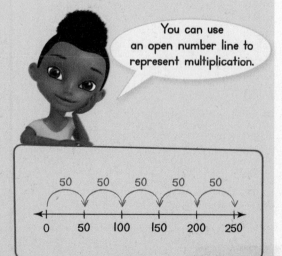

You can use an open number line to represent multiplication.

TOPIC 11 Use Operations with Whole Numbers to Solve Problems

You can use unknowns and bar diagrams to represent steps of a problem.

g = cost of GPS system for the week

g						
$9	$9	$9	$9	$9	$9	$9

c = cost of the car without the GPS

$325	
c	$63

TOPIC 12 Understand Fractions as Numbers

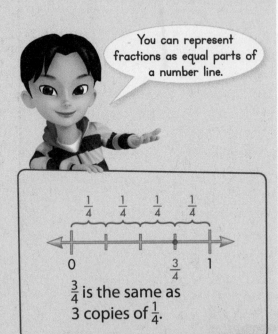

You can represent fractions as equal parts of a number line.

$\frac{3}{4}$ is the same as 3 copies of $\frac{1}{4}$.

TOPIC 13 Fraction Equivalence and Comparison

You can use fraction strips to compare fractions.

$$\frac{5}{8} < \frac{5}{6}$$

TOPIC 14 Solve Time, Capacity, and Mass Problems

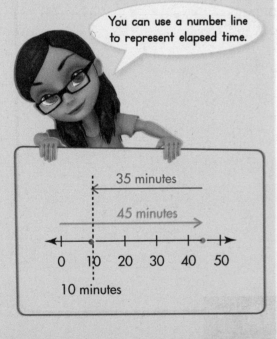

You can use a number line to represent elapsed time.

35 minutes

45 minutes

10 minutes

TOPIC 15 Attributes of Two-Dimensional Shapes

A quadrilateral is a polygon with four sides. These are different quadrilaterals.

Trapezoid   Square   Parallelogram

Rhombus   Rectangle

TOPIC 16 Solve Perimeter Problems

You can find the perimeter of a shape by adding the lengths of its sides.

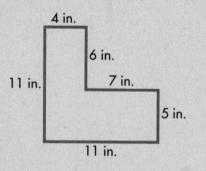

$4 + 6 + 7 + 5 + 11 + 11 = 44$

The perimeter of the figure is 44 inches.

© Pearson Education, Inc. 3

STEP UP to Grade 4

These lessons help prepare you for Grade 4.

Problem Solving Handbook

Math Practices

1. **Make sense of problems and persevere in solving them.**

2. **Reason abstractly and quantitatively.**

3. **Construct viable arguments and critique the reasoning of others.**

4. **Model with mathematics.**

5. **Use appropriate tools strategically.**

6. **Attend to precision.**

7. **Look for and make use of structure.**

8. **Look for and express regularity in repeated reasoning.**

There are good Thinking Habits for each of these math practices.

1 Make sense of problems and persevere in solving them.

Good math thinkers make sense of problems and think of ways to solve them.

If they get stuck, they don't give up.

Mia has $36. Kate has $17 less than Mia. Do Mia and Kate together have enough money to buy a bike for $54?

Here I listed what I know and what I am trying to find.

What I know:
- Mia has $36.
- Kate has $17 less than $36.
- The bike costs $54.

What I need to find:
- Whether Kate and Mia have at least $54 in all.

Thinking Habits

Be a good thinker! These questions can help you.

- What do I need to find?
- What do I know?
- What's my plan for solving the problem?
- What else can I try if I get stuck?
- How can I check that my solution makes sense?

2 Reason abstractly and quantitatively.

Good math thinkers know how to think about words and numbers to solve problems.

I drew a bar diagram that shows how things in the problem are related.

Jake bought a coat for $47. He also bought a shirt. Jake spent $71 in all. How much did he spend on the shirt?

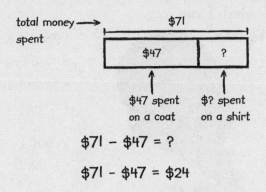

total money spent → $71

| $47 | ? |

↑ $47 spent on a coat   ↑ $? spent on a shirt

$71 – $47 = ?

$71 – $47 = $24

Thinking Habits

Be a good thinker! These questions can help you.

- What do the numbers and symbols in the problem mean?

- How are the numbers or quantities related?

- How can I represent a word problem using pictures, numbers, or equations?

3 Construct viable arguments and critique the reasoning of others.

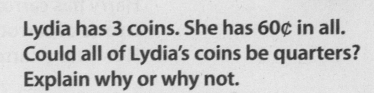

Good math thinkers use math to explain why they are right. They can talk about the math that others do, too.

I wrote a clear argument with words, numbers, and symbols.

Lydia has 3 coins. She has 60¢ in all. Could all of Lydia's coins be quarters? Explain why or why not.

Marta's Work

Lydia's coins cannot all be quarters.

1 quarter is 25¢.

3 quarters is 25¢, 50¢, 75¢.

75¢ > 60¢

So, 3 quarters is more money than Lydia actually has.

Thinking Habits

Be a good thinker! These questions can help you.

- How can I use numbers, objects, drawings, or actions to justify my argument?

- Am I using numbers and symbols correctly?

- Is my explanation clear and complete?

- What questions can I ask to understand other people's thinking?

- Are there mistakes in other people's thinking?

- Can I improve other people's thinking?

4 Model with mathematics.

Good math thinkers choose and apply math they know to show and solve problems from everyday life.

Harry has carrots in his garden. Harry has 5 rows of carrots with 4 carrots in each row. How many carrots are in Harry's garden?

I used what I know about arrays and addition. I drew a picture to help.

$$4 + 4 + 4 + 4 + 4 = 20$$

There are 20 carrots in Harry's garden.

Thinking Habits

Be a good thinker! These questions can help you.

- How can I use math I know to help solve this problem?

- How can I use pictures, objects, or an equation to represent the problem?

- How can I use numbers, words, and symbols to solve the problem?

5 Use appropriate tools strategically.

Good math thinkers know how to pick the right tools to solve math problems.

I decided to use place-value blocks to help me compare. I can use them to show the hundreds, the tens, and the ones.

Carla has 234 stickers. Dan has 242 stickers. Who has more stickers?

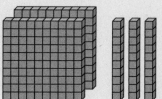 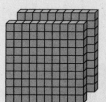 

242 is greater than 234.
Dan has more stickers.

Thinking Habits

Be a good thinker! These questions can help you.

- Which tools can I use?

- Why should I use this tool to help me solve the problem?

- Is there a different tool I could use?

- Am I using the tool appropriately?

Attend to precision.

Good math thinkers are careful about what they write and say, so their ideas about math are clear.

I was precise with my measurements and the way that I wrote my solution.

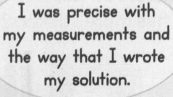

Which of these two paths is longer? How much longer?

Blue path: 3 cm + 3 cm = 6 cm
Yellow path: 4 cm + 1 cm = 5 cm
6 cm – 5 cm = 1 cm
The *blue* path is 1 cm longer than the yellow path.

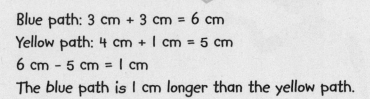

Thinking Habits

Be a good thinker! These questions can help you.

- Am I using numbers, units, and symbols appropriately?

- Am I using the correct definitions?

- Am I calculating accurately?

- Is my answer clear?

7 Look for and make use of structure.

Good math thinkers look for patterns or relationships in math to help solve problems.

A store has 123 apples. 67 apples are sold. How many apples does the store have left?

123 − 67 = ?

I know 67 = 60 + 7.
123 − 60 = 63
63 − 7 = 56

So, 123 − 67 = 56.
The store has 56 apples left.

I broke apart 67 to solve 123 − 67.

Thinking Habits

Be a good thinker! These questions can help you.

- What patterns can I see and describe?

- How can I use the patterns to solve the problem?

- Can I see expressions and objects in different ways?

8 Look for and express regularity in repeated reasoning.

Good math thinkers look for things that repeat, and they make generalizations.

I used reasoning to generalize about calculations.

Find the sum for each of these addends.

$185 + 100 = ?$

$? = 292 + 100$

$100 + 321 = ?$

Daniel's Work

185 + 100 = 285

392 = 292 + 100

100 + 321 = 421

100 is added in each problem.

Adding 100 makes the hundreds digit go up by 1.

Thinking Habits

Be a good thinker! These questions can help you.

- Are any calculations repeated?

- Can I generalize from examples?

- What shortcuts do I notice?

Problem Solving Guide

These questions can help you solve problems.

Make Sense of the Problem

Reason Abstractly and Quantitatively

- What do I need to find?
- What given information can I use?
- How are the quantities related?

Think About Similar Problems

- Have I solved problems like this before?

Persevere in Solving the Problem

Model with Math

- How can I use the math I know?
- How can I represent the problem?
- Is there a pattern or structure I can use?

Use Appropriate Tools Strategically

- What math tools could I use?
- How can I use those tools strategically?

Check the Answer

Make Sense of the Answer

- Is my answer reasonable?

Check for Precision

- Did I check my work?
- Is my answer clear?
- Did I construct a viable argument?
- Did I generalize correctly?

Some Ways to Represent Problems

- Draw a Picture
- Make a Bar Diagram
- Make a Table or Graph
- Write an Equation

Some Math Tools

- Objects
- Grid Paper
- Rulers
- Technology
- Paper and Pencil

Problem Solving Recording Sheet

This sheet helps you organize your work.

Name **Carlos**

Teaching Tool
1

Problem Solving Recording Sheet

Problem:
Cory wants to buy a video game that costs $60. He has $48 saved. On Monday he used part of his savings to buy a shirt for $15. How much more money does Cory need to save to buy the video game?

MAKE SENSE OF THE PROBLEM

Need to Find

Money needed to buy video game

Given

Video game costs $60
Saved $48
Used $15 of savings

PERSEVERE IN SOLVING THE PROBLEM

Some Ways to Represent Problems

- ☐ Draw a Picture
- ☑ Make a Bar Diagram
- ☐ Make a Table or Graph
- ☐ Write an Equation

Some Math Tools

- ☐ Objects
- ☐ Grid Paper
- ☐ Rulers
- ☐ Technology
- ☑ Paper and Pencil

Solution and Answer

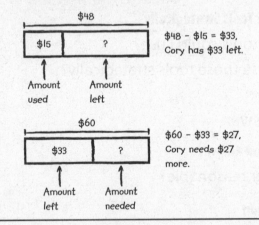

$48 − $15 = $33,
Cory has $33 left.

$60 − $33 = $27,
Cory needs $27 more.

CHECK THE ANSWER

Estimate
50 − 20 = 30   60 − 30 = 30
Check
33 + 15 = 48   27 + 33 = 60

My answer is reasonable and makes sense.
My answer is correct.

T1

Bar Diagrams

You can draw a **bar diagram** to show how the quantities in a problem are related. Then you can write an equation to solve the problem.

Add To

Draw this **bar diagram** for situations that involve *adding* to a quantity.

Result →

	82	
15	67	

↑ Start   ↑ Change

Result Unknown

Greg bought a baseball and a baseball glove. How much did he pay for both?

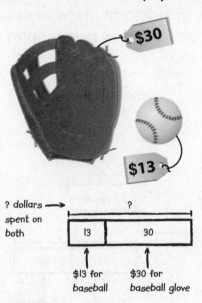

$30

$13

? dollars spent on both →

?	
13	30

↑ $13 for baseball   ↑ $30 for baseball glove

$13 + 30 = ?$

Greg spent $43 on both.

Start Unknown

Robin had some rings. Her sister gave her the rings shown below. After that, Robin had 90 rings. How many rings did Robin start with?

90 rings →

90	
?	34

↑ ? rings to start   ↑ 34 rings added

$? + 34 = 90$

Robin started with 56 rings.

Bar Diagrams

You can use bar diagrams to make sense of addition and subtraction problems.

Take From

Draw this **bar diagram** for situations that involve *taking* from a quantity.

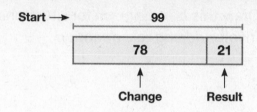

Start → 99

78 21

Change Result

Result Unknown

Maurice had 78 e-mails. He deleted 49 of them. How many e-mails did Maurice keep?

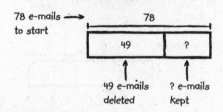

78 e-mails → 78
to start

49 ?

49 e-mails   ? e-mails
deleted   kept

$78 - 49 = ?$

Maurice kept 29 e-mails.

Start Unknown

Layla picked some apples at an orchard. She gave the apples below to her grandmother. Now Layla has 29 apples left. How many apples did Layla pick?

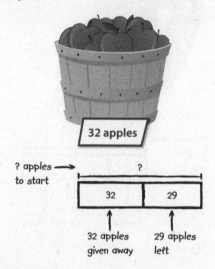

32 apples

? apples → ?
to start

32 29

32 apples   29 apples
given away   left

$? - 32 = 29$

Layla had 61 apples before she gave some to her grandmother.

The **bar diagrams** on this page can help you make sense of more addition and subtraction situations.

Put Together/Take Apart

Draw this **bar diagram** for situations that involve *putting together* or *taking apart* quantities.

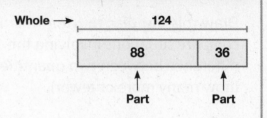

Whole → 124

| 88 | 36 |

↑ Part   ↑ Part

Whole Unknown

The bar graph shows how far Lana drove her car for 3 days. How many total miles did she drive?

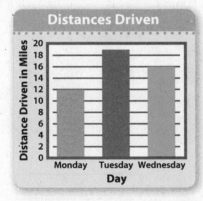

Distances Driven

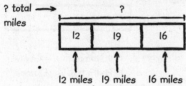

? total miles →   ?

| 12 | 19 | 16 |

↑ 12 miles ↑ 19 miles ↑ 16 miles

$12 + 19 + 16 = ?$

Lana drove a total of 47 miles.

Part Unknown

Pier school collected a total of 46 toys during two weeks of a toy drive for charity. How many toys were collected during the second week?

28 toys collected first week

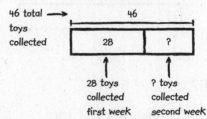

46 total toys collected →   46

| 28 | ? |

↑ 28 toys collected first week   ↑ ? toys collected second week

$28 + ? = 46$ or $46 - 28 = ?$

Pier school collected 18 toys during the second week.

Bar Diagrams

Pictures help you understand a problem.

Compare: Addition and Subtraction

Draw this **bar diagram** for *compare* situations involving the difference between two quantities (how many more or fewer).

Bigger quantity →

96

37	59

↑ Smaller quantity   ↑ Difference

Difference Unknown

The larger dog weighs 82 pounds. The smaller dog weighs 6 pounds. How many more pounds does the larger dog weigh?

82 pounds →

82

6	?

6 pounds   ? more pounds

$6 + ? = 82$ or $82 - 6 = ?$

The larger dog weighs 76 more pounds.

Smaller Unknown

Tim has 12 more postage stamps than Pedro. Tim has 30 postage stamps. How many postage stamps does Pedro have?

30 stamps Tim has →

30

?	12

? stamps Pedro has   12 more stamps

$30 - 12 = ?$ or $? + 12 = 30$

Pedro has 18 postage stamps.

The **bar diagrams** on this page can help you solve problems involving multiplication and division.

Equal Groups: Multiplication and Division

Draw this **bar diagram** for situations that involve *equal groups*.

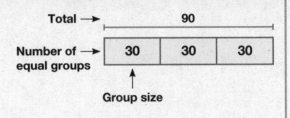

Number of Groups Unknown

Josie spent $40 on tickets to a movie for herself and some friends on Saturday. How many tickets did Josie buy?

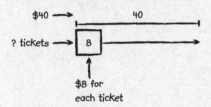

$? \times 8 = 40$ or $40 \div 8 = ?$

Josie bought 5 tickets.

Group Size Unknown

Marie placed an equal number of marbles in each bag below. She has 36 total marbles. How many marbles did Marie place in each bag?

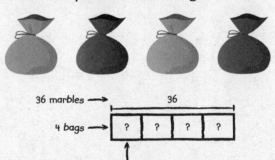

$4 \times ? = 36$ or $36 \div 4 = ?$

Marie placed 9 marbles in each bag.

TOPIC 8

Use Strategies and Properties to Add and Subtract

Essential Question: How can sums and differences be estimated and found mentally?

The fur of an arctic fox changes color during the year.

In the winter an arctic fox has white fur. During the summer it can have gray or brown fur.

Where something lives can affect its traits. Here's a project on plant and animal traits and the environment.

Math and Science Project: Traits and the Environment

Do Research Use the Internet or other sources to find out about how the environment can influence plants or animals. Describe a trait in an animal or plant that can change due to the environment.

Journal: Write a Report Include what you found. Also in your report:

- Make a table that includes the plant or animal, the trait, and changes in the environment. Record any related data about the environment, such as temperature or rainfall.

- Include information about why the trait is useful.

- Write and solve addition problems using your data. Use estimation to check for reasonableness.

Name _____

Review What You Know

A-Z Vocabulary

Choose the best term from the box.
Write it on the blank.

• number line   • difference
• equation   • sum

1. The amount that is left after you subtract is the _____.

2. A line that shows numbers in order from left to right is a(n) _____.

3. The total when you add is the _____.

4. Both sides of a(n) _____ are equal.

Addition and Subtraction Strategies

Find the sum or difference. Show your work.

5. $32 + 58$

6. $27 + 46$

7. $73 - 52$

8. $63 + 16$

9. $88 - 28$

10. $76 - 49$

Numerical Expressions

11. Atif puts 45 rocks in a display box. He has 54 rocks in all. Which expression can be used to find how many rocks are not in the display box?

    Ⓐ $45 + 54$ Ⓑ $45 + 45$ Ⓒ $54 - 45$ Ⓓ $54 - 54$

Counting Money

12. Tony has the coins shown at the right. Does he have enough money to buy a toy car that costs 86¢? Explain.

My Word Cards   Use the examples for each word on the front of the card to help complete the definitions on the back.

A-Z Glossary

Commutative (Order) Property of Addition

34 + 52 = 86
52 + 34 = 86

Identity (Zero) Property of Addition

29 + 0 = 29
35 + 0 = 35
63 + 0 = 63

Associative (Grouping) Property of Addition

(4 + 3) + 8 = 15
4 + (3 + 8) = 15
(4 + 3) + 8 = 4 + (3 + 8)

round

42 rounded to the nearest 10 is 40.

42

40   45   50

compatible numbers

255 ⟶ 250
+ 298 ⟶ 300
        550

inverse operations

addition	subtraction
14 + 12 = 26 ⟷	26 − 12 = 14
multiplication	division
8 × 9 = 72 ⟷	72 ÷ 9 = 8

place value

946
↑
hundreds

My Word Cards

Complete each definition. Extend learning by writing your own definitions.

The _____ _____ states that the sum of any number and zero is that same number.

Numbers can be added in any order and the sum remains the same because of the _____ _____.

When you _____, you can use the multiple of ten or hundred that is nearest to a number.

Addends can be regrouped and the sum remains the same because of the _____ _____.

Two operations that undo each other are called _____ _____.

Numbers that are easy to add, subtract, multiply, or divide mentally are called _____.

_____ is the value given to a place a digit has in a number.

Name _____

Solve & Share

Olivia has cups of buttons. On each cup she writes how many buttons are inside. Does Olivia have more buttons in the 3 cups on the left or in the 3 cups on the right? Explain your answer.

I can ...
use properties to understand addition.

I can also generalize from examples.

Are you making the same calculations more than once? What can you generalize?

18   24   26   18   26   24

$18 + 24 + 36 = 68$ $18 + 26 + 24 = 68$

$18 + 24 + 2$

Look Back! **Use Structure** What is different about the numbers on the left cups and the numbers on the right cups?

Essential Question · What Are Some Properties of Addition?

A

You can use properties of addition to join groups.

Parentheses show what to do first.

Associative (Grouping) Property of Addition: You can group addends in any way and the sum will be the same.

$$(18 + 14) + 15 = 47$$

$$18 + (14 + 15) = 47$$

$$(18 + 14) + 15 = 18 + (14 + 15)$$

B **Commutative (Order) Property of Addition:** You can add numbers in any order and the sum will be the same.

$$57 + 35 = 35 + 57$$

C **Identity (Zero) Property of Addition:** The sum of zero and any number is that same number.

$$39 + 0 = 39$$

Convince Me! **Use Structure** Pick one of the properties above. Explain how you can use a number line to show an example of that property.

☆ Guided Practice ☆

Practice Buddy   Tools   Assessment

Do You Understand?

1. Ralph says he can rewrite $(4 + 5) + 21$ as $9 + 21$. Do you agree? Why or why not?

2. What property is shown with this equation? How do you know?

$$65 + (18 + 38) = (18 + 38) + 65$$

Do You Know How?

In **3** and **4**, identify each property.

3. $4 + (15 + 26) = (4 + 15) + 26$

4. $17 + 0 = 17$

In **5–7**, write each missing number.

5. ____ $+ 90 = 90$

6. $42 + 23 = 23 +$ ____

7. $(2 +$ ____ $) + 36 = 2 + (23 + 36)$

☆ Independent Practice ☆

In **8–11**, identify each property.

8. $19 + 13 = 13 + 19$

9. $18 + 0 = 18$

10. $16 + (14 + 13) = (16 + 14) + 13$

11. $(39 + 12) + 8 = (12 + 39) + 8$

In **12–19**, write each missing number.

12. $25 + 62 =$ ____ $+ 25$

13. $(22 + 32) + 25 =$ ____ $+ (22 + 32)$

14. $23 +$ ____ $+ 11 = 23 + 11$

15. $10 + (45 + 13) = ($ ____ $+ 45) + 13$

16. $($ ____ $+ 0) + 14 = 7 + 14$

17. $(12 + 2) + 20 =$ ____ $+ 20$

18. $34 + (2 + 28) = ($ ____ $+ 28) + 34$

19. $(50 + 30) +$ ____ $= 50 + (30 + 20)$

Problem Solving

20. Make Sense and Persevere Gino packs his blue and green pencils into boxes. He puts 8 pencils in each box. How many boxes does Gino use?

Color	Number of Pencils
Red	14
Blue	23
Green	17

21. Use Structure Group the addends below in a different way to get the same sum. Write the new equation.

$(42 + 14) + 6 = 62$

22. **A-Z Vocabulary** How is the Commutative Property of Addition like the Commutative Property of Multiplication?

23. Math and Science A lionfish has 13 spines on its back, 2 near the middle of its underside, and 3 on its underside near its tail. Using a property of addition, write two different equations to find how many spines a lionfish has. What property did you use?

24. Higher Order Thinking Barry says he can subtract numbers in any order and the difference will stay the same. Is Barry correct? Give an example to support your answer.

Assessment

25. On Monday, a vegetable stand sold 12 cucumbers, 15 pumpkins, and 23 squash. On Tuesday, it sold 17 cucumbers, 25 pumpkins, and 13 squash. Complete the bar graph and use properties to show how many vegetables were sold on each day.

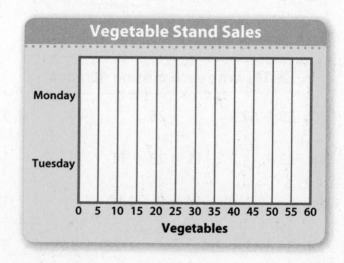

Vegetable Stand Sales

Name _____

Homework & Practice 8-1
Addition Properties

Another Look!

Commutative (Order) Property of Addition
You can add numbers in any order and the sum will be the same.

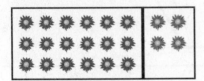

$$18 + 4 = 22$$

$$4 + 18 = 22$$

Associative (Grouping) Property of Addition
You can group numbers in any way and the sum will be the same.

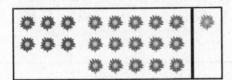

$$(6 + 15) + 1 = 22$$

$$6 + (15 + 1) = 22$$

Identity (Zero) Property of Addition
The sum of any number and zero equals that same number.

$$0 + 14 = 14$$

Addition properties make it easier to add numbers.

In **1–7**, write each missing number.

1.

(____ + 15) + ____ = 29

____ + (____ + ____) = ____

2. $30 + 40 = 40 +$ ____

3. ____ $+ 32 = 32$

4. $(48 + 27) + 3 =$ ____ $+ (27 + 3)$

5. $29 + (22 + 27) = (29 + 22) +$ ____

6. $89 +$ ____ $= 89$

7. $35 + 49 =$ ____ $+ 35$

8. Construct Arguments Jake says adding 0 to an addend does not change a sum. Is he correct? Explain. Include an equation in your explanation.

9. Draw lines onto the hexagon below to show how you can cut it into new shapes. What are the shapes you made?

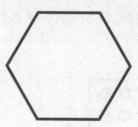

10. Use Structure Troy wants to buy pants, shoes, and a cap. Use the Associative Property of Addition to show two ways he can add the prices to find the total cost. Then find the total.

DATA	Clothing Sale	
	Pants	$35
	Cap	$15
	Shoes	$49

11. Higher Order Thinking Does $65 - (45 - 20) = (65 - 45) - 20$? How do you know?

12. Model with Math Minnie has 16 old posters and 25 new posters. Amanda has 25 old posters and 16 new posters. Who has more posters? Explain.

✓ **Assessment**

13. Evan has 23 basketball cards, 37 football cards, and 10 hockey cards. Alan has 8 basketball cards, 14 football cards, and 38 hockey cards. Complete the bar graph and use properties to show how many total sports cards each person has.

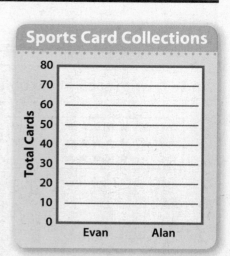

Sports Card Collections

Total Cards: 0, 10, 20, 30, 40, 50, 60, 70, 80

Evan   Alan

Name _____

Solve & Share

Shade 3 sums that are next to each other on the addition table. Add the first and third sums you shaded. How is the total you get related to the second sum you shaded? Is this true for other sums?

I can ...
find and explain addition patterns.

I can also look for patterns to solve problems.

+	0	1	2	3	4	5	6	7	8	9
0	0	1	2	3	4	5	6	7	8	9
1	1	2	3	4	5	6	7	8	9	10
2	2	3	4	5	6	7	8	9	10	11
3	3	4	5	6	7	8	9	10	11	12
4	4	5	6	7	8	9	10	11	12	13
5	5	6	7	8	9	10	11	12	13	14
6	6	7	8	9	10	11	12	13	14	15
7	7	8	9	10	11	12	13	14	15	16
8	8	9	10	11	12	13	14	15	16	17
9	9	10	11	12	13	14	15	16	17	18

← These are addends.

These are addends.

These are sums.

You can look for relationships in the addition table. The numbers in the shaded column and shaded row are addends. The other numbers are the sums.

Look Back! **Generalize** Explain what you did to test if the relationship is always true.

Essential Question **How Can You Find Addition Patterns?**

A

Helen notices a pattern in the addition table. The sums change between even and odd as she reads across a row or down a column. Explain this pattern.

+	0	1	2	3	4	5	6	7	8	9
0	0	1	2	3	4	5	6	7	8	9
1	1	2	3	4	5	6	7	8	9	10
2	2	3	4	5	6	7	8	9	10	11
3	3	4	5	6	7	8	9	10	11	12
4	4	5	6	7	8	9	10	11	12	13
5	5	6	7	8	9	10	11	12	13	14
6	6	7	8	9	10	11	12	13	14	15
7	7	8	9	10	11	12	13	14	15	16
8	8	9	10	11	12	13	14	15	16	17
9	9	10	11	12	13	14	15	16	17	18

Remember, an even number can be shown as two equal groups, so it can be written as a double. An odd number cannot be shown as two equal groups.

B Think about even and odd numbers.

An even number of things can be paired.

When you add 1 to an even number, you get an odd number.

When you add 1 to an odd number, you get an even number.

As 1 more is added to each sum on the addition table, the sums change between even and odd.

C You can use the Associative Property of Addition to explain.

+	4	5	6
4	8	9	10
5	9	10	11
6	10	11	12

As you read across or down in the addition table, 1 more is added to the sum each time.

For example, 4 + 5 is 1 more than 4 + 4.

$(4 + 4) + 1 = 4 + (4 + 1)$
$= 4 + 5$

Convince Me! **Generalize** Sebastian said that an even number plus an even number is always even. Is Sebastian's pattern always true? Explain.

Name _____

☆ Guided Practice*

Do You Understand?

1. **Generalize** Is the sum of two odd numbers odd or even? Explain why the pattern is always true.

Do You Know How?

2. Look at the addition table in Box A on page 412. What pattern do you see in the highlighted sums? Explain.

☆ Independent Practice ☆

In **3** and **4**, use the table at the right.

3. Look at the sums that are shaded the same color. Describe a pattern shown by these sums. Explain why this pattern is true.

+	2	3	4	5	6	7	8	9
2	4	5	6	7	8	9	10	11
3	5	6	7	8	9	10	11	12
4	6	7	8	9	10	11	12	13
5	7	8	9	10	11	12	13	14
6	8	9	10	11	12	13	14	15
7	9	10	11	12	13	14	15	16
8	10	11	12	13	14	15	16	17
9	11	12	13	14	15	16	17	18

4. Find other sums with a similar pattern. Shade them on the table. Explain why you chose those sums.

In **5** and **6**, use the table at the right.

5. Shade the table to show a pattern you see. Describe your pattern.

+	0	1	2	3	4	5	6	7
4	4	5	6	7	8	9	10	11
5	5	6	7	8	9	10	11	12
6	6	7	8	9	10	11	12	13
7	7	8	9	10	11	12	13	14
8	8	9	10	11	12	13	14	15
9	9	10	11	12	13	14	15	16

6. Explain why your pattern is true.

Problem Solving

7. **Look for Relationships** Greg drew a rectangle on the addition table at the right. He colored the corners. Find the sum of the green corners. Find the sum of the orange corners. What pattern do you notice?

+	3	4	5	6	7
1	4	5	6	7	8
2	5	6	7	8	9
3	6	7	8	9	10
4	7	8	9	10	11
5	8	9	10	11	12

8. **Generalize** Draw another rectangle on the addition table. See if Greg's pattern is true for this rectangle.

9. Explain why Greg's pattern works.

10. Which multiplication fact does the number line show? Write a related division fact.

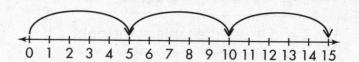

0 1 2 3 4 5 6 7 8 9 10 11 12 13 14 15

11. **Higher Order Thinking** Pierre made an addition table using only even addends. Write a pattern that you found in another problem. Does that pattern work for Pierre's table? Find an example. Explain why it does or does not work.

+	2	4	6	8	10	12	14
2	4	6	8	10	12	14	16
4	6	8	10	12	14	16	18
6	8	10	12	14	16	18	20
8	10	12	14	16	18	20	22
10	12	14	16	18	20	22	24
12	14	16	18	20	22	24	26
14	16	18	20	22	24	26	28

✓ Assessment

12. Look at the row shaded in green.

+	5	6	7	8	9
0	5	6	7	8	9
1	6	7	8	9	10
2	7	8	9	10	11
3	8	9	10	11	12
4	9	10	11	12	13

Part A

What pattern do you notice?

Part B

Explain why the pattern works.

Name _____

☆ ☆
Solve & Share

Think about ways to find numbers that tell *about* how much or *about* how many. Derek has 277 stickers. What number can you use to describe *about how many* stickers Derek has? Explain how you decided.

I can ...
use place value and a number line to round numbers.

I can also be precise in my work.

280 because it said "what number can you use to descibe aboct how many stickers" so, I thoth 280.

Think about how precise you need to be.

Look Back! **Make Sense and Persevere** Can you use another number to tell about how many stickers Derek has? Explain.

A

About how many rocks does Tito have? Round 394 to the nearest ten.

When you round to the nearest ten, you are finding the closest multiple of ten for a given number.

Place value is the value of the place a digit has in a number. Think about the place value of the digits in 394.

Donna 350 rocks

Carl 345 rocks

Tito 394 rocks

B You can use place-value understanding and a number line to round to the nearest ten.

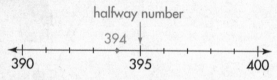

halfway number

394

390   395   400

394 is closer to 390 than 400, so 394 rounds to 390.

Tito has about 390 rocks.

C About how many rocks does Donna have? Round 350 to the nearest hundred.

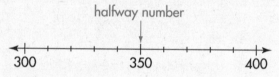

halfway number

300   350   400

If a number is halfway between, round to the greater number.

350 is halfway between 300 and 400, so 350 rounds to 400.

Donna has about 400 rocks.

Convince Me! **Make Sense and Persevere** Susan says, "I am thinking of a number that has a four in the hundreds place and a two in the ones place. When you round it to the nearest hundred, it is 500."

What number could Susan be thinking of? What else could be Susan's number?

Name _____

Another Example

Round 345 to the nearest ten and the nearest hundred.

- Find the digit in the rounding place.
- Look at the next digit to the right. If it is 5 or greater, add 1 to the rounding digit. If it is less than 5, leave the rounding digit alone.
- Change all the digits to the right of the rounding place to 0.

tens place   hundreds place

345   **345**
↓↓↓   ↓↓↓
350   **300**

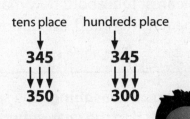

You can use place value to round numbers.

☆ Guided Practice*

Do You Understand?

1. What number is halfway between 200 and 300?

2. Sheri rounds 678 to 680. What place does she round to?

3. Tito adds one more rock to his collection on page 418. About how many rocks does he have, rounded to the nearest ten? Rounded to the nearest hundred? Explain.

Do You Know How?

In **4–6**, round to the nearest ten.

4.
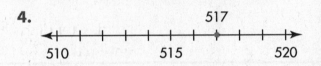
517

510   515   520

5. 149   6. 732

In **7–9**, round to the nearest hundred.

7.
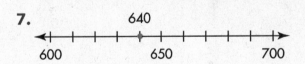
640

600   650   700

8. 305   9. 166

☆ Independent Practice ☆

In **10–12**, round to the nearest ten.

10. 88   11. 531   12. 855

In **13–15**, round to the nearest hundred.

13. 428   14. 699   15. 750

Problem Solving

16. The Leaning Tower of Pisa in Italy has 294 steps. To the nearest ten, about how many steps are there? To the nearest hundred, about how many steps are there?

17. Critique Reasoning Zoe says 247 rounded to the nearest hundred is 300 because 247 rounds to 250 and 250 rounds to 300. Is Zoe correct? Explain.

18. Use the number line to show a number that rounds to 200 when it is rounded to the nearest ten.

⟵─────────────────────⟶

19. Name the least number of coins you can use to show $0.47. What are the coins?

20. Suppose you are rounding to the nearest hundred. What is the greatest number that rounds to 600? What is the least number that rounds to 600?

21. Higher Order Thinking A 3-digit number has the digits 2, 5, and 7. To the nearest hundred, it rounds to 800. What is the number? Show how you found the answer.

22. Make Sense and Persevere Emil says, "I am thinking of a number that is greater than 142, rounds to 100 when rounded to the nearest hundred, and has a 5 in the ones place." What is Emil's number?

What else can you try if you get stuck?

✔ **Assessment**

23. When rounded to the nearest hundred dollars, a computer game costs $100. Which could be the actual cost of the game? Choose all that apply.

☐ $10   ☑ $110

☐ $89   ☑ $150

☑ $91

24. Mandy rounds these numbers to the nearest ten. Which does she round to a lesser number? Choose all that apply.

☑ 46   ☐ 351

☑ 72   ☐ 833

☐ 200

Name _____

Help   Practice   Tools   Games
       Buddy

Homework & Practice 8-3
Round Whole Numbers

Another Look!

You can use number lines and what you know about place value to help round numbers.

If a number is halfway between, round to the greater number.

Round 483 to the nearest ten.

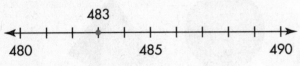

483 is closer to 480 than 490, so 483 rounds to 480.

Round 483 to the nearest 100.

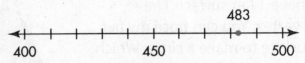

483 is closer to 500 than 400, so 483 rounds to 500.

---

1. Round 328 to the nearest ten.

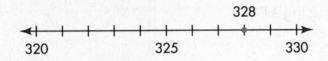

2. Round 630 to the nearest hundred.

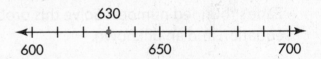

3. Round 649 to the nearest hundred.

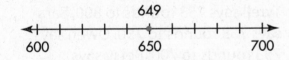

4. Round 155 to the nearest ten.

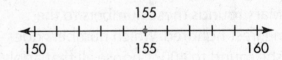

5. Round 262 to the nearest ten.

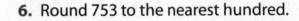

6. Round 753 to the nearest hundred.

7. Round 429 to the nearest ten and hundred.

8. Round 234 to the nearest ten and hundred.

Digital Resources at PearsonRealize.com   **Topic 8** | Lesson 8-3   421

9. Use the number line to show a number which rounds to 170 when it is rounded to the nearest ten.

←————————————————→

10. Higher Order Thinking When this 3-digit number is rounded to the nearest hundred, it rounds to 900. The digit in the ones place is the fifth odd number you count beginning with 1. The sum of the digits is 22. What is the number?

11. Make Sense and Persevere
I have 1 flat surface. I have 1 vertex. You can trace my flat surface to make a circle. Which shape am I? Circle the correct solid figure.

12. Algebra There are 254 counties in Texas. Zane rounds the number of counties to the nearest ten. What is the difference between the actual number of counties and Zane's rounded number? Solve this problem using an equation and an unknown.

✓ **Assessment**

13. Mary rounds these numbers to the nearest hundred. Which numbers does she round to 400? Choose all that apply.

☐ 351
☐ 369
☐ 401
☐ 413
☐ 448

14. Tyrell says 753 rounds to 800. Sara says 753 rounds to 750. Owen says 753 rounds to 700. Betsy says 753 rounds to 740. Mo says 753 cannot be rounded. Which people are correct? Choose all that apply.

☐ Tyrell
☐ Sara
☐ Owen
☐ Betsy
☐ Mo

Name _____

Solve & Share

A school store sold 436 pencils last week and 28 pencils today. Use mental math to find how many pencils were sold in all. Explain how you found your answer.

I can ...
use mental math to add.

I can also look for patterns to solve problems.

Look at the structure of the quantities in this problem.

I found the answer by using mentle math.

$$436 + 28 = 464 \checkmark$$

Look Back! **Make Sense and Persevere** What is another way you can find 436 + 28 using mental math?

A

Essential Question **How Can You Add with Mental Math?**

Dr. Gomez recorded how many whales, dolphins, and seals she saw. How many whales did she see during the two years?

Find 325 + 114 using mental math.

Marine Animals Seen		
Animal	**Year 1**	**Year 2**
Whales	325	114
Dolphins	228	171
Seals	434	212

You can use mental math to add and solve this problem. Properties of Addition let you reorder and group by place value.

B **One Way**

Add on to the first addend.

- Break apart 114.
  114 = 100 + 10 + 4

- Add 100 to 325.
  325 + 100 = 425

- Add 10 to 425.
  425 + 10 = 435

- Add 4 to 435.
  435 + 4 = 439

325 + 114 = 439

Dr. Gomez saw 439 whales.

C **Another Way**

- Break apart both addends.
  325 = 300 + 20 + 5
  114 = 100 + 10 + 4

- Add the hundreds: (300 + 100) = 400
  Add the tens: (20 + 10) = 30
  Add the ones: (5 + 4) = 9

- Then add the hundreds, tens, and ones.
  400 + 30 + 9 = 439

325 + 114 = 439

Dr. Gomez saw 439 whales.

Convince Me! **Model with Math** Show how you could use the same two ways above to find the total number of dolphins seen.

Practice Buddy   Tools   Assessment

Another Example!

You can make a ten to add mentally. Find 228 + 117.

- Break apart 117. $117 = 100 + 15 + 2$
- Add 2 to 228 to make a ten. $228 + 2 = 230$
- Add 100 to 230. $230 + 100 = 330$
- Add 15 to 330. $330 + 15 = 345$

So, $228 + 117 = 345$.

> There are many strategies you can use to add!

☆ Guided Practice*

Do You Understand?

1. Compare the One Way and Another Way on page 424. How are they the same? How are they different?

2. Use mental math to find how many animals Dr. Gomez saw during Year 2. Show your work.

Do You Know How?

3. Make a ten to add 738 + 126.

   $126 = 2 + 24 + 100$

   $738 + \underline{\quad} = 740$

   $740 + \underline{\quad} = 764$

   $764 + \underline{\quad} = 864$

   So, $738 + 126 = \underline{\quad}$

4. Use breaking apart to add 325 + 212.

   $212 = 200 + 10 + 2$

   $325 + 200 = \underline{\quad}$

   $525 + 10 = \underline{\quad}$

   $\underline{\quad} + 2 = 537$

   So, $325 + 212 = \underline{\quad}$

☆ Independent Practice ☆

In **5–8**, find each sum using mental math.

5. $252 + 44$ 6. $236 + 243$ 7. $651 + 150$ 8. $378 + 542$

Problem Solving

9. **Higher Order Thinking** Maxine earns $8 each hour that she works as a cashier. She starts with $233. Today she cashiers for 6 hours. How much does she have at the end of the day? Explain how you found your answer.

10. **Be Precise** Lauren sorted the 4 solids into 2 groups. Use mathematical terms to explain how she sorted the solids.

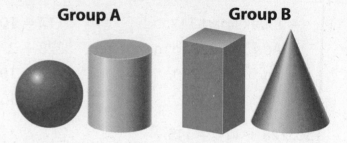

Group A   **Group B**

11. **Be Precise** The Rodriguez family drives 229 miles on Friday and 172 miles on Saturday. Explain how you can break apart both addends to find the total number of miles the Rodriguez family drives.

12. **Critique Reasoning** Is Bill's work correct? Explain why or why not. If not, find the correct answer.

Find 438 + 107.
I'll think of 7 as 2 + 5.
438 + 2 = 440
440 + 7 = 447
437 + 100 = 547
So, 438 + 107 is 547.

✓ **Assessment**

13. The table to the right shows the number of people who attend a movie on Friday and Saturday. How can you reorder to find the total number of people for both days?

　Ⓐ　(3 + 2 + 1) + (1 + 6 + 4)

　Ⓑ　(3 + 20 + 100) + (1 + 60 + 400)

　Ⓒ　300 + 100 + 60 + 4

　Ⓓ　(300 + 100) + (20 + 60) + (1 + 4)

DATA	Day	Number of People
	Friday	164
	Saturday	321

Name _____

Solve & Share

Peyton wants to buy an item that originally cost $635. If she gets the discount shown on the sign below, what is the sale price? Explain how you can use mental math to find your answer.

DISCOUNT:
$170 off
original price

I can ...
use mental math to subtract.

I can also make math arguments.

Even when you use mental math, you should still show your work! You can construct arguments using mental math.

Look Back! **Make Sense and Persevere** What is another way you can use mental math to solve the problem?

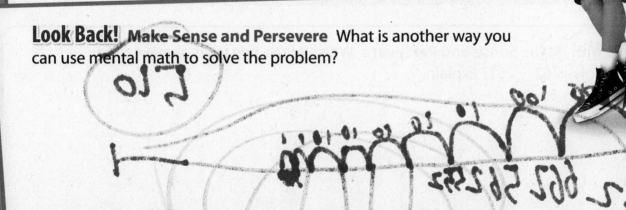

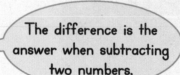

Essential Question # How Can You Subtract with Mental Math?

A

A store is having a sale on jackets. A jacket is on sale for $197 less than the original price. What is the sale price?

Find $352 - 197$.

~~$352~~
$197 off!

You can use mental math to subtract and solve this problem.

The difference is the answer when subtracting two numbers.

B **One Way**

$352 - 197 = ?$

It's easier to subtract 200.
$352 - 200 = 152$

If you subtract 200, you subtract 3 more than 197. You must add 3 to the answer.

$152 + 3 = 155$

$352 - 197 = 155$

The sale price is $155.

C **Another Way**

$352 - 197 = ?$

Make a simpler problem by changing each number in the same way.

You can change 197 to 200 because it's easier to subtract 200. So, add 3 to both 197 and 352.

$$352 \quad - \quad 197 \quad = \quad ?$$
$$\downarrow +3 \qquad \downarrow +3$$
$$355 \quad - \quad 200 \quad = \quad 155$$
$352 - 197 = 155$

The sale price is $155.

Convince Me! **Make Sense and Persevere** Which of the two ways above would you use to solve $762 - 252$? Explain.

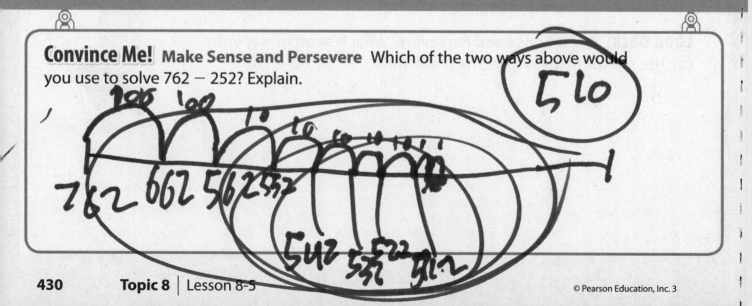

© Pearson Education, Inc. 3

Practice Buddy   Tools   Assessment

Another Example!

You can count on to subtract mentally. Find $300 - 155$.

$155 + 5 = 160$
$160 + 40 = 200$
$200 + 100 = 300$

$5 + 40 + 100 = 145$

So, $300 - 155 = 145$.

If you get stuck using one strategy, another strategy may be easier!

☆ Guided Practice *

Do You Understand?

1. In the One Way example on page 430, why do you add 3 to 152 instead of subtracting 3 from 152?

2. Suppose a computer costs $573. If you buy it today, it costs $498. What is the discount? Show your work.

Do You Know How?

In **3–6**, find using mental math.

3. $846 - 18$
   $848 - 20 = $ _____

4. $534 - 99$
   $535 - 100 = $ _____

5. $873 - 216$
   $877 - 220 = $ _____

6. $782 - 347$
   $785 - 350 = $ _____

7. Find $400 - 138$ mentally by counting on.

   $138 + $ _____ $= 140$

   $140 + $ _____ $= 200$

   $200 + $ _____ $= 400$

   _____ $+$ _____ $+$ _____ $=$ _____

☆ Independent Practice ☆

In **8–19**, find each difference using mental math.

8. $128 - 19$

9. $887 - 18$

10. $339 - 117$

11. $468 - 224$

12. $784 - 515$

13. $354 - 297$

14. $853 - 339$

15. $638 - 372$

16. $400 - 250$

17. $430 - 216$

18. $705 - 255$

19. $687 - 323$

*For another example, see Set E on page 462.   **Topic 8 | Lesson 8-5**

Problem Solving

20. Paolo has read 158 pages in a book. The book is 214 pages long. How many pages does Paolo have left to read? Use mental math to solve.

21. Model with Math Jessica has an array with 9 columns. There are 36 counters in the array. How many rows does her array have? Show how to represent the problem and find the answer.

22. Look for Relationships Nina wrote the following number pattern. Describe a pattern rule. What are the next three numbers in the pattern?

653   553   453   353

23. Of the students at Paul's school, 270 are girls and 298 are boys. There are 354 students at Alice's school. How many more students are there at Paul's school than at Alice's school?

24. Higher Order Thinking To find $357 - 216$, Tom added 4 to each number, and then subtracted. Saul added 3 to each number, and then subtracted. Will both ways work to find the correct answer? Explain.

25. Number Sense Aubrey is comparing 369 and 382. Which place-value digits does she need to compare? Which number would be farther right on a number line? Explain.

✓ **Assessment**

---

26. Sarah has $350. How much money will she have after buying the computer at the sale price? Describe how you can use mental math to find the answer.

$299 SALE! Take $58 off the original price.

Help   Practice   Tools   Games
Buddy

Homework & Practice 8-5

Mental Math: Subtraction

Another Look!

You can use properties of operations to change numbers to make subtraction easier.

Megan has 372 buttons. She used 14 buttons to make a collage and 49 buttons to make an ornament. How many buttons does Megan have now?

First find $372 - 14$.

You can add 6 to both 372 and 14.

$$372 + 6 \rightarrow 378$$
$$\underline{-\ 14 + 6 \rightarrow\ \ 20}$$
$$358$$

Adding the same amount to each number does not change the difference.

Then find $358 - 49$.

You can add 1 to both 358 and 49.

$$358 + 1 \rightarrow 359$$
$$\underline{-\ 49 + 1 \rightarrow\ \ 50}$$
$$309$$

So, $358 - 49 = 309$.

Megan has 309 buttons.

In **1–20**, find each difference using mental math.

1. $232 - 117$
$$232 + 3 \rightarrow 235$$
$$\underline{-\ 117 + 3 \rightarrow\ \underline{\ \ \ }}$$

2. $940 - 109$
$$940 + 1 \rightarrow \underline{\ \ \ }$$
$$\underline{-\ 109 + 1 \rightarrow 110}$$

3. $281 - 112$
$$281 + 8 \rightarrow 289$$
$$\underline{-\ 112 + 8 \rightarrow\ \underline{\ \ \ }}$$

4. $309 - 195$
$$309 + 5 \rightarrow \underline{\ \ \ }$$
$$\underline{-\ 195 + 5 \rightarrow 200}$$

5. $656 - 127$
$$659 - 130 = \underline{\ \ \ }$$

6. $781 - 536$
$$785 - 540 = \underline{\ \ \ }$$

7. $228 - 119$
$$229 - 120 = \underline{\ \ \ }$$

8. $647 - 355$
$$652 - 360 = \underline{\ \ \ }$$

9. $153 - 37$

10. $777 - 135$

11. $841 - 281$

12. $976 - 918$

13. $959 - 415$

14. $604 - 406$

15. $543 - 132$

16. $975 - 242$

17. $490 - 255$

18. $460 - 212$

19. $800 - 325$

20. $769 - 428$

21. **Generalize** Cassie has 20 bracelets. How many can she give to her sister if she wants to keep 11 or more bracelets? What repeats in the possibilities?

22. **Make Sense and Persevere** Gillian started to find 888 − 291. This is what she did.

$$888 - 291 = ?$$
$$888 - 300 = 588$$

What should Gillian do next?

23. **Math and Science** Julie recorded the heights of three different trees in this table. Use mental math to find how much taller the Redwood tree is than the Sequoia tree.

Tree Heights	
Tree	**Height (ft)**
Sequoia	173
Tanbark	75
Redwood	237

24. Cary wants to upload 316 pictures from his digital camera and 226 pictures from his computer. So far, he has uploaded 191 of all the pictures. How many more pictures does Cary have left to upload?

25. Martin has 1 quarter, 5 dimes, 2 nickels, and 4 pennies. Tim has 2 quarters, 2 dimes, and 3 nickels. How much money does each boy have? Who has more money?

26. **Higher Order Thinking** Use mental math to find how many more total raffle tickets Ms. Hudson's and Mr. Nealy's classes sold than Mrs. Robertson's class. Explain.

Some problems have more than one step to solve.

Raffle Tickets Sold	
Class	**Number of Tickets**
Ms. Hudson	352
Mr. Nealy	236
Mrs. Robertson	429

27. A box of tiles contains 625 tiles. Mai needs 363 tiles for her art project, and her friend Beth needs 272 tiles for her project. If they buy one box of tiles, do they have enough for both projects? Explain.

© Pearson Education, Inc. 3

Name _____

Solve & Share

Look at the table below. Is the weight of a female and male sun bear together more or less than the weight of one female black bear? Without finding an exact answer, explain how you can decide. **Solve this problem any way you choose.**

I can ...
use what I know about addition and place value to estimate sums.

I can also be precise in my work.

$78 = 70 + 8$
$+ 95 = 90 + 3$ 161

160

You can use symbols, numbers, and words to write a precise explanation. *Show your work in the space below!*

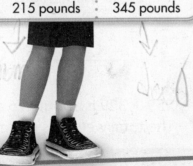

Type of Bear	Weight	
	Female	**Male**
Sun Bear	78 pounds	95 pounds
Black Bear	215 pounds	345 pounds

DATA

I think it is less than because I used mentle math and it gave me 161.

Look Back! **Reasoning** Why is an exact answer not needed to solve the problem?

Essential Question **How Can You Estimate Sums?**

A

Do the two pandas together weigh more than 500 pounds?

Estimate 255 + 329.

You can estimate to find about how much the two pandas weigh.

Female
255 pounds

Male
329 pounds

B **One Way**

Round to the nearest hundred.

$255 \rightarrow 300$
$+329 \rightarrow 300$
$ 600$

255 + 329 is about 600.
600 > 500

The pandas together weigh more than 500 pounds.

C **Another Way**

Use compatible numbers.

Compatible numbers are numbers that are close to the addends, but easy to add mentally.

$255 \rightarrow 250$
$+329 \rightarrow 325$
$ 575$

255 + 329 is about 575 and 575 > 500.
The total weight is more than 500 pounds.

Convince Me! **Be Precise** Sandy said, "Just look at the numbers. 200 and 300 is 500. The pandas weigh over 500 pounds because one panda weighs 255 pounds and the other weighs 329 pounds."

What do you think she means? Use numbers, words, or symbols to explain.

Name _____

Another Example!

Suppose one panda ate 166 pounds of bamboo in a week and another ate 158 pounds. About how many pounds of bamboo did the two pandas eat?

You can estimate 166 + 158 by rounding to the nearest ten.

$$166 \rightarrow 170$$
$$+\ 158 \rightarrow 160$$
$$330$$

The pandas ate about 330 pounds of bamboo in a week.

☆ Guided Practice

Do You Understand?

1. Two addends are rounded to greater numbers. Is the estimate greater than or less than the actual sum?

2. Mary and Todd estimate 143 + 286. They have different answers. Can they both be correct? Explain why or why not.

Do You Know How?

Round to the nearest ten to estimate.

3. 218 + 466   ____ + ____ = ____

4. 108 + 223   ____ + ____ = ____

Round to the nearest hundred to estimate.

5. 514 + 258   ____ + ____ = ____

6. 198 + 426   ____ + ____ = ____

☆ Independent Practice ☆

In **7–10**, round to the nearest ten to estimate.

7. 138 + 435   8. 563 + 289   9. 644 + 172   10. 376 + 295

In **11–14**, round to the nearest hundred to estimate.

11. 403 + 179   12. 462 + 251   13. 274 + 443   14. 539 + 399

In **15–18**, use compatible numbers to estimate.

15. 175 + 126   16. 167 + 27   17. 108 + 379   18. 145 + 394

Problem Solving

Use the table to answer **19** and **20**.

19. Ms. Tyler drove from Albany to Boston, and then from Boston to Baltimore. To the nearest ten miles, about how many miles in all did she drive?

20. Ms. Tyler drove from Boston to New York and back again. To the nearest hundred miles, about how many miles did she drive?

Distance from Boston, MA

City	Miles Away
Albany, NY	166
Baltimore, MD	407
Philadelphia, PA	313
New York, NY	211
Norfolk, VA	577

21. Reasoning Jen has $236. Dan has $289. Do Jen and Dan have more than $600 in all? Estimate to solve. Explain.

22. Model with Math Ralph has 75¢. How much more money does he need to buy a pencil for 90¢? Complete the diagram.

90¢

75¢	

Money Ralph has   Money needed

23. Higher Order Thinking Susan drove 247 miles on Wednesday morning. Then she drove 119 miles on Wednesday afternoon. On Thursday, Susan drove 326 miles. About how far did Susan drive in all? Explain the method you used to estimate.

Remember that you learned different methods to estimate.

Assessment

24. Liam rounds some sums to the nearest hundred. Does he round correctly? Choose *Yes* or *No*.

24a. 273 + 365 is about 700.   ○ Yes   ○ No

24b. 154 + 152 is about 300.   ○ Yes   ○ No

24c. 542 + 338 is about 880.   ○ Yes   ○ No

24d. 535 + 294 is about 800.   ○ Yes   ○ No

Name _____

Another Look!

There is more than one
way you can estimate.

The students at Silver School are saving cereal box tops.

Fruit & Crunch

136
box tops

Bran Swirls

178
box tops

About how many box tops have the students saved?
When you find *about* how many, you estimate.

Estimate by rounding each addend. Then, add the rounded numbers.

Round to the nearest ten.

$136 \rightarrow 140$
$+ 178 \rightarrow 180$
$ 320$

The students have saved about
320 box tops.

Round to the nearest hundred.

$136 \rightarrow 100$
$+ 178 \rightarrow 200$
$ 300$

The students have saved about
300 box tops.

In **1–4**, round to the nearest ten to estimate.

1. $144 \rightarrow$ ____
    $+ 298 \rightarrow$ ____
    _____

2. $271 \rightarrow$ ____
    $+ 487 \rightarrow$ ____
    _____

3. $225 \rightarrow$ ____
    $+ 294 \rightarrow$ ____
    _____

4. $359 \rightarrow$ ____
    $+ 107 \rightarrow$ ____
    _____

In **5–8**, round to the nearest hundred to estimate.

5. $291 + 268$

6. $378 + 136$

7. $436 + 309$

8. $365 + 487$

9. **Critique Reasoning** Sun-Yi estimated 270 + 146 and got 320. Is her estimate reasonable? Explain.

10. **A-Z Vocabulary** Miguel has 334 baseball cards and 278 football cards. He says, "I have 612 cards in all." Is that reasonable? Explain using the words *round* and *estimate*.

11. Paige and her friend Karla planted 4 types of rosebushes for the Dundee Community Center. The bar graph at the right shows the color and number of each bush the girls planted. How many more red and pink rosebushes were planted than yellow and white rosebushes?

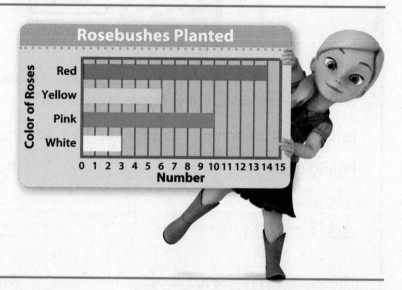

12. **Higher Order Thinking** On Monday, Cheryl drove from Austin to Fort Worth and back to Austin. On Tuesday, she drove from Austin to Jackson. Find about how far Cheryl drove to the nearest ten miles and to the nearest hundred miles.

Distances from Austin, TX	
City	Miles Away
Memphis, TN	643
Fort Worth, TX	189
Jackson, MS	548

13. Angelina rounds some sums to the nearest ten. Does she round correctly? Choose *Yes* or *No*.

13a. 468 + 124 is about 590.   ○ Yes   ○ No

13b. 233 + 521 is about 750.   ○ Yes   ○ No

13c. 323 + 224 is about 550.   ○ Yes   ○ No

13d. 241 + 476 is about 700.   ○ Yes   ○ No

Name _____

Sara collected 356 aluminum cans to recycle. Pierre collected 112 cans. About how many more cans did Sara collect? **Solve this problem any way you choose.**

You can make sense and persevere. What is a good plan for solving this problem? *Show your work in the space below!*

Lesson 8-7
Estimate Differences

I can ...
use what I know about subtraction and place value to estimate differences.

I can also make sense of problems.

Look Back! Generalize Which strategy gives an estimate that is closest to the exact answer? How did you decide?

Essential Question # How Can You Estimate Differences?

A

All of the tickets for a concert were sold. So far, 126 people have arrived at the concert. About how many people who have tickets have not arrived?

Estimate 493 — 126 by rounding.

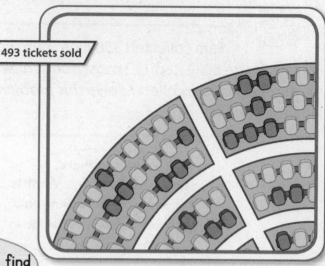

493 tickets sold

You can estimate to find *about* how many.

B **One Way**

Round each number to the nearest hundred and subtract.

$$493 \rightarrow 500$$
$$-126 \rightarrow 100$$
$$\overline{\qquad 400}$$

About 400 people have not yet arrived.

C **Another Way**

Round each number to the nearest ten and subtract.

$$493 \rightarrow 490$$
$$-126 \rightarrow 130$$
$$\overline{\qquad 360}$$

About 360 people have not yet arrived.

Convince Me! **Model with Math** Suppose 179 people have arrived at the concert. Use the two ways shown above to estimate how many people have not arrived.

© Pearson Education, Inc. 3

Name _____

Another Example!

You can use compatible numbers to estimate differences.

Estimate 372 − 149.

$$372 \rightarrow 375$$
$$-\ 149 \rightarrow 150$$
$$\overline{\qquad\quad 225}$$

375 and 150 are compatible numbers for 372 and 149.

Guided Practice

Do You Understand?

1. Does rounding to the nearest ten or nearest hundred give an estimate closer to the exact answer for 295 − 153?

2. A theater sells 408 tickets. 273 people arrive. About how many more people are expected to arrive? Use compatible numbers. Show your work.

Do You Know How?

In **3** and **4**, round to the nearest hundred to estimate.

3. 321 − 182   **4.** 655 − 189

In **5** and **6**, round to the nearest ten to estimate.

5. 763 − 471   **6.** 816 − 297

Independent Practice

In **7–10**, round to the nearest hundred to estimate.

7. 286 − 189   **8.** 461 − 216   **9.** 891 − 686   **10.** 724 − 175

In **11–14**, round to the nearest ten to estimate.

11. 766 − 492   **12.** 649 − 487   **13.** 241 − 117   **14.** 994 − 679

In **15–18**, use compatible numbers to estimate.

15. 760 − 265   **16.** 355 − 177   **17.** 481 − 105   **18.** 794 − 556

Problem Solving

19. **Reasoning** The Grand Concert Hall sold 100 more tickets on Sunday than on Friday. On what day did it sell about 150 tickets more than it sold on Sunday?

Think about what the numbers mean.

Grand Concert Hall	
Day	Number of Tickets Sold
Wednesday	506
Thursday	323
Friday	251
Saturday	427
Sunday	?

20. **Model with Math** Find the total number of tickets sold on Thursday and Friday. Explain what math you used.

21. **Algebra** Anna and Joe write reports for their science class. Anna's report is 827 words long. Joe's report is 679 words long. Round each report length to the nearest ten and estimate about how many more words Anna writes. Then write an equation that shows exactly how many more words Anna writes.

22. **Higher Order Thinking** To earn some extra money, Mrs. Runyan helps a carpenter. One week she earned $486, and the next week she earned $254. If Mrs. Runyan wanted to earn $545, about how much extra money did she earn? Show how you used estimation to find your answers.

✓ **Assessment**

23. About how many inches longer was a *Brachiosaurus* than a *Tyrannosaurus rex*?

Tyrannosaurus rex
468 inches

Brachiosaurus
972 inches

Part A

Use compatible numbers to estimate.

Part B

Explain how you found your answer.

Name _____

Another Look!

You can use rounding to estimate differences.

Members of the Biology Club caught 288 butterflies and 136 grasshoppers in their nets. About how many more butterflies than grasshoppers did the club catch?

When you find *about* how many, you estimate. You can estimate by rounding.

Round to the nearest hundred.

$$288 \rightarrow 300$$
$$-\ 136 \rightarrow 100$$
$$\overline{\hphantom{-\ 136 \rightarrow\ } 200}$$

There were about 200 more butterflies than grasshoppers caught.

Round to the nearest ten.

$$288 \rightarrow 290$$
$$-\ 136 \rightarrow 140$$
$$\overline{\hphantom{-\ 136 \rightarrow\ } 150}$$

There were about 150 more butterflies than grasshoppers caught.

In **1–8**, round to the nearest hundred to estimate.

1. $584 \rightarrow$ ____
   $-\ 347 \rightarrow$ ____

2. $274 \rightarrow$ ____
   $-\ 147 \rightarrow$ ____

3. $615 \rightarrow$ ____
   $-\ 523 \rightarrow$ ____

4. $831 \rightarrow$ ____
   $-\ 143 \rightarrow$ ____

5. $422 - 142$

6. $725 - 278$

7. $682 - 224$

8. $363 - 187$

In **9–16**, round to the nearest ten to estimate.

9. $146 \rightarrow$ ____
   $-\ 118 \rightarrow$ ____

10. $428 \rightarrow$ ____
    $-\ 332 \rightarrow$ ____

11. $588 \rightarrow$ ____
    $-\ 491 \rightarrow$ ____

12. $351 \rightarrow$ ____
    $-\ 106 \rightarrow$ ____

13. $654 - 585$

14. $355 - 186$

15. $274 - 207$

16. $522 - 330$

17. Number Sense Duncan says, "Since 6 is greater than 3, the number 65 is greater than 344." Do you agree? Explain.

18. On Friday, 537 people attended a play. On Saturday, 812 people attended the same play. About how many more people attended the play on Saturday than on Friday? How did you estimate? Show your work.

19. Andrew has the coins shown at the right. He wants to buy a comic book for $1.00. How much more money does he need to make 1 dollar?

20. Model with Math Lori lives 272 miles from her grandparents, 411 miles from her aunt, and 39 miles from her cousins. About how much closer does Lori live to her grandparents than to her aunt? Explain what math you used.

21. Higher Order Thinking Carl is estimating $653 - 644$. His work is shown below.

$$700 - 600 = 100$$

What is the actual difference? Is Carl's estimate reasonable? If not, how could he have made a closer estimate?

✓ **Assessment**

22. Tyrel recorded the elevations of three cities.

Part A

Use rounding to the nearest ten to estimate about how many more feet Dallas's elevation is than Waco's.

Part B

Write an equation to show how you solved the problem.

Solve

Solve & Share

The Eat Healthy Café prepared 326 breakfasts and 584 lunches during one month. Some lunches were salads and the rest were sandwiches. There were 253 salad lunches. How many lunches were sandwiches? **Solve this problem any way you choose.**

I can ...
use the relationship between addition and subtraction to solve problems.

I can also model with math to solve problems.

You can model with math. How can you use what you know about addition and subtraction to help solve this problem? *Show your work in the space below!*

Look Back! **Critique Reasoning** Ryan solves the problem by finding 584 − 253. He says 330 of the lunches were sandwiches. Is Ryan's answer correct? Show a way to check his work.

Essential Question

How Can the Relationship Between Addition and Subtraction Help You Solve Problems?

A

A company has already asked 253 people the same question. How many more people need to answer the question to reach the goal?

Goal: 775 people

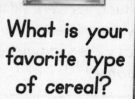
What is your favorite type of cereal?

☐ Hot cereal
☐ Cold cereal

775 people for goal

253	?

253 people asked   ? more people

$253 + ? = 775$

You know the whole and one part.

B Addition and subtraction are related. You can use an addition equation or a subtraction equation to solve this problem.

$253 + ? = 775$

$775 - 253 = ?$

$775 - 253 = 522$

522 more people must answer the question.

The equations show the same whole, the same known part, and the same missing part.

C Operations that undo each other are inverse operations. Subtracting 253 and adding 253 are inverse operations.

Add to check a subtraction problem.

The numbers match the subtraction.

$$\begin{array}{r} 522 \\ + 253 \\ \hline 775 \end{array}$$

522 more people must answer the question.

Convince Me! **Model with Math** Could you still use addition or subtraction to solve the problem if the goal was 943 people instead? What equations would you use?

Name _____

☆ Guided Practice*

Do You Understand?

1. Reasoning How does knowing $557 - 232 = 325$ help you solve $325 + ? = 557$?

> In **2** and **3**, add or subtract. Then use the inverse operation to check your answer.

2.
```
   7 8 4            ☐☐☐
 − 2 3 2    →    + 2 3 2
   ☐☐☐            ☐☐☐
```

3.
```
   4 3 2            ☐☐☐
 + 3 5 7    →    − 3 5 7
   ☐☐☐            ☐☐☐
```

Do You Know How?

4. Grade 3 students brought in 134 coupons on Friday. This brought their total up to 556 coupons. How many coupons had the students brought in before Friday? Complete the bar diagram and solve the problem.

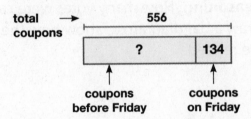

total → 556
coupons

| ? | 134 |

coupons before Friday   coupons on Friday

☆ Independent Practice ☆

> In **5** and **6**, complete the bar diagram and solve the problem.

5. Gerardo's book has 634 pages. So far he has read 379 pages. How many more pages does Gerardo need to read to finish his book?

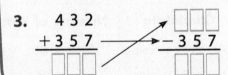

6. Nisha scored some points on a video game. Joanne scored 472 points. Together they scored 896 points. How many points did Nisha score?

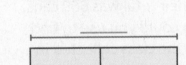

> In **7** and **8**, add or subtract. Then use the inverse operation to check your answer.

7.
```
   3 6 9
 − 1 5 9
   ☐☐☐
```

8.
```
   3 2 5
 + 5 4 3
   ☐☐☐
```

Problem Solving

9. **Model with Math** Jason puts $382 into his bank account. Now he has $594 in his bank account. How much money did Jason have in his bank account to start? Show how you can use addition and subtraction to solve.

10. Mandi's class has recess in the morning at the time shown on the clock. What time does her class have recess? Use A.M. or P.M. in your answer.

11. **Reasoning** How many votes were cast in all? Draw a bar diagram to show how the numbers are related.

12. **Higher Order Thinking** How many more votes did Abraham Lincoln receive than the total votes of the other three candidates? Explain how you found and checked your answer.

DATA

1860 Electoral Votes

Candidate	Number of Votes
Abraham Lincoln	180
Stephen Douglas	12
John Breckinridge	72
John Bell	39

✓ Assessment

13. Gino's class collected cans for a food drive that lasted 2 weeks. The class collected 363 cans in week 1. By the end of week 2 their total was 659 cans. Which equation could you use to find how many cans the class collected in week 2?

   Ⓐ ? + 363 = 659 or ? − 659 = 363

   Ⓑ ? − 363 = 659 or 659 + 363 = ?

   Ⓒ 363 + ? = 659 or 659 − 363 = ?

   Ⓓ 363 + ? = 659 or 363 − 659 = ?

14. Destiny calculated 357 − 102 = 255. How could she check her answer? What will she find?

   Ⓐ Subtract 357 − 100 = 257.
   Her original answer was correct.

   Ⓑ Add 102 + 255 = 357.
   Her original answer was correct.

   Ⓒ Add 102 + 357 = 459.
   Her original answer was incorrect.

   Ⓓ Subtract 255 − 102 = 153.
   Her original answer was incorrect.

Help Practice Tools Games
      Buddy

Homework & Practice 8-8
Relate Addition and Subtraction

Another Look!

Ian ran 251 meters. Ian and Julie ran for 672 meters in all. How many meters did Julie run?

> You can use an addition equation or a subtraction equation to solve.

> You can use addition to check subtraction and subtraction to check addition.

$251 + ? = 672$

$672 - 251 = ?$

$672 - 251 = 421$

Check your work.
Since you subtracted, use addition to check.

```
  672              421    Use the difference as one addend.
- 251            + 251    Use the number you subtracted as the other addend.
  421              672    The sum should match the number you subtracted from.
```

1. Teri earns $227 this week. Now she has $569. How much money did Teri have to start?

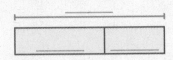

2. Arif drives 184 miles on Monday. He drives a total of 391 miles on Monday and Tuesday. How many miles did he drive on Tuesday?

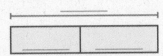

In **3–6**, add or subtract. Then use the inverse operation to check your answer.

3.
```
  4 4 5            □□□
- 1 2 1          + 1 2 1
  □□□              □□□
```

4.
```
  2 1 6            □□□
+ 6 6 3          - 6 6 3
  □□□              □□□
```

5.
```
  9 7 7
- 4 5 2
  □□□
```

6.
```
  2 6 3
+ 5 2 2
  □□□
```

In **7** and **8**, use the table at the right. Show how you can use addition and subtraction to solve.

7. On Monday, 134 customers ordered orange juice. How many customers did not order orange juice?

Daily Diner Customers	
Day	**Customers**
Monday	275
Tuesday	210
Wednesday	395
Thursday	240

DATA

8. **Reasoning** How many more customers were there on the day with the most customers than on the day with the fewest customers?

How can you represent a problem using numbers?

---

9. Draw lines into the circle and rectangle to divide each of them into four equal parts.

10. **Higher Order Thinking** Becky added 273 + 416 and got 688. Then she checked her answer by adding 688 + 416. What error did Becky make? Was the sum she found for the original problem correct? Explain.

---

11. By 1 o'clock, 452 total runners had finished a marathon race. By 2 o'clock 584 total runners had finished. Which could you use to find how many runners finished the race between 1 o'clock and 2 o'clock?

Ⓐ $? - 452 = 584$ or $584 + 452 = ?$

Ⓑ $? + 452 = 584$ or $? - 584 = 452$

Ⓒ $452 + ? = 584$ or $452 - 584 = ?$

Ⓓ $452 + ? = 584$ or $584 - 452 = ?$

12. Mary's work is shown below. How can she use inverse operations to check her work?

$$\begin{array}{r} 332 \\ + 131 \\ \hline 463 \end{array}$$

Ⓐ   Subtract 131 from 463.

Ⓑ   Subtract 131 from 332.

Ⓒ   Add 332 to 463.

Ⓓ   Add 131 to 463.

Name _____

Solve & Share

A pond has 458 rosy red minnows, 212 white cloud minnows, and 277 goldfish. How many more minnows than goldfish live in the pond? **Solve this problem any way you choose.**

Solve

I can ...
apply the math I know to solve problems.

I can also solve multi-step problems.

Thinking Habits

Be a good thinker!
These questions can help you.

• How can I use math I know to help solve this problem?

• How can I use pictures, objects, or an equation to represent the problem?

• How can I use numbers, words, and symbols to solve the problem?

Look Back! Model with Math Explain what math you used to solve this problem.

Essential Question **How Can You Model with Math?**

A

David has $583 to spend on soccer uniforms. He buys this soccer jersey and 2 soccer shorts. How much money does David spend?

Shorts $35

Jersey $109

What math do I need to use to solve the problem?

I need to show what I know and then choose the needed operations.

B **How can I model with math?**
I can

- apply math I know to solve the problem.

- use a bar diagram and equations to represent the problem.

- use an unknown to represent the number I am trying to find.

C
Here's my thinking...

I will use a bar diagram and an equation.

The hidden question is: How much does David spend on shorts?

? for both shorts

35	35

35 + 35 = ?
35 + 35 = $70. The shorts cost $70.

So I need to find the total including the jersey.

? total

70	109

$70 + $109 = ?
70 + 109 = $179. David spends $179.

Convince Me! **Model with Math** How does the bar diagram help you model with math?

Name _____

☆ Guided Practice *

Model with Math

Harris's office building has 126 windows. Morgan's bank has 146 windows. Devon's bank has 110 windows. How many more windows do the banks have than the office building?

> You can model with math by using bar diagrams to represent each step of a two-step problem.

1. What is the hidden question you need to answer before you can solve the problem?

2. Solve the problem. Complete the bar diagrams. Show the equations you used.

? windows in banks

_____	_____

banks
_____

office
	? more
_____	

☆ Independent Practice ☆

Model with Math

Regina's bakery makes 304 pies in January. Her bakery made 34 fewer pies in February. How many pies did her bakery make in both months?

3. What is the hidden question you need to answer before you can solve the problem?

_____

4. Solve the problem. Complete the bar diagrams. Show the equations you used.

_____

_____

_____

5. How would your equations change if the bakery made 34 more pies in February than January?

Problem Solving

Skyscraper Heights

The Empire State Building in New York is 159 meters taller than the Republic Plaza in Denver. The John Hancock Building in Chicago is 122 meters taller than the Republic Plaza. The Empire State Building is 712 miles away from the Hancock Building. The Hancock Building is 920 miles away from the Republic Plaza.

Manuel wants to know how tall the Hancock Building is. Answer Exercises 6–9 to solve the problem.

Empire State Building
381 meters

6. **Construct Arguments** To solve the problem, should you add 159 to the height of the Empire State Building? Explain why or why not.

7. **Model with Math** What is the hidden question you need to solve in this problem? Draw a bar diagram and write an equation to represent the hidden question.

8. **Model with Math** Solve the problem. Show the equations you used.

9. **Use Appropriate Tools** Which tool would you use to represent and explain how to solve the problem: counters, cubes, or place-value blocks? Explain.

Model with math means you apply math you have learned to solve problems.

© Pearson Education, Inc. 3

Help   Practice   Tools   Games
        Buddy

Another Look!

Don sold 180 books in the morning, 293 books in the afternoon, and 104 books in the evening. How many books did he sell in all?

Tell how you can model with math.

- I can use the math that I know.

- I can use a bar diagram and equations to represent and choose the operations I need.

> You can model with math by using bar diagrams to show the relationships between quantities in a problem.

Represent and solve this problem.

Find the hidden question:
How many books did Don sell in the morning and the evening?

? books sold in morning and evening

180	104

$180 + 104 = ?$
I can break apart by place value.
$(100 + 80) + (100 + 4)$
$= (100 + 100) + 80 + 4$
$= 284$ books

Use the answer to solve the problem.
How many books did Don sell in all?

? books sold in all

284	293

$284 + 293 = ?$
I can make a ten. $293 + 7 = 300$
$284 - 7 = 277$
$300 + 277 = 577$ books in all

Model with Math

Vanessa spends $273. She donates $119. Vanessa had $685.
How much money does she have left?

1. Explain how you can represent this problem.

2. What is the hidden question you need to answer before you can solve the problem?

3. Solve the problem. Draw bar diagrams to represent the problem. Show any equations you used.

Stamp Collection

Scott has collected stamps for 4 years. The table at the right shows the number of stamps from foreign countries in Scott's stamp collection. Scott has 315 more stamps from the U.S. than from Canada. Each stamp from the U.S. is worth 49 cents. Scott wants to know the total number of stamps he has in his collection.

Stamps from Foreign Countries	
Country	**Number of Stamps**
Canada	55
Mexico	221

DATA

4. **Reasoning** How are the numbers in this problem related?

5. **Model with Math** What is the hidden question you need to answer before you can solve the problem? Draw a bar diagram and write an equation to represent the hidden question.

6. **Model with Math** Solve the problem. Show the equations you used.

> Diagrams and equations can help you model with math.

7. **Make Sense and Persevere** What are two ways that Scott can check that his answer is correct? Use one of those ways to check your answer.

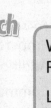

Find a Match

Work with a partner. Point to a clue. Read the clue.

Look below the clues to find a match. Write the clue letter in the box next to the match.

Find a match for every clue.

I can ...
divide within 100.

Clues

A The missing number is 9.

E The missing number is 7.

B The missing number is 10.

F The missing number is 4.

C The missing number is 3.

G The missing number is 8.

D The missing number is 6.

H The missing number is 5.

$42 \div \underline{} = 6$	$24 \div 8 = \underline{}$	$\underline{} \div 5 = 2$	$18 \div 3 = \underline{}$
$\underline{}\overline{)30}$ 6	$\underline{} \div 2 = 4$	$40 \div \underline{} = 10$	$7\overline{)63}$

Vocabulary Review

A-Z Glossary

Word List

- Associative Property of Addition
- Commutative Property of Addition
- compatible numbers
- estimate
- Identity Property of Addition
- inverse operations
- mental math
- place value
- round

Understand Vocabulary

Circle the property of addition shown in the following examples.

1. $17 + 14 = 14 + 17$

Associative Property   Commutative Property   Identity Property

2. $93 + 0 = 93$

Associative Property   Commutative Property   Identity Property

3. $8 + (5 + 9) = (8 + 5) + 9$

Associative Property   Commutative Property   Identity Property

4. $65 + 0 = 0 + 65$

Associative Property   Commutative Property   Identity Property

Choose the best term from the box. Write it in the blank.

5. You _____ when you use the nearest multiple of ten or hundred.

6. Addition and subtraction are _____.

7. _____ is the value given to the place a digit has in a number.

8. Numbers that are easy to compute mentally are _____.

9. You do not need pencil and paper when using _____.

Use Vocabulary in Writing

10. Jim found that $123 + 284$ is about 400. Explain what Jim did. Use at least 3 terms from the Word List in your answer.

Name _____

Set A pages 405–410

You can use properties of addition to help solve addition problems.

The Commutative Property of Addition

$12 + \boxed{} = 15 + 12$

$12 + 15 = 15 + 12$

You can order addends in any way, and the sum will be the same.

The Associative Property of Addition

$3 + (7 + 8) = (3 + \boxed{}) + 8$

$3 + (7 + 8) = (3 + 7) + 8$

You can group addends in any way, and the sum will be the same.

The Identity Property of Addition

$30 + \boxed{} = 30$

$30 + 0 = 30$

The sum of any number and zero is that same number.

Remember that both sides of the equal sign must have the same value.

In **1–6**, write each missing number.

1. $18 + \underline{} = 18$

2. $14 + (16 + 15) = (\underline{} + 16) + 15$

3. $\underline{} + 13 = 13 + 17$

4. $28 + (\underline{} + 22) = 28 + (22 + 25)$

5. $62 + 21 + 0 = 62 + \underline{}$

6. $\underline{} + (26 + 78) = (31 + 26) + 78$

7. Use the numbers 78 and 34 to write an equation that shows the Commutative Property of Addition.

Set B pages 411–416

You can find patterns using an addition table.

+	4	5	6	7
3	7	8	9	10
4	8	9	10	11
5	9	10	11	12
6	10	11	12	13
7	11	12	13	14
8	12	13	14	15

3 more than an even number is always an odd number.
3 is an odd number.
An even number plus an odd number is an odd number.

Use examples to make generalizations!

Remember that properties can help you understand patterns.

+	0	1	2	3	4	5	6	7
0	0	1	2	3	4	5	6	7
1	1	2	3	4	5	6	7	8
2	2	3	4	5	6	7	8	9
3	3	4	5	6	7	8	9	10
4	4	5	6	7	8	9	10	11
5	5	6	7	8	9	10	11	12

1. Find the doubles-plus-2 facts. What pattern do you notice about the sums?

2. Explain why your pattern works.

You can use a number line to round.

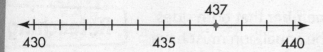

437

430   435   440

Nearest ten: 437 rounds to 440.

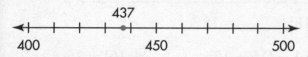

437

400   450   500

Nearest hundred: 437 rounds to 400.

Think about place value when you round.

Remember that if a number is halfway between, round to the greater number.

1. Round 374 to the nearest ten and the nearest hundred.

2. Round 848 to the nearest ten and the nearest hundred.

3. Mark's family traveled 565 miles. Rounded to the nearest ten, about how many miles did they travel?

4. Sara collected 345 shells. Rounded to the nearest hundred, about how many shells did she collect?

Use mental math to find 374 + 238.

Break apart 374 and 238.
300 + 70 + 4 and 200 + 30 + 8

Add hundreds, tens, and ones.
(300 + 200) + (70 + 30) + (4 + 8)

500 + 100 + 12 = 612

So, 374 + 238 = 612.

Remember that you can break apart both addends when finding sums mentally.

1. 302 + 56   2. 463 + 418

3. 222 + 725   4. 689 + 115

Use mental math to find 400 − 168.

Count on.

168 + 2 = 170
170 + 30 = 200
200 + 200 = 400
2 + 30 + 200 = 232

So, 400 − 168 = 232.

Remember that you can count on when subtracting mentally.

1. 523 − 163   2. 847 − 372

3. 768 − 259   4. 282 − 125

Name _____

Set F pages 435–440

Estimate 478 + 112.

Round each addend to the nearest ten.

478 → 480
+ 112 → 110
590

Round each addend to the nearest hundred.

478 → 500
+ 112 → 100
600

Use compatible numbers.

478 → 475
+ 112 → 110
585

Remember that compatible numbers are numbers close to the actual numbers and are easier to add mentally.

Round to the nearest hundred.

1. 367 + 319   **2.** 737 + 127

Round to the nearest ten.

3. 298 + 542   **4.** 459 + 85

Use compatible numbers.

5. 372 + 173   **6.** 208 + 164

7. Will rounding to the nearest ten or the nearest hundred give a closer estimate of 314 + 247? Explain your answer.

Set G pages 441–446

Estimate 486 − 177.

Round each number to the nearest hundred.

486 → 500
− 177 → 200
300

Round each number to the nearest ten.

486 → 490
− 177 → 180
310

Use compatible numbers.

486 → 475
− 177 → 175
300

Remember that an estimate is close to the actual answer.

Round to the nearest hundred.

1. 527 − 341   **2.** 872 − 184

Round to the nearest ten.

3. 387 − 298   **4.** 659 − 271

Use compatible numbers.

5. 472 − 228   **6.** 911 − 347

7. Will rounding to the nearest ten or the nearest hundred give a closer estimate of 848 − 231? Explain your answer.

Set H pages 447–452

A theater sells 128 tickets on Friday. The theater has sold a total of 679 tickets. How many tickets had the theater sold before Friday?

You can use an addition equation or a subtraction equation to solve this problem.

$? + 128 = 679$

$679 - 128 = ?$

Find the difference. Then use addition to check your subtraction.

$$\begin{array}{r} 679 \\ -\ 128 \\ \hline 551 \end{array} \qquad \begin{array}{r} 551 \\ +\ 128 \\ \hline 679 \end{array}$$

The numbers in the addition and subtraction match, so 551 is the correct difference.

Remember that you can use inverse operations to check your work.

Add or subtract. Check your work.

1.
$$\begin{array}{r} 7\ 4\ 6 \\ -\ 5\ 3\ 2 \\ \hline \square\square\square \end{array} \qquad \begin{array}{r} \square\square\square \\ +\ 5\ 3\ 2 \\ \hline \square\square\square \end{array}$$

2.
$$\begin{array}{r} 2\ 3\ 7 \\ +\ 4\ 1\ 2 \\ \hline \square\square\square \end{array} \qquad \begin{array}{r} \square\square\square \\ -\ 4\ 1\ 2 \\ \hline \square\square\square \end{array}$$

3. Toni read 131 pages on Monday and some pages on Tuesday. She read 289 pages in all. How many pages did Toni read on Tuesday?

Set I pages 453–458

Think about these questions to help you **model with math**.

Thinking Habits

- How can I use math I know to help solve this problem?

- How can I use pictures, objects, or an equation to represent the problem?

- How can I use numbers, words, and symbols to solve the problem?

Remember to apply the math you know to solve problems.

Elena has $265. She buys a jacket that costs $107 and a sweater that costs $69. How much money does Elena have left?

1. What is the hidden question you need to answer before you can solve the problem?

2. Solve the problem. Draw bar diagrams to represent the problem. Show the equations you used.

Name _____

1. Write the numbers that make this equation true.

$(2 + 1) + 3 = 2 + (\underline{} + \underline{})$

2. A mother elephant at the zoo ate 171 pounds of food one day. A baby elephant ate 69 pounds of food that day. Choose all the equations that show a reasonable estimate for how much they ate all together.

☐ $175 + 70 = 245$

☐ $100 + 60 = 160$

☐ $170 + 70 = 240$

☐ $175 + 75 = 250$

☐ $130 + 70 = 200$

3. Brianna wants to subtract $382 - 148$ mentally. Which of the following should she do first to find the difference?

Ⓐ Add 2 to 148 and add 2 to 382.

Ⓑ Add 2 to 148 and subtract 2 from to 382.

Ⓒ Subtract 8 from 148 and subtract 2 from 382.

Ⓓ Subtract 12 from 382 and add 12 to 148.

4. Estimate the difference of 765 and 333.

5. Look at the sums in the shaded column. Look at the addends. What pattern do you see? Explain why this pattern is always true.

+	0	1	2	3	4	5
0	0	1	2	3	4	5
1	1	2	3	4	5	6
2	2	3	4	5	6	7
3	3	4	5	6	7	8
4	4	5	6	7	8	9
5	5	6	7	8	9	10

6. Kayla wants to use mental math to add 332 and 154. Which of these shows how to break apart the numbers into hundreds, tens, and ones?

Ⓐ Break 332 into $320 + 12$. Break 154 into $125 + 29$.

Ⓑ Break 332 into $100 + 230 + 2$. Break 154 into $100 + 52 + 2$.

Ⓒ Break 332 into $300 + 16 + 16$. Break 154 into $100 + 27 + 27$.

Ⓓ Break 332 into $300 + 30 + 2$. Break 154 into $100 + 50 + 4$.

7. Christopher's school has 634 students. 528 students live within two miles of school. Use mental math to find how many students live farther than two miles from school.

8. Choose all the equations that are true.

☐ $32 + 56 + 10 = 10 + 56 + 32$

☐ $(49 + 28) + 5 = 49 + (28 + 5)$

☐ $56 + 890 = 890 + 56$

☐ $82 + 0 = 82$

☐ $45 + 27 = 27 + 35$

9. The table shows the scores for 4 teams on Sports Day.

Sports Day	
Team	**Score**
A	**168**
B	**153**
C	**161**
D	**179**

Write the letter A, B, C, or D above the number line to show each team's score rounded to the nearest ten.

```
←+——+——+——+——+——+——+→
  150   160   170   180   190   200
```

10. José subtracted 57 from 169. His work is shown below.

$$
\begin{array}{r}
169 \\
- \quad 57 \\
\hline
112
\end{array}
$$

Do the strategies below show a way to check his work using inverse operations? Choose *Yes* or *No*.

10a. Add 57 and 169. ○ Yes ○ No

10b. Add 112 and 169. ○ Yes ○ No

10c. Subtract 112 from 169. ○ Yes ○ No

10d. Add 112 and 57. ○ Yes ○ No

11. Kara wanted to round to the nearest ten to estimate the sum of 405 and 385. She wrote $400 + 400 = 800$. Do you agree with Kara? Explain why or why not.

12. Amy subtracts 342 from 456 and gets 114. What addition equation can she use to check her answer? Draw a bar diagram to show how the numbers in this problem are related.

Name _____

13. Adrian wants to buy a tablet computer for $350 and a storage case for $62. He wants to install software that costs $199.

Part A

Draw a bar diagram that you can use to find the total cost of the items.

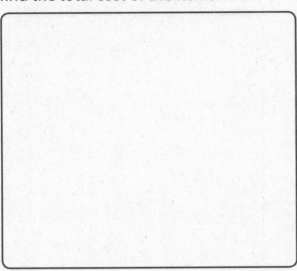

Part B

What is the first step you would do to solve this problem using mental math?

14. Allie wants to subtract 341 − 97 mentally. First she adds 3 to 97 to get 100. What should Allie's next step be? What is the difference?

Ⓐ Add 6 to 341. The difference is 247.

Ⓑ Add 200 to 100. The difference is 100.

Ⓒ Subtract 3 from 341. The difference is 238.

Ⓓ Add 3 to 341. The difference is 244.

15. Draw lines to match each number on the left with the number on the right that shows rounding to the nearest hundred.

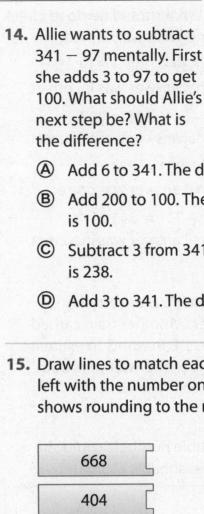

668		600
404		700
649		400
489		500

16. Explain how to use mental math to find 620 − 278.

17. Emil found $693 - 231$. The difference he got was 464. What should he do to check his answer, and what will he find?

Ⓐ Subtract $639 - 300 = 339$. His original answer was incorrect.

Ⓑ Subtract $464 - 231 = 233$. His original answer was incorrect.

Ⓒ Add $693 + 231 = 924$. His original answer was correct.

Ⓓ Add $464 + 231 = 695$. His original answer was incorrect.

18. A train came into Dallas carrying 392 passengers. Another train carried 259 passengers. Erin wants to estimate the total number of passengers both trains carried.

Part A

What compatible numbers could she add to get a reasonable estimate?

Part B

Estimate the total number of passengers in two different ways.

19. At the School Fair, Grade 3 raises $84 more than Grade 4. Grade 4 raises $112 more than Grade 2. Grade 3 raises $360. How much money does Grade 2 raise?

Part A

Use a bar diagram to represent the hidden question. Then answer the hidden question.

Part B

Use an equation to represent the main question. Then answer the main question.

Name _____

Vacation Trip
Mia is planning a vacation in Orlando, FL.
The **Mia's Route** table shows her route and the miles she will drive.

Use the **Mia's Route** table to answer Questions 1–3.

1. Round each distance to the nearest ten to show about how many
   miles Mia will drive on each part of her trip.

   Memphis, TN, to Birmingham, AL:

   Birmingham, AL, to Gainesville, FL:

   Gainesville, FL, to Orlando, FL:

Mia's Route		
City 1	**City 2**	**Miles**
Memphis, TN	Birmingham, AL	237
Birmingham, AL	Gainesville, FL	422
Gainesville, FL	Orlando, FL	183

2. Use mental math to find the actual number of miles Mia will drive to
   reach Gainesville. Show your work.

3. Mia says, "Birmingham is 185 miles closer to Memphis than to Gainesville."
   Her brother says, "No, it is 175 miles closer."
   Use mental math to decide who is correct. Show your work.

Mia has to book a hotel and buy theme park tickets. The **Hotel Prices** and **Theme Park Prices** tables show the total prices for Mia's stay.
The **Mia's Options** list shows two plans that Mia can choose from.

Hotel Prices

Hotel	Price for Mia's Stay
Hotel A	$362
Hotel B	$233
Hotel C	$313

4. Mia has $600 to spend on a hotel and tickets.

Part A

Which option does Mia have enough money for? Explain using estimation.

Theme Park Prices

Theme Park	Price for a Ticket
Theme Park X	$331
Theme Park Y	$275
Theme Park Z	$302

Part B

Create a new option for Mia. Fill out the table with a hotel and a theme park. Explain why Mia has enough money for this plan.

Mia's Options

Option	Hotel	Theme Park
1	A	Z
2	B	Y
3		

5. One theme park has a special offer. For each ticket Mia buys, she gets another ticket free. Shade the squares in the table at the right to show this pattern. Explain why the pattern is true.

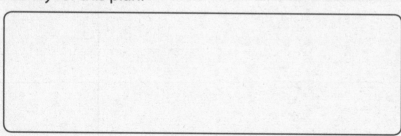

+	0	1	2	3	4	5
0	0	1	2	3	4	5
1	1	2	3	4	5	6
2	2	3	4	5	6	7
3	3	4	5	6	7	8
4	4	5	6	7	8	9
5	5	6	7	8	9	10

Fluently Add and Subtract within 1,000

Essential Question: What are standard procedures for adding and subtracting whole numbers?

Forest fires cause many changes within an environment.

A forest fire can be destructive. But it also helps a new forest start to grow.

My knowledge is growing! Here's a project on changing environments and populations.

Math and Science Project: Changing Environments

Do Research Forest fires destroy, but they also make room for new growth. Use the Internet or other sources to find information about forest fires. Describe the effect of forest fires on plant and animal populations.

Journal: Write a Report Include data with numbers for the population you researched. Also include:

- Choose a kind of animal or plant. Tell how a change in the environment can affect the number of animals or plants.

- Write and solve a subtraction problem using your data.

- Write and solve an addition problem using your data.

Name _____

Review What You Know

A-Z Vocabulary

Choose the best term from the box.
Write it on the blank.

- Commutative Property of Addition
- Associative Property of Addition
- compatible numbers
- inverse operations

1. _____
   are easy to add or subtract
   mentally.

2. According to the _____, the grouping of
   addends can be changed, and the sum will remain the same.

3. Addition and subtraction are _____.

Rounding

Round each number to the nearest ten.

4. 57   **5.** 241   **6.** 495

Round each number to the nearest hundred.

7. 732   **8.** 81   **9.** 553

Estimating Sums

Use compatible numbers to estimate each sum.

10. 27 + 12   **11.** 133 + 102

12. 504 + 345   **13.** 52 + 870

14. 293 + 278   **15.** 119 + 426

Estimating Differences

16. Tony and Kim play a video game. Tony scores 512 points. Kim scores
768 points. About how many more points does Kim score than Tony?
Which estimation method did you use?

17. Which number sentence shows the most reasonable estimate for 467 − 231?

    Ⓐ 425 − 250 = 175   Ⓒ 400 − 300 = 100

    Ⓑ 500 − 200 = 300   Ⓓ 470 − 230 = 240

My Word Cards

Use the examples for each word on the front of the card to help complete the definitions on the back.

A-Z Glossary

regroup

28 = 28 ones

28 = 1 ten 18 ones

28 = 2 tens 8 ones

conjecture

353 + 287 (>) 375 + 243

Conjecture: The expression on the left has the greater sum.

Complete the definition. Extend learning by writing your own definitions.

A _____ is a statement that is believed to be true, but it has not been proved.

When you _____ numbers, you are naming whole numbers in a different way using place value.

Name _____

☆ *Solve & Share*

Find the sum of 327 + 241. Think about place value. **Solve this problem any way you choose.**

I can ...
use place value to break apart and add numbers.

I can also look for patterns to solve problems.

You can use structure. You can break apart the problem to show each of the addends in expanded form. *Show your work in the space below!*

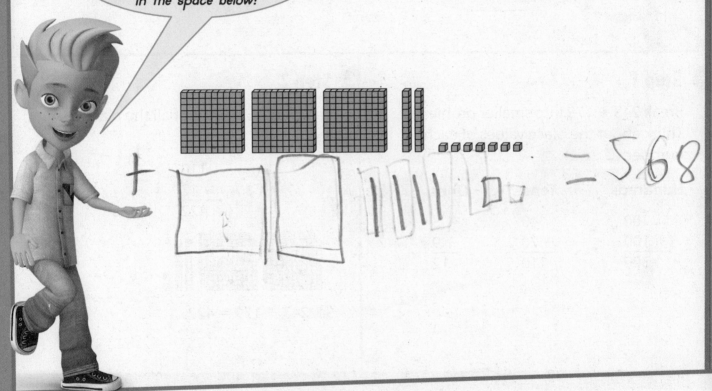

$= 568$

Look Back! **Use Appropriate Tools** Is it easier to use place-value blocks or counters to help you solve this 3-digit addition problem? Explain.

How Can You Break Large Addition Problems into Smaller Ones?

A

Find the sum of 243 + 179. Each digit in the numbers can be modeled with place-value blocks.

You can use place value to add the numbers.

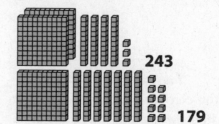

243

179

B ## Step 1

Break 243 + 179 into smaller problems. Think about the place values of each number.

Hundreds	Tens	Ones
200	40	3
+ 100	+ 70	+ 9
300	110	12

C ## Step 2

Then, add the sums of all the places.

```
  300
  110
+  12
─────
  422
```

So, 243 + 179 = 422.

Convince Me! **Critique Reasoning** Lexi says, "To solve 243 + 179, I can just count on with place-value blocks to find the answer: 100, 200, 300, another hundred from the 11 tens is 400, one more ten and 12 ones is 422!" How is Lexi's way like Steps 1 and 2 above?

Name _____

☆ Guided Practice *

Do You Understand?

1. Use Structure Suppose you were adding 527 + 405. What numbers would you combine when adding the tens? Why?

2. Write the smaller problems you could use to find 623 + 281. What is the sum?

Do You Know How?

In **3**, use place value to find the sum.

3. 365 + 422

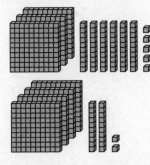

Hundreds	Tens	Ones	Total
300	60	5	_____
+ 400	+ 20	+ 2	_____
		+	_____

☆ Independent Practice ☆

Leveled Practice In **4–11**, find each sum.

4. 356 + 123

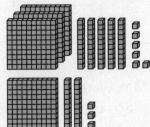

Hundreds	Tens	Ones	Total
300	50	6	_____
+ 100	+ 20	+ 3	_____
		+	_____

5. 550 + 423

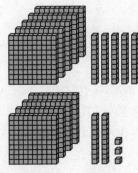

Hundreds	Tens	Ones	Total
500	50	0	_____
+ 400	+ 20	+ 3	_____
		+	_____

6. 185 + 613

7. 730 + 168

8. 546 + 143

9. 362 + 524

10. 644 + 101

11. 463 + 315

Problem Solving

12. Model with Math John read a book with 377 pages. Jess read a book with 210 pages. How many pages did John and Jess read? Draw a bar diagram to represent and solve the problem.

13. Construct Arguments Explain how the solids shown in Group A and Group B could have been sorted.

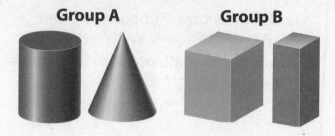

Group A   Group B

14. Critique Reasoning Henry believes the sum of 275 + 313 is 598. Is Henry correct? Explain.

?	
275	313

15. Higher Order Thinking A school cafeteria sold 255 lunches on Monday, 140 lunches on Tuesday, and 226 lunches on Wednesday. Did the cafeteria sell more lunches on Monday and Tuesday or on Tuesday and Wednesday? Explain.

✔ Assessment

16. Nina wants to find 622 + 247 using place value. Which shows the correct way to break apart this addition problem?

    Ⓐ   600 + 200; 22 + 40; 2 + 7

    Ⓑ   600 + 300; 20 + 40; 2 + 7

    Ⓒ   600 + 200; 20 + 40; 2 + 7

    Ⓓ   600 + 200; 20 + 47; 2 + 7

17. Max wants to add 331 + 516 using place value. He begins by breaking the problem into smaller problems. He writes (300 + 500) + (30 + 10) + (1 + 6). Which shows the correct sums of the hundreds, tens, and ones?

    Ⓐ   800 + 40 + 6

    Ⓑ   800 + 40 + 7

    Ⓒ   700 + 40 + 8

    Ⓓ   400 + 80 + 8

Name _____

Another Look!

"You can use place-value blocks to represent each number."

Find 234 + 451.

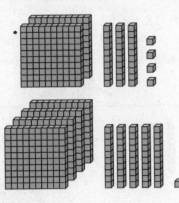

Break the problem into smaller problems.

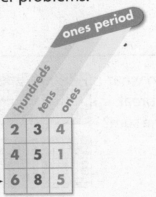

ones period

hundreds | tens | ones

2	3	4
4	5	1
Sums → 6	8	5

Add the sums. | **Total**
Hundreds ⟶ 600
Tens ⟶ 80
Ones ⟶ + 5
234 + 451 = 685

In **1**, complete the steps to find the sum.

1.

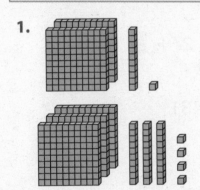

211 + 334

Hundreds	Tens	Ones	Total
200	10	1	_____
+ 300	+ 30	+ 4	_____
		+	_____

In **2–10**, find each sum.

2. 516 + 142

3. 439 + 520

4. 721 + 176

5. 631 + 245

6. 580 + 315

7. 714 + 144

8. 128 + 441

9. 214 + 253

10. 661 + 127

11. **Make Sense and Persevere** Estimate first, then use counting on to solve mentally. How many more students are in eighth grade than sixth grade at North Middle School? Is your answer reasonable? Explain.

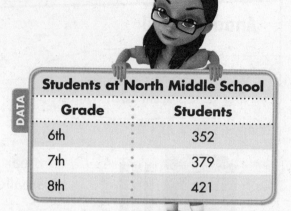

Students at North Middle School	
Grade	Students
6th	352
7th	379
8th	421

12. Bill needs to find 318 + 230. Into what three smaller problems can Bill break this addition problem? What is the sum?

You can use place value to add.

13. **Higher Order Thinking** The Smith family took a vacation. They drove 256 miles on the first day and 287 miles on the second day. If they drove the same number of total miles on their return trip, how many miles did they drive on their entire trip?

14. **Critique Reasoning** Is Dale's work correct? If not, tell why and write a correct answer.

Find 64 − 27.
I can add 3 to 27 to get 30.
64 − 30 = 34
34 − 3 = 31
So, 64 − 27 = 31.

15. Shariq wants to find 415 + 583 using place value. Which shows the correct way to break apart this addition problem?

Ⓐ 400 + 800; 10 + 50; 5 + 3

Ⓑ 400 + 500; 10 + 83; 5 + 3

Ⓒ 400 + 580; 10 + 80; 5 + 3

Ⓓ 400 + 500; 10 + 80; 5 + 3

16. Katrina uses place value to find the sum of 627 + 361. She begins by breaking the problem into smaller problems. She writes (600 + 300) + (20 + 60) + (7 + 1). Which shows the correct sums of the hundreds, tens, and ones?

Ⓐ 800 + 80 + 9   Ⓒ 900 + 80 + 8

Ⓑ 800 + 90 + 8   Ⓓ 900 + 90 + 8

Name _____

Solve

Solve & Share

Suppose a bus travels 276 miles on Monday and 248 miles on Tuesday. How many miles does the bus travel? *Solve this problem any way you choose.*

I can ...
use different strategies to regroup when adding 3-digit numbers.

I can also choose and use a math tool to solve problems.

You can use tools, such as place-value blocks, to add larger numbers. What other strategies can you use to solve this problem? *Show your work!*

Look Back! **Make Sense and Persevere** Why would it be a good idea to estimate first before you solved this problem?

Essential Question **How Can You Use Addition to Solve Problems?**

A

Jason's family drove from Niagara Falls to Albany. They drove 119 miles in the morning and 187 miles in the afternoon. How far did Jason's family drive?

Find 119 + 187.

Estimate by rounding to the nearest hundred.
100 + 200 = 300
So, 119 + 187 is about 300 miles.

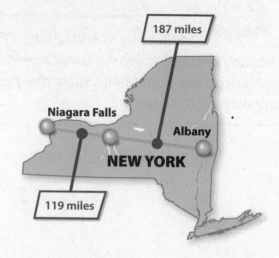

187 miles

Niagara Falls

Albany

NEW YORK

119 miles

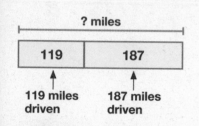

? miles

| 119 | 187 |

119 miles driven   187 miles driven

An estimate can help you check whether or not your answer is reasonable.

B ## Step 1

Add the ones.
9 ones + 7 ones = 16 ones
Regroup.
16 ones = 1 ten 6 ones

$$\begin{array}{r} {}^{1} \\ 119 \\ + 187 \\ \hline 6 \end{array}$$

When you regroup, you name a whole number in a different way.

C ## Step 2

Add the tens.
1 ten + 1 ten + 8 tens
= 10 tens

Regroup.
10 tens = 1 hundred 0 tens

$$\begin{array}{r} {}^{1\,1} \\ 119 \\ + 187 \\ \hline 06 \end{array}$$

D ## Step 3

Add the hundreds.
1 hundred + 1 hundred
+ 1 hundred = 3 hundreds

$$\begin{array}{r} {}^{1\,1} \\ 119 \\ + 187 \\ \hline 306 \end{array}$$

Jason's family drove 306 miles.

The answer is reasonable since 306 is close to 300.

Convince Me! **Model with Math** Draw or use place-value blocks to show how Steps 1, 2, and 3 above work. What did you find out?

Practice Buddy Tools Assessment

☆ Guided Practice ☆

Do You Understand?

1. Sue scored 236 points during the first half of her basketball season. She scored 285 points during the second half. How many points did she score during the entire season?

? points	
236	285

2. **Make Sense and Persevere** In Exercise 1, how can you tell if your answer is reasonable?

Do You Know How?

In **3–6**, estimate by rounding to the nearest ten. Then find each sum. You may use place-value blocks or drawings to help.

3.
```
   1 2 6
 + 1 7 1
 2 □ □
```

4.
```
     □
   5 3 8
 + 4 2 9
   □ □ 7
```

5.
```
     □
   4 1 5
 + 1 6 8
   □ 8 □
```

6.
```
   □ □
   3 9 1
 + 6 0 9
 □ □ □ 0
```

☆ Independent Practice ☆

Leveled Practice In **7–18**, estimate by rounding to the nearest ten. Then find each sum.

7.
```
   1 3 6
 + 2 5 2
 3 □ □
```

8.
```
   □ □
   6 7 8
 + 1 2 9
   □ □ 7
```

9.
```
     □
   5 6 4
 + 2 8 3
 8 □ □
```

10.
```
     □
   1 1 8
 + 3 3 5
   □ 5 □
```

11.
```
   1 7 2
 + 5 3 4
```

12.
```
   3 2 4
 + 5 0 8
```

13.
```
   3 0 9
 + 2 8 7
```

14.
```
   4 6 5
 + 2 8 5
```

15. 582 + 230

16. 207 + 238

17. 424 + 391

18. 678 + 143

Problem Solving

In **19** and **20**, use the table at the right.

19. **Model with Math** How many soup can labels did Grades 1 and 2 collect? Estimate by rounding to the nearest hundred. Then solve. Write an equation that represents the problem.

Soup Can Labels Collected	
Grades	**Number**
Grade 1	385
Grade 2	294
Grade 3	479
Grade 4	564

20. **Make Sense and Persevere** Is your answer to Exercise 19 reasonable? Explain.

21. **Number Sense** The roller coaster Kingda Ka is 192 feet taller than the first Ferris wheel. Use the symbols < and > to compare the heights of the two rides in two different ways.

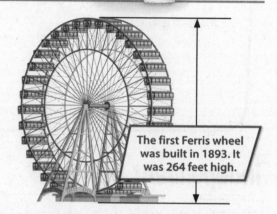

The first Ferris wheel was built in 1893. It was 264 feet high.

22. **Higher Order Thinking** Pete can run 178 yards in one minute. Sharon can run 119 more yards than Pete in one minute. How many yards can they both run in one minute?

? yards

178	178 + 119

↑ yards Pete runs   ↑ yards Sharon runs

 Assessment

23. There were 126 tomato plants at the nursery. The owner planted 229 pepper plants. Complete the problem to find the total number of plants in the nursery. Show regrouping, if necessary.

```
    □
  1 2 6
+ 2 2 9
  □□□
```

24. Josh was playing a board game. He scored 248 points in the first game and 273 points in the second game. Complete the problem to find the total number of points Josh scored. Show regrouping, if necessary.

```
  □□
  2 4 8
+ 2 7 3
  □□□
```

Name _____

Another Look!
Find 237 + 186.

You can use place-value blocks to model each number you are adding.

237

186

Step 1
$$\begin{array}{r} \overset{1}{237} \\ + 186 \\ \hline 3 \end{array}$$

Step 2
$$\begin{array}{r} \overset{1\,1}{237} \\ + 186 \\ \hline 23 \end{array}$$

Step 3
$$\begin{array}{r} \overset{1\,1}{237} \\ + 186 \\ \hline 423 \end{array}$$

In **1**, use the place-value blocks to help add.

1. 345 + 276

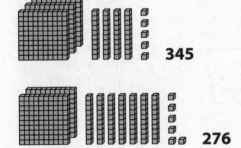

345

276

Add the ones and regroup.
$$\begin{array}{r} 3\ 4\ 5 \\ +\ 2\ 7\ 6 \\ \hline \square \end{array}$$

Add the tens and regroup.
$$\begin{array}{r} 3\ 4\ 5 \\ +\ 2\ 7\ 6 \\ \hline \square\square \end{array}$$

Add the hundreds.
$$\begin{array}{r} 3\ 4\ 5 \\ +\ 2\ 7\ 6 \\ \hline \square\square\square \end{array}$$

In **2–5**, estimate by rounding to the nearest hundred. Then find each sum.

2. 118
   + 146

3. 283
   + 147

4. 542
   + 109

5. 220
   + 479

In **6** and **7**, use the table at the right.

6. **Model with Math** How many points were scored by Howie and Theo? Estimate by rounding to the nearest hundred. Then solve. Write an equation that represents the problem.

Points Scored	
Player	**Points**
Howie	272
Theo	325
Isabel	288

7. **Make Sense and Persevere** Is your answer to Exercise 6 reasonable? Explain.

8. **A-Z Vocabulary** Maria and her family drove 885 miles on their summer vacation. The first 8 on the left in this number has a _____ of 800.

9. **Critique Reasoning** Marc thinks a hexagon has 5 sides and 5 angles. Is Marc correct? Explain.

10. **Higher Order Thinking** Sarah and Angela have a collection of pennies and nickels in their piggy banks. Which girl has more coins in her bank? Explain how you know using numbers and symbols.

Sarah
149 pennies
127 nickels

Angela
173 pennies
105 nickels

✓ **Assessment**

11. There were 252 horses in the pasture. The rancher added 163 new horses to the pasture. Complete the problem to find how many horses are now in the pasture. Show regrouping, if needed.

```
   □
   2 5 2
 + 1 6 3
 □□□
```

12. Mrs. Collins bought a $256 plane ticket in March and a $125 ticket in April. Complete the problem to find how much Mrs. Collins spent on plane tickets. Show regrouping, if needed.

```
     □
   $2 5 6
 + $1 2 5
 $□□□
```

Name _____

Solve & Share

There were 565 rubber ducks in the Rubber Ducky Race last year. There were 237 more rubber ducks this year. How many rubber ducks were there in this year's race? **Solve this problem any way you choose.**

I can ...
use regrouping to add 3-digit numbers.

I can also reason about math.

Use reasoning.
Think about the operation that will give you the answer to this problem.

Look Back! **Make Sense and Persevere** Show how to use estimation to check that your answer is reasonable.

How Can You Use Addition to Solve Problems?

A

A riverboat carried 124 more passengers on Sunday than on Saturday. How many passengers were there on Sunday?

288 passengers on Saturday

Sunday passengers →

?

288	124

↑ 288 passengers on Saturday   ↑ 124 more passengers on Sunday

You can estimate by rounding each number to the nearest hundred:
$300 + 100 = 400$.

B **Step 1**

Add the ones.
8 ones + 4 ones = 12 ones

Regroup.
12 ones = 1 ten 2 ones

$$
\begin{array}{r}
1 \\
288 \\
+\,124 \\
\hline
2
\end{array}
$$

C **Step 2**

Add the tens.
1 ten + 8 tens + 2 tens
= 11 tens

Regroup.
11 tens = 1 hundred 1 ten

$$
\begin{array}{r}
1\,1 \\
288 \\
+\,124 \\
\hline
12
\end{array}
$$

D **Step 3**

Add the hundreds.
1 hundred + 2 hundreds
+ 1 hundred = 4 hundreds

$$
\begin{array}{r}
1\,1 \\
288 \\
+\,124 \\
\hline
412
\end{array}
$$

There were 412 passengers on Sunday.

The answer is reasonable because it is close to the estimate of 400.

Convince Me! **Use Structure** Use a different method to add 288 + 136.

Another Example!

The Yellowstone River is 692 miles long. It is 51 miles shorter than the Kansas River. How long is the Kansas River?

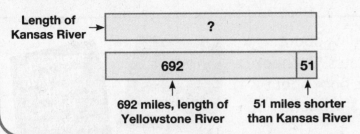

Length of Kansas River →

?

692 | 51

692 miles, length of Yellowstone River

51 miles shorter than Kansas River

Line up the digits by place value. Add the ones, add the tens, and add the hundreds, regrouping as needed.

$$\begin{array}{r} \overset{1}{6}92 \\ +\ 51 \\ \hline 743 \end{array}$$

The Kansas River is 743 miles long.

Guided Practice

Do You Understand?

1. **Generalize** When you add 3-digit numbers, how do you know if you need to regroup?

2. **Reasoning** To add 546 + 327, would you need to regroup? Explain.

Do You Know How?

In **3–6**, estimate by rounding to the nearest ten. Then find each sum.

3. 516
   + 325

4. 163
   + 50

5. 255
   + 189

6. 303
   + 597

Independent Practice

In **7–14**, estimate by rounding to the nearest ten or to the nearest hundred. Then find each sum.

7. 209
   + 469

8. 634
   + 87

9. 418
   + 351

10. 787
    + 151

11. 630 + 178

12. 273 + 727

13. 360 + 58

14. 575 + 366

For another example, see Set C on page 526.

Topic 9 | Lesson 9-3

Problem Solving ☆

15. Mrs. Morris drove 116 more miles on Tuesday than on Monday. On Monday, she drove 235 miles. How many miles did she drive on Tuesday?

16. At a puppet show there are 56 chairs arranged in rows and columns. Tonya places the chairs in 7 rows. How many columns are there?

17. Make Sense and Persevere Gwen is reading about the rivers and mountains of the United States. The book about rivers has 137 fewer pages than the book about mountains. How many pages are there in the book about mountains?

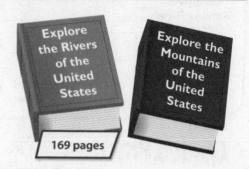

169 pages

18. Critique Reasoning Jackson says that when you add 567 to 358 you only need to regroup once. Abby says that you need to regroup two times. Who is correct? Explain.

19. Higher Order Thinking The students at Cleveland School are collecting soda can tabs. The goal of each class is to collect 500 tabs. So far, the second graders have collected 315 tabs. The third graders have collected 190 more tabs than the second graders. Have the third graders reached their goal? Explain.

✓ Assessment

20. Choose all of the expressions that need regrouping to solve.

- ☐ 613 + 326
- ☐ 481 + 276
- ☐ 135 + 295
- ☐ 503 + 296
- ☐ 823 + 176

21. Choose all of the expressions that do **NOT** need regrouping to solve.

- ☐ 243 + 708
- ☐ 681 + 107
- ☐ 259 + 662
- ☐ 680 + 210
- ☐ 324 + 572

Homework & Practice 9-3
Continue to Add 3-Digit Numbers

Another Look!

In August, there were 568 people who went whitewater rafting in the state park. That was 245 fewer people than in July. How many people went whitewater rafting in July?

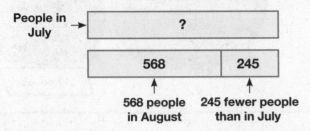

People in July → [?]

[568 | 245]

568 people in August   245 fewer people than in July

You can estimate by rounding each number to the nearest ten:
570 + 250 = 820

Step 1

Add the ones.

Regroup 13 ones as 1 ten 3 ones.

$$\begin{array}{r} \overset{1}{568} \\ + 245 \\ \hline 3 \end{array}$$

Step 2

Add the tens.

Regroup 11 tens as 1 hundred 1 ten.

$$\begin{array}{r} \overset{11}{568} \\ + 245 \\ \hline 13 \end{array}$$

Step 3

Add the hundreds.

$$\begin{array}{r} \overset{11}{568} \\ + 245 \\ \hline 813 \end{array}$$

In July, 813 people went whitewater rafting.

The answer is reasonable because it is close to the estimate of 820.

In **1–12**, estimate by rounding to the nearest ten or to the nearest hundred. Then find each sum.

1. 238
   + 481

2. 506
   + 127

3. 356
   + 52

4. 59
   + 264

5. 279 + 600

6. 165 + 561

7. 922 + 39

8. 504 + 109

9. 311 + 619

10. 694 + 116

11. 527 + 450

12. 285 + 258

In **13** and **14**, use the picture on the right.

13. **Reasoning** At the county fair, the red-ribbon pumpkin weighed 108 pounds less than the blue-ribbon pumpkin. How much did the blue-ribbon pumpkin weigh?

14. **Make Sense and Persevere** What is the total weight of the two pumpkins?

317 pounds

In **15–17**, use the graph on the right.

15. How many students read more than 20 books over the summer?

16. **Be Precise** How many fewer books did Frannie read than Kenny?

17. **Higher Order Thinking** In all, did the students read at least 100 books? How can you tell without using addition?

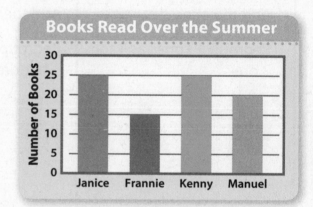

Books Read Over the Summer

Number of Books — Janice, Frannie, Kenny, Manuel

✓ **Assessment**

18. Choose all of the expressions that need regrouping to solve.

☐ 815 + 125
☐ 266 + 548
☐ 436 + 352
☐ 480 + 125
☐ 376 + 613

19. Choose all of the expressions that do **NOT** need regrouping to solve.

☐ 703 + 108
☐ 56 + 367
☐ 173 + 405
☐ 653 + 325
☐ 442 + 536

Name _____

☆ ☆
Solve & Share

A pet store has 162 goldfish, 124 angelfish, and 53 pufferfish. How many fish are there in all? How might an estimate help you solve the problem? **Solve this problem any way you choose.**

I can ...
add three or more numbers using what I know about adding 3-digit numbers.

I can also generalize from examples.

You can generalize. Use what you know about adding two numbers to add three numbers. *Show your work in the space below!*

Look Back! Reasoning How can the 3 numbers in the problem help you find the answer?

Essential Question **How Can You Add More Than 2 Numbers?**

A

Different kinds of birds are for sale at a pet store. How many birds are for sale?

Find 137 + 155 + 18.

Round to the nearest ten to estimate:
140 + 160 + 20 = 320.

Parrots
18

Canaries
137

Parakeets
155

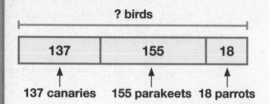

? birds

137	155	18

137 canaries   155 parakeets   18 parrots

A bar diagram can
show 3 addends.

B **Step 1**

Line up ones, tens,
and hundreds.

```
  137
  155
+  18
```

C **Step 2**

Add the ones.
Regroup.

```
   2
  137
  155
+  18
    0
```

D **Step 3**

Add the tens.
Regroup.

```
  1 2
  137
  155
+  18
   10
```

The answer is
reasonable since 310
is close to 320.

E **Step 4**

Add the hundreds.

```
  1 2
  137
  155
+  18
  310
```

In all, 310 birds
are for sale.

Convince Me! **Model with Math** Suppose the pet store gets
46 lovebirds to sell. How many birds are for sale at the pet store now?
Write an equation to show how you solved this problem.

Name _____

 Guided Practice *

Do You Understand?

In **1** and **2**, look at the example on page 494.

1. **Reasoning** Why is there a 2 above the tens place in Step 2?

2. If you add the numbers in this order, do you get the same sum? Explain why or why not.

```
    1 5 5
    1 3 7
  + 1 8
```

Do You Know How?

In **3–6**, find each sum.

3.
```
       1
    1 2 3
    1 6 8
  +   3 6
  □ □ 7
```

4.
```
    5 1 0
      4 5
  +   2 7
  5 □ □
```

5.
```
    2 4 7
    3 6 2
  +   4 9
```

6. 56 + 183 + 269

You can use estimation to check if your sums are reasonable.

Independent Practice

Leveled Practice In **7–17**, find each sum.

7.
```
      6 4
      4 2
  +   8 8
  □ □ □
```

8.
```
    3 5 4
      8 5
  +   7 2
  □ □ □
```

9.
```
    3 0 7
      3 7
  + 2 3 4
  □ □ □
```

10.
```
    7 1 4
    1 6 3
  +   9 9
  □ □ □
```

11.
```
    602
    125
  + 231
```

12.
```
    246
     54
    233
  + 205
```

13.
```
    164
     68
  +  35
```

14.
```
    125
     35
    124
  + 239
```

15. 32 + 9 + 56 + 8

16. 481 + 78 + 42

17. 398 + 219 + 23 + 251

Problem Solving

18. **Model with Math** Use the picture at the right to find the height of President Washington's head carved in Mt. Rushmore. Write an equation to solve the problem.

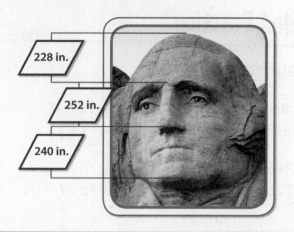

228 in.

252 in.

240 in.

19. **Number Sense** Compare the numbers 212 and 209. Use <, >, or =. Explain how you decided.

20. Ramos has 12 one-dollar bills, 225 pennies, 105 nickels, and 65 dimes. How many coins does he have?

21. **Algebra** Jada spends $74 on a hat, shoes, and shorts. If the hat costs $22 and the shoes cost $33, how much were the shorts? Write and solve an equation. Use an unknown to represent the cost of the shorts.

22. **Higher Order Thinking** Meg says 95 + 76 + 86 is greater than 300, but less than 400. Is Meg correct? Why or why not?

✓ **Assessment**

23. Karin had cereal, a glass of milk, and a banana for breakfast. How many calories were in her meal? Round to the nearest ten to estimate and then solve. Write a number sentence that includes your solution.

banana: 105 calories
bowl of dry cereal: 110 calories
glass of milk: 150 calories

Name _____

Another Look!

Find 137 + 201 + 109.

?		
137	201	109

To add three numbers, you can add two numbers first. Then, add the sum of those two numbers and the third number.

You can break the problem into two smaller problems.

Step 1

Add 137 + 201.

```
  137
+ 201
  338
```

Step 2

Add 338 + 109.

```
   1
  338
+ 109
  447
```

So, 137 + 201 + 109 = 447.

In **1** and **2**, complete the smaller problems to find the sum.

1. 35 + 63 + 76

```
  3 5          ▢
+ ▢▢        + 7 6
  ▢▢          ▢▢▢
```

2. 149 + 22 + 314

```
      ▢
  1 4 9        ▢▢▢
+   ▢▢      + 3 1 4
  ▢▢▢          ▢▢▢
```

In **3–8**, find the sum.

3.
```
  127
   39
+  87
```

4.
```
  293
  312
+  78
```

5.
```
   25
  238
   75
+ 180
```

6. 150 + 125 + 350

7. 382 + 164 + 267

8. 46 + 461 + 309

9. **Critique Reasoning** Justine has 162 red buttons, 98 blue buttons, and 284 green buttons. By estimating she says she knows she has more than 500 buttons. Do you agree? Explain.

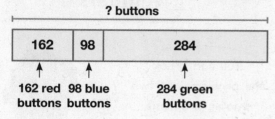

? buttons

| 162 | 98 | 284 |

↑ 162 red buttons   ↑ 98 blue buttons   ↑ 284 green buttons

10. **Generalize** To subtract 178 − 135 mentally, Carmine adds 5 to each number. Karen adds 2 to each number. Will both methods work to find the correct answer? Why or why not?

11. **Higher Order Thinking** On Friday, 215 people went to the street fair. On Saturday, 163 more people went to the street fair than on Friday. On Sunday, 192 people went. In total how many people went to the fair? What are two ways you can use to find the answer?

12. **Model with Math** Kyle was playing a new video game. He scored 128 points on his first game. He scored 305 points on his second game, and 490 points on his third game. How many points did Kyle score? Draw a bar diagram and write an equation to solve.

✓ **Assessment**

13. The table shows what Carlos had for breakfast. How many calories did Carlos consume? Write an equation to solve the problem.

Food	Amount	Calories
Bran flakes	1 ounce	90
Banana	1	105
Orange juice	1 cup	110
Milk	1 cup	150

DATA

Name _____

Find the difference of 534 − 108. Think about how place value can help you subtract. **Solve this problem any way you choose.**

I can ...
use place value to solve simpler problems when subtracting multi-digit numbers.

I can also look for patterns to solve problems.

You can use structure. How could you use place value to break this problem into smaller subtraction problems? *Show your work in the space below!*

Look Back! **Generalize** How can using place value help you solve this subtraction problem?

Essential Question ## How Can You Break Large Subtraction Problems into Smaller Ones?

A

At the end of the fourth round of a game of Digit Derby, Marco's score was 462 points. During the fifth round of the game, Marco loses points. What is Marco's score at the end of the fifth round?

Find 462 − 181.

End of Round 4

Marco has 462 points.

End of Round 5

Marco loses 181 points.

> Place value can help you break a subtraction problem into smaller problems.

B ## Step 1

Start with 462.

Subtract the **hundreds**.
462 − 100 = 362

So far, 100 has been subtracted.

C ## Step 2

Next, start with 362.

Subtract the **tens**.

You need to subtract 8 tens, but there are not enough tens. First, subtract 6 tens.
362 − 60 = 302

Then, subtract the remaining 2 tens.
302 − 20 = 282

So far, 100 + 60 + 20 = 180 has been subtracted.

D ## Step 3

That leaves just 1 to subtract.

Subtract the **ones**.
282 − 1 = 281

100 + 60 + 20 + 1 = 181 has been subtracted.

At the end of the fifth round, Marco's score is 281 points.

Convince Me! **Be Precise** Find 453 − 262. Explain how place value can help you solve.

© Pearson Education, Inc. 3

☆ Guided Practice*

Do You Understand?

1. Why do you need to record the numbers you subtract at each step?

2. Ana is trying to find 634 − 210. She decides to start by subtracting 10 from 634. Do you agree with Ana? Explain.

Do You Know How?

In **3** and **4**, use place value to help break the problem into smaller problems.

3. Find 374 − 236.

374 − 200 = ____

174 − 30 = ____

144 − 4 = ____

140 − 2 = ____

4. Find 369 − 175.

369 − 100 = ____

269 − 60 = ____

209 − 10 = ____

199 − 5 = ____

Independent Practice ☆

Leveled Practice In **5–10**, follow the steps to find each difference. Show your work.

5. 738 − 523

First, subtract 500.

____ − ____ = 238

Then, subtract 20.

238 − ____ = ____

Then, subtract 3.

____ − 3 = ____

6. 755 − 315

First, subtract 300.

755 − ____ = ____

Then, subtract 10.

____ − 10 = ____

Then, subtract 5.

____ − ____ = 440

7. 336 − 217

First, subtract 200.

____ − 200 = ____

Then, subtract 10.

____ − 10 = ____

Then, subtract 6.

____ − ____ = 120

Then, subtract 1.

____ − 1 = ____

8. 455 − 182

9. 865 − 506

10. 794 − 355

Problem Solving

11. Don's book has 316 pages. He read 50 pages last week. He read another 71 pages this week. How many more pages does Don have left to read?

12. **Vocabulary** Explain how you would *regroup* the tens when adding 172 + 264.

13. **Use Structure** Beth had a necklace with 128 beads. The string broke, and she lost 43 beads. How many beads does Beth have left? Explain how you can break the problem into smaller problems to solve.

14. Write the time shown on the clock in 2 different ways.

15. **Higher Order Thinking** Which weighs more, two Basset Hounds or one Great Dane? Show the difference in pounds between two Basset Hounds and a Great Dane. Draw bar diagrams to represent and help you solve the problem.

Great Dane: 145 pounds

Basset Hound: 66 pounds

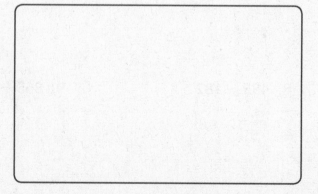

✓ **Assessment**

16. There are 183 students in the school lunchroom. Near the end of lunch, 128 students leave. How many students are left in the lunchroom? Explain how you can break the problem into smaller problems to find the difference.

Name _____

Another Look!

Greenwood School has 248 musical instruments. The students use 156 instruments for a concert. How many instruments are not used for the concert?

What You Think
I need to find $248 - 156$.   156 is the same as $100 + 50 + 6$.   I can subtract each addend, starting with hundreds and ending with ones.   There are not enough tens, so I'll break apart 5 tens into 4 tens and 1 ten.

What You Write
$248 - 100 = 148$ $148 - 40 = 108$ $108 - 10 = 98$ $98 - 6 = 92$ 92 instruments are not used for the concert.

In **1–4**, subtract.

1. Follow the steps to find $365 - 138$.

   First, subtract 100. $365 - 100 =$ _____

   Then, subtract 30. _____ $-$ _____ $= 235$

   Then, subtract 5. $235 -$ _____ $=$ _____

   Then, subtract 3. _____ $- 3 =$ _____

2. Follow the steps to find $217 - 118$.

   First, subtract 100. $217 - 100 =$ _____

   Then, subtract 10. $117 - 10 =$ _____

   Then, subtract 7. $107 - 7 =$ _____

   Then, subtract 1. $100 - 1 =$ _____

3. Follow the steps to find $568 - 293$.

   First, subtract 200. _____ $-$ _____ $= 368$

   Then, subtract 60. _____ $- 60 =$ _____

   Then, subtract 30. $308 -$ _____ $=$ _____

   Then, subtract 3. _____ $- 3 =$ _____

4. Follow the steps to find $928 - 374$.

   First, subtract 300. _____ $- 300 =$ _____

   Then, subtract 20. _____ $-$ _____ $= 608$

   Then, subtract 50. _____ $- 50 =$ _____

   Then, subtract 4. _____ $-$ _____ $= 554$

Leveled Practice In **5–7**, write the steps used to find each difference.

5. $756 - 642$

   $756 - 600 = 156$

6. $848 - 276$

   $848 - 200 = 648$

7. $641 - 139$

8. How many vertices does the cube below have?

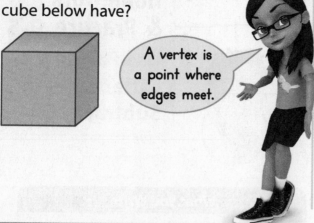

A vertex is a point where edges meet.

9. Critique Reasoning Tamara needs to find 455 − 364. Her work is below. Explain what is incorrect and find the correct answer.

$455 - 300 = 155$
$155 - 50 = 105$
$105 - 4 = 101$

10. Students in the third-grade class at Lowell Elementary were asked which breakfast they like best from the three choices shown in the bar graph. How many more students chose eggs or fruit than cereal?

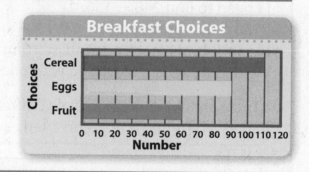

Breakfast Choices

11. Math and Science Water boils at 212 degrees Fahrenheit. It freezes at 32 degrees Fahrenheit. How many degrees difference is there between these two temperatures? Explain how you found your answer.

12. Higher Order Thinking Tom had 347 marbles. He traded 28 of them for some marbles that he really wanted. Now he has 336 marbles. How many marbles did Tom get from the trade? Explain how you found the answer.

✔ **Assessment**

13. Rachel had 251 pennies, and got more from her sister. Now she has 534 pennies. How many pennies did Rachel get? Explain how to break the problem into smaller problems.

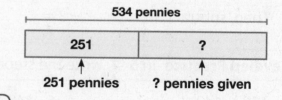

534 pennies

| 251 | ? |

251 pennies   ? pennies given

Name _____

Solve & Share

Last year, there were 347 houses for sale in Mill County and 289 houses for sale in Hunter County. Of the houses for sale in Mill County, 162 were sold. How many houses in Mill County were not sold?
Solve this problem any way you choose.

I can ...
use place-value reasoning to subtract 3-digit numbers.

I can also look for patterns to solve problems.

You can generalize when you subtract 3-digit numbers. You know how to show regrouping with and without place-value blocks when you add. How can you do the same when you subtract? *Show your work in the space below!*

Look Back! Use Appropriate Tools How can you use place-value blocks to show how to regroup in this problem?

How Can You Use Subtraction to Solve Problems?

A

Mike and Linda play a game. How many more points does Linda have than Mike?

Find 528 − 341.

Estimate by rounding to the nearest ten:
530 − 340 = 190.

Linda has → 528 points

528

341	?

Mike has   ? more points
341 points   Linda has

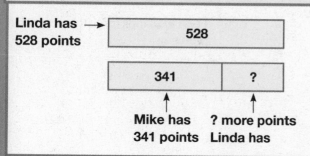

B Subtract the ones.

8 ones > 1 one
You do not regroup.
8 ones − 1 one = 7 ones

```
  5 2 8
− 3 4 1
      7
```

You can use place value to subtract using an algorithm.

C Subtract the tens.

Since 2 tens < 4 tens, regroup
1 hundred into 10 tens.
12 tens − 4 tens = 8 tens

```
   4 12
  5 2 8
− 3 4 1
   8 7
```

D Subtract the hundreds.

4 hundreds − 3 hundreds
= 1 hundred

```
   4 12
  5 2 8
− 3 4 1
  1 8 7
```

Linda has 187 more points.

187 is close to the estimate, 190. The answer is reasonable.

Convince Me! **Use Appropriate Tools** In Box C above, 5 hundreds, 2 tens, 8 ones are regrouped as 4 hundreds, 12 tens, 8 ones. How could you regroup those numbers using place-value blocks? Which method is easier?

Another Example!

You may have to regroup twice when you subtract.
Find 356 − 189.

Subtract the ones. Regroup if needed.	Subtract the tens. Regroup if needed.	Subtract the hundreds.

6 ones < 9 ones. So, regroup 1 ten into 10 ones.

$$\begin{array}{r} \overset{4,16}{3\cancel{5}\cancel{6}} \\ -189 \\ \hline 7 \end{array}$$

4 tens < 8 tens. So, regroup 1 hundred into 10 tens.

$$\begin{array}{r} \overset{14}{\underset{2\ \cancel{4}\ 16}{\cancel{3}\cancel{5}\cancel{6}}} \\ -189 \\ \hline 67 \end{array}$$

$$\begin{array}{r} \overset{14}{\underset{2\ \cancel{4}\ 16}{\cancel{3}\cancel{5}\cancel{6}}} \\ -189 \\ \hline 167 \end{array}$$

So, 356 − 189 = 167.

☆ Guided Practice*

Do You Understand?

1. In the example on page 506, explain how to decide if regrouping is necessary.

Do You Know How?

In **2** and **3**, subtract.

2.	374		3.	856
	− 176			− 219

Independent Practice ☆

In **4–11**, estimate by rounding to the nearest ten. Then find each difference. Check answers for reasonableness.

4.	431	5.	276	6.	516	7.	526
	− 145		− 97		− 402		− 238

8. 574 − 86

9. 629 − 453

10. 979 − 569

11. 764 − 237

Problem Solving

12. At the end of their game, Lora had 426 points, and Theo had 158 points. How many more points did Lora have than Theo?

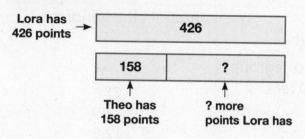

Lora has 426 points →

426

158	?

↑ Theo has 158 points ↑ ? more points Lora has

13. Model with Math Zac and Malcolm each wrote short stories. Zac's story is 272 lines long. Malcolm's story is 145 lines longer than Zac's. How long is Malcolm's story? Explain what operation you used to solve this problem.

14. The world's largest basket is 186 feet tall from the base to the top of the handles. What is the height of the handles?

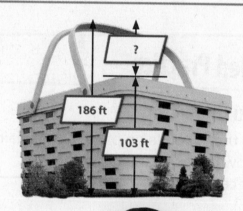

?

186 ft

103 ft

15. Higher Order Thinking How many more swimmers signed up for the 1st session at Oak Pool than the 1st and 2nd sessions at Park Pool combined? Write an equation that represents the problem and includes the solution.

DATA

Swim Class Enrollment

Pool	Number of Swimmers	
	1st session	2nd session
Oak	763	586
Park	314	179
River	256	163

✔ **Assessment**

16. Mr. Johnson drove his car 231 miles on Monday. After 5 days he had driven 729 miles. Complete the problem to show how many miles Mr. Johnson drove his car from Tuesday through Friday. Show regrouping, if necessary.

```
  □ □ □
  7 2 9
- □ □ □
_____
  □ □ □
```

Help Practice Tools Games
      Buddy

Another Look!

Find 726 − 238.
Estimate by rounding to the
nearest ten: 730 − 240 = 490.

Step 1

First, subtract the ones.
6 ones < 8 ones
Regroup 1 ten into 10
ones.

$$
\begin{array}{r}
7\overset{1\ 16}{2\!\!\!/6} \\
-\ 238 \\
\hline
8
\end{array}
$$

Step 2

Subtract the tens.
1 ten < 3 tens
Regroup 1 hundred into
10 tens.

$$
\begin{array}{r}
\overset{11}{6\overset{1\ 16}{7\!\!\!/2\!\!\!/6}} \\
-\ 238 \\
\hline
88
\end{array}
$$

Use your
estimate to
generalize.

Step 3

Subtract the hundreds.

$$
\begin{array}{r}
\overset{11}{6\overset{1\ 16}{7\!\!\!/2\!\!\!/6}} \\
-\ 238 \\
\hline
488
\end{array}
$$

This answer
is reasonable because
488 is close to the
estimate, 490.

Leveled Practice In **1–16**, estimate by rounding to the nearest ten. Then find each difference.

1. $\begin{array}{r} 9\ 1\ 4 \\ -\ 4\ 8\ 2 \\ \hline \square\ \square\ 2 \end{array}$

2. $\begin{array}{r} 8\ 8\ 3 \\ -\ 3\ 8\ 8 \\ \hline 4\ \square\ \square \end{array}$

3. $\begin{array}{r} 3\ 7\ 5 \\ -\ 1\ 8\ 3 \\ \hline \square\ \square\ 2 \end{array}$

4. $\begin{array}{r} 7\ 3\ 6 \\ -\ 2\ 9\ 5 \\ \hline 4\ \square\ \square \end{array}$

5. $\begin{array}{r} 4\ 7\ 8 \\ -\ 1\ 5\ 2 \\ \hline \end{array}$

6. $\begin{array}{r} 2\ 4\ 6 \\ -\ 1\ 2\ 7 \\ \hline \end{array}$

7. $\begin{array}{r} 8\ 1\ 6 \\ -\ 3\ 0\ 4 \\ \hline \end{array}$

8. $\begin{array}{r} 9\ 1\ 9 \\ -\ 2\ 8\ 4 \\ \hline \end{array}$

9. 318 − 123

10. 441 − 187

11. 334 − 275

12. 597 − 384

13. 732 − 455

14. 412 − 83

15. 828 − 615

16. 649 − 367

17. Reasoning A greenhouse grew tomato plants. It sold 276 tomato plants and 307 roses. There are 187 tomato plants left. How many tomato plants did the greenhouse originally grow? Explain which numbers and operation you used to solve.

18. Texas has 254 counties. California has 58 counties. Florida has 67 counties. How many more counties does Texas have than the number of counties in California and Florida combined?

19. Make Sense and Persevere How many miles closer to Omaha is Chicago than Dallas? Use the table and follow the steps below to solve.

a. Estimate the answer.
b. Write the solution to the problem in word form.
c. Explain why your answer is reasonable.

Routes to Omaha	
Trip	**Miles**
Dallas to Omaha	644
Chicago to Omaha	459
Tulsa to Omaha	387

DATA

20. Higher Order Thinking Jill is going on a trip from Chicago to Omaha, and then from Omaha to Tulsa. Bill will travel from Dallas to Omaha. How much farther will Jill travel than Bill? Explain how you solved the problem.

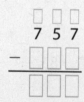

You can use an inverse operation to check your solution to each part of a problem.

 **Assessment**

21. Toby rode his bike 757 miles from May through July. He rode 398 miles in May. Complete the problem to show how many miles he rode in June and July. Regroup if needed.

$$\begin{array}{r} \square\ \square\ \square \\ 7\ 5\ 7 \\ -\ \square\ \square\ \square \\ \hline \square\ \square\ \square \end{array}$$

Name _____

Solve

Solve & Share

Rick is allowed to receive 1,000 text messages each month. How many more text messages did Rick receive this week than last week? *Solve this problem any way you choose.*

I can ...
use place-value reasoning to subtract 3-digit numbers.

I can also reason about math.

Rick's Text Messages
Last week: 125
This week: 213

Use reasoning. First think about the operation you should use.

Look Back! **Make Sense and Persevere** How can you check the answer to any subtraction problem? Is your answer to the question about Rick correct?

Essential Question

How Can You Subtract from a Number with One or More Zeros?

A

There are 136 fewer cell phone towers in Jurloe County than in Fraser County. How many cell phone towers are there in Jurloe County?

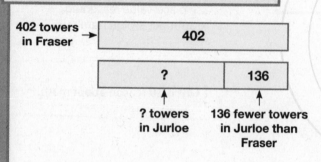

402 towers in Fraser →

402

?	136

? towers in Jurloe

136 fewer towers in Jurloe than Fraser

You can estimate by rounding each number to the nearest hundred: 400 − 100 = 300. Then you can check if your answer is reasonable.

Fraser County has 402 cell phone towers.

B ## Step 1

Subtract the ones.
2 ones < 6 ones, so regroup.

Since there are no tens in 402, regroup 1 hundred into 10 tens.

4 hundreds 0 tens =
3 hundreds 10 tens

$$\begin{array}{r} \overset{3\ 10}{4\,\cancel{0}\,2} \\ -1\,3\,6 \\ \hline \end{array}$$

C ## Step 2

Regroup 1 ten into 10 ones.

10 tens 2 ones =
9 tens 12 ones

$$\begin{array}{r} \overset{\ \ \ 9}{\overset{3\ \cancel{10}\ 12}{4\,\cancel{0}\,\cancel{2}}} \\ -1\,3\,6 \\ \hline \end{array}$$

D ## Step 3

Subtract the ones, the tens, and then the hundreds.

$$\begin{array}{r} \overset{\ \ \ 9}{\overset{3\ \cancel{10}\ 12}{4\,\cancel{0}\,\cancel{2}}} \\ -1\,3\,6 \\ \hline 2\,6\,6 \end{array}$$

There are 266 cell phone towers in Jurloe County.

The answer is reasonable because it is close to the estimate of 300.

Convince Me! **Use Appropriate Tools** Show how to use another tool to model the problem above.

Practice Buddy   Tools   Assessment

Another Example!

You may have to subtract from a number that has two zeros. Find 600 − 164.

Subtract the ones. 0 ones < 4 ones, so regroup. You cannot regroup 0 tens. So regroup the hundreds. 6 hundreds 0 tens = 5 hundreds 10 tens $\begin{array}{c} {\scriptstyle 5\ 10} \\ 6\ 0\ 0 \\ -\ 1\ 6\ 4 \end{array}$	Now regroup the tens. 10 tens 0 ones = 9 tens 10 ones. $\begin{array}{c} {\scriptstyle \quad 9} \\ {\scriptstyle 5\ 10\ 10} \\ 6\ 0\ 0 \\ -\ 1\ 6\ 4 \end{array}$	Subtract the ones, the tens, and then the hundreds. $\begin{array}{c} {\scriptstyle \quad 9} \\ {\scriptstyle 5\ 10\ 10} \\ 6\ 0\ 0 \\ -\ 1\ 6\ 4 \\ \hline 4\ 3\ 6 \end{array}$ So, 600 − 164 = 436.

☆ Guided Practice*

Do You Understand?

1. To subtract 507 − 348, how can you regroup the tens if there are 0 tens?

2. **Generalize** Do you need to regroup every time you subtract from a number with a zero? Explain.

Do You Know How?

In **3–6**, find each difference.

3.	816 − 335	4.	703 − 246
5.	900 − 375	6.	508 − 247

☆ Independent Practice ☆

In **7–14**, find each difference. Then use estimation to check your answer.

7.	549 − 167	8.	411 − 238	9.	560 − 144	10.	783 − 68

11. 400 − 219   12. 904 − 703   13. 700 − 604   14. 807 − 308

Problem Solving

15. Model with Math How much more money does the Elm School Art Club need to raise? Complete the bar diagram and solve the problem.

Elm School Art Club Fundraiser!

GOAL — $305

Raised $178

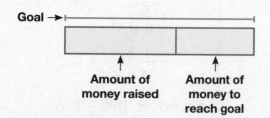

Goal →

Amount of money raised   Amount of money to reach goal

---

16. There were some ears of corn for sale at the farmers' market. 388 ears of corn were sold. At the end there were 212 ears left. How many ears of corn were for sale at the start?

17. Dina was adding books to the library shelves. She put 117 nonfiction books on the shelves. Then there were 204 nonfiction books. How many nonfiction books were on the shelves before?

---

18. Construct Arguments Terri has 10 pencils. How many can she put in her pink pencil case and how many in her white pencil case? Explain.

19. Higher Order Thinking Dylan had $405 in his savings account and spent $253. Brian had $380 in his savings account and spent $48 less than Dylan. Now who has more money in his savings account? How much more?

✓ **Assessment**

20. Which shows how to regroup 706 in order to subtract 706 − 169?

Ⓐ 6 hundreds 9 tens 16 ones

Ⓑ 6 hundreds 10 tens 16 ones

Ⓒ 7 hundreds 9 tens 16 ones

Ⓓ No regrouping is needed.

21. At Yellowstone National Park, Irene took 65 more pictures than her brother. Irene took 300 pictures. How many pictures did her brother take?

Ⓐ 365 pictures

Ⓑ 335 pictures

Ⓒ 245 pictures

Ⓓ 235 pictures

Help Practice Tools Games
      Buddy

Another Look!

Find 207 − 98.

Remember, you can use addition to check your answer or use estimation to see if your answer is reasonable.

Step 1	Step 2	Step 3
Subtract the ones. 7 ones < 8 ones, so regroup. Since there are no tens in 207, regroup the hundreds.	Regroup the tens.	Subtract the ones, the tens, and then the hundreds.

Step 1

Subtract the ones.
7 ones < 8 ones, so regroup.
Since there are no tens in 207, regroup the hundreds.

2 hundreds 0 tens =
1 hundred 10 tens

$$\begin{array}{r} \overset{1\ \ 10}{2\ \cancel{0}\ 7} \\ -\ \ 9\ 8 \end{array}$$

Step 2

Regroup the tens.

10 tens 7 ones =
9 tens 17 ones

$$\begin{array}{r} \overset{1\ \ \overset{9}{10}\ 17}{2\ \cancel{0}\ 7} \\ -\ \ 9\ 8 \end{array}$$

Step 3

Subtract the ones, the tens, and then the hundreds.

$$\begin{array}{r} \overset{1\ \ \overset{9}{10}\ 17}{2\ \cancel{0}\ 7} \\ -\ \ 9\ 8 \\ \hline 1\ 0\ 9 \end{array}$$

In **1–16**, find each difference. Then use addition to check your answer or use estimation to see if your answer is reasonable.

1. 518
   − 339

2. 401
   − 137

3. 856
   − 92

4. 800
   − 523

5. 946
   − 441

6. 530
   − 157

7. 600
   − 75

8. 916
   − 850

9. 155 − 109

10. 815 − 248

11. 922 − 39

12. 504 − 208

13. 300 − 145

14. 709 − 643

15. 200 − 188

16. 480 − 252

17. Make Sense and Persevere At a baseball game the Gordon family bought 4 ham sandwiches and 4 drinks. How much did they pay for the food and drinks?

Ham sandwich	$4
Tuna sandwich	$5
Soft pretzel	$2
Drink	$1

18. Some seniors signed up for dance classes for the fall. Then 117 stopped taking classes. 189 seniors continued taking classes. How many seniors started taking classes in the fall?

19. Reasoning Write a story for 105 − 58. Then find the difference.

20. Higher Order Thinking Party Palace receives an order for 505 party favors. It packages 218 favors on Monday and 180 favors on Tuesday. How many more party favors does it still need to package? Show two different ways to solve the problem.

21. Math and Science A scientist was observing a group of wildebeests over two years. One year the herd consisted of 200 animals. In the next year there were 155 wildebeests. How many more animals were in the herd during the first year?

✔ **Assessment**

22. Which shows how to regroup 500 in order to subtract 500 − 228?

  Ⓐ 5 hundreds 9 tens 10 ones

  Ⓑ 4 hundreds 9 tens 10 ones

  Ⓒ 4 hundreds 10 tens 10 ones

  Ⓓ No regrouping is needed.

23. This year, 403 children attended the Fun Fair. Last year, 115 fewer children attended. How many children attended the Fun Fair last year?

  Ⓐ 388 children

  Ⓑ 298 children

  Ⓒ 288 children

  Ⓓ 278 children

Name _____

Solve & Share

Use each of the digits 0, 1, 2, 3, 4, and 5 only once. Write the digits in the space below to make two 3-digit addends with the greatest sum. Write the sum of the 2 addends. How do you know you have made the greatest sum?

$$
\begin{array}{r}
\square\,\square\,\square \\
+\ \square\,\square\,\square \\
\hline
\end{array}
$$

Problem Solving

Lesson 9-8
Construct Arguments

I can ...
construct math arguments using what I know about addition and subtraction.

I can also add and subtract to solve problems.

Thinking Habits

Be a good thinker! These questions can help you.

- How can I use numbers, objects, drawings, or actions to justify my argument?

- Am I using numbers and symbols correctly?

- Is my explanation clear and complete?

Look Back! **Construct Arguments** If you added your two addends in a different order, would the sum be greater or less than your original sum? How do you know?

Essential Question **How Can You Construct Arguments?**

A

Nancy has $457 in her savings account and wants to have $500 by the end of the year. Christopher has $557 in his savings account and wants to have $600 by the end of the year. Who needs to save more money by the end of the year?

My conjecture: They both need to save the same amount.

> A conjecture is a statement that you think is true. It needs to be proved or disproved.

How can I explain why my conjecture is correct?

I need to construct an argument to justify my conjecture.

> Here's my thinking...

B **How can I construct an argument?**

I can

- use numbers, objects, drawings, or actions correctly to explain my thinking.

- make sure my explanation is simple, complete, and easy to understand.

C I will use drawings and numbers to explain my thinking.

The distance from 457 to 500 on the number line is the same as the distance from 557 to 600.

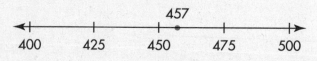

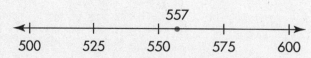

The number lines show that it takes the same amount of money to get from $457 to $500 that it takes to get from $557 to $600.

So, $500 - 457 = 600 - 557$. My conjecture is correct.

Convince Me! **Construct Arguments** Use objects to construct another math argument to justify the conjecture above. Think about how you can use place-value blocks.

Name _____

☆ Guided Practice ☆

Construct Arguments

Mr. Lee had $375 in the bank. Then he spent $242. Ms. Davis had $675 in the bank and then spent $542. Who has more money left?
Conjecture: They both have the same amount of money left.

1. Draw a diagram to justify the conjecture.

Diagrams can help you support an argument.

2. Use your diagram to justify the conjecture.

☆ Independent Practice ☆

Construct Arguments

A Grade 2 class has made 165 paper cranes and wants to reach a total of 250.
A Grade 3 class has made 255 paper cranes and wants to reach a total of 350.
Which class has fewer paper cranes left to make to reach its goal?
Conjecture: The Grade 2 class has to make fewer paper cranes to reach its goal.

3. Draw a diagram at the right to help you justify the conjecture.

4. Use your diagram to justify the conjecture.

5. Explain another way you could justify the conjecture.

Problem Solving

✓ **Performance Assessment**

Band Practice

Some musicians set goals for the number of minutes they want to practice before a concert, which is 5 days away. They want to know who has to practice the fewest number of minutes to reach his or her goal.

Student	Aria	Dexter	Yin	Sawyer
Minutes Practiced	608	612	604	612
Goal in Minutes	700	650	625	675

6. **Make Sense and Persevere** How can you find the number of minutes Aria has to practice to reach her goal?

7. **Look for Relationships** So far Dexter and Sawyer have both practiced the same number of minutes. Do they need the same amount of practice time to reach their goals? Explain.

> When you construct arguments, you explain why your work is right.

8. **Reasoning** Who has the fewest number of minutes left to practice to reach his or her goal?

9. **Construct Arguments** Construct a math argument to explain why your answer to **8** is correct.

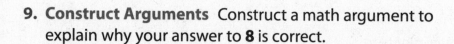

520   **Topic 9** | Lesson 9-8

© Pearson Education, Inc. 3

Another Look!

During the last two weeks Max exercised for 446 minutes.
During the first week he exercised for 220 minutes.
Did he exercise more during the first or second week?
Conjecture: Max exercised more during the second week.

Tell how you can justify the conjecture.

- I can use numbers, objects, drawings, or actions to explain.

- I can make sure my argument is simple, complete, and easy to understand.

Construct an argument to justify the conjecture.

I can use place-value blocks to see that if Max exercised the same amount the second week, the time would only be 440 minutes. So Max must have exercised for more minutes the second week to get to a total of 446 minutes.

> When you construct an argument, you use reasoning to give a logical explanation.

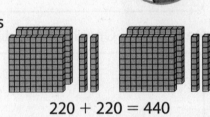

$$220 + 220 = 440$$

Construct Arguments

Central School has 758 students. There are 2 lunch periods at Central School.
371 students eat during the first lunch period. Which lunch period has more students?
Conjecture: More students eat lunch during the second lunch period.

1. Tell how you can justify the conjecture.

2. Construct an argument to justify the conjecture.

3. Explain another way you could justify the conjecture.

Family Vacation

The Willis family has 4 members. Some mornings and evenings the family traveled to different cities on their vacation. Below are the distances they drove. Mrs. Willis is trying to find which day they drove the most.

DATA	Saturday	Monday	Wednesday	Friday
Morning	174 miles	112 miles	121 miles	172 miles
Evening	106 miles	165 miles	168 miles	113 miles

4. **Model with Math** Write equations to represent the distances the family drove on the given days.

5. **Reasoning** On which day did the family drive the most?

6. **Construct Arguments** Construct a math argument to explain why your answer to **5** is correct.

You can use numbers, objects, drawings, or actions to construct an argument.

7. **Make Sense and Persevere** How can you check that your answer is reasonable?

Name _____

I can ...
add within 1,000.

Find a partner. Get paper and a pencil. Each partner chooses a different color: light blue or dark blue.

Partner 1 and Partner 2 each point to a black number at the same time. Both partners add those numbers.

If the answer is on your color, you get a tally mark. Work until one partner has seven tally marks.

Partner 1

| 400 |
| 120 |
| 233 |
| 275 |
| 412 |

812	591	520
687	758	824
800	240	353
675	508	532
645	770	633
395	550	478

Partner 2

| 358 |
| 275 |
| 412 |
| 400 |
| 120 |

Tally Marks for Partner 1

Tally Marks for Partner 2

Vocabulary Review

Glossary

Word List

- conjecture
- estimate
- inverse operations
- place value
- regroup
- round

Understand Vocabulary

Draw a line to match each term to an example.

1. place value $515 + 141$ is about 660.

2. estimate $305 + 299 = 604$ and
                                $604 - 299 = 305$

3. regroup $232 = 2$ hundreds 3 tens 2 ones

4. inverse operations $47 = 3$ tens 17 ones

Write *always*, *sometimes*, or *never*.

5. When *rounding* to the nearest ten, a number with a 5 in the ones digit
_____ rounds to the next ten.

6. A *conjecture* is _____ true.

7. A digit with a greater *place value* is _____
written to the right of a digit with a lesser place value.

8. A ten can _____ be *regrouped* as 10 hundreds.

Use Vocabulary in Writing

9. Explain how to find $600 - 281$, and then explain how to
check that the difference is correct. Use at least 2 terms
from the Word List in your explanation.

Name _____

Set A | pages 475–480

Find the sum of 257 + 186.

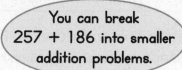

You can break 257 + 186 into smaller addition problems.

Break each number by place value and find the sum of the numbers in each place.

Hundreds	Tens	Ones
200	50	7
+ 100	+ 80	+ 6
300	130	13

Then add the sums.

```
  300
  130
+  13
  443
```

So, 257 + 186 = 443.

Remember you can use place value to add numbers by breaking large addition problems into smaller addition problems.

In **1–5**, find each sum. Break each problem into smaller problems.

1. 135 + 152   2. 650 + 138

3. 535 + 423   4. 475 + 264

5. Yvette takes 137 photographs on Friday. She takes 248 photographs on Saturday. How many did she take on both days?

Set B | pages 481–486

Find 235 + 187.

Estimate by rounding to the nearest ten: 240 + 190 = 430.

Add the ones.   Add the tens.
Regroup if needed.   Regroup if needed.

```
  1                      1 1
  235                    235
+ 187                  + 187
    2                     22
```

Add the hundreds.

```
 1 1
 235
+187
 422
```

The answer is reasonable since 422 is close to 430.

So, 235 + 187 = 422.

Remember that an estimate can help you check whether your answer is reasonable.

In **1–6**, estimate by rounding to the nearest ten. Then find each sum.

1.   236   2.   407
   + 217   + 436

3. 235 + 59   4. 584 + 326

5. 196 + 243   6. 465 + 357

Chad has a new video game. He scores 128 points on the first level. He scores 218 points on the second level. How many points does Chad score on both levels?

You can use a bar diagram.

?	
128	218

Estimate and solve.

$$130 + 220 = 350$$

$$\begin{array}{r} \overset{1}{1}28 \\ + 218 \\ \hline 346 \end{array}$$

The sum is reasonable. It is close to the estimate.

Chad scores 346 points on both levels.

Remember to regroup when you have more than 10 in a place value.

In **1** and **2**, estimate. Then find each sum.

1. Mike's Café sells 237 sandwiches on Friday. It sells 448 sandwiches on Saturday. How many sandwiches are sold on both days?

2. 2 planes leave an airport. Each plane has 239 seats. The first plane has 224 passengers. The second plane has 189 passengers. How many passengers are on both planes?

Find $124 + 32 + 238$.

Estimate by rounding to the nearest ten: $120 + 30 + 240 = 390$.

Add the ones. Regroup if needed.

$$\begin{array}{r} \overset{1}{1}24 \\ 32 \\ + 238 \\ \hline 4 \end{array}$$

Add the tens. Regroup if needed.

$$\begin{array}{r} \overset{1}{1}24 \\ 32 \\ + 238 \\ \hline 94 \end{array}$$

Add the hundreds.

$$\begin{array}{r} \overset{1}{1}24 \\ 32 \\ + 238 \\ \hline 394 \end{array}$$

The answer is reasonable since 394 is close to 390.

So, $124 + 32 + 238 = 394$.

Remember that adding three numbers is like adding two numbers. Line up the digits and add by place value.

In **1–5**, estimate by rounding to the nearest ten. Then find each sum.

1. $\begin{array}{r} 209 \\ 48 \\ + 312 \\ \hline \end{array}$

2. $\begin{array}{r} 412 \\ 273 \\ + 139 \\ \hline \end{array}$

3. $146 + 86 + 53$

4. $125 + 224 + 306$

5. A flower shop has 124 tulips, 235 roses, and 85 carnations. How many flowers does the flower shop have?

Set E | pages 499–504

Use place value to help find 548 − 263.

Subtract the hundreds.	$548 - 200 = 348$
Subtract the tens. Start with 348. There are not enough tens in the tens place. So, first subtract 4 tens.	$348 - 40 = 308$
Then subtract 2 more tens.	$308 - 20 = 288$
Subtract the ones.	$288 - 3 = 285$

So, $548 - 263 = 285$.

Remember that place value can help you break a subtraction problem into smaller problems.

In **1–6**, find each difference. Break each problem into smaller problems.

1. $489 - 253$ **2.** $544 - 162$

3. $856 - 328$ **4.** $349 - 98$

5. $873 - 184$ **6.** $526 - 207$

Set F | pages 505–510

Find $416 - 243$.
Estimate by rounding to the nearest ten:
$420 - 240 = 180$.

Subtract the ones.
Regroup if needed.

$$\begin{array}{r} 416 \\ -\ 243 \\ \hline 3 \end{array}$$

Subtract the tens.
Regroup if needed.

$$\begin{array}{r} {}^{3\ 11}\ \\ 4\cancel{1}6 \\ -\ 243 \\ \hline 73 \end{array}$$

Subtract the hundreds.

$$\begin{array}{r} {}^{3\ 11}\ \\ \cancel{4}\cancel{1}6 \\ -\ 243 \\ \hline 173 \end{array}$$

So, $416 - 243 = 173$.

The answer is reasonable since 173 is close to 180.

Remember to regroup if necessary.

In **1–5**, estimate by rounding to the nearest ten. Then find each difference.

1.
$$\begin{array}{r} 458 \\ -\ 176 \\ \hline \end{array}$$

2.
$$\begin{array}{r} 236 \\ -\ 79 \\ \hline \end{array}$$

3.
$$\begin{array}{r} 863 \\ -\ 526 \\ \hline \end{array}$$

4.
$$\begin{array}{r} 748 \\ -\ 279 \\ \hline \end{array}$$

5. $400 - 227$ **6.** $306 - 198$

Set G pages 511–516

273 people have finished a marathon.
A total of 458 people entered the marathon.
How many people are still running?

You can use a bar diagram.

458	
273	?

Estimate and solve.

$$460 - 270 = 190$$

$$\begin{array}{r} \overset{3\ \ 15}{4\,\cancel{5}\,8} \\ -\ 2\,7\,3 \\ \hline 1\,8\,5 \end{array}$$

The difference is reasonable. It is close to the estimate.

185 people are still running.

Remember to regroup when subtracting across zeros.

In **1** and **2**, estimate. Then find each sum.

1. Damian's conservation club wants to plant 640 seedlings. They have 172 seedlings that they still need to plant to meet their goal. How many seedlings have they planted so far?

2. The Smith family is driving to Dallas. The trip is 450 miles. So far, they have driven 315 miles. How many miles are left in the trip?

Set H pages 517–522

Think about these questions to help you **construct arguments**.

Thinking Habits

• How can I use numbers, objects, drawings, or actions to justify my argument?

• Am I using numbers and symbols correctly?

• Is my explanation clear and complete?

Remember that a conjecture needs to be proved to be true.

Emma has $191. She spends $105. She donates $52 to charity. Can Emma save $30?

Conjecture: Emma can save $30.

1. Draw a diagram to justify the conjecture.

2. Use your diagram to justify the conjecture.

Name _____

TOPIC 9

✓ Assessment

1. Jorge is finding the sum of 337 + 285 by breaking it into smaller problems. He uses place value and finds the sums of the hundreds, tens, and ones. Write each digit to show the correct place value. Then show how to break apart the addends to solve.

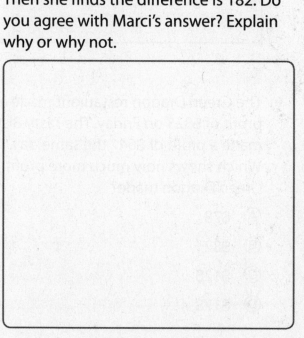

Hundreds	Tens	Ones

2   3   5   7   3   8

2. Marci finds the difference of 431 − 249. First she estimates using compatible numbers. She finds 425 − 250 = 175. Then she finds the difference is 182. Do you agree with Marci's answer? Explain why or why not.

3. For 3a–3d, choose Yes or No to say if the addends are broken apart correctly.

3a. 320 + 148
(300 + 100) + (20 + 40) + (20 + 8)

○ Yes   ○ No

3b. 270 + 341
(2 + 70) + (3 + 4 + 1)

○ Yes   ○ No

3c. 318 + 393
300 + (10 + 90) + (8 + 3)

○ Yes   ○ No

3d. 532 + 360
(500 + 300) + (30 + 60) + 2

○ Yes   ○ No

4. A play begins at 7:00 P.M. At 6:40 P.M., the first 176 people arrive. At 6:50 P.M., another 204 people arrive. At 7:00 P.M., the last 59 people arrive. How many people attend the play?

Ⓐ 329 people

Ⓑ 339 people

Ⓒ 429 people

Ⓓ 439 people

Topic 9 | Assessment   **529**

5. The girls' volleyball team raised $276 during a fundraiser. The boys' basketball team raised $289. Each team worked 28 hours to raise the money. How much did the two teams raise?

Ⓐ $509

Ⓑ $537

Ⓒ $565

Ⓓ $593

6. Tricia has 302 prize tickets. She trades 237 of the tickets for a stuffed animal, and 20 tickets for a drink. How many prize tickets does Tricia have left?

7. Chickens at the Lapp chicken farm laid 300 eggs this morning. So far the Lapps have sold 168 of these eggs. There are 400 chickens on the farm. How many of the eggs do they have left to sell?

Ⓐ 32

Ⓑ 122

Ⓒ 132

Ⓓ 142

8. The residents of Elm City own 346 cats. They own 268 dogs and 37 birds.

Part A

Is the number of dogs and birds together greater than the number of cats? Make a conjecture.

Part B

Construct an argument to prove your conjecture.

9. The Green Dragon restaurant made a profit of $825 on Friday. The Tasty Bistro made a profit of $647 the same day. Which shows how much more profit the Green Dragon made?

Ⓐ $78

Ⓑ $82

Ⓒ $128

Ⓓ $178

Name _____

10. Mr. Jackson buys a package of 600 napkins. He uses 335 napkins for family dinners. Then he throws a birthday party and uses another 108 napkins. He uses 12 napkins to clean up a spill. How many napkins does he have left?

11. Yasmin earned $283 from her babysitting job and $45 from walking dogs. She spent $139 of this money on a wedding present for her aunt. How can Yasmin find how much money she has left? Choose all that apply.

☐ Add $45 and $283, then subtract $139

☐ Subtract $139 from $283, then add $45

☐ Add $283 and $45, then subtract $139

☐ Subtract $45 from $283, then add $139

☐ Add $139 and $45, then subtract $283

12. Describe how to regroup to solve the subtraction problem below. What is the difference?

$$\begin{array}{r} 316 \\ -\ 226 \\ \hline \end{array}$$

13. Mitch is finding the difference between 254 − 125.

Part A

Does Mitch need to regroup? If he does, explain how he should regroup. If he does not, explain why he does not.

Part B

Find the difference.

14. Put the steps in order to find 756 − 345.

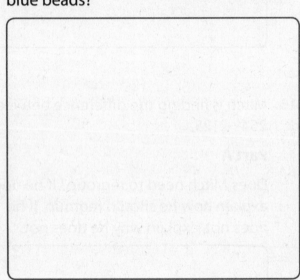

Subtract 416 − 5   1st step

Subtract 756 − 300   2nd step

Subtract 456 − 40   3rd step

15. Maggie makes jewelry out of beads. She buys 408 red beads, 240 green beads, and 259 blue beads. How many more red and green beads does Maggie buy than blue beads?

16. Luisa uses place value to subtract 737 − 639. How many times does she need to regroup?

Ⓐ 3

Ⓑ 2

Ⓒ 1

Ⓓ 0

17. The Smith family spent $457 on groceries last month. The Wilson family spent $291. The Moore family spent $338. How much less did the Moores spend on groceries than the Smiths?

Ⓐ $109

Ⓑ $119

Ⓒ $121

Ⓓ $129

18. Edison School has 332 students. Du Bois School has 246 students. Turner School has 199 students. How many more students does Edison School have than Du Bois School?

Name _____

Video Arcade

Nita, Arif, and Sarah have been playing games at the video arcade.
The **Tickets Estimates** list below shows the number of tickets each
friend estimated they would win before they started playing.
The **Tickets Won** table shows the numbers of tickets each friend won.

Tickets Estimates

• Nita estimated she would win 165 tickets.
• Arif estimated he would win 150 tickets
• Sarah estimated she would win 175 tickets.

The friends want to compare the tickets
they won to their estimates. Use the **Tickets
Estimates** list and **Tickets Won** table to answer
Questions 1 and 2.

Tickets Won		
Name	**Tickets Won Playing Sports Games**	**Tickets Won Playing Action Games**
Nita	96	112
Arif	94	91
Sarah	104	117

1. How many tickets did each of the friends
   win in all?

2. Show how many more tickets each friend won than his or her estimate.

3. Arif says if he won 24 more tickets, he would have won more tickets
   than Nita. Is he correct? Explain.

4. The three friends put all of their tickets together.
   How many tickets did they win in all?

Tickets can be used to get prizes. The **Arcade Prizes** table shows how many tickets each prize costs.

Use the **Arcade Prizes** table to answer Question 5.

5. Use the total number of tickets you found in Question 4. The 3 friends will use this number of tickets to get 1 prize each and 1 more prize as a gift.

There are 2 rules the friends must follow.

- They cannot use more than their total number of tickets.
- After their purchases they do not want more than 50 tickets remaining.

Part A

Arif starts a prize log to record the prizes they will get. In the table below, record some prizes the friends could choose, the cost of the prize, and show how many tickets they will have left.

Arcade Prizes	
Prize	**Cost (Tickets)**
Board Game	138
Stuffed Animal	85
Action Figures	73
Wristwatch	170
Calculator	142
Mystery Book	92
Video Game	235
Photo Album	79

Prize	Cost (Tickets)	Number of Tickets Left
Wristwatch	170	_____ $-170 = 444$

Part B

If the friends made your choices from Part A, how many of their tickets would they use to get prizes? Explain how you found the answer.

Multiply by Multiples of 10

Essential Question: What are ways to multiply by multiples of 10?

Digital Resources

Solve Learn Glossary Practice Buddy

Tools Assessment Help Games

The insect in this picture is hiding to avoid being eaten.

Animals that have a better camouflage color than others are more likely to survive.

It's like playing hide-and-seek! Here's a project on animal and plant characteristics and multiplication.

Math and Science Project: Animal and Plant Characteristics

Do Research Use the Internet or other sources to find information about how the characteristics of some plants and animals help them survive. Think about how characteristics can be different among members of the same species.

Journal: Write a Report Include what you found. Also in your report:

- Tell about an insect that uses camouflage.

- Describe an example of how a plant's thorns help it survive.

- Make up and solve multiplication problems about the animals or plants you research. Use multiples of 10.

Review What You Know

A-Z Vocabulary

Choose the best term from the box.
Write it on the blank.

| • factor | • multiplication |
| • equation | • multiple |

1. A number sentence where the value on the left and right of the equal sign (=) is the same is called a(n) _____.

2. The product of a number and any other whole number is called a(n) _____.

3. _____ is an operation that gives the total number when you join equal groups.

Multiplication Table

Find the value that makes the equations true.
Use the multiplication table to help.

×	0	1	2	3	4	5	6	7
0	0	0	0	0	0	0	0	0
1	0	1	2	3	4	5	6	7
2	0	2	4	6	8	10	12	14
3	0	3	6	9	12	15	18	21
4	0	4	8	12	16	20	24	28
5	0	5	10	15	20	25	30	35
6	0	6	12	18	24	30	36	42
7	0	7	14	21	28	35	42	49
8	0	8	16	24	32	40	48	56
9	0	9	18	27	36	45	54	63

4. $21 \div 7 =$ ____

   $7 \times$ ____ $= 21$

5. $45 \div 5 =$ ____

   $5 \times$ ____ $= 45$

6. $48 \div 6 =$ ____

   $6 \times$ ____ $= 48$

7. $56 \div 8 =$ ____

   $8 \times$ ____ $= 56$

Multiplication Properties

Find each product.

8. $3 \times 3 \times 2 =$ ____

9. $5 \times 1 \times 3 =$ ____

10. $4 \times 2 \times 4 =$ ____

11. $2 \times 2 \times 4 =$ ____

12. $4 \times 0 \times 2 =$ ____

13. $2 \times 5 \times 3 =$ ____

Multiplication on the Number Line

14. Which equation does the number line show?

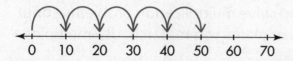

Ⓐ $1 \times 10 = 10$ Ⓑ $3 \times 10 \times 1 = 30$ Ⓒ $4 \times 5 = 20$ Ⓓ $5 \times 10 = 50$

My Word Cards

Use the examples for each word on the front of the card to help complete the definitions on the back.

open number line

$3 \times 10 = 10 + 10 + 10$

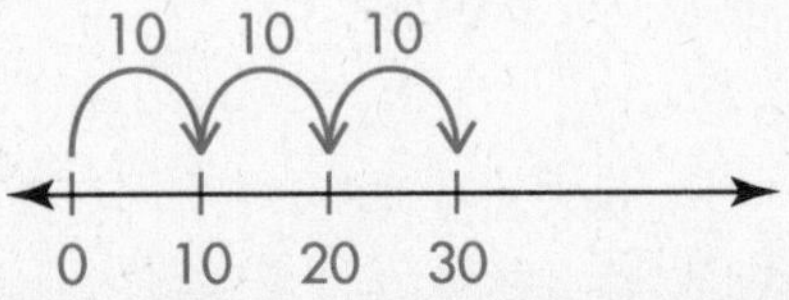

My Word Cards

Complete the definition. Extend learning by writing your own definitions.

An _____ only displays the numbers being computed.

Name _____

☆ ☆
Solve & Share

A case of water has 20 bottles. How many bottles are in the different numbers of cases? Complete the table.

I can ...
use an open number line and patterns to multiply by multiples of 10.

I can also model with math to solve problems.

Number of Cases	Number of Bottles
1	20
2	
3	
4	

0 ————————————————————→

You can model with math. A number line can help you apply the math you know.

Look Back! **Look for Relationships** What pattern do you see when multiplying by 20?

How Can You Multiply on an Open Number Line?

A

Complete the products in the table. Use an open number line to help. Describe any patterns you see.

Factor	Multiple of 10	Product
1	50	50
2	50	
3	50	
4	50	
5	50	

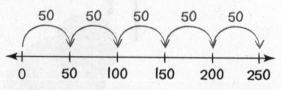

You can use an open number line to multiply.

0

B You can show jumps of 50 on the open number line.

50 50 50 50 50

0   50 100 150 200 250

1 jump of 50 is 50. $1 \times 50 = 50$

2 jumps of 50 are 100. $2 \times 50 = 100$

3 jumps of 50 are 150. $3 \times 50 = 150$

4 jumps of 50 are 200. $4 \times 50 = 200$

5 jumps of 50 are 250. $5 \times 50 = 250$

C

Factor	Multiple of 10	Product
1	50	50
2	50	100
3	50	150
4	50	200
5	50	250

The pattern in the products is like the pattern when you multiply by 5, but with an extra 0 in the ones place.

Convince Me! **Use Structure** Suppose the multiple of 10 in the table above was 40 instead of 50. Show how the open number line would look. Explain how this open number line is different from the open number line above.

Practice Buddy · Tools · Assessment

☆ Guided Practice *

Do You Understand?

1. Explain how to use a number line to multiply 9×50.

2. Generalize How are the products in Box C on page 540 like skip counting by 5?

Do You Know How?

3. Use the open number line to multiply 4×60.

0

4. Jon says, "4×6 is 4 groups of 6 ones. 4 times 6 equals 24."
Complete the sentences to describe 4×60 in a similar way.

4×60 is 4 groups of 6 _____.
4 times 60 equals _____.

☆ Independent Practice ☆

Leveled Practice In **5–8**, use an open number line to find the product.

5. 3×70

0

6. 8×20

0

7. 9×30

8. 5×60

9. Rick says "9×3 is 9 groups of 3 ones. 9 times 3 equals 27."
Complete the sentences to describe 9×30 in a similar way.

9×30 is 9 groups of 3 _____.
9 times 30 equals _____.

Problem Solving

10. **Model with Math** The Aztecs had a solar calendar. How many days are in 7 of the longer months? Show how to use a number line to solve.

The longer months of the calendar are each 20 days long. After the longer months, there is a period of 5 days.

11. **Higher Order Thinking** On one open number line, show 4 × 30. On the other open number line, show 3 × 40. How are the number lines alike? How are they different?

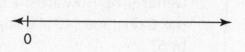

0

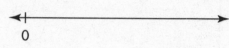

0

12. **Reasoning** Martina has $504. She spends $199 on new computer software. Use mental math to find how much money she has left.

13. **Generalize** List 4 multiples of 40. What is the same in each of the multiples you listed?

14. A package of crepe paper streamers has 2 rolls. Yen bought 3 packages. How many inches of crepe paper did he get?

70 inches long

15. Amanda has 4 boxes of beads. There are 70 beads in each box.

Part A

How many beads does Amanda have in all? Show how to use a number line to solve.

Part B

Amanda gets 2 more boxes of 70 beads. Explain how you can change your number line from Part A to show this. How many beads does Amanda have now?

© Pearson Education, Inc. 3

Name _____

Solve & Share

Three students found 5 × 30 in different ways. Which student is correct? Explain.

I can ...
use properties of multiplication to find a product when one factor is a multiple of 10.

I can also critique other people's math work.

Janice

I imagined 5 jumps of 30 on a number line and counted by 30s just like counting by 3s.
30, 60, 90, 120, 150

Earl

30 = 3 × 10. So, 5 × 30 = 5 × 3 × 10.
I multiplied 5 × 3 first to get 15.
Then, I multiplied 15 × 10 to get 150.

Properties can help you critique the reasoning of someone else.

Clara

It's easier to count by 5 than 3.
I multiplied the 5 × 10 first to get 50, and then found 3 × 50 by counting 50, 100, 150.

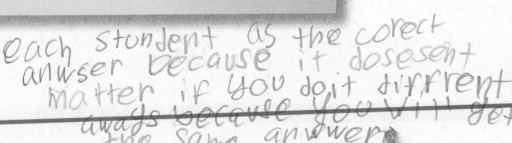

each stondent as the corect anwser because it dosesent matter if you doit dirrrent aways because you vill get the same answer

Look Back! Be Precise What property of multiplication did Earl use in his reasoning?

Essential Question **How Can You Use Properties to Multiply by Multiples of 10?**

A

How can you find the product of 4 × 20?

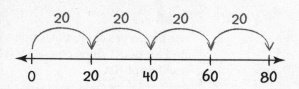

You know how to use an open number line to model multiplication.

You can use properties to explain a rule for finding a product when one factor is a multiple of 10.

Remember the 10s facts pattern. Think about the product of a number and 10. The product has a zero in the ones place. The other factor is written to the left of the zero.

B **One Way**

You can use the Associative Property of Multiplication to group the factors.

$4 \times 20 = 4 \times (2 \times 10)$

$4 \times 20 = (4 \times 2) \times 10$

$4 \times 20 = 8 \times 10$

$4 \times 20 = 80$

Think of 20 as 2 × 10.

C **Another Way**

You can use the Distributive Property to decompose a factor.

$4 \times 20 = (2 + 2) \times 20$

$4 \times 20 = (2 \times 20) + (2 \times 20)$

$4 \times 20 = 40 + 40$

$4 \times 20 = 80$

Convince Me! **Construct Arguments** Use properties of multiplication to explain why $3 \times 60 = 18 \times 10$.

☆Guided Practice☆

Do You Understand?

1. Why can you say that
$3 \times 20 = (2 \times 20) + 20$?

2. Why can you say that
$3 \times 20 = (3 \times 2) \times 10$?

Do You Know How?

In **3** and **4**, find the product using properties of multiplication.

3. $9 \times 60 = 9 \times (\underline{\quad} \times 10)$

$9 \times 60 = (9 \times \underline{\quad}) \times 10$

$9 \times 60 = \underline{\quad} \times 10 = \underline{\quad}$

4. $4 \times 90 = (\underline{\quad} + 2) \times 90$

$4 \times 90 = (\underline{\quad} \times 90) + (\underline{\quad} \times 90)$

$4 \times 90 = \underline{\quad} + \underline{\quad} = \underline{\quad}$

Independent Practice ☆

In **5–12**, find the product using properties of multiplication.

5. $7 \times 60 = 7 \times (\underline{\quad} \times 10)$

$7 \times 60 = (7 \times \underline{\quad}) \times 10$

$7 \times 60 = \underline{\quad} \times 10 = \underline{\quad}$

6. $5 \times 40 = \underline{\quad} \times (\underline{\quad} \times 10)$

$5 \times 40 = (\underline{\quad} \times \underline{\quad}) \times 10$

$5 \times 40 = \underline{\quad} \times \underline{\quad} = \underline{\quad}$

7. $8 \times 30 = (\underline{\quad} + 4) \times 30$

$8 \times 30 = (4 \times 30) + (\underline{\quad} \times 30)$

$8 \times 30 = \underline{\quad} + \underline{\quad} = \underline{\quad}$

8. $4 \times 70 = 4 \times (\underline{\quad} \times 10)$

$4 \times 70 = (4 \times \underline{\quad}) \times 10$

$4 \times 70 = \underline{\quad} \times 10 = \underline{\quad}$

9. $5 \times 90 = \underline{\quad} \times (\underline{\quad} \times 10)$

$5 \times 90 = (\underline{\quad} \times \underline{\quad}) \times 10$

$5 \times 90 = \underline{\quad} \times \underline{\quad} = \underline{\quad}$

10. $8 \times 80 = (4 + \underline{\quad}) \times 80$

$8 \times 80 = (4 \times 80) + (4 \times 80)$

$8 \times 80 = \underline{\quad} + \underline{\quad} = \underline{\quad}$

11. $6 \times 40 = (3 + \underline{\quad}) \times 40$

$6 \times 40 = (3 \times \underline{\quad}) + (3 \times \underline{\quad})$

$6 \times 40 = \underline{\quad} + \underline{\quad} = \underline{\quad}$

12. $9 \times 80 = 9 \times (\underline{\quad} \times 10)$

$9 \times 80 = (9 \times \underline{\quad}) \times 10$

$9 \times 80 = \underline{\quad} \times \underline{\quad} = \underline{\quad}$

Problem Solving

13. Look at the picture graph at the right. How many pounds of newspaper did Grade 3 collect?

14. **Make Sense and Persevere** How many pounds of newspaper did Grade 3 and Grade 4 collect together? Explain your plan for solving.

Newspaper Collected to Recycle

Grade 2	▭ ▭
Grade 3	▭ ▭ ▭ ▭
Grade 4	▭ ▭ ▭

Each ▭ = 30 pounds

15. **Higher Order Thinking** Grade 5 collected 150 pounds of newspaper. How many more symbols would be in the row for Grade 5 than Grade 2?

16. **Number Sense** Without finding the products, how can you tell whether 4×60 or 7×40 is greater?

17. Explain how to use mental math to add $521 + 104$.

18. **Construct Arguments** Tikie said that it's easy to count by 50s. Explain how she could use counting by 50s to find 5×60.

Use properties and equations to help you construct an argument!

✓ **Assessment**

19. Which products are equal to 180? Choose all that apply.

☐ 1×80 ☐ 2×80
☐ 6×30 ☐ 8×20
☐ 3×60

20. Which numbers are multiples of 40? Choose all that apply.

☐ 24 ☐ 240
☐ 40 ☐ 290
☐ 160

Help Practice Buddy Tools Games

Another Look!

Find 4×70.

Use equivalent expressions to solve a simpler problem.

It can be easier to multiply by 10! You can use properties to think of the problem as multiplying by 10.

You can group factors.

$4 \times 70 = 4 \times (7 \times 10)$

$4 \times 70 = (4 \times 7) \times 10$

$4 \times 70 = 28 \times 10 = 280$

So, $4 \times 70 = 280$

You can decompose a factor.

$4 \times 70 = (2 + 2) \times 70$

$4 \times 70 = (2 \times 70) + (2 \times 70)$

$4 \times 70 = 140 + 140 = 280$

So, $4 \times 70 = 280$

In **1–6**, find the product using properties of multiplication.

1. $8 \times 40 = 8 \times (\underline{} \times 10)$

$8 \times 40 = (8 \times \underline{}) \times 10$

$8 \times 40 = \underline{} \times 10 = \underline{}$

2. $2 \times 90 = \underline{} \times (\underline{} \times 10)$

$2 \times 90 = (\underline{} \times \underline{}) \times 10$

$2 \times 90 = (\underline{}) \times 10 = \underline{}$

3. $6 \times 20 = (3 + \underline{}) \times 20$

$6 \times 20 = (3 \times \underline{}) + (3 \times \underline{})$

$6 \times 20 = \underline{} + \underline{} = \underline{}$

4. $4 \times 80 = 4 \times (\underline{} \times 10)$

$4 \times 80 = (4 \times \underline{}) \times 10$

$4 \times 80 = \underline{} \times 10 = \underline{}$

5. $7 \times 70 = \underline{} \times (\underline{} \times 10)$

$7 \times 70 = (\underline{} \times \underline{}) \times 10$

$7 \times 70 = \underline{} \times 10 = \underline{}$

6. $8 \times 60 = (4 + \underline{}) \times 60$

$8 \times 60 = (4 \times \underline{}) + (4 \times \underline{})$

$8 \times 60 = \underline{} + \underline{} = \underline{}$

7. **Use Structure** A warehouse has 9 crates. Each crate has 20 boxes of cereal. How many boxes of cereal does the warehouse have? Explain how to use properties to solve the problem.

8. **Construct Arguments** Hank gets 9 cases of CDs. He wants to record his band's song on 250 CDs. There are 30 CDs in a case. Did Hank buy enough CDs? Explain.

9. $32 \div 4 =$ ___
   List 2 other facts that belong to the same fact family.

10. **Algebra** Kelsey writes the equation $6 \times ? = 180$. What value makes Kelsey's equation true?

11. **Be Precise** Josie bikes 40 miles each month for 5 months. She multiplies 40×5. What unit should she use for the product: miles or months? Explain.

12. **Higher Order Thinking** June says that $5 \times 28 = 140$. She uses the reasoning shown below. Explain whether you agree or disagree with June's reasoning.

    $5 \times 28 = 5 \times (4 \times 7)$
    $= (5 \times 4) \times 7$
    $= 20 \times 7 = 140$

✔ **Assessment**

13. Which numbers are multiples of 70? Choose all that apply.

    ☐ 7
    ☐ 14
    ☐ 210
    ☐ 270
    ☐ 560

14. Which products are equal to 300? Choose all that apply.

    ☐ 3×10
    ☐ 6×50
    ☐ 8×40
    ☐ 5×60
    ☐ 30×10

Name _____

Solve & Share

Find the products of 4 × 50, 2 × 40, and 9 × 20. *Solve these problems using any strategy you choose.* Describe the patterns you find.

I can ...
use different strategies to find products when one factor is a multiple of 10.

I can also look for patterns to solve problems.

You can look for relationships. Think about how patterns can help you solve the problems. *Show your work!*

Look Back! **Generalize** Is there a rule you can make for multiplying a number by a multiple of 10?

What Is a Rule for Multiplying by a Multiple of 10?

A

There are 5 boxes of crayons on a shelf. Each box has 30 crayons. How many crayons are there?

Find 5 × 30.

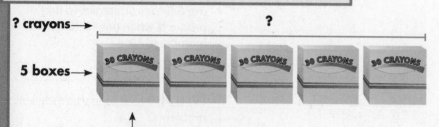

? crayons →

?

5 boxes →

↑ 30 crayons in each box

B Apply the Associative Property of Multiplication.

$5 \times 30 = 5 \times (3 \times 10)$
$5 \times 30 = (5 \times 3) \times 10$
$5 \times 30 = 15 \times 10$
$5 \times 30 = 150$

There are 150 crayons.

You can use basic multiplication facts to multiply by multiples of 10.

C Use a shortcut to multiply.

Find 5 × 30.

Multiply by the digit in the tens place.

$5 \times 3 = 15$

Write one zero after the product.

$5 \times 3\underline{0} = 15\underline{0}$

So, 5 × 30 = 150.

There are 150 crayons.

D Sometimes, the basic multiplication fact makes the rule look different.

Find 5 × 60.

Multiply by the digit in the tens place.

$5 \times 6 = 30$

Write one zero after the product.

$5 \times 6\underline{0} = 30\underline{0}$

So, 5 × 60 = 300.

When the product of a basic fact ends in zero, the answer will have two zeros.

Convince Me! **Make Sense and Persevere** Suppose there are 50 crayons in each of the 5 boxes. Find 5 × 50 using the Associative Property of Multiplication as shown above. How many crayons are in 5 boxes?

Name _____

Practice Buddy Tools Assessment

☆Guided Practice☆

Do You Understand?

1. How can you find the product of 9 × 80? Explain.

2. Sue wants to find the product of 30 × 2. She knows the product of 2 × 30. What property of multiplication could she use to help solve the problem? Explain.

Do You Know How?

In **3–9**, complete each equation.

3. 2 × 70 = 2 × (____ × ____)

2 × 70 = (2 × ____) × ____

2 × 70 = 14 × ____

2 × 70 = ____

4. 6 × 6 = ____   **5.** 7 × 8 = ____

6 × 60 = ____   70 × 8 = ____

6. 5 × 4 = ____   **7.** 8 × 2 = ____

5 × 40 = ____   80 × 2 = ____

8. 4 × 9 = ____   **9.** 3 × 2 = ____

40 × 9 = ____   3 × 20 = ____

☆Independent Practice☆

Leveled Practice In **10–20**, complete each equation.

10. 6 × 70 = 6 × (7 × ____)

6 × 70 = (6 × ____) × ____

6 × 70 = ____ × 10

6 × 70 = ____

11. 9 × 50 = 9 × (____ × 10)

9 × 50 = (9 × ____) × ____

9 × 50 = 45 × ____

9 × 50 = ____

12. 2 × 6 = ____   **13.** 5 × 8 = ____   **14.** 9 × 4 = ____

2 × 60 = ____   5 × 80 = ____   9 × 40 = ____

15. 2 × 30 = ____   **16.** 60 × 9 = ____   **17.** 8 × 20 = ____

18. 80 × 5 = ____   **19.** 90 × 2 = ____   **20.** 30 × 4 = ____

Problem Solving

21. **Critique Reasoning** Adam says the product of 2 × 50 equals 100. Dan says the product is 1,000. Who is correct? Explain.

22. **Model with Math** Juanita buys 7 sheets of postage stamps at the post office. Each sheet has 20 stamps. How many stamps does she buy in all? Explain how you solved the problem. Tell why you chose that method.

23. **Algebra** What value makes the equation below true?

    9 × ? = 630

24. Janet bought 137 green beads. Now she has 349 beads. How many beads did Janet have before?

25. **Higher Order Thinking** Ali and his family are going to the amusement park. If there are 2 adults and 5 children, how much will the tickets cost?

✓ Assessment

26. Mr. Ridley owns a clothing store. The table shows how many pieces of clothing fit on each rack, and the number of racks. Complete the bar graph to show how many articles of clothing fit in Mr. Ridley's store.

DATA

Type	Number of Clothes on Each Rack	Number of Racks
Shirts	50	2
Pants	30	3
Shorts	20	3
Dresses	40	2

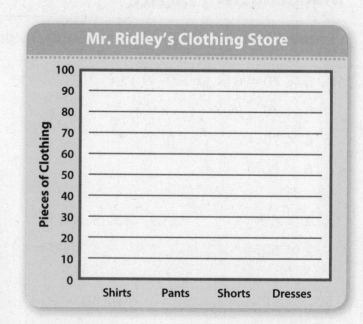

Mr. Ridley's Clothing Store

Another Look!

You can use basic facts to help you multiply by numbers that are multiples of 10.

Find 6×40.

First find 6×4. $6 \times 4 = 24$

Then write one zero after the product. $6 \times 40 = 240$

You can use a basic fact or properties of multiplication to solve 2×70.

Below are different ways to solve 2×70.

2×70	$2 \times 70 = 2 \times (7 \times 10)$
$2 \times 7 = 14$	$2 \times 70 = (2 \times 7) \times 10$
$2 \times 70 = 140$	$2 \times 70 = 14 \times 10$
	$2 \times 70 = 140$

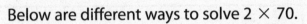

In **1** and **2**, use basic facts to help you multiply.

1. Find 3×80.

Basic fact: $3 \times$ _____ = _____

Show multiplication by 10 by writing a _____ after the product of the fact.

$3 \times 80 =$ _____

2. Find 9×50.

Basic fact: _____ $\times$ _____ = _____

Show multiplication by 10 by writing a _____ after the product of the fact.

$9 \times 50 =$ _____

In **3–11**, complete each equation.

3. $5 \times 6 =$ _____

$50 \times 6 =$ _____

4. $8 \times 7 =$ _____

$80 \times 7 =$ _____

5. $3 \times 6 =$ _____

$3 \times 60 =$ _____

6. $30 \times 9 =$ _____

7. $9 \times 80 =$ _____

8. $60 \times 6 =$ _____

9. $5 \times 50 =$ _____

10. $7 \times 60 =$ _____

11. $4 \times 30 =$ _____

12. Explain why there are two zeros in the product of 5 × 40.

13. Model with Math Tonya lined up 4 rows of train tracks. In each row there are 20 trains. How many trains are there? Explain how you can represent this problem.

14. Use Appropriate Tools Which tool would you use to measure the area of a rectangle: counters, square tiles, or triangle pattern blocks? Explain why you chose that tool.

15. Math and Science There are 3 plots in Kevin's garden. Last year, Kevin planted 10 lilies in one plot. This year, there are 30 lilies on each plot. How many total lilies are on Kevin's land now?

16. Higher Order Thinking Noah takes about 200 steps in an hour. About how many steps does Noah take in 4 hours? Fill in the table. Look for a pattern.

Time	1 hour	2 hours	3 hours	4 hours
Number of Steps				

✓ Assessment

17. Geena has 4 boxes of small paper clips, 3 boxes of medium paper clips, and 5 boxes of large paper clips. Each box has 40 paper clips. Complete the bar graph to show Geena's paper clips.

Geena's Paper Clips

Name _____

Solve

Solve & Share

Stefan says that he could use this multiplication table to help him multiply 3 × 40 to get 120. Explain Stefan's strategy.

×	0	1	2	3	4	5	6
0	0	0	0	0	0	0	0
1	0	1	2	3	4	5	6
2	0	2	4	6	8	10	12
3	0	3	6	9	12	15	18
4	0	4	8	12	16	20	24
5	0	5	10	15	20	25	30
6	0	6	12	18	24	30	36

Thinking Habits

Be a good thinker! These questions can help you.

- What patterns can I see and describe?

- How can I use the patterns to solve the problem?

- Can I see expressions and objects in different ways?

Look Back! **Use Structure** Could Stefan also use the multiplication table to solve 4 × 40 in the same way? Explain how you decided.

A

How Can I Use Structure to Multiply with Multiples of 10?

Find the missing products in the multiplication table.

×	10	20	30	40	50	60	70	80	90
4	40	80				240		320	
5	50		150				350		
6	60		180				420		

You can look for relationships in the multiplication table.

B **How can I make use of structure to solve this problem?**

I can

- look for patterns to help solve a problem.

- describe the patterns that I find.

- identify how numbers are organized.

C

 Here's my thinking...

As I move down the columns, the numbers increase by the value of the column.

As I move across the rows, the numbers increase by the value in the 10 column.

I used patterns I know for multiplying by multiples of 10.

×	10	20	30	40	50	60	70	80	90
4	40	80	120	160	200	240	280	320	360
5	50	100	150	200	250	300	350	400	450
6	60	120	180	240	300	360	420	480	540

Convince Me! **Use Structure** The ones digit never changes in the products in the multiplication table above. Explain why.

Practice Buddy | Tools | Assessment

☆ Guided Practice*

Use Structure

Sean is making muffins. He is choosing to make either 7 or 8 batches. He is also choosing whether to use 40, 50, 60, or 70 raisins for each batch. Sean starts this table to show the total number of raisins he will need for each choice.

You can use the structure of the products and factors to find a pattern.

1. Find the missing products in the table to show how many raisins Sean will use for each batch. Think about patterns or properties you know.

×	40	50	60	70
7			420	
8	320			

2. Sean uses 480 raisins in total. How many batches does he make? How many raisins does he use for each batch?

Independent Practice ☆

Use Structure

Jolene is making a display with equal rows of stickers. She is choosing whether to use 20, 30, 40, or 50 stickers in each row. She is also choosing whether to have 2, 3, or 4 rows. Jolene starts this table to show the total number of stickers she will need for each choice.

3. Find the missing products in the table to show how many stickers Jolene will need for each choice. Think about patterns or properties you know.

×	20	30	40	50
2	40	60		
3	60			
4				200

4. Jolene uses 150 stickers in total. How many rows does she have in her display? How many stickers does she put in each row?

*For another example, see Set D on page 566.

Music Lessons

Four friends each took music lessons for different instruments this month. They want to know who spent the most money on music lessons.

Student	June	Li	Mick	Rita
Price Paid per Lesson (dollars)	60	20	10	40
Length of Lesson (minutes)	60	60	50	90
Number of Lessons	4	8	9	7
Total Cost (dollars)	___	___	___	___

5. **Make Sense and Persevere** What do you need to do to solve the problem?

6. **Use Structure** How can you find the total amount for each student? Think about properties or patterns you know.

Think about and look for relationships to help solve problems.

7. **Model with Math** Use math you know to complete the table. Circle the person who spent the greatest amount.

8. **Construct Arguments** Did the person who spent the most per lesson also spend the greatest amount in total? Explain why or why not.

Another Look!

Find the missing products in the table.

Tell how you can make use of structure to solve this problem.

- I can look for things in common to find a pattern.
- I can describe the patterns I find.
- I can extend a pattern.

Complete the table. Think about patterns or properties you know.

×	10	20	30	40	50	60	70	80	90
3	30	60	90	120	150	180	210	240	270
4	40	80	120	160	200	240	280	320	360
5	50	100	150	200	250	300	350	400	450

One factor is always a multiple of 10. I used patterns I know for multiplying by multiples of 10 to find each missing factor.

> When you use structure, you look for and describe patterns that can be used to solve the problem.

Use Structure

Clifton is making different types of necklaces. The necklaces will have either 10, 20, 30, or 40 beads. Clifton starts the table below to find the number of beads he will need if he makes 6, 7, or 8 of each type of necklace.

1. Tell how you can find the products in the table below.

2. Find the missing products in the table to show how many beads Clifton will need for each type of necklace. Think about patterns or properties you know.

×	10	20	30	40
6	60	120		
7	70			
8	80	160		

Exercise Routine

Bernard is training for a race. He performs the same exercise routine every day. In a 7-day week, does Bernard spend more time weight lifting or jogging? How much more time? Answer Exercises 3–6 to solve the problem.

Activity	Time Each Day (minutes)	Time Each Week (minutes)
Walking	10	_____
Jogging	20	140
Weight lifting	30	_____
Stretching	5	_____

3. **Model with Math** Identify the hidden question in this problem. What operation can you use to answer the hidden question?

4. **Use Structure** Solve the problem. Think about properties or patterns you know. Show your work.

Use structure to understand how a pattern works.

5. **Generalize** What step can you repeat to find the time Bernard spends on each activity in 1 week? Complete the table.

6. **Critique Reasoning** Jacob solves the problem by adding the time Bernard spends each day jogging and weight lifting. Then he multiplies this sum by 7. Does Jacob's reasoning make sense? Explain.

Name _____

Follow the Path

Shade a path from **START** to **FINISH**. Follow the sums or differences that are correct. You can only move up, down, right, or left.

I can ...
add and subtract within 1,000.

Start				
574 + 390 964	999 − 632 331	123 + 612 475	587 + 219 736	501 − 444 95
914 − 627 287	242 + 486 568	794 − 632 162	497 + 493 990	999 − 256 743
399 + 469 868	687 − 413 264	887 − 199 688	718 − 256 262	378 + 511 889
924 − 885 39	653 + 342 995	242 + 547 789	852 − 231 651	593 − 528 65
374 + 469 799	408 − 122 530	523 + 304 821	315 + 411 737	879 − 465 414

Finish

Vocabulary Review

A-Z Glossary

Word List

- Associative Property of Multiplication
- Distributive Property
- equal groups
- factor
- multiple
- open number line
- product

Understand Vocabulary

1. Cross out any numbers below that are **NOT** *multiples* of 20.

20   30   40   50   90

2. Cross out any equations below where 10 is **NOT** a *factor*.

$3 \times 10 = 30$ $10 = 5 \times 2$ $50 = 10 \times 5$ $10 \times 0 = 0$

3. Cross out any equations below that do **NOT** show the *Associative Property of Multiplication.*

$(4 \times 6) \times 7 = 4 \times (6 \times 7)$ $4 \times 3 = 3 \times 4$ $0 = 2 \times 0$

4. Cross out any equations below where 8 is **NOT** the *product*.

$8 = 2 \times 4$ $8 \times 8 = 64$ $2 \times (4 \times 1) = 8$ $2 \times 8 = 16$

Write T for true or F for false.

_____ **5.** An example of the *Distributive Property* is $6 \times 0 = 0$.

_____ **6.** *Equal groups* have the same amount in each group.

_____ **7.** An *open number line* is a plain line that can be used to help you multiply.

Use Vocabulary in Writing

8. Use at least 2 terms from the Word List to explain how to solve 3×30.

Name _____

Set A | pages 539–544 _____

Find 5 × 70.

Show 5 jumps of 70 on the number line.

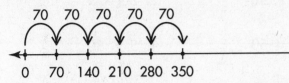

70   70   70   70   70

0   70   140   210   280   350

1 jump of 70 is 70.	1 × 70 = 70
2 jumps of 70 are 140.	2 × 70 = 140
3 jumps of 70 are 210.	3 × 70 = 210
4 jumps of 70 are 280.	4 × 70 = 280
5 jumps of 70 are 350.	5 × 70 = 350

The pattern in the products is like the pattern when you multiply by 7, but with an extra 0 in the ones place.

Remember that you can skip count to show multiplication.

Reteaching

In **1–3**, use an open number line to solve.

1. 4 × 80

0

2. 7 × 20

0

3. 3 × 50

0

Set B | pages 545–550 _____

Find 7 × 80.

Think of 80 as 8 × 10. Then use the Associative Property of Multiplication.

7 × 80 = 7 × (8 × 10)
7 × 80 = (7 × 8) × 10
7 × 80 = 56 × 10
7 × 80 = 560

When you multiply a number by 10, the product has a zero in the ones place. The other factor is written to the left of the zero. So, 56 × 10 = 560.

Remember that the Associative Property of Multiplication lets you regroup factors.

In **1** and **2**, find the product using properties.

1. 5 × 80 = 5 × (____ × 10)

5 × 80 = (5 × ____) × 10

5 × 80 = ____ × 10 = ____

2. 7 × 40 = ____ × (____ × 10)

7 × 40 = (____ × ____) × 10

7 × 40 = ____ × 10 = ____

Set C pages 551–556

You can use patterns and properties to multiply by multiples of 10.

Find 6 × 30.

Multiply by the digit in the tens place.

6 × 3 = 18

Write one zero after the product of the basic fact.

6 × 3<u>0</u> = 18<u>0</u>

Patterns can help you learn a shortcut!

Remember that sometimes your answer will have two zeros.

In **1–10**, find each product.

1. 3 × 30   **2.** 50 × 9

3. 6 × 60   **4.** 5 × 80

5. 8 × 40   **6.** 80 × 7

7. 70 × 4   **8.** 8 × 30

9. 7 × 70   **10.** 60 × 5

Set D pages 557–562

Think about these questions to help you **make use of structure.**

Thinking Habits

- What patterns can I see and describe?

- How can I use the patterns to solve the problem?

- Can I see expressions and objects in different ways?

Remember to use patterns or properties to multiply by multiples of 10.

Christy is making a savings plan. She wants to know how much she will save if she saves $40 for 6, 7, 8, or 9 weeks.

1. How can you use patterns to help solve this problem?

2. Find the total amount Christy would save after 6, 7, 8, or 9 weeks. Think about patterns or properties you know.

Name _____

1. Julia gives a sheet of stickers to 4 of her friends. Each sheet has 20 stickers. How many stickers do her friends have in all? Use the open number line to solve.

2. For questions 2a–2d, choose *Yes* or *No* to tell if the expression is equal to 8×60.

   2a. 48×10 ○ Yes ○ No

   2b. 6×80 ○ Yes ○ No

   2c. $(8 \times 6) \times 10$ ○ Yes ○ No

   2d. $8 \times (8 \times 10)$ ○ Yes ○ No

3. Mrs. Rode bought 80 packs of juice boxes for her school's party. The juice boxes came in packs of 8. How many juice boxes did Mrs. Rode buy? Explain how to solve.

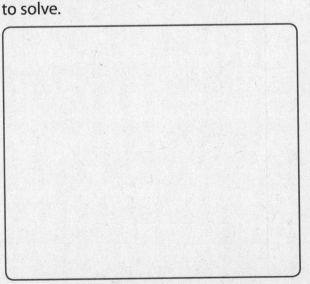

4. The third-grade teachers at Jenny's school need 5 boxes of yellow folders and 4 boxes of red folders. Each box has 40 folders. How many folders do the teachers need?

   Ⓐ 160   Ⓒ 320

   Ⓑ 200   Ⓓ 360

5. Write each expression in the correct answer space to show expressions equal to 6×30 and 3×80.

6×30	3×80

   $(3 \times 8) \times 10$ $6 \times (3 \times 10)$

   $3 \times (6 \times 10)$ 18×10

   24×10 $3 \times (8 \times 10)$

   $8 \times (3 \times 10)$ $(6 \times 3) \times 10$

6. Draw lines to connect equal expressions.

6×60	42×10
6×70	24×10
7×40	36×10
6×40	28×10

7. To solve 4 × 30, Tomas wrote
4 × (3 × 10) = (4 × 3) × 10.
What is 4 × 30?

Ⓐ 22

Ⓑ 34

Ⓒ 120

Ⓓ 160

8. Tyler does 40 push-ups each day. How many push-ups does he do in 5 days? Use the open number line to solve.

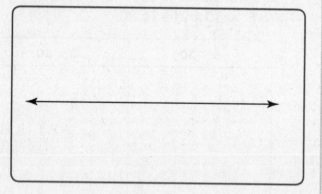

9. The membership to a children's museum is $90 for a year. On Friday 5 families bought memberships. How much did the museum receive for the new memberships? Explain how you can use structure to solve.

10. Choose all of the expressions that are equal to 7 × 50.

☐ 7 × (5 × 10)

☐ 35 × 10

☐ 7 × 5

☐ 75 × 10

☐ (7 × 5) × 10

11. Tyrone drives 30 miles every day. How many miles does Tyrone drive in 7 days?

Part A

Use a number line to solve the problem.

Part B

Show another way to solve the problem.

Name _____

Pet Adoption
Carson and Adriana volunteer at a local animal rescue center.
The adoption fee is different based on the animal and its age.

Carson made an **Adoption Fee** graph to show the fees
for adult dogs, puppies, adult cats, and kittens. Adriana
recorded the number of each animal adopted during the
summer in the **Animals Adopted** table.

Use the **Adoption Fee** graph and the **Animals Adopted**
table to answer Questions 1–3.

1. Carson wants to find the total adoption fees the rescue
   center received for adopted adult dogs. Show how
   Carson can use a number line to do this.

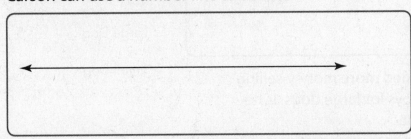

2. Adriana says that she can use (4 × 8) × 10 to find
   the total adoption fees for adopted puppies. Is she correct?
   Explain why or why not. Then find the total.

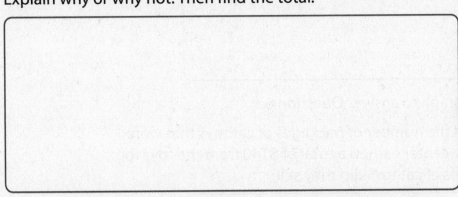

Animals Adopted	
Adult Dog	8
Puppy	4
Adult Cat	5
Kitten	3

3. Find the adoption fees the rescue center received for kittens.
   Think about patterns or properties you know. Show your work.

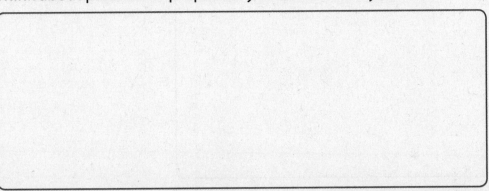

The animal rescue center sells toy packages for pets.

The **Toy Packages** graph shows the amount earned for different types of packages. The **Toy Packages Sold** table shows how many packages were sold in the summer.

Use the **Toy Packages** graph and the **Toy Packages Sold** table to answer Questions 4 and 5.

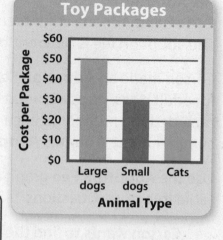

4. How much money did the animal rescue center earn from toys for large dogs? Show your work.

5. Carson says that the center earned more money selling toys for small dogs than from toys for large dogs. Is he correct? Explain why or why not.

Toy Packages Sold	
Large Dog	5
Small Dog	7

Use the **Toy Packages** graph to answer Question 6.

6. Adriana forgot to record the number of packages of cat toys that were sold. She knows that the center earned a total of $140 from the toys for cats. How many packages of cat toys did they sell?

Use Operations with Whole Numbers to Solve Problems

Essential Question: What are ways to solve 2-step problems?

Digital Resources

Solve   Learn   Glossary   Practice Buddy

Tools   Assessment   Help   Games

It's fun to build something that you designed! Here's a project on engineering.

Kites come in many shapes and sizes.

Engineers think about how much material, time, and money they need for a successful design.

Math and Science Project: Engineering Design

Do Research Use the Internet or other sources to find information about kites. Find two designs for building a kite. What materials do you need for each design? How much do those materials cost?

Journal: Write a Report Include what you found. Also in your report:

- Find the total cost for each design.

- Decide which design is cheaper.

- Write an equation to show how much cheaper that design is.

Review What You Know

A-Z Vocabulary

Choose the best term from the box.
Write it on the blank.

• equation   • quotient
• product   • unknown

1. The equal sign shows that the left side of a(n) _____ has the same value as the right side.

2. A question mark can stand for a(n) _____ value.

3. The answer to a division problem is the _____ .

Addition and Subtraction

4. $739 - 104$

5. $512 + 216$

6. $710 - 569$

7. $104 + 67$

8. $664 + 78$

9. $825 - 477$

Multiplication and Division

10. $60 \div 6$

11. 40×4

12. 7×3

13. $(3 \times 10) \times 6 =$

Ⓐ $(3 \times 10) + (6 \times 10)$

Ⓑ $(3 \times 6) + (10 \times 6)$

Ⓒ $3 \times (10 \times 6)$

Ⓓ $(10 + 10 + 10) + 6$

Model with Math

14. Caleb has 8 toy cars. Each car has 4 wheels. He wants to know how many wheels are on all of his cars. Represent this problem using a bar diagram and an equation. Then solve.

Name _____

Solve & Share

Jen buys a backpack and a sleeping bag. She gets $10 off if the total is more than $200. What is the final cost of Jen's order? Complete the bar diagram below. Then draw another diagram to solve the problem.

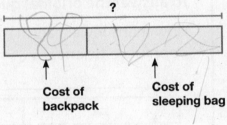

	Item	Price
DATA	Grill	$138
	Backpack	$89
	Lantern	$78
	Sleeping Bag	$128

?

↑ Cost of backpack   ↑ Cost of sleeping bag

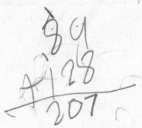

I can ...
draw diagrams and write equations to show how the quantities in a problem are related.

I can also reason about math.

Use reasoning. You can draw more than one diagram and write more than one equation to solve 2-step problems.

Look Back! **Make Sense and Persevere** How can you use an estimate to show that the final cost of the backpack and sleeping bag you found makes sense?

How Can You Use Diagrams to Solve 2-Step Problems?

A

The results of a car survey are shown in the table. How many fewer cars in the survey have poor fuel efficiency than have either good or average fuel efficiency? Use estimation to check the answer.

Survey of Fuel-Efficient Cars	
Fuel Efficiency	Number of Cars
Good	98
Average	165
Poor	224

You can draw bar diagrams to help. You can use a letter to stand for the unknown quantity.

B Step 1

Find and answer the hidden question.

How many total cars in the survey have either good or average fuel efficiency?

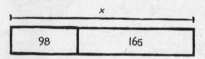

x is the unknown total.

$x = 98 + 165$

$$\begin{array}{r} \overset{1\ 1}{165} \\ +\ \ 98 \\ \hline 263 \end{array}$$

$x = 263$

263 cars have good or average fuel efficiency.

C Step 2

Use the answer to the hidden question to answer the original question.

How many fewer cars in the survey have poor fuel efficiency?

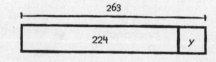

$y = 263 - 224$

$$\begin{array}{r} \overset{5\ 13}{2\cancel{6}\cancel{3}} \\ -\ 224 \\ \hline 39 \end{array}$$

$y = 39$

y is the unknown difference.

39 fewer cars have poor fuel efficiency.

Convince Me! **Critique Reasoning** Jane used estimation to check the reasonableness of the work above. Explain whether Jane's work makes sense.

165 and 98 is about 200.
224 minus 200 equals 24, which is sort of close to 39.

Name _____

Guided Practice

Do You Understand?

1. How do the diagrams help you write equations for the problem on page 574?

Do You Know How?

2. **Model with Math** Josie has $145. She buys a bike for $127. The next week she saves $15. How much money does Josie have now? Complete the bar diagrams and write equations to solve.

m ← Money left after buying a bike

s ← Money now

Independent Practice

In **3**, use the map. Draw diagrams and write equations to solve. Use letters to represent unknown quantities.

3. **Model with Math** Manuel's family drove from Louisville to Indianapolis to Detroit and then directly back to Louisville. How much farther did they drive going to Detroit than returning from Detroit?

Detroit

283 miles

361 miles

Indianapolis

114 miles

Louisville

4. **Make Sense and Persevere** How can you estimate to check if your answer above is reasonable? Explain.

Problem Solving

5. **Model with Math** Write equations to find how many more tickets were sold for the roller coaster on Saturday than for the swings on both days combined.
Use letters to represent the unknown quantities. You can draw diagrams to help.

Number of Tickets Sold		
Ride	Saturday	Sunday
Ferris Wheel	368	302
Roller Coaster	486	456
Swings	138	154

6. **Higher Order Thinking** Write a two-step problem that can be solved using addition or subtraction. Solve your problem.

7. **Math and Science** Lindsay has 6 boxes of toothpicks. There are 80 toothpicks in each box. Lindsay uses all of the toothpicks to build a model arch bridge. How many toothpicks does Lindsay use in all?

8. **Model with Math** Matt has 327 plastic bottles for recycling. He recycled 118 bottles on Monday. He recycled 123 bottles on Tuesday. How many bottles does Matt have left to recycle?
Write equations to solve. Use letters to represent the unknown quantities. Estimate to check your work.

When checking, remember to estimate for each step.

✔ **Assessment**

9. Ukie has 142 leaves in her collection. She gives 25 to her brother and then collects 19 more. Find how many leaves Ukie has now. Write numbers and symbols in the boxes to complete the equations.

$\boxed{}\ \boxed{}\ \boxed{} = x \quad x = \boxed{}$

$\boxed{}\ \boxed{}\ \boxed{} = y \quad y = \boxed{}$

10. Richard had $236 in his savings account. He got $45 for his birthday and saved all but $16 of it. How much is in Richard's savings account now? Write the answer in the box.

$\$\ \boxed{}$

Name _____

Solve

☆ ☆
Solve & Share

Two friends decide to share equally all
of the apples they picked. They filled the bags shown
with 4 apples in each bag. How many apples will each
friend get? *Solve this problem any way you choose.*

I can ...
draw diagrams and write equations
to show how the quantities in a
problem are related.

Use reasoning. You can use
diagrams and equations to show
how the numbers in 2-step
problems are related.

$3 \times 4 = 12$

$4 \times 3 = 12$

I can also reason about math.

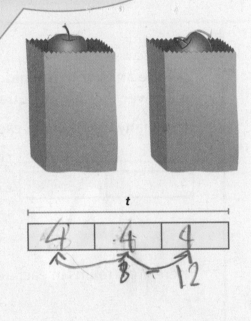

$12 \div 2 = 6$

t

| 4 | 4 | 4 |

8   12

Look Back! **Generalize** Tell why multiplication can be used to
find the total for the bar diagram given above.

How Can You Use Diagrams to Solve 2-Step Problems?

A

The teams for the City Baseball Tournament are divided equally into 3 leagues. Each league is divided into 2 regions with the same number of teams in each region. How many teams are in each region?

You can represent this problem with bar diagrams. You can use a letter to stand for the unknown quantity.

City Baseball Tournament

- 24 teams
- 3 leagues

B ## Step 1

Find and answer the hidden question.

How many teams are in each league?

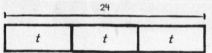

t is the unknown number of teams in each league.

$t = 24 \div 3$

$t = 8$

There are 8 teams in each league.

C ## Step 2

Use the answer to the hidden question to answer the original question.

How many teams are in each region?

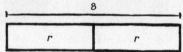

r is the unknown number of teams in each region.

$r = 8 \div 2$

$r = 4$

There are 4 teams in each region.

Convince Me! **Make Sense and Persevere** Another tournament has 2 leagues with 9 teams in each league. An equal number of teams will play on each of the 3 days of the tournament. Each team will play once. How many teams will play on each day?

© Pearson Education, Inc. 3

Name _____

Solve & Share

An aquarium had 75 clownfish in a large water tank. The clownfish represented in the graph were added to this tank. How many clownfish are in the tank now? *Solve this problem any way you choose.* Write and explain how you found the answer.

I can ...
solve two-step word problems involving different operations.

I can also make sense of problems.

Make sense of this problem. Think about the information you need to solve the problem.

Recent Arrivals at the Aquarium

Clownfish	▲ ▲ ▲ ▲ ▲ ▲ ▲ ▲ ▲ = 45
Sea Stars	▲ ▲ ▲ ▲ ▲ = 25
Crabs	▲ ▲ ▲ ▲ ▲ ▲ = 30

Each ▲ = 5 animals

10 20 10 10 20 10 40 45
10 20
10 20 10 5
10 20 10 10
30

75 + 45 = 55
75
+45
[120]

I found the anwser by finding 9×5. Then I added 75+45 and that's how I got this anwser.

Look Back! Reasoning What operations did you use to solve this problem? Tell why you needed those operations.

Essential Question **How Can You Solve 2-Step Problems?**

A

Jill can rent a car and GPS device for $325 for 7 days. What is the cost to rent the car for a week without the GPS device? Use estimation to check the answer.

DATA	**Car Rental Extras**	
	DVD player	$6 a day
	GPS	$9 a day
	Child seat	$10 a day

There are two operations to solve this problem.

c = cost of the car without the GPS

$\$325 - 7 \times \$9 = c$

B

The equation does not have parentheses, so you need to know which of the two operations to do first.

There is an order to do calculations in a problem with no parentheses.

- Start reading the equation from the left side and do any **multiplication** or **division** as you move to the right.

- Then, start back on the left side and do any **addition** or **subtraction**.

C First **multiply**.

$\$325 - 7 \times \$9 = c$

$\$325 - \$63 = c$

Then **subtract**.

$\$325 - \$63 = \$262$

$c = \$262$

The cost without the GPS is $262.

If you subtracted before multiplying, you would not get the correct answer.

Convince Me! **Use Structure** Jill can rent a different car and a DVD player for $384 for 7 days. She wants to know the cost to rent the car for a week without the DVD player.

Explain how this problem is different from the problem above. Then solve.

Name _____

☆Guided Practice*

Do You Understand?

1. **Critique Reasoning** Dotty says you can also use $63 + c = $325 instead of $325 − $63 = c$ for the problem on page 586. Can this equation be used to get the correct answer? Explain.

2. Look at the equation below. Which calculation should you do first to find y?

   $8 \div 4 \times 2 = y$

Do You Know How?

In **3**, write equations to solve. Use a letter to represent the unknown quantity.

3. **Model with Math** Look at Box A on page 586. How much would it cost Jill to rent the car for a week with the GPS and DVD player?

   c = cost of the car with the GPS and DVD player

   _____ + _____ × _____ = c

   _____ + _____ = c

   _____ + _____ = _____

   c = _____

Independent Practice ☆

In **4** and **5**, write equations to solve. Use letters to represent the unknown quantities.

4. **Model with Math** Trish bought 4 yards of rope to make a swing. Judy spent $18 on rope. How much did the two girls spend in all?

   s = total spent

   ____ × ____ + ____ = s

   ____ + ____ = s

   ____ + ____ = ____

   s = ____

5. **Model with Math** Martha has 12 stamps. Toni has 21 stamps. Toni divides her stamps into 3 equal groups. She gives one group to Martha. How many stamps does Martha have now?

   m = Martha's stamps now

   ____ + ____ ÷ ____ = m

   ____ + ____ = m

   ____ + ____ = ____

   m = ____

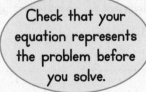

Check that your equation represents the problem before you solve.

*For another example, see Set C on page 600.

Problem Solving

In **6** and **7**, use the fruit shown at the right.

6. **Model with Math** Maurice needs 36 apples for his party. How much will the apples cost? Write equations to solve. Use a letter to represent the unknown quantity.

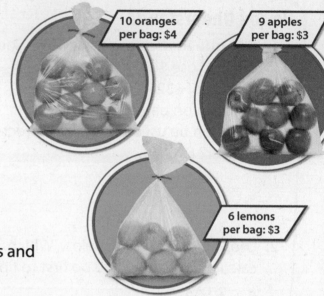

10 oranges per bag: $4

9 apples per bag: $3

6 lemons per bag: $3

7. **Higher Order Thinking** Delia bought 24 lemons and 63 apples. How much did she spend on fruit?

8. **A-Z Vocabulary** Fill in the blank.

When you _____ 72 to the nearest ten, you get 70.

9. **Number Sense** Carla collected 328 shells. Dan collected 176 shells. How can you use compatible numbers to estimate how many shells they collected?

10. **Math and Science** Sasha is building a scratching post for her cat. There will be 3 levels. Sasha spends $10 on the pole. She spends $7 on each level. Sasha's plan to find the total cost is shown at the right. Is she correct? Explain.

$3 \times \$10 + \$7 = c$
I multiply $3 \times \$10$ first.

✓ Assessment

11. Use the fruit from Exercises **6** and **7**. Kaylie bought 4 bags of oranges and 1 bag of apples. How many pieces of fruit did she buy? Write equations to solve. Use letters to represent any unknown quantities.

Name _____

Solve & Share

Solve

Concert tickets for adults cost $12. Concert tickets for students cost $9. Marie has $190. She wants to buy 1 adult and 20 student tickets.

Skip says, "$190 is enough for all the tickets because $9 × 20 = $180 and $180 is less than $190."

Does Skip's reasoning make sense? Explain.

I can ...
critique the reasoning of others using what I know about estimating.

I can also solve multi-step problems.

Thinking Habits
Be a good thinker!
These questions can help you.

- What questions can I ask to understand other people's thinking?

- Are there mistakes in other people's thinking?

- Can I improve other people's thinking?

Look Back! **Critique Reasoning** Was the strategy Skip used to find the total cost of student tickets correct? Explain.

A

Gina has $68. She earns $9 an hour babysitting. She wants to buy a computer program for $130.

Will Gina have enough money to buy the program if she babysits for 6 hours?

Danielle solved this problem.

Her work is shown at the right.

$6 \times \$9 = \$54$, which is about $60.
Gina has $68, which is about $70.
$\$60 + \$70 = \$130$
Gina can buy the program.

What is Danielle's reasoning to support her conclusion?

Danielle used an estimate to add the amount Gina made babysitting to the amount she already had.

B **How can I critique the reasoning of others?**

I can

- ask questions for clarification.

- decide if the strategy used makes sense.

- look for flaws in estimates or calculations.

C

Here's my thinking...

Danielle's reasoning has flaws.

She used estimates that add up to more than the actual amount Gina will have.

$6 \times 9 = \$54$

$\$54 + \$68 = \$122$

Danielle's conclusion is not correct because the actual amount Gina will have is less than $130.

Convince Me! **Critique Reasoning** Tony says that if Gina babysits for 8 hours, she will have enough money. He reasons that $8 \times \$9 = \$72$, which rounds to $70, and $\$70 + \$60 = \$130$. Does that seem reasonable? Explain.

Guided Practice*

Critique Reasoning

Miguel's and Nita's goal is to collect 600 box tops.
Miguel collects 253 box tops in January and 158 box ~~tops in all.~~

~~...~~ more than their goal. She estimates that 250 + ~~___~~ 0 and
400 + 200 = 600.

When you critique reasoning, you can look for good strategies or mistakes. You can see whether you can clarify or improve the reasoning.

1. **What is Teri's argument? How does she support it?**

2. **Does Teri's conclusion make sense? Explain.**

Independent Practice

Critique Reasoning

Gill gets 24 stickers on Monday. She gets the same number of stickers on Tuesday. Gill then shares equally all of her stickers among 8 friends.

Liam concluded that each friend gets fewer than 5 stickers. His work is shown at the right.

3. **What is Liam's argument? How does he support it?**

Liam's work

$8 \times 3 = 24$
So, $24 \div 8 = 3$

Each friend gets 3 stickers.
3 is less than 5.

4. **Does Liam's reasoning make sense? Explain.**

5. **Explain the strategy you would use to improve Liam's work.**

*For another example, see Set D on page 600.   **Topic 11** | Lesson 11-4   **593**

Problem Solving

Selling Buttons

A Grade 3 class is going to buy buttons like the ones shown. Each package costs $8. Each package is 40 cm long. They need to know if $50 is enough money to buy 200 buttons.

30 buttons

Jim's work

6 × 30 = 180 buttons, which is not enough.
7 × 30 = 210 buttons, so the class needs to buy 7 packages.
7 × $8 = $48
48 < 50
$50 is enough.

6. **Make Sense and Persevere** Which given quantity do you not need to solve this problem?

7. **Critique Reasoning** Jim solved the problem as shown above. Does Jim's strategy make sense? Explain.

When you critique reasoning, you need to carefully consider all parts of an argument.

8. **Be Precise** Are Jim's calculations correct? Explain how you decided.

9. **Use Appropriate Tools** Can place-value blocks be used to check whether Jim's math is correct? Explain.

Help Practice Tools Games
      Buddy

Another Look!

Frank needs $169 to buy a bike. He already has $46.
He earns $20 for mowing a lawn.

Dan says Frank needs to mow 6 lawns
to get enough money. His work is
shown at the right.

> **Dan's work**
>
> $6 \times \$20 = \$120$
> $\$120 + \$46$ is about $\$120 + \$50 = \$170$
> $\$170 > \$169$.
> Frank has enough money.

**Tell how you can critique
Dan's reasoning.**

- I can decide if his strategy makes sense.

- I can identify flaws in his thinking.

Critique Dan's reasoning.

The reasoning does not make sense.
Dan rounded $46 to $50, so his estimate of $170 is more than
Frank will have.
Compare the actual sum of $120 + $46 to $169: $166 < $169.

Frank will not have enough money.

> When you critique reasoning, you explain why someone's thinking is correct or incorrect.

Critique Reasoning

A store made $650 on Monday. It made $233 on Tuesday
morning and $378 on Tuesday afternoon.

Leah says the store made more money on Tuesday.
Her work is shown at the right.

> **Leah's work**
>
> $\$233 + \$378$ is about
> $\$300 + \$400 = \$700$.
>
> $\$700 > \$650$
> The store made more money
> on Tuesday.

1. What is Leah's argument? How does she support it?

2. Tell how you can critique Leah's reasoning.

3. Critique Leah's reasoning.

Stocking a Fish Pond

About 200 people visit Mr. Ortiz's park each day. A fish pond in the park contains 636 fish. It cannot hold more than 700 fish. Mr. Ortiz has 7 bags of goldfish like the one at the right. Can Mr. Ortiz put all of his goldfish into the pond?

Jai solved the problem as shown.

700 − 636 is about 700 − 640.
700 − 640 = 60

There are 8 goldfish in each bag.
7 × 8 = 56
Mr. Ortiz has 56 goldfish.
56 < 60

Mr. Ortiz can put all of his goldfish into the pond.

4. **Make Sense and Persevere** Have you seen a problem like this before? If so, how can this help you solve it?

5. **Critique Reasoning** Does Jai's method make sense? Explain.

6. **Be Precise** Are Jai's calculations correct? Explain.

7. **Reasoning** Explain how Jai found the number of goldfish in each bag.

Name _____

☆ **Find a Match** ☆

Work with a partner. Point to a clue. Read the clue.

Look below the clues to find a match. Write the clue letter in the box next to the match.

Find a match for every clue.

I can ...
multiply and divide within 100.

Clues

A The product is between 55 and 60.

E The quotient is less than 5.

B The product is equal to 10 × 2.

F The product is between 30 and 40.

C The quotient has two digits.

G The quotient is a multiple of 3.

D The product is between 50 and 55.

H The quotient is equal to the divisor.

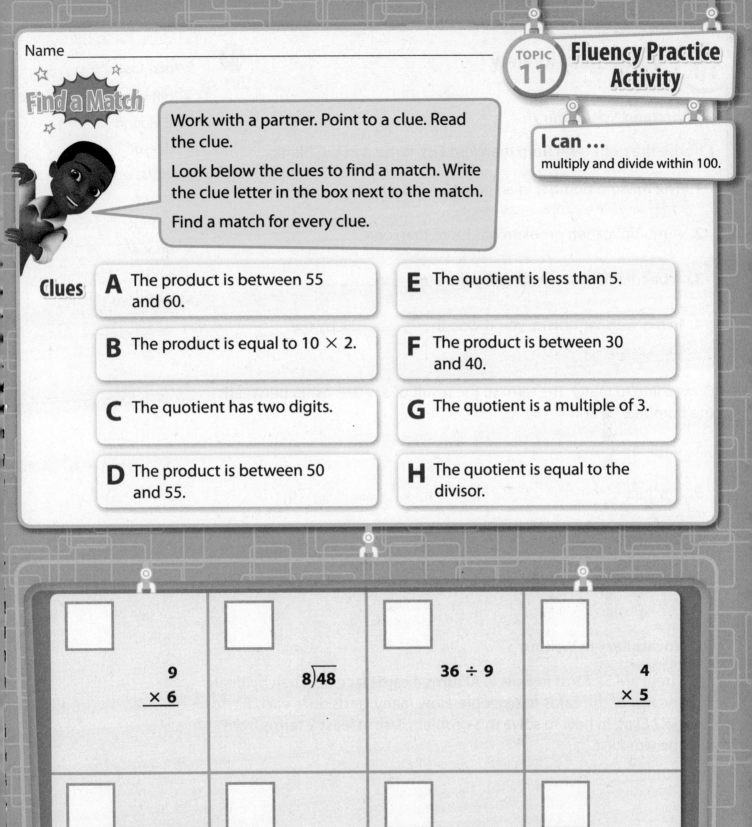

□   9 × 6

□   8)‾48‾

□   36 ÷ 9

□   4 × 5

□   64 ÷ 8

□   7 × 8

□   5)‾50‾

□   5 × 7

 A-Z Glossary

Word List

- difference
- dividend
- divisor
- equation
- factor
- product
- quotient
- sum
- unknown

Understand Vocabulary

Choose the right term from the Word List. Write it in the blank.

1. The missing number in an equation is a(n) _____.

2. A multiplication problem has more than one _____.

3. A bar diagram can help you write a(n) _____.

4. In a division problem, you divide the _____ by the _____.

Draw a line to match the term to the result of a relationship between the numbers 80 and 4.

5. difference   20

6. product   76

7. quotient   84

8. sum   320

Use Vocabulary in Writing

9. There are 52 cards in a deck. Al turns 4 cards face up. Then he deals the rest of the cards to 6 people. How many cards does each person get? Explain how to solve this problem. Use at least 2 terms from the word list.

Set A pages 573–578 _____

You can use more than
1 step to solve
problems.

Use diagrams to
help write equations.

A ship has 439 passengers.
179 new passengers get on at
a port. Then 250 passengers
get off. How many passengers
are on the ship now?

Total passengers → *p*

439	179

$p = 439 + 179; p = 618$
There are 618 passengers in all.

618

250	*l*

← **Passengers left**

$l = 618 - 250; l = 368$
There are 368 passengers left on the ship.

Remember to check for
reasonableness after
each step.

In **1**, draw bar diagrams and write
equations to solve the problems.

1. Mr. Sato has $800. He spends $600 on
   rent. Then he spends $85 on groceries.
   How much money does he have left?

Set B pages 579–584 _____

You can use diagrams and equations to
show how numbers are related.

Roger reads a poem with 16 lines. Each line
has 7 words. The poem is on 2 pages with
the same number of lines on each page.
How many words are on each page?

16

l	*l*

$16 \div 2 = l$ lines on each page

$l = 8$ lines

w

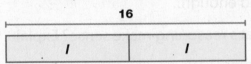

7	7	7	7	7	7	7	7

$8 \times 7 = w$ words on each page

$w = 56$ words

Remember to use unknowns to stand for the
numbers you need to find.

In **1**, draw bar diagrams and write
equations to solve the problems.

1. A rancher has 24 cows. He puts an equal
   number of cows in 4 fields. Each cow
   produces 5 gallons of milk. How much
   milk do the cows in one field produce?

If there are no parentheses in
an equation:

- First, you **multiply** or **divide** from left
  to right.

- Then, you **add** or **subtract** from left
  to right.

Ryan reads a book with 420 pages. He also
reads 7 magazine articles. Each article has
6 pages. How many pages does Ryan read?

p = number of pages Ryan reads

$420 + 7 \times 6 = p$

First **multiply**.

$420 + 7 \times 6 = p$

$420 + 42 = p$

Then **add**.

$420 + 42 = 462$

$p = 462$

Remember to perform the operations in the
correct order for the problem.

In **1**, write equations to solve the
problem. Use letters to stand for
the unknown.

1. Destiny gets $168 for selling mint cookies
   and chocolate cookies. She sells 8 boxes
   of chocolate cookies at $9 per box.
   How much does Destiny get for selling
   mint cookies?

   t = total amount from mint cookies

   _____ − _____ $\times$ _____ = t

   _____ − _____ = t

   _____ − _____ = _____

   $t =$ _____

2. Look at the equation below. Which
   calculation should you do first to find s?

   $16 \div 2 \times 4 = s$

Think about these questions to help you
critique the reasoning of others.

Thinking Habits

- What questions can I ask
  to understand other
  people's thinking?

- Are there mistakes in other
  people's thinking?

- Can I improve other
  people's thinking?

Remember to consider all parts of
an explanation.

Pat needs to practice guitar for at least 40 hours
this month. He has practiced 9 hours a week for
the last 3 weeks. He practiced for 15 hours this
week. Pat says, "3 $\times$ 9 is less than 40. So I have
not practiced enough."

1. Does Pat's reasoning make sense? Explain.

2. How can you clarify or improve
   Pat's reasoning?

Name _____

1. Emma works at a diner. On Monday, she served 7 tables with 6 people at each table. On Tuesday, she served 72 people. She wants to know how many more people she served on Tuesday than on Monday.

   Choose the correct operations to represent this problem using equations. Write each operation on the blanks.

   $7 \_\_ 6 = m$

   $72 \_\_ 42 = d$

   $+ \quad - \quad \times \quad \div$

2. Madison has a jar of 160 jellybeans. She saves 88 for herself. She divides the rest equally among 8 friends. She wants to find how many each friend gets.

   Which equations should she use? Choose all that apply.

   ☐ $80 \div 8 = j$

   ☐ $88 - 8 = k$

   ☐ $160 - 88 = l$

   ☐ $160 \div 80 = m$

   ☐ $72 \div 8 = n$

3. Alberto sells magazine subscriptions to his neighbors. 3 neighbors each buy 3 subscriptions. There are 8 issues in each subscription. Write equations to find the total number of magazine issues all of his neighbors get.

4. Hailey's restaurant has a jar of 585 toothpicks. 315 toothpicks are used at lunch. 107 toothpicks are used at dinner. Hailey says that $315 - 107 = t$ toothpicks are used in all, and that $585 - 208 = r$ toothpicks are left. Is her answer reasonable? Explain why or why not.

5. Tyler has 127 trading cards in his collection. Chloe has 63 cards in her collection. Then Chloe gives her collection away. She divides it equally among Tyler and 8 other friends. How many cards does Tyler have now?

6. Ten people each bring 4 platters of food to a family reunion. The 120 guests all share the platters equally.

Part A

How many guests share 1 platter?

Part B

Landon thinks that the answer is 12 guests. He says, "10 + 4 = 14, and 14 rounds to 10. Then 10 × 12 = 120." Do you agree with his reasoning? Explain why or why not.

7. Jeri collects flags of the United Nations. She wants to know how many cases she needs to display her collection. She can fit 9 flags in one case. There are 193 countries in the United Nations. Jeri does not have flags for 130 countries. Which equation should she use first to solve this problem?

(A) $c = 193 + 130$ (C) $f = 72 \div 9$

(B) $c = 193 - 130$ (D) $f = 9 \times 7$

8. Mrs. Lazio lives 8 miles from her office. She drives to her office and back 5 days each week. On Saturday she also drives 173 miles to visit her sister. Draw bar diagrams to represent how many miles Mrs. Lazio drives each week.

9. José is a bird-watcher. He wants to know how many more birds he saw this month than in the past 3 months. First he adds up the number of birds he saw in the past 3 months. He calls this number b. What should José do next?

(A) Add b to the number of birds he saw this month.

(B) Subtract b from the number of birds he saw this month.

(C) Multiply b by 3.

(D) Multiply b by the number of birds he saw this month.

10. For questions 10a–10d, choose *Yes* or *No* to tell if the estimate is reasonable to solve this problem: $j = 9 \times 6$; $342 - j$.

10a. 50   ○ Yes ○ No

10b. 290   ○ Yes ○ No

10c. 300   ○ Yes ○ No

10d. 390   ○ Yes ○ No

Name _____

Filmmaking Camp

Mrs. Radner and Mr. Yu teach filmmaking at a summer camp. The students work in crews to make movies. The summer ends with the crew and actors watching all the movies.

Class Details

- Mrs. Radner helps the students who make the action and drama films.
- Mr. Yu helps the students who make the comedy films.
- There are 246 actors in all.

	Film Types	
Type	**Number of Films**	**Pages of Script per Film**
Action	2	126
Comedy	3	178
Drama	4	157

Use the **Class Details** list and **Film Types** table to answer Questions 1–3.

1. There are 20 actors working on each Drama film. How many actors are not working on Drama films?

2. Mrs. Radner has read 139 pages of the action-film scripts. How many more pages does she need to read to finish reading all of the action-script pages?

3. Mr. Yu says, "I have read 169 pages of the scripts for each comedy film. I need to read 27 more pages to finish reading all of the pages." Do you agree with his reasoning? Explain why or why not.

4. Mrs. Radner wants to find t, the total time to watch all the student films. Use the **Film Lengths** table to answer the following questions.

Film Lengths

Length (min)	Number of Films	Crew per Film
30	1	12
60	3	10
90	5	20

Part A

Mrs. Radner estimates $t = 810$ minutes. She reasons, "There are 9 films. Most of the films are 90 minutes long. 9 times 90 equals 810." Do you agree with her reasoning? Explain why or why not.

Part B

Use bar diagrams or equations to represent t. Then find t.

5. Mrs. Radner sets up chairs for the crew and actors from the audition to watch the films. Use the **Film Lengths** table and **Class Details** list to answer the following questions.

Part A

How many students are in the crew in all?

Part B

Find the number of chairs Mrs. Radner needs if 147 students cannot watch the films. Use estimation to check your work.

Understand Fractions as Numbers

Essential Question: What are different interpretations of a fraction?

Digital Resources

Solve Learn Glossary Practice Buddy

Tools Assessment Help Games

Most fossils form when living things die and get buried in sediment.

Scientists dig up and study fossils. They help to show a picture of Earth's past environments.

Dig it! So finding fossils of mammals and plants in Antarctica tells us that the environment there has changed. Here's a project about fossils and environment.

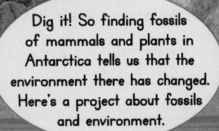

Math and Science Project: Fossils and Environment

Do Research Use the Internet or other sources to find out more about what fossils tell us about past environments. Research and make a booklet of fossils found in your state. Find at least 5 fossils and use one page for each fossil. Include where each fossil was found and what type of environment each location is now.

Write a Report: Journal Include what you found. Also in your report:

- List the types of food each of the 5 creatures ate when they were alive.

- Explain whether each of the 5 creatures on your list could live in today's environment.

- Find the lengths of different fossils to the nearest half inch. Record the lengths in a line plot.

Review What You Know

A-Z Vocabulary

Choose the best term from the box.
Write it on the blank.

• inch	• halves
• thirds	• yard

1. If a shape is divided into 2 equal parts, the parts can be called _____.

2. The tip of your thumb is about 1 _____ long.

3. If a shape is divided into 3 equal parts, the parts can be called _____.

Skip Counting on the Number Line

Skip count on the number line. Write the missing numbers.

4.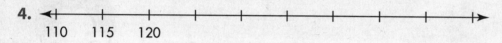
110   115   120

5.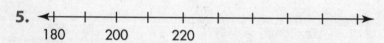
180   200   220

Equal Parts

6. Circle the shapes that show halves.

7. Circle the shapes that show fourths.

Measurement

8. How long is this object to the nearest inch?
Explain how you know.

My Word Cards

Use the examples for each word on the front of the card to help complete the definitions on the back.

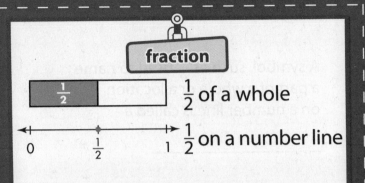

fraction

$\frac{1}{2}$ of a whole

$\frac{1}{2}$ on a number line

unit fraction

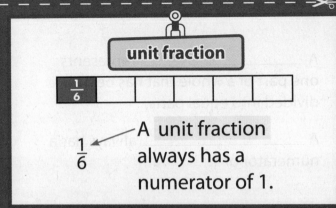

A unit fraction always has a numerator of 1.

numerator

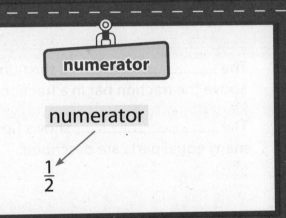

numerator

$\frac{1}{2}$

denominator

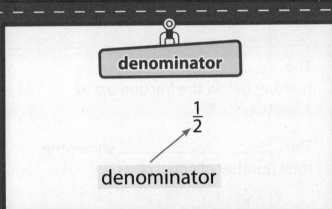

$\frac{1}{2}$

denominator

line plot

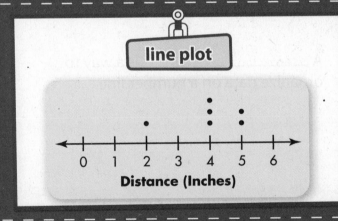

Distance (Inches)

nearest half inch

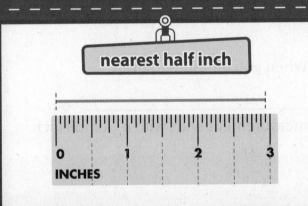

INCHES

nearest fourth inch

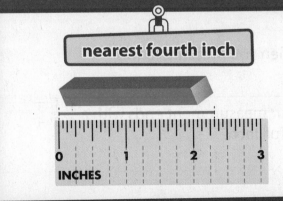

INCHES

My Word Cards

A _____ represents one part of a whole that has been divided into equal parts.

A _____ always has a numerator of 1.

A symbol, such as $\frac{1}{2}$, used to name a part of a whole or a location on a number line is called a

_____.

The _____ is the number below the fraction bar in a fraction.

The _____ shows the total number of equal parts.

The _____ is the number above the fraction bar in a fraction.

The _____ shows how many equal parts are described.

When you measure to the

_____, your measurement ends with a $\frac{1}{2}$ or full inch.

A _____ is a way to organize data on a number line.

When you measure to the

_____, your measurement ends with a $\frac{1}{4}$, $\frac{1}{2}$, $\frac{3}{4}$, or full inch.

Solve

Lesson 12-1
Divide Regions into Equal Parts

Solve & Share

Show two different ways to divide a 2 × 6 region into 6 equal parts. Color the 6 parts of each region a different color. How do you know the parts are equal?

I can ...
read and write a unit fraction.

I can also be precise in my work.

Be precise. Think about the area of each part as you divide the regions.

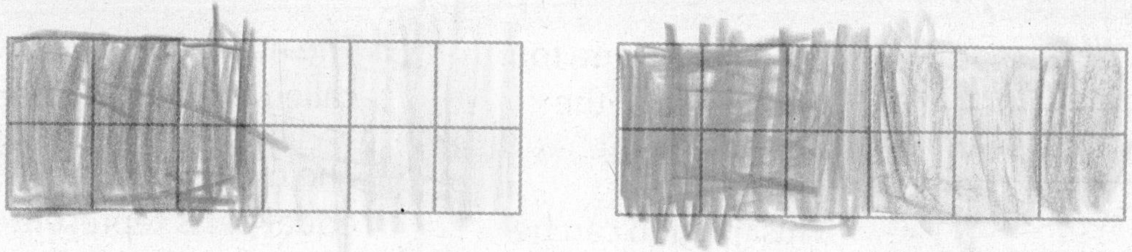

Look Back! Use Structure How are the parts of the regions alike? How are they different?

Essential Question **How Can You Name the Equal Parts of a Whole?**

Divide a whole into fourths. What fraction can you write to represent one fourth of a whole?

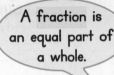 A fraction is an equal part of a whole.

B

one fourth

one fourth

one fourth

one fourth

Each part is made up of 3 unit squares. All parts have equal area.

C

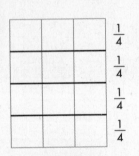

$\frac{1}{4}$
$\frac{1}{4}$
$\frac{1}{4}$
$\frac{1}{4}$

Each part is **one** fourth of the area of the whole shape.

This fraction can be written as $\frac{1}{4}$.

$\frac{1}{4}$ is a unit fraction. A unit fraction represents one of the equal parts.

D The number above the bar in a fraction is called the **numerator**.

The numerator shows the number of equal parts represented by that fraction.

numerator $\longrightarrow$ $\frac{1}{4}$
denominator $\longrightarrow$

The number below the bar in a fraction is called the **denominator**.

The denominator shows the total number of equal parts in that whole.

Convince Me! **Critique Reasoning** Kim says that the figure at the right is divided into fourths because there are 4 equal parts. Carrie says it is not divided into fourths because the parts are not the same shape. Who is correct? Explain.

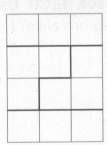

Name _____

☆ Guided Practice ☆

Do You Understand?

1. In the example in Box B on page 610, explain how you know the four parts are equal.

In **2** and **3**, tell if each shows equal or unequal parts. If the parts are equal, label one of the parts using a unit fraction.

2.

3.

Do You Know How?

4. Draw lines to divide the shape into 8 equal parts. Then write the fraction that represents one equal part.

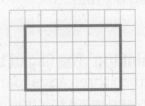

Independent Practice ☆

In **5–7**, tell if each shows equal or unequal parts. If the parts are equal, label one of the parts using a unit fraction.

5.

6.

7.

In **8–10**, draw lines to divide the shape into the given number of equal parts. Then write the fraction that represents one equal part.

8. 6 equal parts

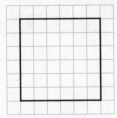

9. 3 equal parts

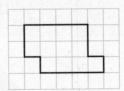

10. 4 equal parts

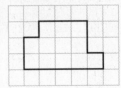

Problem Solving

In **11–14**, use the table of flags.

11. **Be Precise** What fraction represents the white part of Nigeria's flag?

12. Which nation's flag is $\frac{1}{2}$ red?

13. **Higher Order Thinking** The flag of this nation has more than three equal parts. Which nation is it, and what fraction represents one part of its flag?

14. Which nation's flag does **NOT** have equal parts?

Flags of Different Nations

Nation	Flag
Mauritius	
Nigeria	
Poland	
Seychelles	

15. **Model with Math** Maryann buys 24 cans of soda. The soda comes in packs of 6 cans. How many packs did she purchase? Write a multiplication equation and a division equation to show your answer.

16. **Make Sense and Persevere** Jim has stickers in an array of 8 rows and 4 columns. He also has a packet of 14 stickers. How many stickers does Jim have in all?

✓ **Assessment**

17. Draw lines to show how to divide this cake into 8 equal pieces. What fraction represents 1 of the pieces? Explain how you know.

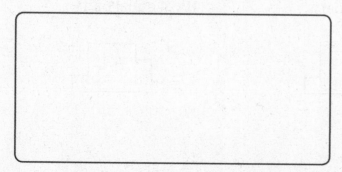

Name _____

☆ ✦ ☆
Solve & Share

    Pat made a garden in the shape of a rectangle and divided it into 4 equal-size parts. She planted flowers in 3 of the parts. Draw a picture of what Pat's garden might look like.

I can ...
use a fraction to represent multiple copies of a unit fraction.

I can also model with math to solve problems.

Model with math. You can use what you know to draw a picture to represent Pat's garden.

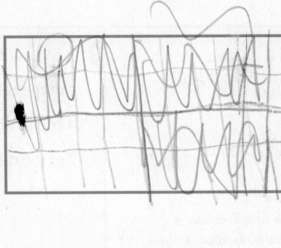

Look Back! **Reasoning** How many parts of Pat's garden do **NOT** have flowers? Explain.

Essential Question **How Can You Show and Name Parts of a Region?**

A

Mr. Peters served part of a pan of enchilada casserole to a friend. What does each part of the whole pan of casserole represent? What part was served? What part is left?

You can use fractions to represent more than one of the equal parts.

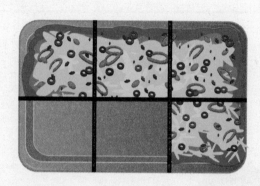

B The whole casserole is divided into 6 equal parts. Each part is $\frac{1}{6}$ of the whole.

6 copies of $\frac{1}{6}$ is $\frac{6}{6}$.

So, the whole is $\frac{6}{6}$.

The unit fraction is $\frac{1}{6}$. The numerator is the number of copies of the unit fraction.

C 2 copies of $\frac{1}{6}$ is $\frac{2}{6}$.

$\frac{2}{6}$ of the casserole was served.

4 copies of $\frac{1}{6}$ is $\frac{4}{6}$.

$\frac{4}{6}$ of the casserole is left.

Convince Me! **Be Precise** Below is a picture of a pie pan. Draw lines and use shading to show that five $\frac{1}{8}$-pieces are still in the pan, and that three $\frac{1}{8}$-pieces were eaten. Use a fraction to label the part of the pie that is in the pan.

☆ Guided Practice *

Do You Understand?

1. In the problem in Box A on page 616, what fraction names all of the pieces in the casserole?

2. Mrs. Patel made a cake. What fraction of the whole cake does each piece represent?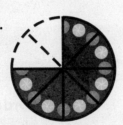

3. In the picture in Exercise 2, how many $\frac{1}{8}$-pieces were eaten? What fraction of the whole cake was eaten?

Do You Know How?

In **4–6**, use the figure below.

4. How many $\frac{1}{3}$-parts are blue?

5. What fraction of the whole is blue?

6. What fraction names *all* of the parts in the whole?

☆ Independent Practice ☆

In **7–10**, write the unit fraction that represents each part of the whole. Then write the number of blue parts and the fraction of the whole that is blue.

7.

8.

9.

10.

11. Draw a rectangle that shows 6 equal parts. Write the unit fraction that represents each part. Then shade $\frac{2}{6}$ of the rectangle. Explain how you know you shaded $\frac{2}{6}$ of the rectangle.

Problem Solving

12. **Vocabulary** George cut a cake into eight pieces. Explain what the unit fraction of the cake is.

13. **Be Precise** Divide the grid below into fourths. Shade three of the parts. Write the unit fraction that represents each part of the whole. Then write a fraction that represents the shaded area.

14. **Model with Math** Christine has 6 red scarves and 3 blue scarves. Each scarf has 2 fringes. How many fringes does Christine have on her scarves? Write equations to represent and solve the problem.

15. **Higher Order Thinking** Draw a circle that shows 6 equal parts. Shade more than $\frac{3}{6}$ of the circle, but less than $\frac{5}{6}$ of the circle. What fraction have you shaded?

16. **Number Sense** What is the area of the baseball card?

10 cm

7 cm

✓ **Assessment**

17. Write fractions to show 3 parts of each of these vegetable trays. How are the fractions alike and different? Explain.

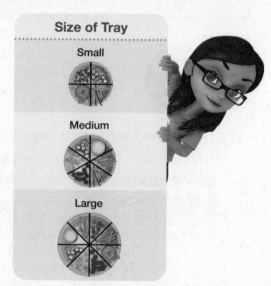

Size of Tray

Small

Medium

Large

© Pearson Education, Inc. 3

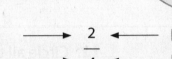

Another Look!

A fraction can be used to name part of a whole.

The denominator shows the total number of equal parts in a whole. The numerator shows how many equal parts are described.

2 copies of $\frac{1}{4}$ is $\frac{2}{4}$. $\frac{2}{4}$ of the rectangle is shaded green.

Number of $\frac{1}{4}$-parts shaded ⟶ 2 ⟵ Numerator

Total number of equal parts ⟶ 4 ⟵ Denominator

In **1–6**, write the unit fraction that represents each part of the whole. Next write the number of shaded parts. Then write the fraction of the whole that is shaded.

1.

2.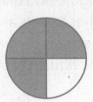

3.

4.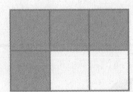

5.

6.

7. Draw a rectangle that shows 2 equal parts. Shade $\frac{1}{2}$ of the rectangle.

8. Draw a circle that shows 8 equal parts. Shade $\frac{2}{8}$ of the circle.

9. Model with Math There are 6 cookies in 1 bag. How many cookies are in 5 bags? Use the bar diagram to write and solve an equation.

? cookies → | ? |
5 bags → | 6 | 6 | 6 | 6 | 6 |

↑
6 cookies in each bag

10. A banner is made of 8 equal parts. Five of the parts are green. Three of the parts are yellow. Draw and color the banner.

11. Make Sense and Persevere Three friends go bowling. Artie's score is 52 points greater than Matthew's score. Matthew's score is 60 points less than Greg's score. If Greg's score is 122, what is Artie's score?

12. Circle all the figures that show $\frac{3}{4}$.

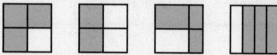

13. Higher Order Thinking Rashad draws a figure and divides it into equal parts. Two of the parts are red. The other 4 parts are blue. Rashad says that $\frac{2}{4}$ of the figure is red. What error is he making? Explain. Then write the correct fraction of the figure that is red.

You can draw a picture to help you solve this problem.

14. Write the unit fraction that represents one purple square. What fraction represents the whole? Explain how you know.

$\frac{\square}{\square} ; \frac{\square}{\square}$

Name _____

☆ ☆
Solve & Share

Mrs. Garcia's third-grade class is planting a flower garden and a vegetable garden.

Draw a picture of the whole flower garden and the whole vegetable garden based on the parts shown. How did you decide what the whole of each garden looked like?

$\frac{1}{3}$ of the flower garden

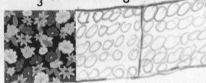

$\frac{2}{4}$ of the vegetable garden

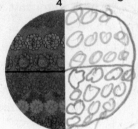

Lesson 12-3
Understand the Whole

I can ...
identify the whole by seeing a part.

I can also reason about math.

You can use reasoning. Think about the parts you know and how many parts you need to make the whole.

Look Back! Use Structure What do the fractions $\frac{1}{3}$ and $\frac{2}{4}$ tell you about the number of equal parts in the whole?

Essential Question **How Can You Use a Fractional Part to Find the Whole?**

A

Anya and Novi are running in different races. The diagrams below show how much of their races each runner has completed. Draw a picture of the whole of each track. Write a fraction to represent the whole.

You can look at the fraction to find how many parts will make up the whole.

Anya ⊢——$\frac{1}{6}$——⊣

Novi ⊢————$\frac{1}{6}$————⊣

B You know Anya and Novi have each completed $\frac{1}{6}$ of their races.

Six lengths of $\frac{1}{6}$ make $\frac{6}{6}$, or 1 whole.

These diagrams show the whole of Anya's and Novi's races. The sixths are different sizes because the tracks for the races (the wholes) are different sizes.

Anya ⊢ $\frac{1}{6}$ | $\frac{1}{6}$ | $\frac{1}{6}$ | $\frac{1}{6}$ | $\frac{1}{6}$ | $\frac{1}{6}$ ⊣

Novi ⊢ $\frac{1}{6}$ | $\frac{1}{6}$ | $\frac{1}{6}$ | $\frac{1}{6}$ | $\frac{1}{6}$ | $\frac{1}{6}$ ⊣

$1 = \frac{6}{6}$

Convince Me! **Reasoning** Why is Novi's track longer than Anya's track?

© Pearson Education, Inc. 3

Name _____

Another Example!

The part of a race Rob has completed is shown at the right. You can use fractional parts like this to identify the whole.

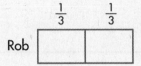

Rob

$\frac{2}{3}$ is 2 copies of $\frac{1}{3}$. Divide Rob's track into 2 equal parts.

| $\frac{1}{3}$ | $\frac{1}{3}$ |

Rob

Three copies of $\frac{1}{3}$ make $\frac{3}{3}$ or 1 whole. Draw one more third.

$1 = \frac{3}{3}$

| $\frac{1}{3}$ | $\frac{1}{3}$ | $\frac{1}{3}$ |

Rob

☆ Guided Practice *

Do You Understand?

1. **Reasoning** If the distance Anya ran was $\frac{1}{5}$ of the length of the track, what fraction would you use to represent the whole track?

2. **Generalize** What is true about the numerator and denominator of each fraction that represents one whole?

Do You Know How?

3. Draw a picture and write a fraction to represent the whole.

$\frac{2}{8}$

Independent Practice ☆

In **4–7**, draw a picture and write a fraction to represent the whole.

4. $\frac{2}{3}$

5. $\frac{1}{2}$

6. $\frac{3}{4}$

7. $\frac{2}{6}$

*For another example, see Set C on page 660.

Problem Solving

8. Critique Reasoning Ronnie and Gina were shown $\frac{1}{2}$ of a table. They each drew a picture of the whole table. Which drawing is correct? Explain.

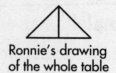

$\frac{1}{2}$ of table

Ronnie's drawing of the whole table

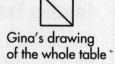

Gina's drawing of the whole table

---

9. Higher Order Thinking If the part shown in **8** is $\frac{1}{4}$ of a table, what could the whole table look like? Draw a picture and write a fraction to represent the whole.

10. Number Sense Mike has 8 nickels and 4 dimes. How much money does he have?

---

11. Construct Arguments Jenna and Jamal are making rugs. They have finished the parts shown. Draw pictures to show each whole rug. Whose rug will be longer when it is finished? Explain.

$\frac{1}{3}$ of Jenna's rug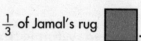

$\frac{1}{3}$ of Jamal's rug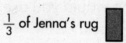

 Assessment

12. The picture shows $\frac{2}{3}$ of a granola bar.

Which shows the whole granola bar?

Ⓐ

Ⓑ

Ⓒ

Ⓓ

13. Each part below is $\frac{1}{2}$ of a different whole. Which is part of the largest whole?

Ⓐ

Ⓑ

Ⓒ

Ⓓ

Name _____

Solve

Solve & Share

At a state park, there is a 1-mile hiking path between the park entrance and the beach. Scenic lookouts are located at points $\frac{1}{3}$ and $\frac{2}{3}$ of the distance from the park entrance to the beach. Show about where the lookout points are located on the line below.

ENTRANCE
State Park

BEACH

0          $\frac{1}{3}$ $\frac{2}{3}$ 1
                                              mile

Model with math. You can represent this problem on a number line.

Lesson 12-4
Number Line: Fractions Less Than 1

I can ...
represent fractions on a number line.

I can also model with math to solve problems.

Look Back! **Construct Arguments** If you know about where the $\frac{1}{3}$ point is located, how can you find about where the $\frac{2}{3}$ point is located?

A

How Can You Record Fractions on a Number Line?

Mr. Singer is picking up his daughter, Greta, from school to go to soccer practice. Greta's school is located at $\frac{3}{4}$ of the distance from the Singers' house to the soccer field. How can you represent $\frac{3}{4}$ on a number line?

Every number on a number line represents a distance from 0.

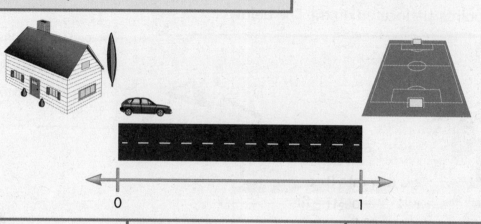

B ## Step 1

Draw a number line from 0 to 1.

0 represents the Singers' house.

1 represents the distance from the Singers' house to the soccer field.

C ## Step 2

Divide the distance from 0 to 1 into 4 equal parts. Each length is $\frac{1}{4}$ of the whole distance between 0 and 1.

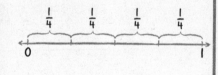

D ## Step 3

Start at 0. Draw a point at the end of the third fourth on the line. Write $\frac{3}{4}$. This represents the distance from the Singers' house to Greta's school.

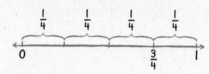

$\frac{3}{4}$ is the same as 3 lengths of $\frac{1}{4}$.

Convince Me! Critique Reasoning

Jenna and Benito each marked $\frac{1}{4}$ on a number line. The length of the part from 0 to $\frac{1}{4}$ on Jenna's number line is shorter than on Benito's. Did someone make a mistake? Explain your thinking.

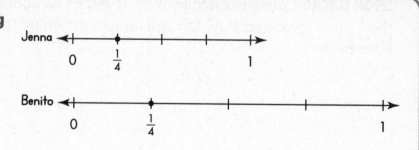

Name _____

☆ Guided Practice ☆

Do You Understand?

1. **Construct Arguments** Maliya divides a number line from 0 to 1 into 6 equal lengths. What unit fraction represents each equal length? What should Maliya label the tick mark just to the left of 1? Explain.

2. **Construct Arguments** Josh divides a number line from 0 to 1 into 8 equal lengths. What should he label the first tick mark to the right of 0? Explain.

Do You Know How?

In **3** and **4**, divide the number line into the given number of equal lengths. Then mark and label the given fraction on the number line.

3. 2 equal lengths; $\frac{1}{2}$

4. 4 equal lengths; $\frac{2}{4}$

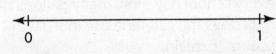

☆ Independent Practice ☆

Leveled Practice In **5** and **6**, divide the number line into the given number of equal lengths. Then mark and label the given fraction on the number line.

5. 3 equal lengths; $\frac{2}{3}$

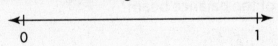

6. 6 equal lengths; $\frac{2}{6}$

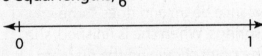

In **7** and **8**, draw a number line. Divide the number line into equal lengths for the given fraction. Then mark and label the given fraction on the number line.

7. $\frac{4}{6}$

8. $\frac{5}{8}$

For another example, see Set D on page 660.

Topic 12 | Lesson 12-4   **629**

Problem Solving

9. Construct Arguments Terrance and Dana each drew a number line and marked $\frac{3}{4}$. Did each person represent $\frac{3}{4}$ on the lines? Explain.

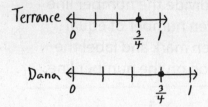

10. Be Precise Jerry stopped at $\frac{3}{6}$ of the distance from his home to school. The 0 represents home, and the 1 represents school on the number line below. Divide the number line into equal lengths and label the point where Jerry stopped.

11. The school cafeteria sells 5 gallons of plain milk and 3 gallons of flavored milk every school day. How many gallons of milk does the cafeteria use in 9 days of school? Explain.

12. Higher Order Thinking Show 3 ways you can represent three-eighths.

13. A gymnast starts at the left end of the balance beam and does some handsprings. When she is finished, she is at the point shown on the diagram. Which fraction represents how far she went on the balance beam?

Ⓐ $\frac{7}{8}$ Ⓒ $\frac{2}{8}$

Ⓑ $\frac{6}{8}$ Ⓓ $\frac{1}{8}$

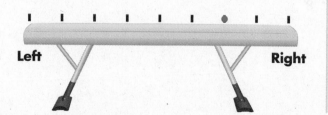

14. Which fraction represents the right end of the balance beam?

Ⓐ 0

Ⓑ $\frac{1}{8}$

Ⓒ $\frac{5}{8}$

Ⓓ $\frac{8}{8}$

Name _____

Another Look!

Show $\frac{3}{8}$ on a number line.

Start by drawing a number line from 0 to 1. Put tick marks at the ends. Label the tick marks 0 and 1.

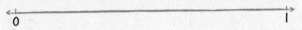

Divide the number line into 8 equal lengths. Each length is $\frac{1}{8}$ of the whole.

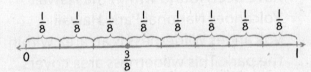

Start at 0. Go to the right until you come to the third tick mark. That mark represents $\frac{3}{8}$. Draw a point at $\frac{3}{8}$ on the line. Label the point $\frac{3}{8}$.

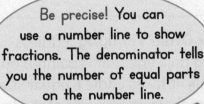

Be precise! You can use a number line to show fractions. The denominator tells you the number of equal parts on the number line.

In **1** and **2**, divide the number line into the given number of equal lengths. Then mark and label the given fraction on the number line.

1. 3 equal lengths; $\frac{2}{3}$

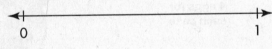

2. 6 equal lengths; $\frac{5}{6}$

In **3–6**, draw a number line. Divide the number line into equal lengths for the given fraction. Then mark and label the fraction on the number line.

3. $\frac{3}{4}$

4. $\frac{4}{8}$

5. $\frac{1}{6}$

6. $\frac{7}{8}$

7. **Algebra** Ted writes the following equation. Write the number that makes the equation correct.

$$824 = 20 + ? + 4$$

? = _____

8. **Critique Reasoning** Craig says that this number line shows $\frac{1}{3}$. Do you agree with Craig? Explain why or why not.

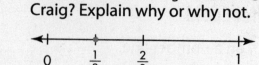

0        $\frac{1}{3}$ $\frac{2}{3}$ 1

9. **Higher Order Thinking** Eddie is walking on a line that is painted on the sidewalk. It takes Eddie 8 equal-size steps to get from one end of the line to the other. After Eddie has taken 5 steps, what fraction of the line is behind him? What fraction of the line is still in front of him?

10. **Math and Science** Fossilized footprints have been found within the Hawaii Volcanoes National Park. Hawaii Volcanoes Wilderness is an area within the park. This wilderness area covers about $\frac{1}{2}$ of the park. Draw a number line. Then mark and label $\frac{1}{2}$ on it.

11. **Model with Math** Marty has 1 dozen eggs. He needs 4 eggs to bake a cake. How many cakes can he bake? Complete the bar diagram and write an equation to represent and solve the problem.

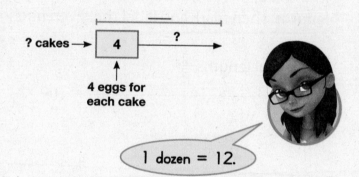

? cakes → | 4 | ?

4 eggs for each cake

1 dozen = 12.

12. James put a point at $\frac{3}{8}$ on a number line. Which number line shows $\frac{3}{8}$?

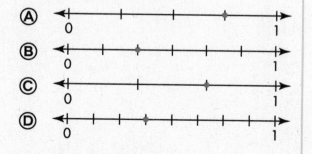

Ⓐ 0 ——————— 1

Ⓑ 0 ——————— 1

Ⓒ 0 ——————— 1

Ⓓ 0 ——————— 1

13. What fraction does the point on this number line represent?

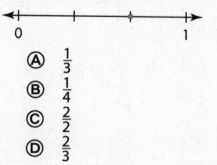

0 ——————— 1

Ⓐ $\frac{1}{3}$

Ⓑ $\frac{1}{4}$

Ⓒ $\frac{2}{2}$

Ⓓ $\frac{2}{3}$

Name _____

 Solve

Solve & Share

The length of one strip of paper is 1 whole unit. Fold two strips of paper in half. Open the strips and place them end-to-end.

How many halves do you have?
How can you use halves to name the fold lines?
Tell how you decided. Draw a picture to show your work.

I can ...
represent fractions equal to or greater than 1 on a number line.

I can also choose and use a math tool to solve problems.

Use appropriate tools. Think about how your paper strips show copies of unit fractions.

$\frac{1}{2}$ $\frac{2}{2}$ $\frac{4}{2}$ $\frac{4}{2}$

Look Back! **Generalize** If you added a third strip of paper folded in half, how could you use halves to name the fold lines? Explain.

Essential Question

How Can You Use a Number Line to Represent Fractions Greater Than 1?

A

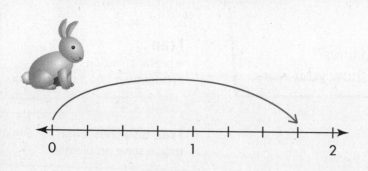

A bunny hopped $\frac{7}{4}$ the distance of a trail. How can you show this on a number line?

Number lines can also represent fractions that are greater than 1.

B The whole is the distance between 0 and 1.

The denominator is 4.

Divide the whole into 4 equal lengths.

Each length is $\frac{1}{4}$ of the whole.

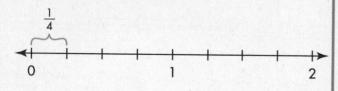

C The numerator is 7.
There are 7 lengths of $\frac{1}{4}$.

The point showing 7 lengths of $\frac{1}{4}$ can be labeled as $\frac{7}{4}$.

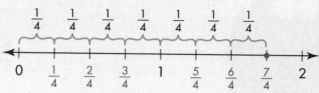

$\frac{7}{4}$ is greater than 1!

Convince Me! **Be Precise** One point on the number line below has been named with the fraction $\frac{2}{3}$. On the number line the lengths marked are equal. Write a fraction for the other points shown.

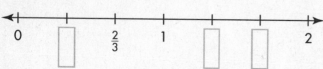

© Pearson Education, Inc. 3

☆ **Guided Practice** *

Do You Understand?

1. Name a fraction that is to the right of the point for 2 on a number line.

2. **Critique Reasoning** Quinn says that $\frac{10}{8}$ comes to the right of $\frac{9}{8}$ on a number line. Do you agree? Why or why not?

Do You Know How?

In **3** and **4**, each number line has equal lengths marked. Write the missing fractions.

3.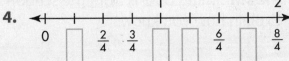

4.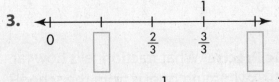

☆ Independent Practice ☆

Leveled Practice In **5–7**, each number line has equal lengths marked. Write the missing fractions.

5.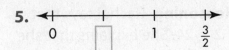

6.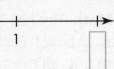

7.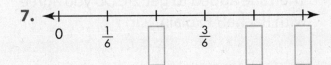

In **8** and **9**, divide the number lines into equal lengths. Write the missing fractions.

> The size of each length depends on the size of the whole.

8.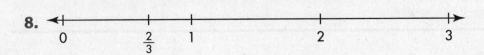

9.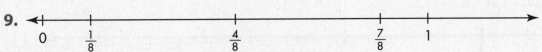

Problem Solving

In **10** and **11**, use the number line below.

School   Grocery Store   Post Office   Swimming Pool

The distance from 0 to 1 is 1 mile.

0    $\frac{1}{6}$ $\frac{2}{6}$ $\frac{3}{6}$ $\frac{4}{6}$ $\frac{5}{6}$ 1 mile

10. Be Precise What fraction tells how far the swimming pool is from the school? Explain how you know.

11. Higher Order Thinking The hospital is halfway between the grocery store and the post office. What fraction tells how far the hospital is from the school? Explain.

12. Model with Math Tim has 78 board games. He has 10 boxes. Each box holds 9 games. If Tim puts all the games he has into the boxes, how many more games can he fit? Complete the bar diagram and solve the problem.

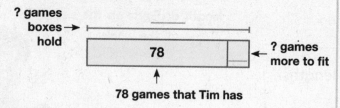

? games
boxes → hold

78

← ? games more to fit

↑
78 games that Tim has

13. Critique Reasoning Rachel says that $(7 \times 5) \times 2 = 24$. She explains that she used the Distributive Property to find $(7 \times 2) + (5 \times 2)$, which equals $14 + 10$. Then she added to get 24. Do you agree with Rachel? Explain.

✓ Assessment

14. Draw lines to divide the number line into fourths. Show a point at $\frac{3}{4}$. Show another point at $\frac{10}{4}$.

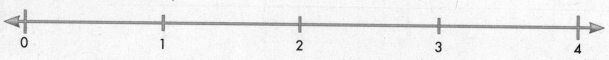

0   1   2   3   4

Name _____

☆Guided Practice*

Do You Understand?

1. Measure the length of this line to the nearest fourth inch.

   _____

2. Describe how you would show this measurement on a line plot.

Do You Know How?

3. Draw a line plot to show the data.

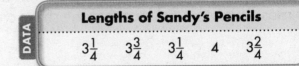

DATA	Lengths of Sandy's Pencils				
	$3\frac{1}{4}$	$3\frac{3}{4}$	$3\frac{1}{4}$	4	$3\frac{2}{4}$

4. Measure your pencil to the nearest fourth inch. Show the length on your line plot.

Independent Practice ☆

5. Daisy measured the lengths of her toy dinosaurs to the nearest fourth inch. She listed the lengths. Make a line plot to show the data.

   $1\frac{2}{4}$ in., $2\frac{1}{4}$ in., 1 in., $1\frac{2}{4}$ in., $1\frac{3}{4}$ in.

6. Measure the lengths of the toy dinosaurs at the right to the nearest fourth inch. Write the length for each toy. Show the lengths on your line plot.

Problem Solving

In **7** and **8**, use the line plot at the right.

7. Arty made a line plot to show the inches different snails crawled in a 5-minute race. What was the most common distance that the snails crawled?

8. **Higher Order Thinking** How many more times did snails crawl more than $8\frac{3}{4}$ inches compared to less than $8\frac{3}{4}$ inches?

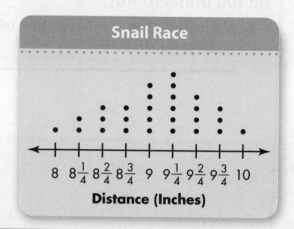

Snail Race

$8 \quad 8\frac{1}{4} \quad 8\frac{2}{4} \quad 8\frac{3}{4} \quad 9 \quad 9\frac{1}{4} \quad 9\frac{2}{4} \quad 9\frac{3}{4} \quad 10$

Distance (Inches)

9. Measure the lengths of 10 classroom objects to the nearest fourth inch. Choose objects that are between 1 and 5 inches long. Record your measurements.

10. On grid paper, draw a line plot to show your data.

11. **Make Sense and Persevere** Jackson bought 5 books that cost $7 each. How much change did he get from $40?

12. **Number Sense** Use the digits 2, 6, and 8 to make as many 3-digit numbers as you can. Put the numbers in order from least to greatest.

✓ Assessment

Tonya is making headbands. She recorded lengths of different bows that she bought.

Each dot on the line plot represents a different bow Tonya bought.

13. Which lengths did Tonya buy the most of? Choose all that apply.

☐ 1 inch

☐ $1\frac{1}{4}$ inches

☐ $1\frac{2}{4}$ inches

☐ $1\frac{3}{4}$ inches

☐ 2 inches

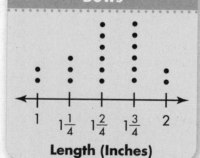

Lengths of Different Bows

$1 \quad 1\frac{1}{4} \quad 1\frac{2}{4} \quad 1\frac{3}{4} \quad 2$

Length (Inches)

Name _____

Another Look!

The blue marks on this ruler show fourth-inch marks. Serena used the ruler to measure a ribbon to the nearest fourth inch.

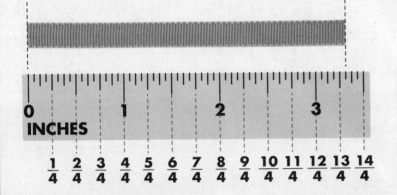

To the nearest fourth inch: the length of the ribbon is $3\frac{1}{4}$ inches.

Serena recorded the measurements of all the ribbons she has. Then she made a line plot.

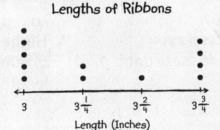

Lengths of Ribbons

Length (Inches)

A ruler can help you be precise when measuring. A line plot can organize the data.

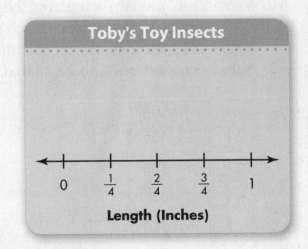

---

1. Toby's toy insects are shown at the right. Use a ruler to measure each insect to the nearest fourth inch. Record each measurement.

6 beetles   7 ladybugs   5 butterflies

2. How many dots, or data points, should be on the line plot to show all of Toby's toy insects?

3. Complete the line plot to show the data.

4. How many more dots did you draw for beetles than for butterflies?

Toby's Toy Insects

0    $\frac{1}{4}$ $\frac{2}{4}$ $\frac{3}{4}$ 1

Length (Inches)

In **5–7**, use the table at the right. The table shows the lengths to the nearest fourth inch of fish that scientists studied.

5. Make a line plot to show the data.

DATA	Fish Lengths					
	$9\frac{1}{4}$ in.	$9\frac{3}{4}$ in.	11 in.	$9\frac{3}{4}$ in.	$8\frac{3}{4}$ in.	10 in.
	$8\frac{3}{4}$ in.	$9\frac{2}{4}$ in.	$10\frac{2}{4}$ in.	$8\frac{2}{4}$ in.	$9\frac{3}{4}$ in.	11 in.
	$10\frac{1}{4}$ in.	9 in.	10 in.	$8\frac{3}{4}$ in.	$10\frac{3}{4}$ in.	$9\frac{3}{4}$ in.

6. **Reasoning** How many dots do you show for $9\frac{3}{4}$ inches? What do these dots represent?

7. **Higher Order Thinking** What is the difference in length between the greatest length and the least length?

8. Owen arranges 48 beads into an array. There are 6 rows of beads. How many columns are there?

9. **Make Sense and Persevere** On Wednesday, Connor spent $65. On Thursday, he spent $130. Connor has $311 left. How much money did Connor have to start?

✔️ **Assessment**

10. Isabella recorded the lengths of the pencils in her collection to the nearest fourth inch. Which lengths of pencils are the most common in Isabella's collection? Choose all that apply.

   ☐ 3 inches

   ☐ $3\frac{3}{4}$ inches

   ☐ 4 inches

   ☐ $4\frac{1}{4}$ inches

   ☐ $4\frac{2}{4}$ inches

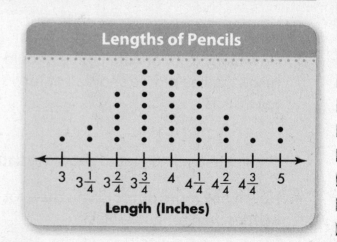

Lengths of Pencils

Length (Inches)

© Pearson Education, Inc. 3

Name _____

Measure each side of the pentagon.

Then use the line plot below to show the length of each side. Which length is most common?

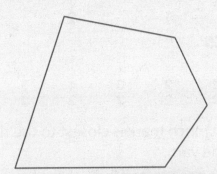

I can ...
measure to the nearest half inch and show the data on a line plot.

I can also be precise in my work.

Be precise. Think about which unit you need to use when you measure the lengths of the sides.

Lengths of Sides

0    $\frac{1}{2}$ 1 $1\frac{1}{2}$ 2

Length (Inches)

Look Back! Use Appropriate Tools What tool did you use to measure the length of the sides? How did you use this tool?

How Can You Measure Lengths and Use Line Plots To Show the Data?

A

Julio is measuring some lengths of yarn. How can he use a ruler to measure to the nearest half inch?

The distance between each whole number on this ruler is 1 inch. Each red mark shows $\frac{1}{2}$ inch. So, you can think of each whole inch as two $\frac{1}{2}$ inches.

Line up one end of the object with 0.

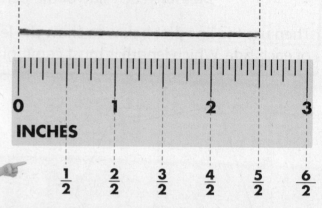

The fifth $\frac{1}{2}$-inch mark is closest to the right end of the yarn.

So, to the nearest half inch, the yarn measures $\frac{5}{2}$ inches.

This is two whole inches and one $\frac{1}{2}$ inch. You can write this as $2\frac{1}{2}$ inches.

B Julio measured 9 other lengths of yarn.
The lengths of all the yarn Julio measured are shown below.
He then recorded the data in a line plot.

$2\frac{1}{2}$ $3\frac{1}{2}$ 3 $3\frac{1}{2}$ 4 3 3 $3\frac{1}{2}$ 4 $3\frac{1}{2}$

You can use this line plot to see that the length that occurred most often was $3\frac{1}{2}$ inches. The length that occurred least often was $2\frac{1}{2}$ inches.

Lengths of Yarns

Length (Inches)

Convince Me! Reasoning Suppose you measured a length of yarn that was about $4\frac{1}{2}$ inches. How would you need to change the line plot above to record this length?

© Pearson Education, Inc. 3

Name _____

☆ Guided Practice *

Do You Understand?

1. Draw a line that is $1\frac{1}{2}$ inches long.

2. If a line measures $3\frac{1}{4}$ inches and you need to measure to the nearest $\frac{1}{2}$ inch, what length would you record? Why?

Do You Know How?

3. Measure the length of each of your fingers. List the measurements to the nearest half inch.

4. Make a line plot to show the measurements of your fingers.

☆ Independent Practice ☆

5. Measure the lengths of the yarn at the right to the nearest half inch. Write the length for each piece.

6. Draw a line to represent another length of yarn. Measure your line to the nearest half inch.

7. Make a line plot to show the measurements of the yarn.

Problem Solving

8. Measure the lengths of 10 classroom objects to the nearest half inch. Choose objects that are between 1 and 6 inches long. Record your measurements.

9. On grid paper, draw a line plot to show your data.

10. **Make Sense and Persevere** Raymond weighed his three dogs. The oldest dog weighs 74 pounds. The other two dogs each weigh 34 pounds. How many more pounds does the oldest dog weigh than the other two dogs combined?

11. Marcus arranged 16 pencils into an array. The array has 2 columns. How many rows are there?

In **12** and **13**, use the table at the right.

12. **Be Precise** How many more of the shortest paper chains does Rico have compared to the longest paper chain? Explain.

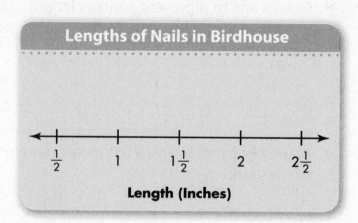

Rico's Paper Chains	
Number of Paper Chains	Length
3	$6\frac{1}{2}$ in.
2	$7\frac{1}{2}$ in.
4	8 in.
1	$8\frac{1}{2}$ in.

13. **Higher Order Thinking** Look at Rico's measurements. Can you tell if he measured the paper chains to the nearest half inch or to the nearest fourth inch? Explain.

✓ **Assessment**

14. Jessica built a birdhouse. The three different sizes of nails she used are shown below. Jessica used 4 of Nail A, 2 of Nail B, and 3 of Nail C. Measure each nail to the nearest half inch. Then complete the line plot to show the size of the nails.

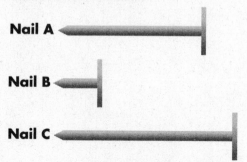

Lengths of Nails in Birdhouse

$\frac{1}{2}$ 1 $1\frac{1}{2}$ 2 $2\frac{1}{2}$

Length (Inches)

Name _____

Another Look!

The red marks on this ruler show half-inch marks. Franco used the ruler to measure a hexagon to the nearest half inch.

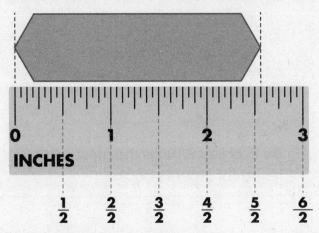

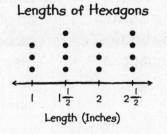

To the nearest half inch: the length of the hexagon is $2\frac{1}{2}$ inches.

Franco recorded the lengths of other hexagons he measured. Then he made a line plot. The most common lengths were $1\frac{1}{2}$ inches and $2\frac{1}{2}$ inches.

Lengths of Hexagons

Length (Inches)

You can use a line plot to compare data.

1. Measure the length of each rectangle to the nearest half inch.

☐
☐
☐

2. Jamal drew 5 of the green rectangles, 3 of the orange rectangles, and 4 of the purple rectangles. How many dots, or data points, should be on the line plot?

3. Complete the line plot to show the data.

Lengths of Rectangles

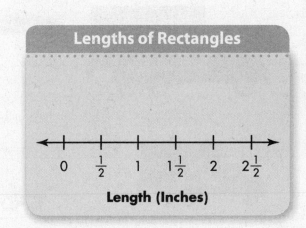

0   $\frac{1}{2}$ 1 $1\frac{1}{2}$ 2 $2\frac{1}{2}$

Length (Inches)

4. Japera measured the lengths of her books to the nearest fourth inch and listed their lengths. Make a line plot that displays the lengths of Japera's books.

$8\frac{1}{2}$ in., $9\frac{1}{2}$ in., $8\frac{1}{2}$ in., $9\frac{1}{2}$ in., 10 in., $9\frac{1}{2}$ in., $8\frac{1}{2}$ in., 9 in., $9\frac{1}{2}$ in.

5. Eli has double the number of books that Japera has. How many books does Eli have?

6. Be Precise What is the most common length of Japera's books?

7. Model with Math Peter bought 8 sets of paint. He gives half of his sets to his sister. Each set has 5 bottles. How many bottles does Peter's sister have? Write equations and solve.

8. Higher Order Thinking Dan measures an object to the nearest fourth inch. He records the length as $4\frac{1}{4}$ inches. Geri measures the same object to the nearest half inch. Could Dan and Geri get the same measurement? Explain.

✓ **Assessment**

9. Robert measured the cars and trucks in his toy collection to the nearest half inch. Find the measurements of each type. Then complete the line plot to show the data.

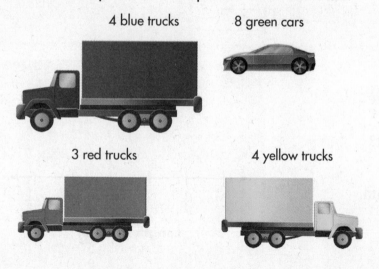

4 blue trucks

8 green cars

3 red trucks

4 yellow trucks

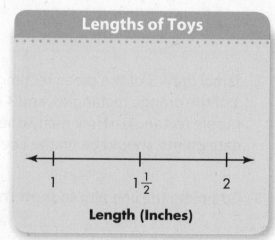

Lengths of Toys

1    $1\frac{1}{2}$ 2

Length (Inches)

Name _____

Solve

Solve & Share

Marcus, Mariah, and Tony painted a mural. They divided it into equal parts. Marcus painted 2 parts, Mariah painted 3 parts, and Tony painted the rest. What fraction of the mural did each student paint?

Decide if this problem has any missing or extra information. If information you need is missing, make up some reasonable information and then solve the problem.

I can ...
make sense of problems and keep working if I get stuck.

I can also decide if I have enough information to solve a problem.

Thinking Habits
Be a good thinker!
These questions can help you.

• What do I need to find?

• What do I know?

• What's my plan for solving the problem?

• What else can I try if I get stuck?

• How can I check that my solution makes sense?

Look Back! **Make Sense and Persevere** What information was not given in the problem? How did you still solve the problem?

Essential Question **How Can You Make Sense of a Problem and Persevere in Solving It?**

A

Suki divides her garden into 6 equal parts. She plants daisies, roses, and violets. It takes Suki 1 hour to plant the flowers. She plants daisies in 1 part, roses in 2 parts, and violets in the rest of the garden.

In what fraction of the garden does Suki plant violets?

What is a good plan for solving the problem?

I need to make sense of the given information. I need to think about what I can use to help me solve the problem.

To persevere you can check your strategy and your work.

B

How can I make sense of and solve this problem?

I can

- identify the quantities given.

- understand which quantities are needed to solve the problem.

- choose and implement an appropriate strategy.

- check to be sure my work and answer make sense.

C

Here's my thinking...

1 hour to plant the flowers is not needed to solve the problem.

I used a picture to help.

Suki plants daises and roses in 3 equal parts. There are 3 equal parts left for violets.

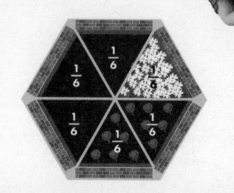

3 copies of $\frac{1}{6}$ is $\frac{3}{6}$. So, Suki plants violets in $\frac{3}{6}$ of the garden.

Convince Me! **Make Sense and Persevere** How can you check to make sure the work and answer given above make sense?

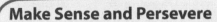

☆ Guided Practice*

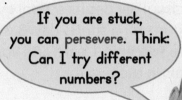

Make Sense and Persevere

Keira and Matt cut a sandwich into four equal parts. They each ate one part. Keira is 9 years old. Matt is the same age as Keira. What fraction of the sandwich is not eaten?

If you are stuck, you can persevere. Think: Can I try different numbers?

1. Is there any missing or extra information? Explain.

2. Solve the problem. If information you need is missing, make up some reasonable information for the problem.

☆ Independent Practice ☆

Make Sense and Persevere

Marni planted a vegetable garden. She put lettuce in 1 part, carrots in 4 parts, and broccoli in the rest of her garden. In what fraction of the garden did Marni plant broccoli?

3. Is there any missing or extra information?

4. Solve the problem. If information you need is missing, make up some reasonable information for the problem.

5. Can you use a different number of parts and still solve the problem? Explain.

Problem Solving

Sports Day

Green School divides its school gym into 8 equal parts for a sports day. Basketball is in 2 parts, soccer in 1 part, and volleyball and tennis in the rest.

Green School Sports Day		
Sport	**Parts of the Gym Needed**	**Number of Coaches Needed**
Basketball	2	2
Soccer	1	1
Tennis	?	3
Volleyball	?	2

6. **Make Sense and Persevere** The gym teacher wants to know what fraction of the gym is used for tennis. What missing information do you need to solve the problem?

In **7** and **8**, draw a picture to represent the number of parts in each plan.

7. **Reasoning** What fraction of the gym would be used for tennis if 2 parts were for volleyball?

8. **Reasoning** What fraction of the gym would be used for tennis if 3 parts were used for volleyball?

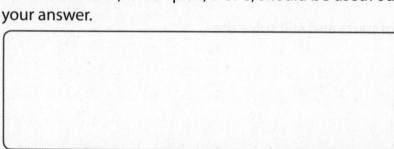

You can look for extra or missing information to help make sense of a problem.

9. **Construct Arguments** To have the same fraction for tennis as for basketball, which plan, **7** or **8**, should be used? Justify your answer.

Another Look!

Becky divides a rectangle into 8 equal parts. She colors 4 parts yellow. The rectangle has 4 sides and 4 vertices. Becky colors 1 part red and the rest blue. What fraction of the rectangle did Becky color blue?

Tell how to make sense of the problem.

- I can identify the quantities given.

- I can understand which quantities are needed to solve the problem.

Use what you know to solve the problem.

The rectangle has 4 sides and 4 vertices is extra information. There are 8 equal parts. So, each part is $\frac{1}{8}$. There are 3 parts left to color blue. 3 copies of $\frac{1}{8}$ is $\frac{3}{8}$. So, $\frac{3}{8}$ are blue.

Make sense of the information in the problem by identifying the quantities. Then use what you know to solve the problem.

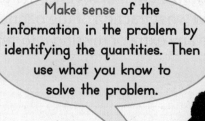

Make Sense and Persevere

Three friends get to a party at 2 o'clock. They cut a pizza into 4 pieces. The friends eat one slice of pizza each. What fraction of the pizza is left?

1. Tell how to make sense of the problem.

2. Is there any missing or extra information? Explain.

3. Solve the problem. If information you need is missing, make up some reasonable information for the problem. You can draw a picture to help.

School Banner

Four students are making the banner shown at the right. They have 1 week to finish the banner. Anja makes the green parts. Michael makes the white part. Adeeba makes the same number of parts as Lee.

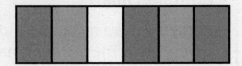

4. **Make Sense and Persevere** The teacher wants to know what fraction of the banner Lee makes. Is there any extra or missing information?

5. **Reasoning** What fraction of the banner does Anja make?

6. **Reasoning** What fraction of the banner does Michael make?

If you are stuck, you can persevere. Think: Can I try different numbers?

7. **Be Precise** Explain how you know the fraction of the banner that is **not** made by either Anja or Michael.

8. **Construct Arguments** What fraction of the banner does Lee make? Explain.

Name _____

Shade a path from **START** to **FINISH**. Follow the sums and differences where the digit in the hundreds place is greater than the digit in the tens place. You can only move up, down, right, or left.

I can ...
add and subtract within 1,000.

Start				
822 − 514	814 − 128	499 + 182	210 + 484	580 − 434
753 − 536	768 + 29	723 − 461	555 − 320	253 + 234
951 − 96	195 + 474	964 − 532	672 − 127	725 − 314
125 + 424	244 − 147	279 + 531	365 − 97	230 + 757
921 − 614	989 − 239	572 + 346	992 − 539	495 + 485

Finish

TOPIC 12 · Vocabulary Review

A-Z Glossary

Word List

- denominator
- fraction
- line plot
- nearest fourth inch
- nearest half inch
- numerator
- unit fraction

Understand Vocabulary

1. Circle each *unit fraction*.

$\frac{1}{4}$ $\frac{3}{8}$ $\frac{1}{6}$ $\frac{1}{8}$ $\frac{2}{3}$

2. Circle each fraction where 6 is the *denominator*.

$\frac{3}{6}$ $\frac{6}{8}$ $\frac{1}{6}$ $\frac{5}{6}$ $\frac{4}{8}$

3. Circle each fraction where 4 is the *numerator*.

$\frac{2}{4}$ $\frac{4}{8}$ $\frac{1}{4}$ $\frac{3}{4}$ $\frac{4}{6}$

4. Circle the lengths that could be measurements to the *nearest half inch*.

$2\frac{1}{2}$ in.   4 in. $3\frac{3}{4}$ in. $7\frac{1}{4}$ in.   6 in.

5. Circle the lengths that could be measurements to the *nearest fourth inch*.

$8\frac{3}{4}$ in. $1\frac{1}{4}$ in.   11 in. $7\frac{1}{4}$ in.   6 in.

Write *always*, *sometimes*, or *never*.

6. The numerator in a fraction is _____?_____ greater than the denominator. _____

7. A fraction _____?_____ has a numerator and denominator. _____

8. A line plot _____?_____ shows a measurement of lengths. _____

Use Vocabulary in Writing

9. Use at least 2 terms from the Word List to explain how to find the unit fraction of the shape shown below.

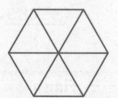

Name _____

Set A | pages 609–614 _____

This is one way to divide a whole into fourths.

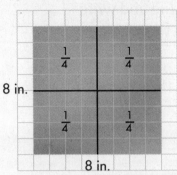

Since each of the 4 parts has the same area, each part is one fourth of the whole shape.

You can write this fraction as $\frac{1}{4}$.

A unit fraction represents one of the equal parts. $\frac{1}{4}$ is a unit fraction.

$$\frac{\text{numerator}}{\text{denominator}} = \frac{\text{number of parts the fraction represents}}{\text{total number of equal parts}} = \frac{1}{4}$$

Remember that fractions can name equal parts of a whole.

Reteaching

In **1** and **2**, draw lines to divide the shape into the given number of equal parts. Then write the fraction that represents one part.

1. 6 equal parts   2. 2 equal parts

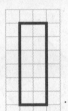   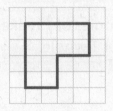

3. Martin divides a shape into 3 equal parts. What unit fraction can he write to represent 1 part?

Set B | pages 615–620 _____

What fraction of this rectangle is shaded?

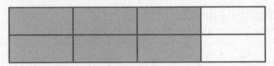

The rectangle is divided into 8 equal parts. So, the unit fraction of the rectangle is $\frac{1}{8}$.

In the whole rectangle there are 8 parts of $\frac{1}{8}$.

8 copies of $\frac{1}{8}$ is $\frac{8}{8}$.

For the shaded part there are 6 parts of $\frac{1}{8}$.

6 copies of $\frac{1}{8}$ is $\frac{6}{8}$.

So, $\frac{6}{8}$ of the rectangle is shaded.

Remember that you need to think about how many parts there are in all and how many parts are shaded.

In **1–4**, write the unit fraction that represents each part of the whole. Next write the number of shaded parts. Then write the fraction of the whole that is shaded.

1.   2.

3.   4.

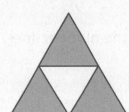   

pages 621–626

This shape is $\frac{2}{4}$ of a fabric Tina used in a quilt. You can draw a picture and write a fraction to represent the whole quilt.

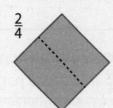
$\frac{2}{4}$

$\frac{2}{4}$ is 2 copies of $\frac{1}{4}$.

Divide the fabric into 2 equal parts.

4 copies of $\frac{1}{4}$ makes $\frac{4}{4}$, or 1 whole.

$1 = \frac{4}{4}$

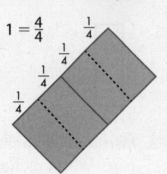
$\frac{1}{4}$ $\frac{1}{4}$ $\frac{1}{4}$ $\frac{1}{4}$

Remember that the denominator shows the total number of equal parts in a whole.

In **1** and **2**, draw a picture and write a fraction to represent the whole.

1. $\frac{1}{4}$

2. $\frac{3}{8}$

---

pages 627–632

You can show fractions on a number line.

The fraction $\frac{5}{6}$ is labeled. What are the missing fractions?

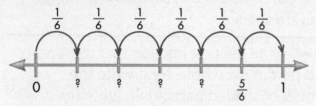
$\frac{1}{6}$ $\frac{1}{6}$ $\frac{1}{6}$ $\frac{1}{6}$ $\frac{1}{6}$ $\frac{1}{6}$

0   ?   ?   ?   ? $\frac{5}{6}$ 1

First, find the unit fraction. The line is divided into six equal lengths. So, the number line shows sixths.

Each jump represents $\frac{1}{6}$. So, the first tick mark is labeled $\frac{1}{6}$. The second tick mark is labeled $\frac{2}{6}$, and so on.

The missing fractions on the number line are $\frac{1}{6}, \frac{2}{6}, \frac{3}{6},$ and $\frac{4}{6}$.

Remember to start by deciding what unit fraction is shown on each number line.

In **1** and **2**, write the missing fractions on each number line.

1.

0   ☐ $\frac{2}{4}$ ☐   1

2.

0   ☐   ☐ $\frac{3}{8}$ ☐   ☐ $\frac{6}{8}$ ☐   1

3. Divide the number line below into 3 equal parts and mark $\frac{2}{3}$ on the line.

0   1

---

660   **Topic 12** | Reteaching   © Pearson Education, Inc. 3

Name _____

Set E | pages 633–638 _____

Number lines can have fractions greater than 1.

The number line below is divided into thirds.

The denominator is 3 because the unit fraction is $\frac{1}{3}$. The numerator shows how many copies of the unit fraction each point is.

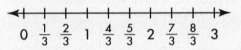

Remember that the numerator increases by 1 because each part of the number line is 1 more copy of the unit fraction.

1. The number line has equal lengths marked. Write the missing fractions.

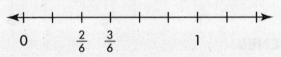

2. Divide the number line into fourths. Label each point.

Set F | pages 639–644 _____

You can use a line plot to show data, such as lengths measured to the nearest half inch.

Steps to make a line plot:

- Draw a number line and choose a scale.
- The scale should show data values from the least to greatest.
- Write a title for the line plot.
- Mark a dot for each value.

Lengths of Lilly's Ribbons				
$5\frac{1}{2}$ in.	4 in.	$5\frac{1}{2}$ in.	$4\frac{1}{2}$ in.	$4\frac{3}{4}$ in.

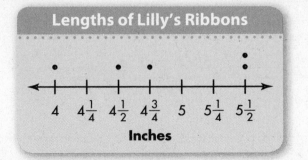

Remember to mark a dot for each length. Check your completed line plot against the data in the chart.

Lengths of Carl's Strings				
3 in.	$2\frac{3}{4}$ in.	$2\frac{1}{2}$ in.	$2\frac{1}{2}$ in.	4 in.
$2\frac{1}{2}$ in.	$3\frac{1}{4}$ in.	$3\frac{3}{4}$ in.	$3\frac{3}{4}$ in.	3 in.

1. Draw a line plot to show the data.

2. How many strings does Carl have in all?

3. Draw a line that is the same length as the most common string length.

You can measure to different lengths, such as the nearest half inch.

The closest half-inch mark to the right of the rectangle is the $2\frac{1}{2}$-inch mark.

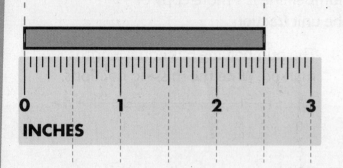

INCHES

The lengths can be shown on a line plot.

Remember to think about the scale of the line plot. It needs to include the least and greatest values.

1. Measure and record the lengths of 5 classroom objects to the nearest half inch. Use objects that are between 1 and 3 inches long.

2. Draw a line plot to show your data.

Think about these questions to help you **make sense and persevere** in solving problems.

Thinking Habits

- What do I need to find?

- What do I know?

- What's my plan for solving the problem?

- What else can I try if I get stuck?

- How can I check that my solution makes sense?

Remember to make sense of the problem by identifying the quantities. Then use what you know to solve.

Gavin divided his notebook into 8 equal parts. He plans to use 3 parts to take notes for math and 2 parts for reading. He has school from 8:30 A.M. to 3:30 P.M. What fraction of his notebook does he have left?

1. Is there any missing or extra information? Explain.

2. Solve the problem. If information you need is missing, make up some reasonable information for the problem. You can draw a picture to help.

Name _____

1. What fraction of the whole is colored green?

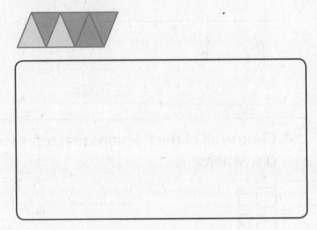

2. Write a fraction to name the equal parts of the whole pizza.

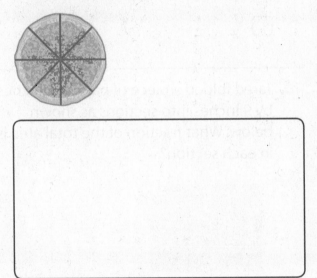

3. This picture represents $\frac{1}{3}$ of the distance from Mal's house to the library. Which represents the whole distance?

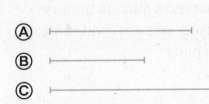

Ⓐ ├────────────┤

Ⓑ ├──────┤

Ⓒ ├──────────┤

Ⓓ ├──┤

4. The distance from Al's home to the park is $\frac{3}{6}$ mile. Which point is at $\frac{3}{6}$ on the number line?

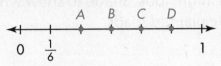

Ⓐ Point *A*

Ⓑ Point *B*

Ⓒ Point *C*

Ⓓ Point *D*

5. Ricky says each of the fractions below would be to the right of 1 on a number line. Do you agree? Choose Yes or No.

5a. $\frac{3}{4}$ ○ Yes   ○ No

5b. $\frac{5}{4}$ ○ Yes   ○ No

5c. $\frac{4}{2}$ ○ Yes   ○ No

5d. $\frac{1}{3}$ ○ Yes   ○ No

6. Dominic's garden is the shape of a rectangle. He divided his garden into 4 equal parts. He planted seeds in $\frac{2}{4}$ of his garden.

Part A

Draw a picture to show how Dominic's garden might look. Shade to show where Dominic planted seeds.

Part B

Explain how you knew you had shaded the correct amount of your picture.

7. Jeremy put pepperoni on half of a pizza. He put olives on $\frac{1}{3}$ of the pizza. What fraction of the pizza did **NOT** have pepperoni?

8. One point on the number line below has been named with the fraction $\frac{2}{4}$. Write a fraction for the other points shown.

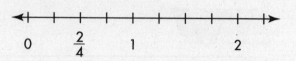

9. Choose all of the fractions that represent one whole.

☐ $\frac{8}{8}$

☐ $\frac{4}{4}$

☐ $\frac{1}{4}$

☐ $\frac{1}{1}$

☐ $\frac{1}{2}$

10. Jared folded a piece of paper 12 inches by 9 inches into sections as shown below. What fraction of the total area is in each section?

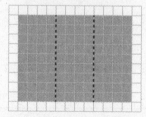

Ⓐ $\frac{1}{2}$

Ⓑ $\frac{1}{3}$

Ⓒ $\frac{2}{3}$

Ⓓ Cannot use a fraction because the paper was not divided into equal parts.

Name _____

11. Divide the number line into halves. Write each fraction in the correct location on the number line.

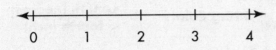

0   1   2   3   4

$\frac{7}{2}$ $\frac{1}{2}$ $\frac{5}{2}$ $\frac{3}{2}$

12. Lane's class is painting a mural. They spent 45 minutes painting on each of 2 days. On the first day, the class painted $\frac{1}{6}$ of the mural. The next day, the class painted another $\frac{1}{6}$ of the mural. What fraction of the mural have they painted so far?

Ⓐ $\frac{1}{6}$

Ⓑ $\frac{2}{6}$

Ⓒ $\frac{3}{6}$

Ⓓ $\frac{4}{6}$

13. Mr. Kim needs $\frac{5}{8}$ yard of wire for a project. He has a stick that is $\frac{1}{8}$ yard long. How many $\frac{1}{8}$-yard lengths does he need to measure to get $\frac{5}{8}$ yard of wire? Use the diagram below to help.

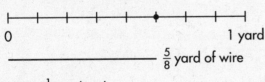

0   1 yard

———————— $\frac{5}{8}$ yard of wire

══ $\frac{1}{8}$ yard stick

Ⓐ 1

Ⓑ 3

Ⓒ 5

Ⓓ 8

14. Which point represents 6 lengths of $\frac{1}{8}$ on the number line?

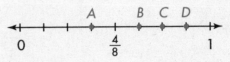

A   B   C   D

0          $\frac{4}{8}$ 1

Ⓐ Point A   Ⓒ Point C

Ⓑ Point B   Ⓓ Point D

15. Marco divided the circle below into 8 equal parts. Show how Marco could have done this. What fraction does each part represent?

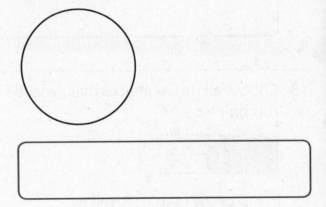

16. $\frac{2}{4}$ of this shape is shown below. Draw a picture to show the whole shape and write a fraction to represent the whole.

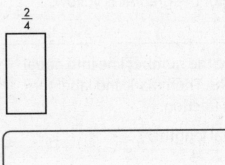

$\frac{2}{4}$

17. Mara believes the point marked on the number line is $\frac{2}{3}$. Is she correct?

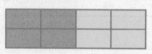

0   1

18. Choose all the sentences that describe this graphic.

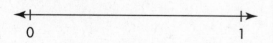

☐ $\frac{8}{8}$ of the graphic is yellow.

☐ $\frac{8}{8}$ represents the whole.

☐ $\frac{5}{8}$ of the graphic is green.

☐ $\frac{4}{8}$ of the graphic is green.

☐ $\frac{4}{8}$ of the graphic is yellow.

19. Divide the number line into equal lengths. Then mark and label the given fraction.

6 equal lengths; $\frac{5}{6}$

0   1

20. Tony collects colored strings. The table shows the lengths of some of his strings.

Lengths of Tony's Strings	
String Colors	**Length (nearest fourth inch)**
Black String	$3\frac{1}{2}$ in.
Blue String	3 in.
White String	$3\frac{1}{2}$ in.
Yellow String	$2\frac{1}{4}$ in.
Green String	$2\frac{3}{4}$ in.

Part A

Measure the lengths of the red and brown strings to the nearest half inch.

_____

_____

_____

_____

Part B

Draw a line plot to show the lengths of Tony's 7 strings to the nearest fourth inch.

Name _____

Art Display

Three students, Zach, Allie, and Paige, are making an art display.

Use the design at the right and the **Paint Colors** list to answer Questions 1–4.

1. The display will be divided into 8 equal parts. Draw lines to show one way to do this. Then write the fraction that describes the area of the total shape that is represented by 1 equal part.

Paint Colors
- Allie is painting the blue parts.
- Paige is painting the red parts.
- Zach is painting the yellow parts.
- Each student will paint at least 2 parts.

2. Shade the parts blue, yellow, or red to show how many parts each student could paint. Write fractions to show how much of the total display Allie and Paige painted.

3. Divide the number line into the number of equal parts of the display. Then show the fraction of the display that Zach painted on the number line.

0   1

4. Which fraction represents the whole display? Explain. Then mark a dot to show where this fraction is located on the number line above.

Use the **Ribbon Lengths** diagram on the right and the
Number of Ribbons table below to answer question 5.

5. The students will use the ribbon lengths at the right in
   their display.

   Part A

   Measure and record the lengths of each of these ribbons to
   the nearest fourth inch.

   Part B

   The **Ribbons** table shows how many of each color ribbon
   will be used. Draw a line plot to show this data.

Number of Ribbons	
Color	**Number Used**
Blue	4
Green	4
Red	2

6. In order to complete the display, the students recorded the
   number of half-hour sessions they spent working together.

   The number line below is divided into equal parts. Each part
   represents half an hour. Write the missing fractions on the
   number line.

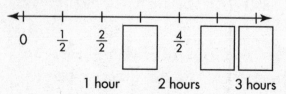

© Pearson Education, Inc. 3

TOPIC 13

Fraction Equivalence and Comparison

Essential Question: What are different ways to compare fractions?

Digital Resources

Solve Learn Glossary Practice Buddy

Tools Assessment Help Games

Some animals and plants even change their forms.

Animals and plants change and grow during their life cycles.

A caterpillar changes into a butterfly! Here's a project on life cycles and fractions.

Math and Science Project: Life Cycles

Do Research A frog egg hatches into a tadpole that lives in water. The tadpole will change and eventually become an adult frog. Use the Internet or another source to gather information about the life cycle of a frog and other animals.

Journal: Write a Report Include what you found. Also in your report:

- Tell about what is in a frog's habitat to support changes the frog goes through in its life cycle.

- Compare the life cycles of the different animals you studied.

- For the animals you studied, make up and solve problems using fractions. Draw fraction strips to represent the fractions.

Name _____

Review What You Know

A-Z Vocabulary

Choose the best term from the box. Write it on the blank.

| • < | • numerator |
| • > | • unit fraction |

1. The symbol _____ means *is greater than*.

2. The symbol _____ means *is less than*.

3. The number above the fraction bar in a fraction is called the _____.

Comparing Whole Numbers

Compare. Write <, >, or =.

4. 48 ◯ 30   **5.** 6 ◯ 6   **6.** 723 ◯ 732

7. 152 ◯ 183   **8.** 100 ◯ 10   **9.** 189 ◯ 99

10. 456 ◯ 456   **11.** 123 ◯ 223   **12.** 421 ◯ 399

13. 158 ◯ 185   **14.** 117 ◯ 117   **15.** 900 ◯ 893

Identifying Fractions

For each shape, write the fraction that is shaded.

16.   **17.**   **18.**

Division

Divide.

19. 30 ÷ 5   **20.** 72 ÷ 8   **21.** 28 ÷ 4

22. 48 ÷ 6   **23.** 81 ÷ 9   **24.** 45 ÷ 5

25. 32 ÷ 8   **26.** 42 ÷ 6   **27.** 49 ÷ 7

28. How can you check if the answer to 40 ÷ 5 is 8?

My Word Cards

Use the examples for each word on the front of the card to help complete the definitions on the back.

A-Z
Glossary

equivalent fractions

$$\frac{1}{2} = \frac{2}{4}$$

My Word Cards

Complete the definition. Extend learning by writing your own definitions.

Fractions that name the same part of a whole or the same location on a number line are called

_____

Name _____

☆ Solve & Share ☆

Gregor threw a softball $\frac{3}{4}$ of the length of the yard in front of his house. Find as many fractions as you can that name the same part of the length that Gregor threw the ball. *Solve this problem any way you choose. Explain how you decided.*

I can ...
find equivalent fractions that name the same part of a whole.

I can also choose and use a math tool to solve problems.

You can use tools. Think about what you need to find. Think about the tools you can use to help solve the problem.

Gregor's yard

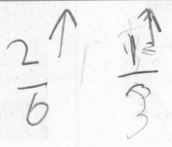

$\frac{2}{6}$ ↑ $\frac{1}{3}$ ↑

Look Back! **Use Appropriate Tools** How can fraction strips help you tell if a fraction with a denominator of 2, 3, or 6 would name the same part of a whole as $\frac{3}{4}$?

A

How Can Different Fractions Name the Same Part of a Whole?

The Chisholm Trail was used to drive cattle to market. Ross's herd has walked $\frac{1}{2}$ the distance to market. What is another way to name $\frac{1}{2}$?

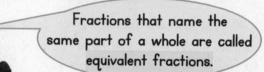

> **Different fractions can name the same part of a whole.**

> **Fractions that name the same part of a whole are called equivalent fractions.**

B $\frac{1}{2} = \dfrac{\square}{\square}$ You can use fraction strips.

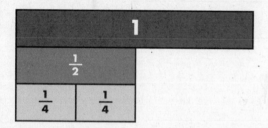

The fractions $\frac{1}{2}$ and $\frac{2}{4}$ represent the same part of the whole.

Two $\frac{1}{4}$ strips are equal to $\frac{1}{2}$, so $\frac{1}{2} = \frac{2}{4}$.

Another name for $\frac{1}{2}$ is $\frac{2}{4}$.

C   You can find other equivalent fractions. Think about fractions that name the same part of the whole.

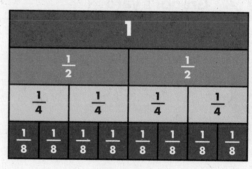

$\frac{1}{2} = \frac{4}{8}$ $\frac{3}{4} = \frac{6}{8}$

Convince Me! **Look for Relationships** In the examples above, what pattern do you see in the numerators and denominators of the fractions that are equivalent to $\frac{1}{2}$? What is another name for $\frac{1}{2}$ that is not shown above?

Practice Buddy · Tools · Assessment

Another Example!

You can find an equivalent fraction for $\frac{4}{6}$ using an area model.

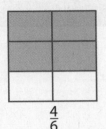

$\frac{4}{6}$

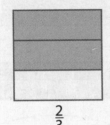

$\frac{2}{3}$

Both area models have the same-size whole.
One is divided into sixths. The other shows thirds.
The shaded parts show the same part of a whole.

Because $\frac{4}{6} = \frac{2}{3}$, another name for $\frac{4}{6}$ is $\frac{2}{3}$.

☆ Guided Practice*

Do You Understand?

1. Divide the second area model into sixths. Shade it to show a fraction equivalent to $\frac{1}{3}$.

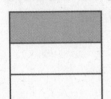 

$\frac{1}{3} = \boxed{}$

Do You Know How?

2. Use the fraction strips to help you find an equivalent fraction.

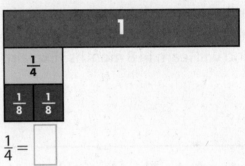

$\frac{1}{4} = \boxed{}$

☆ Independent Practice ☆

3. Use the fraction strips to help you find an equivalent fraction.

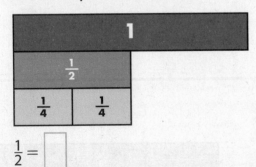

$\frac{1}{2} = \boxed{}$

4. Divide the second area model into eighths. Shade it to show a fraction equivalent to $\frac{1}{2}$.

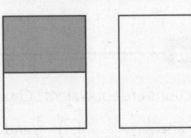

$\frac{1}{2} = \boxed{}$

In **5–8**, find each equivalent fraction. Use fraction strips or draw area models to help.

5. $\frac{3}{4} = \frac{\boxed{}}{8}$ 6. $\frac{6}{6} = \frac{\boxed{}}{8}$ 7. $\frac{2}{6} = \frac{\boxed{}}{3}$ 8. $\frac{4}{8} = \frac{\boxed{}}{2}$

Problem Solving

In **9** and **10**, use the fraction strips at the right.

9. Marcy used fraction strips to show equivalent fractions. Complete the equation.

$$\frac{\square}{4} = \square$$

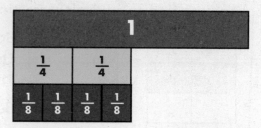

10. **Model with Math** Rita says the fraction strips show fractions that are equivalent to $\frac{1}{2}$. Explain what you could do to the diagram to see if she is correct.

> Both fractions represent the same part of the whole.

11. **Reasoning** A band learns 4 to 6 new songs every month. What is a good estimate for the number of songs the band will learn in 8 months? Explain.

12. Three eighths of a playground is covered by grass. What fraction of the playground is **NOT** covered by grass?

13. **Higher Order Thinking** Aiden folded two strips of paper into eighths. He shaded a fraction equal to $\frac{1}{4}$ on the first strip and a fraction equal to $\frac{3}{4}$ on the second strip. Show the fractions Aiden shaded on the pictures to the right. Which fraction of each strip did he shade?

✅ **Assessment**

14. Which fractions are equivalent? Choose all that apply.

   ☐ $\frac{1}{4}$ and $\frac{1}{8}$ ☐ $\frac{3}{4}$ and $\frac{3}{8}$

   ☐ $\frac{1}{4}$ and $\frac{2}{8}$ ☐ $\frac{3}{4}$ and $\frac{6}{8}$

   ☐ $\frac{2}{4}$ and $\frac{4}{8}$

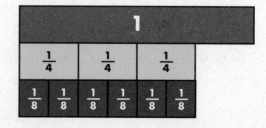

Name _____

Another Look!

You can use fraction strips to find equivalent fractions.

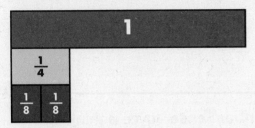

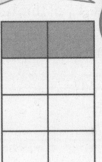

You can see that two $\frac{1}{8}$ strips show the same part of the whole as one $\frac{1}{4}$ strip.

$\frac{1}{4}$ and $\frac{2}{8}$ are equivalent fractions because they name the same amount. You can write $\frac{1}{4} = \frac{2}{8}$.

You can also use area models to show that $\frac{1}{4}$ and $\frac{2}{8}$ are equivalent. You can see the two fractions name the same part of the whole.

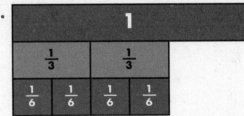

In **1–8**, find the equivalent fractions. Use fraction strips or draw area models to help.

1.

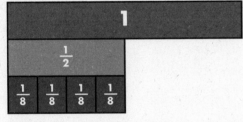

$\frac{1}{2} = \boxed{}$

2.

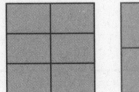

$\frac{2}{3} = \boxed{}$

3.

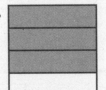

$\frac{6}{6} = \boxed{}$

4.

$\frac{3}{4} = \boxed{}$

5. $\frac{1}{3} = \dfrac{\boxed{}}{6}$

6. $\frac{4}{4} = \dfrac{\boxed{}}{3}$

7. $\frac{1}{2} = \dfrac{\boxed{}}{4}$

8. $\frac{3}{6} = \dfrac{\boxed{}}{2}$

9. 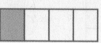 **Vocabulary** Explain what equivalent fractions are and give an example.

10. Use Appropriate Tools When you use fraction strips, how can you tell if two fractions are **NOT** equivalent?

---

11. Taylor colored $\frac{1}{4}$ of this rectangle. Draw an area model showing a fraction equivalent to $\frac{1}{4}$. Use the picture to help.

12. Number Sense Joyce is thinking of a 3-digit number. Her number has the digits 8, 4, and 6. To the nearest hundred, it rounds to 600. What is the number?

---

13. Model with Math Dinner plates are arranged on 5 shelves, with 8 plates on each shelf. How many dinner plates are on all of the shelves? Draw a bar diagram and write an equation to solve.

14. Higher Order Thinking Fred says that $\frac{1}{2}$ and $\frac{7}{8}$ are equivalent fractions. Draw area models for $\frac{1}{2}$ and $\frac{7}{8}$ to show if Fred's statement is correct. Name two fractions that you know are equivalent to $\frac{1}{2}$.

✔ **Assessment**

15. Which fraction pairs are **NOT** equivalent? Choose all that apply.

☐ $\frac{1}{3}$ and $\frac{1}{6}$ ☐ $\frac{4}{6}$ and $\frac{2}{3}$

☐ $\frac{1}{3}$ and $\frac{3}{6}$ ☐ $\frac{2}{3}$ and $\frac{3}{6}$

☐ $\frac{2}{6}$ and $\frac{1}{3}$

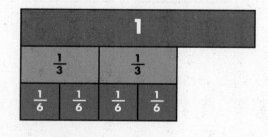

© Pearson Education, Inc. 3

Name _____

The top number line shows a point at $\frac{1}{4}$.
Write the fraction for each of the points labeled A, B,
C, D, E, and F. Which of these fractions show the same
distance from 0 as $\frac{1}{4}$?

I can ...
use number lines to represent
equivalent fractions.

I can also model with math to solve
problems.

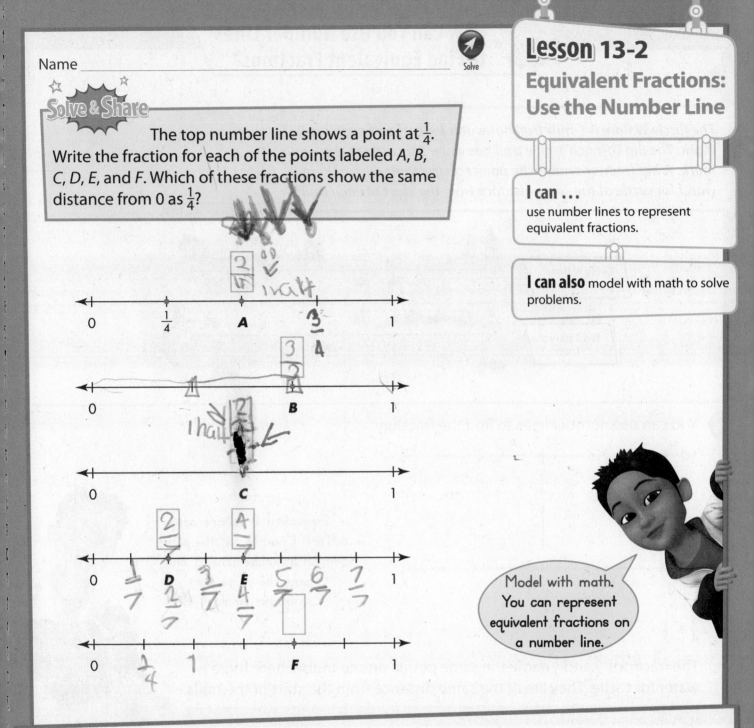

Model with math.
You can represent
equivalent fractions on
a number line.

Look Back! **Construct Arguments** How can number lines
show that two fractions are equivalent?

Essential Question **How Can You Use Number Lines to Find Equivalent Fractions?**

A

The Circle W Ranch 1-mile trail has water for cattle at each $\frac{1}{4}$-mile mark. The Big T Ranch 1-mile trail has water for cattle at the $\frac{1}{2}$-mile mark. What fractions name the points on the trails where there is water for cattle at the same distance from the start of each trail?

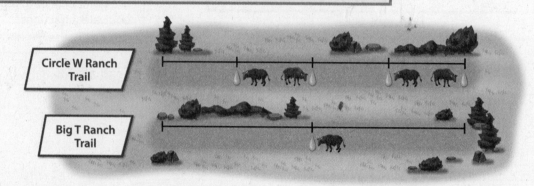

Circle W Ranch Trail

Big T Ranch Trail

B   You can use number lines to find the fractions.

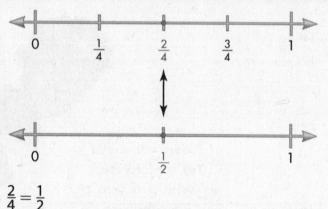

$$\frac{2}{4} = \frac{1}{2}$$

Equivalent fractions are different names for the same point on a number line. $\frac{2}{4}$ and $\frac{1}{2}$ name the same part of the whole.

The fractions $\frac{2}{4}$ and $\frac{1}{2}$ name the same points on the trails where there is water for cattle. They are at the same distance from the start of the trails.

Convince Me! **Model with Math** Ian paints $\frac{6}{8}$ of a fence. Anna paints $\frac{3}{4}$ of another fence of equal size and length. Draw a number line to show that Ian and Anna have painted the same amount of each fence.

☆Guided Practice*

Do You Understand?

1. Complete the number line to show that $\frac{2}{6}$ and $\frac{1}{3}$ are equivalent fractions.

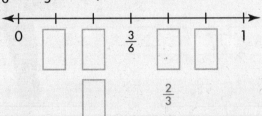

2. Sheila makes a number line to see if $\frac{4}{6}$ and $\frac{4}{8}$ are equivalent. She discovers that the fractions are **NOT** equivalent. How did Sheila know?

Do You Know How?

In **3** and **4**, write two fractions that name the same location on the number line.

3.

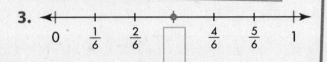

4.

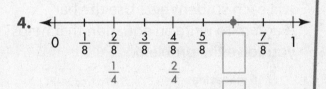

Independent Practice ☆

In **5–8**, write two fractions that name the same location on the number line.

5.

6.

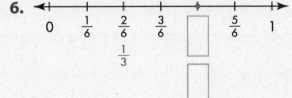

7.

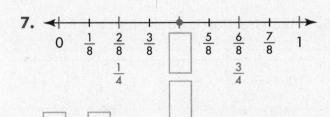

8.

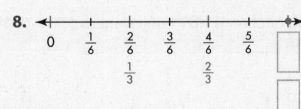

Problem Solving

9. **Number Sense** Bradley had 40 slices of pizza to share. How many pizzas did he have? Explain how you solved the problem.

Each of Bradley's pizzas was cut into 8 slices.

10. **Model with Math** Ms. Owen has 15 magazines to share among 5 students for an art project. How many magazines will each student get? Use the bar diagram to write an equation that helps you solve the problem.

15 magazines

| ? | ? | ? | ? | ? | ← 5 students

11. Yonita has 28 different apps on her computer. Casey has 14 music apps and 20 game apps on his computer. How many more apps does Casey have than Yonita?

12. **Construct Arguments** How can you tell, just by looking at the fractions, that $\frac{2}{4}$ and $\frac{3}{4}$ are **NOT** equivalent?

13. **Higher Order Thinking** Fiona and Gabe each had the same length of clay. Fiona used $\frac{2}{3}$ of her clay. Using sixths, what fraction of the length of clay will Gabe need to use to match the amount Fiona used? Draw a number line as part of your answer.

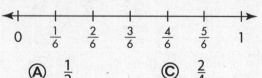 Assessment

14. Which fraction is **NOT** equivalent to $\frac{3}{6}$?

0    $\frac{1}{6}$ $\frac{2}{6}$ $\frac{3}{6}$ $\frac{4}{6}$ $\frac{5}{6}$ 1

Ⓐ $\frac{1}{2}$ Ⓒ $\frac{2}{4}$

Ⓑ $\frac{2}{3}$ Ⓓ $\frac{4}{8}$

15. Which fraction is equivalent to $\frac{4}{8}$?

0    $\frac{1}{8}$ $\frac{2}{8}$ $\frac{3}{8}$ $\frac{4}{8}$ $\frac{5}{8}$ $\frac{6}{8}$ $\frac{7}{8}$ 1

Ⓐ $\frac{3}{8}$ Ⓒ $\frac{2}{4}$

Ⓑ $\frac{3}{4}$ Ⓓ $\frac{1}{4}$

Name _____

Solve & Share

Maria and Evan are both jogging a mile. Maria has jogged $\frac{7}{8}$ mile, and Evan has jogged $\frac{3}{8}$ mile. Who has jogged a shorter distance? *Solve this problem any way you choose. Explain how you decided.*

I can ...
compare fractions that refer to the same-sized whole and have the same denominator by comparing their numerators.

I can also model with math to solve problems.

You can use appropriate tools. Think about fraction strips and why they can be good tools to show fractions. *Show your work in the space below!*

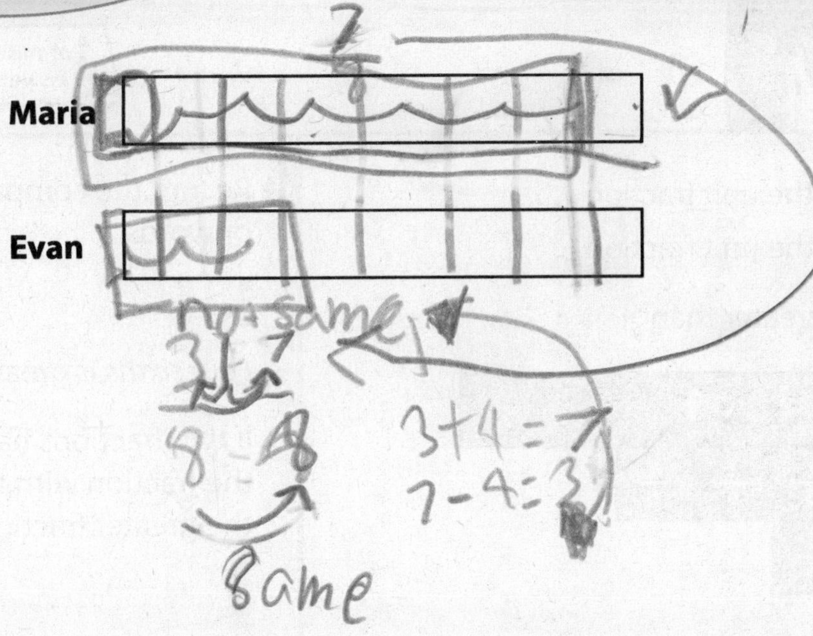

Maria

Evan

not same

$\frac{3}{8} < \frac{7}{8}$

$3+4 = 7$
$7-4 = 3$

same

Look Back! **Construct Arguments** Would your answer change if Evan had jogged $\frac{5}{8}$ of a mile instead? Explain.

Essential Question **How Can You Compare Fractions with the Same Denominator?**

A

Two banners with positive messages are the same size. One banner is $\frac{4}{6}$ yellow, and the other banner is $\frac{2}{6}$ yellow. Which is greater, $\frac{4}{6}$ or $\frac{2}{6}$?

Remember, comparisons are valid, or true, only if they refer to the same-sized whole.

Use fraction strips to reason about the sizes of these two fractions.

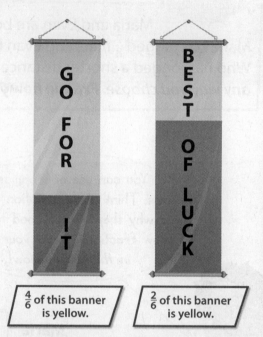

$\frac{4}{6}$ of this banner is yellow.

$\frac{2}{6}$ of this banner is yellow.

B

$\frac{4}{6}$ is 4 of the unit fraction $\frac{1}{6}$.

$\frac{2}{6}$ is 2 of the unit fraction $\frac{1}{6}$.

So, $\frac{4}{6}$ is greater than $\frac{2}{6}$.

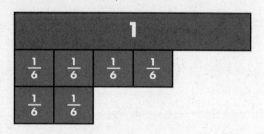

C Record the comparison using symbols or words.

$\frac{4}{6} > \frac{2}{6}$

Four sixths is greater than *two sixths*.

If two fractions have the same denominator, the fraction with the greater numerator is the greater fraction.

Convince Me! **Reasoning** Write a number for each numerator to make each comparison true. Use a picture and words to explain how you decided.

$\frac{\boxed{}}{8} < \frac{\boxed{}}{8}$ $\frac{\boxed{}}{3} > \frac{\boxed{}}{3}$

Name _____

☆ Guided Practice ☆

Do You Understand?

1. **Use Appropriate Tools** Explain how you can use fraction strips to show whether $\frac{5}{6}$ or $\frac{3}{6}$ of the same whole is greater.

2. Which is greater, $\frac{3}{4}$ or $\frac{2}{4}$? Draw $\frac{1}{4}$-strips to complete the diagram and answer the question.

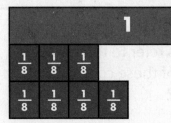

Do You Know How?

In **3** and **4**, compare. Write $<$, $>$, or $=$. Use the fraction strips to help.

3.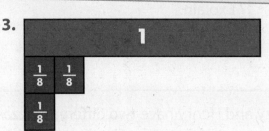

$\frac{2}{8} \bigcirc \frac{1}{8}$

4.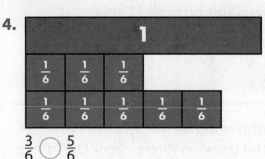

$\frac{3}{6} \bigcirc \frac{5}{6}$

☆ Independent Practice ☆

Leveled Practice In **5–14**, compare. Write $<$, $>$, or $=$. Use or draw fraction strips to help. The fractions refer to the same whole.

5.

$\frac{3}{8} \bigcirc \frac{4}{8}$

6.

$\frac{3}{4} \bigcirc \frac{3}{4}$

7. $\frac{6}{8} \bigcirc \frac{3}{8}$

8. $\frac{5}{8} \bigcirc \frac{7}{8}$

9. $\frac{1}{2} \bigcirc \frac{1}{2}$

10. $\frac{1}{3} \bigcirc \frac{2}{3}$

11. $\frac{6}{6} \bigcirc \frac{3}{6}$

12. $\frac{2}{8} \bigcirc \frac{3}{8}$

13. $\frac{3}{3} \bigcirc \frac{1}{3}$

14. $\frac{1}{4} \bigcirc \frac{3}{4}$

*For another example, see Set C on page 724.   **Topic 13** | Lesson 13-3   **687**

Problem Solving

In **15** and **16**, use the pictures of the strips that have been partly shaded.

15. Compare. Write $<$, $>$, or $=$.
The green strips show $\frac{1}{6}$ ◯ $\frac{2}{6}$.

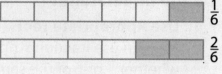

$\frac{1}{6}$

$\frac{2}{6}$

16. Construct Arguments Do the yellow strips show $\frac{2}{4} > \frac{3}{4}$? Explain.

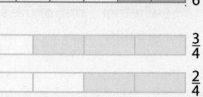

$\frac{3}{4}$

$\frac{2}{4}$

17. Izzy and Henry have two different pizzas. Izzy ate $\frac{3}{8}$ of her pizza. Henry ate $\frac{3}{8}$ of his pizza. Izzy ate more pizza than Henry. How is this possible? Explain.

18. Generalize Two fractions are equal. They also have the same denominator. What must be true of the numerators of the fractions? Explain.

19. Number Sense Mr. Domini had $814 in the bank on Wednesday. On Thursday, he withdrew $250, and on Friday, he withdrew $185. How much money did he have in the bank then?

20. Higher Order Thinking Tom's parents let him choose whether to play his favorite board game for $\frac{7}{8}$ hour or for $\frac{8}{8}$ hour. Explain which amount of time you think Tom should choose, and why.

Assessment

21. The pictures below show tile designs. Which shows less than $\frac{4}{8}$ of the whole shaded?

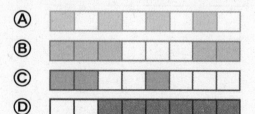

22. These fractions refer to the same whole. Which of these comparisons is **NOT** correct?

Ⓐ $\frac{5}{6} > \frac{3}{6}$

Ⓑ $\frac{2}{4} < \frac{3}{4}$

Ⓒ $\frac{3}{8} > \frac{1}{8}$

Ⓓ $\frac{2}{3} < \frac{1}{3}$

Name _____

Another Look!

You can use fraction strips to compare fractions that have the same denominator.

Compare $\frac{1}{4}$ and $\frac{3}{4}$.

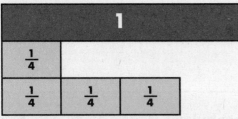

Fractions that you compare must be part of the same whole or of equal-sized wholes.

The denominator for each fraction is 4.
Use fraction strips to help you compare the fractions.

Use one $\frac{1}{4}$ strip to show $\frac{1}{4}$ and three $\frac{1}{4}$ strips to show $\frac{3}{4}$.
More $\frac{1}{4}$ strips are used to show $\frac{3}{4}$. So, $\frac{3}{4} > \frac{1}{4}$ and $\frac{1}{4} < \frac{3}{4}$.

In **1–12**, compare. Write $<$, $>$, or $=$. Use or draw fraction strips to help. The fractions refer to the same whole.

1.

$\frac{4}{8}$ ◯ $\frac{5}{8}$

2.
$\frac{3}{4}$ ◯ $\frac{2}{4}$

3.
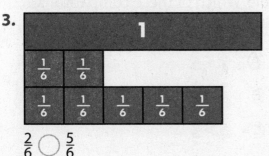
$\frac{2}{6}$ ◯ $\frac{5}{6}$

4.
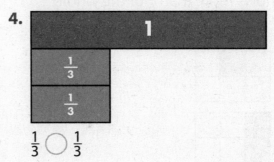
$\frac{1}{3}$ ◯ $\frac{1}{3}$

5. $\frac{4}{8}$ ◯ $\frac{4}{8}$

6. $\frac{2}{4}$ ◯ $\frac{1}{4}$

7. $\frac{7}{8}$ ◯ $\frac{1}{8}$

8. $\frac{2}{6}$ ◯ $\frac{3}{6}$

9. $\frac{5}{6}$ ◯ $\frac{5}{6}$

10. $\frac{1}{8}$ ◯ $\frac{2}{8}$

11. $\frac{4}{6}$ ◯ $\frac{2}{6}$

12. $\frac{1}{6}$ ◯ $\frac{5}{6}$

13. Be Precise Ali is comparing fractions using fraction strips. Using the symbols > and <, write two different comparisons for the fractions.

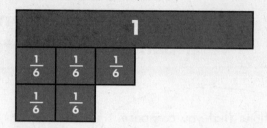

14. Use Appropriate Tools How could you use fraction strips to help you decide which fraction is greater, $\frac{5}{8}$ or $\frac{6}{8}$?

15. Number Sense Keisha has 10 coins. Two of the coins are nickels, 6 are pennies, and the rest are dimes. What is the value of Keisha's coins?

16. Vocabulary Write a fraction that has 6 as the denominator. Write a fraction that does not have 6 as the denominator.

17. Higher Order Thinking Draw fraction strips to show the following fractions: $\frac{4}{6}$, $\frac{1}{6}$, and $\frac{5}{6}$. Then, write the three fractions in order from least to greatest.

Fraction strips can help you order fractions.

Assessment

18. The pictures below show tile designs. Which shows more than $\frac{3}{6}$ of the whole shaded?

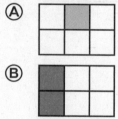

Ⓐ

Ⓑ

Ⓒ

Ⓓ

19. These fractions refer to the same whole. Which of these comparisons is **NOT** correct?

Ⓐ $\frac{2}{4} < \frac{3}{4}$

Ⓑ $\frac{5}{8} > \frac{7}{8}$

Ⓒ $\frac{2}{3} > \frac{1}{3}$

Ⓓ $\frac{1}{6} < \frac{5}{6}$

Name _____

Solve

Solve & Share

Carrie and Alan had the same amount of vegetables to eat. Carrie ate $\frac{1}{4}$ of her vegetables. Alan ate $\frac{1}{3}$ of his vegetables. Who ate more vegetables? *Solve the problem any way you choose. Explain how you decided.*

I can ...
compare fractions that refer to the same whole and have the same numerator by comparing their denominators.

I can also be precise in my work.

Be precise.
Use pictures, words, and symbols to represent and compare fractions in different ways. *Show your work in the space below!*

Look Back! **Construct Arguments** If Carrie ate $\frac{2}{4}$ of her vegetables and Alan ate $\frac{2}{3}$ of his vegetables, would your answer change? Use reasoning about the size of fractions to explain.

Learn   Glossary

Essential Question

How Can You Compare Fractions with the Same Numerator?

A

Two scarves are the same size. One scarf is $\frac{5}{6}$ orange, and the other scarf is $\frac{5}{8}$ orange. Which is less, $\frac{5}{6}$ or $\frac{5}{8}$?

$\frac{5}{6}$ of this scarf is orange.

$\frac{5}{8}$ of this scarf is orange.

B ## What You Show

Use fraction strips to reason about the size of $\frac{5}{6}$ compared to the size of $\frac{5}{8}$.

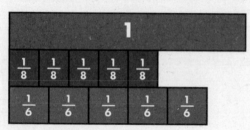

C ## What You Write

Justify the comparison using symbols or words.

$$\frac{5}{8} < \frac{5}{6}$$

Five eighths is less than *five sixths*.

If two fractions have the same numerator, the fraction with the greater denominator is less than the other fraction.

You can compare fractions that have the same numerator by reasoning about their size.

Convince Me! **Critique Reasoning** Julia says $\frac{1}{8}$ is greater than $\frac{1}{4}$ because 8 is greater than 4. Is she correct? Explain.

☆Guided Practice☆

Do You Understand?

1. **Reasoning** How can fraction strips help you reason about size to find whether $\frac{4}{6}$ or $\frac{4}{8}$ of the same whole is greater?

2. Which is greater, $\frac{1}{4}$ or $\frac{1}{6}$? Draw fraction strips to complete the diagram and answer the question.

1

Do You Know How?

In **3** and **4**, compare. Write $<$, $>$, or $=$. Use fraction strips to help.

3.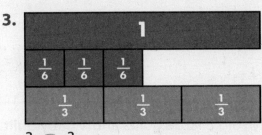

$\frac{3}{6}$ ◯ $\frac{3}{3}$

4.

$\frac{4}{8}$ ◯ $\frac{4}{6}$

☆Independent Practice☆

Leveled Practice In **5–14**, compare. Write $<$, $>$, or $=$. Use or draw fraction strips to help. The fractions refer to the same whole.

5.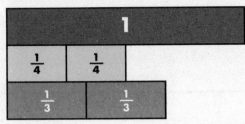

$\frac{2}{3}$ ◯ $\frac{2}{4}$

6.

1

$\frac{4}{4}$ ◯ $\frac{4}{6}$

7. $\frac{2}{3}$ ◯ $\frac{2}{2}$ 8. $\frac{4}{8}$ ◯ $\frac{4}{8}$ 9. $\frac{5}{6}$ ◯ $\frac{5}{8}$ 10. $\frac{1}{4}$ ◯ $\frac{1}{3}$

11. $\frac{1}{3}$ ◯ $\frac{1}{6}$ 12. $\frac{4}{6}$ ◯ $\frac{4}{6}$ 13. $\frac{1}{8}$ ◯ $\frac{1}{2}$ 14. $\frac{2}{6}$ ◯ $\frac{2}{3}$

Problem Solving

15. Critique Reasoning James uses blue and white tiles to make the two designs shown here. Each design is the same size. James says that the blue area in the top design is the same as the blue area in the bottom design. Is he correct? Explain.

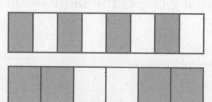

Each whole is the same size. So, you can compare the fractions the blue tiles represent in each whole.

16. Amy sold 8 large quilts and 1 baby quilt. How much money did she make from selling quilts?

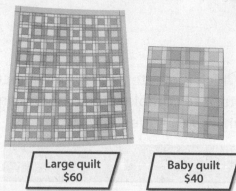

Large quilt $60   Baby quilt $40

17. Be Precise Write two comparison statements about the fractions shown below.

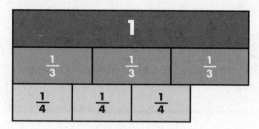

18. Higher Order Thinking John says that when you compare two fractions with the same numerator, you look at the denominators because the fraction with the greater denominator is greater. Is he correct? Explain, and give an example.

Assessment

19. These fractions refer to the same whole. Which of these comparisons are correct? Choose all that apply.

☐ $\frac{5}{6} < \frac{5}{8}$ ☐ $\frac{2}{4} > \frac{2}{3}$

☐ $\frac{1}{2} > \frac{1}{4}$ ☐ $\frac{5}{6} = \frac{5}{6}$

☐ $\frac{3}{4} > \frac{3}{6}$

© Pearson Education, Inc. 3

Name _____

☆ Guided Practice ☆

Do You Understand?

1. Tina used benchmark numbers to decide that $\frac{3}{8}$ is less than $\frac{7}{8}$. Do you agree? Explain.

2. **Reasoning** Write two fractions with a denominator of 6 that are closer to 0 than to 1.

3. **Reasoning** Write two fractions with a denominator of 8 that are closer to 1 than to 0.

Do You Know How?

In **4–6**, choose from the fractions $\frac{1}{8}$, $\frac{1}{4}$, $\frac{6}{8}$, and $\frac{3}{4}$. Use fraction strips to help.

4. Which fractions are closer to 0 than to 1?

5. Which fractions are closer to 1 than to 0?

6. Use the two fractions with a denominator of 8 to write a true statement: ■ < ■.

☆ Independent Practice ☆

In **7** and **8**, choose from the fractions $\frac{2}{3}$, $\frac{7}{8}$, $\frac{1}{4}$, $\frac{2}{6}$.

7. Which of the fractions are closer to 0 than to 1?

8. Which of the fractions are closer to 1 than to 0?

In **9–14**, compare. Write <, >, or =.

9. $\frac{5}{8}$ ◯ $\frac{7}{8}$

10. $\frac{5}{8}$ ◯ $\frac{2}{8}$

11. $\frac{3}{4}$ ◯ $\frac{3}{6}$

12. $\frac{4}{6}$ ◯ $\frac{4}{8}$

13. $\frac{2}{6}$ ◯ $\frac{2}{4}$

14. $\frac{2}{3}$ ◯ $\frac{1}{3}$

Problem Solving

In **15–17**, use the table at the right.

15. Who has walked closer to 1 mile than to 0 miles?

16. Who has walked closer to 0 miles than to 1 mile?

17. **Construct Arguments** Who has walked a fraction of a mile that is closer to neither 0 nor 1? Explain.

Name	Fraction of mile walked
Mrs. Avery	$\frac{1}{6}$
Mr. Nunez	$\frac{5}{6}$
Ms. Chang	$\frac{1}{3}$
Mr. O'Leary	$\frac{4}{8}$
Miss Lee	$\frac{4}{6}$

18. **Critique Reasoning** Rahul compares two wholes that are the same size. He says that $\frac{2}{6} < \frac{2}{3}$ because $\frac{2}{6}$ is less than $\frac{1}{2}$, and $\frac{2}{3}$ is greater than $\frac{1}{2}$. Is he correct? Explain.

Think about fractions that are equivalent to one half.

19. **Make Sense and Persevere** Manish drives 265 more miles than Janice. Manish drives 642 miles. How many miles does Janice drive?

20. **Algebra** Nika has 90 pencils. 40 of them are yellow, 13 are green, 18 are red, and the rest are blue. How many blue pencils does Nika have?

21. **Higher Order Thinking** Omar says that $\frac{2}{3} < \frac{4}{6}$ because $\frac{2}{3}$ is between 0 and $\frac{1}{2}$, and $\frac{4}{6}$ is between $\frac{1}{2}$ and 1. Is he correct? Explain.

Think about equivalent fractions you know.

✓ **Assessment**

22. Write each fraction in the correct answer space to show whether the fraction is closer to 0 or to 1.

Closer to 0 than to 1	Closer to 1 than to 0

$\frac{1}{8}$　$\frac{6}{8}$　$\frac{2}{3}$　　　$\frac{3}{4}$　$\frac{2}{6}$　$\frac{1}{6}$

Name _____

Homework & Practice 13-5

Compare Fractions: Use Benchmarks

Another Look!

Compare $\frac{3}{8}$ and $\frac{7}{8}$.

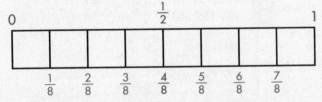

0                    $\frac{1}{2}$ 1

$\frac{1}{8}$ $\frac{2}{8}$ $\frac{3}{8}$ $\frac{4}{8}$ $\frac{5}{8}$ $\frac{6}{8}$ $\frac{7}{8}$

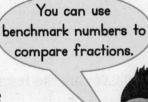

You can use benchmark numbers to compare fractions.

The denominator for each fraction is 8. Use the benchmark numbers $0, \frac{1}{2}$, and 1 to reason about the relative sizes of the numerators in $\frac{3}{8}$ and $\frac{7}{8}$.

$\frac{1}{2}$ and $\frac{4}{8}$ are equivalent fractions. $\frac{3}{8}$ is less than $\frac{4}{8}$ and closer to 0.

$\frac{7}{8}$ is greater than $\frac{4}{8}$ and closer to 1. So, $\frac{3}{8}$ is less than $\frac{7}{8}$.

In **1** and **2**, choose from the fractions $\frac{1}{3}, \frac{5}{6}, \frac{3}{4}, \frac{3}{8}$.

1. Which of the fractions are closer to 1 than to 0?

2. Which of the fractions are closer to 0 than to 1?

3. Write two fractions with a denominator of 8 that are closer to 0 than to 1.

4. Use the benchmark $\frac{1}{2}$ and the fractions $\frac{1}{8}$ and $\frac{5}{8}$ to write three comparison statements.

In **5–10**, compare. Write $<$, $>$, or $=$.

5. $\frac{2}{6} \bigcirc \frac{2}{4}$

6. $\frac{1}{4} \bigcirc \frac{1}{8}$

7. $\frac{3}{6} \bigcirc \frac{5}{6}$

8. $\frac{2}{3} \bigcirc \frac{2}{3}$

9. $\frac{1}{6} \bigcirc \frac{1}{4}$

10. $\frac{3}{3} \bigcirc \frac{3}{8}$

11. The 3rd grade classes at Haines Elementary are each making a class banner. The banners are all the same size. The table shows how much of a banner each class has completed so far. Has Ms. Holmes class or Mrs. Johnson's class completed the greater fraction of a banner?

DATA	Class	Fraction of Class Banner Completed
	Ms. Holmes	$\frac{6}{8}$
	Mr. Cline	$\frac{3}{6}$
	Mr. Gomez	$\frac{1}{3}$
	Mrs. Johnson	$\frac{7}{8}$
	Ms. Park	$\frac{3}{4}$

12. In whose classes are the fractions of the banners completed equivalent?

13. In whose classes is the fraction of a completed banner closer to 1 than to 0?

14. Construct Arguments In whose class is the fraction of a completed banner closer to neither 0 nor 1? Use benchmark numbers to explain.

15. Using the denominators 2, 3, 6, or 8, write two fractions less than 1. Then tell if the fractions are closer to 0 than to 1.

16. Make Sense and Persevere Natalie has 28 erasers. She divided some of her erasers equally among 3 friends. Natalie has 10 erasers left. How many erasers did each friend get?

17. Higher Order Thinking Write two fractions using the numbers from the cards at the right. One fraction should be closer to 0 than to 1. The other fraction should be closer to 1 than to 0. Explain which fraction meets each rule.

| 1 | 2 | 3 | 4 |

✓ **Assessment**

18. Write each fraction in the correct answer space to show whether the fraction is closer to 0 or to 1.

Closer to 0 than to 1	Closer to 1 than to 0

$\frac{5}{6}$ $\frac{3}{8}$ $\frac{1}{4}$ $\frac{1}{3}$ $\frac{2}{8}$ $\frac{4}{6}$

Name _____

Solve & Share

Tanya, Riaz, and Ryan each used a bag of flour to make modeling clay. The bags were labeled $\frac{3}{4}$ lb, $\frac{1}{4}$ lb, and $\frac{2}{4}$ lb. Show these fractions on a number line. How can you use the number line to compare two of these fractions?

Lesson 13-6
Compare Fractions: Use the Number Line

I can ...
compare two fractions by locating them on a number line.

I can also reason about math.

You can use reasoning to compare fractions. Think about the size of the fractions.

$$0 \qquad \frac{1}{4} \qquad \frac{2}{4} \qquad \frac{3}{4} \qquad 1 \;\; \frac{4}{4}$$

$\frac{1}{4}$

$\frac{3}{4}$

$\frac{2}{4} \quad \frac{2}{4}$ is the less

Look Back! **Use Structure** If the bags were labeled $\frac{4}{8}$ lb, $\frac{3}{8}$ lb, and $\frac{6}{8}$ lb, how could a number line help you solve this problem?

How Can You Compare Fractions Using the Number Line?

A

Talia has two different lengths of blue and red ribbon. Does she have more blue ribbon or more red ribbon?

$\frac{2}{3}$ yard $\frac{1}{3}$ yard

Look at the numerators and the denominators of each fraction.

B   The fractions both refer to 1 yard of ribbon. This is the whole.

You can use a number line to compare $\frac{1}{3}$ and $\frac{2}{3}$.

The farther to the right a fraction is on the number line, the greater the fraction.

0          $\frac{1}{3}$ $\frac{2}{3}$ 1

On the number line, $\frac{2}{3}$ is farther to the right than $\frac{1}{3}$.

So, $\frac{2}{3} > \frac{1}{3}$.

Talia has more blue ribbon than red ribbon.

Convince Me! Use Structure Talia has an additional length of green ribbon that measures $\frac{3}{6}$ yard. How can you use the number line to compare the length of the green ribbon to the lengths of the blue and red ribbons?

☆ Guided Practice*

Do You Understand?

1. **Use Structure** When two fractions refer to the same whole, what do you notice when the denominators you are comparing are the same?

2. **Reasoning** Write a problem that compares two fractions with different numerators.

Do You Know How?

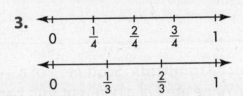

In **3–5**, compare fractions using <, >, or =. Use the number lines to help.

3.
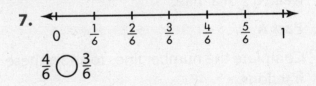

$\frac{2}{4} \bigcirc \frac{2}{3}$

4.
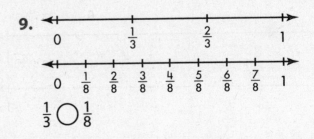

$\frac{2}{6} \bigcirc \frac{1}{3}$

5.

$\frac{5}{8} \bigcirc \frac{3}{8}$

☆ Independent Practice ☆

In **6–9**, use the number lines to compare the fractions. Write >, <, or =.

6.
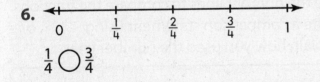

$\frac{1}{4} \bigcirc \frac{3}{4}$

7.

$\frac{4}{6} \bigcirc \frac{3}{6}$

8.
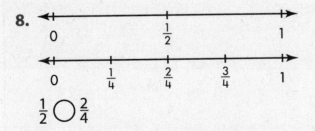

$\frac{1}{2} \bigcirc \frac{2}{4}$

9.

$\frac{1}{3} \bigcirc \frac{1}{8}$

Problem Solving

10. **Number Sense** Randy wants to save $39. The table shows how much money he has saved. Explain how you can use estimation to decide if he has saved enough money.

Money Saved	
Month	**Amount**
March	$14
April	$11
May	$22

DATA

---

11. **Construct Arguments** Scott ate $\frac{2}{8}$ of a fruit bar. Anne ate $\frac{4}{8}$ of a different fruit bar. Can you tell who ate more of the fruit bar, Scott or Anne? Explain.

12. **Be Precise** Matt and Adara have identical pieces of cardboard for an art project. Matt uses $\frac{2}{3}$ of his piece. Adara uses $\frac{2}{6}$ of her piece. Who uses more, Matt or Adara? Draw two number lines to help explain your answer.

---

13. **Higher Order Thinking** Some friends shared a pizza. Nicole ate $\frac{2}{8}$ of the pizza. Chris ate $\frac{1}{8}$ more than Johan. Mike ate $\frac{1}{8}$ of the pizza. Johan ate $\frac{1}{8}$ more than Mike. Who ate the most pizza?

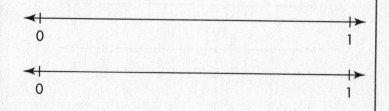

14. Inez has 2 rows of plants. There are 8 plants in each row. Each plant has 3 flowers. How many flowers are there in all?

✔ Assessment

15. Daniel has walked $\frac{3}{4}$ of a mile. Theo has walked $\frac{5}{8}$ of a mile.

Part A

Complete the number lines to show these fractions.

```
←|————————————————|→
  0                1

←|————————————————|→
  0                1
```

Part B

Use the number lines to compare the fractions. Write a comparison statement using $<$, $>$, or $=$. Explain how you used the number lines.

Name _____

Help Practice Tools Games
       Buddy

Homework
& Practice 13-6
Compare Fractions:
Use the Number Line

Another Look!

Ben has $\frac{1}{2}$ yard of string. John has $\frac{1}{3}$ yard of string.
Who has more string?

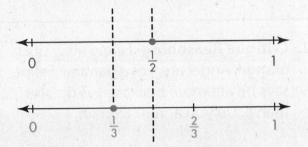

You can draw two number
lines of equal length to compare
fractions with different
denominators.

Mark 0 and 1 on both number lines.
Divide the first number line into 2 equal parts. Mark $\frac{1}{2}$.
Divide the second number line into 3 equal parts. Mark $\frac{1}{3}$.
$\frac{1}{2}$ is farther to the right than $\frac{1}{3}$.
So, $\frac{1}{2} > \frac{1}{3}$. Ben has more string than John.

In **1–4**, use the number lines to compare the fractions. Write $>$, $<$, or $=$.

1. ◄—+—+—+—+—+—+—+—►
   0 $\frac{1}{8}$ $\frac{2}{8}$ $\frac{3}{8}$ $\frac{4}{8}$ $\frac{5}{8}$ $\frac{6}{8}$ $\frac{7}{8}$ 1

   $\frac{7}{8}$ ◯ $\frac{4}{8}$

2. ◄—+—+—+—+—+—►
   0 $\frac{1}{6}$ $\frac{2}{6}$ $\frac{3}{6}$ $\frac{4}{6}$ $\frac{5}{6}$ 1

   $\frac{1}{6}$ ◯ $\frac{3}{6}$

3. ◄—+———+———+———►
   0    $\frac{1}{3}$ $\frac{2}{3}$ 1

   ◄—+—+—+—+—+—►
   0 $\frac{1}{6}$ $\frac{2}{6}$ $\frac{3}{6}$ $\frac{4}{6}$ $\frac{5}{6}$ 1

   $\frac{1}{3}$ ◯ $\frac{1}{6}$

4. ◄—+————+————►
   0      $\frac{1}{2}$ 1

   ◄—+—+—+—+—+—+—+—►
   0 $\frac{1}{8}$ $\frac{2}{8}$ $\frac{3}{8}$ $\frac{4}{8}$ $\frac{5}{8}$ $\frac{6}{8}$ $\frac{7}{8}$ 1

   $\frac{1}{2}$ ◯ $\frac{4}{8}$

In **5–8**, compare the fractions. Use number lines to help. Write $>$, $<$, or $=$.

5. $\frac{1}{4}$ ◯ $\frac{1}{8}$

6. $\frac{3}{6}$ ◯ $\frac{3}{4}$

7. $\frac{4}{8}$ ◯ $\frac{4}{6}$

8. $\frac{2}{3}$ ◯ $\frac{2}{4}$

9. Number Sense Angela drove 82 miles on Monday. She drove 94 miles on Tuesday. To the nearest hundred, how many miles did Angela drive over the two days?

10. I have 4 sides. The lengths of all my sides are equal. Which shape am I?

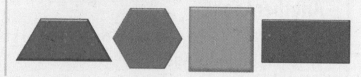

11. Be Precise Dylan and Javier had the same size serving of vegetables for dinner. Dylan finished $\frac{2}{3}$ of his vegetables. Javier ate $\frac{4}{6}$ of his serving. Who ate more vegetables? Draw two number lines to justify your answer.

12. Critique Reasoning Felipe ate $\frac{7}{8}$ of an orange. Angel ate $\frac{5}{8}$ of a banana. Felipe says he ate more because $\frac{7}{8}$ is greater than $\frac{5}{8}$. Do you agree? Explain.

13. Higher Order Thinking Some friends are sharing a watermelon. Simone eats $\frac{2}{6}$ of the watermelon. Ken eats $\frac{3}{6}$ of the watermelon and Claire eats the rest. Alex has his own watermelon equal in size to the one shared by his friends. He eats $\frac{5}{6}$ of his watermelon. Which of the friends eats the least amount of watermelon?

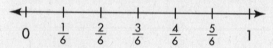

The number line shows the whole.

✓ **Assessment**

14. Molly's dad is grilling burgers. He uses $\frac{1}{4}$ lb of beef in each burger for Molly and her mother. He uses $\frac{1}{3}$ lb of beef to make a burger for himself.

Part A

Complete number lines to show these fractions.

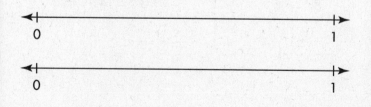

Part B

Use the number lines to compare the fractions. Then write a comparison statement using $<$, $>$, or $=$. Explain how you used the number lines.

Name _____

Solve & Share

Jamie ate six pieces of apple pie during the week. Each piece was $\frac{1}{6}$ of the whole pie. How much of the pie did Jamie eat? How much pie is left over? *Solve this problem any way you choose. Explain how you decided.*

I can ...
use representations to find fraction names for whole numbers.

I can also reason about math.

Use reasoning. Think about the size of each piece and the size of the whole pie. *Show your work!*

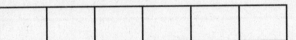

Look Back! **Construct Arguments** Jamie cuts another pie into smaller pieces. Each piece of pie is $\frac{1}{8}$ of the whole. Jamie gives away eight pieces. Does Jamie have any pie left over? Explain how you know.

How Can You Use Fraction Names to Represent Whole Numbers?

A

What are some equivalent fraction names for 1, 2, and 3?

You can write a whole number as a fraction by writing the whole number as the numerator and 1 as the denominator.

The number line shows 3 wholes. Each whole is divided into 1 equal part.

1 whole divided into 1 equal part can be written as $\frac{1}{1}$.
2 wholes each divided into 1 equal part can be written as $\frac{2}{1}$.
3 wholes each divided into 1 equal part can be written as $\frac{3}{1}$.

$1 = \frac{1}{1}$
$2 = \frac{2}{1}$
$3 = \frac{3}{1}$

B You can find other equivalent fraction names for whole numbers.

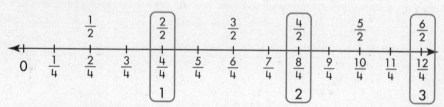

$1 = \frac{1}{1} = \frac{2}{2} = \frac{4}{4}$

$2 = \frac{2}{1} = \frac{4}{2} = \frac{8}{4}$

$3 = \frac{3}{1} = \frac{6}{2} = \frac{12}{4}$

There are many fraction names for whole numbers!

Convince Me! **Reasoning** What equivalent fraction names can you write for 4 using denominators of 1, 2, or 4?

Another Example!

You can use fractions to name whole numbers.

1	1
$\frac{1}{6}$ $\frac{1}{6}$ $\frac{1}{6}$ $\frac{1}{6}$ $\frac{1}{6}$ $\frac{1}{6}$	$\frac{1}{6}$ $\frac{1}{6}$ $\frac{1}{6}$ $\frac{1}{6}$ $\frac{1}{6}$ $\frac{1}{6}$

Twelve $\frac{1}{6}$ fraction strips equal 2 whole fraction strips.

All whole numbers have fraction names. You can write $2 = \frac{12}{6}$.

You also know $2 = \frac{2}{1}$, so you can write $2 = \frac{2}{1} = \frac{12}{6}$.

☆ Guided Practice *

Do You Understand?

1. **Reasoning** Explain how you know that $\frac{4}{1} = 4$.

Do You Know How?

2. Complete the number line.

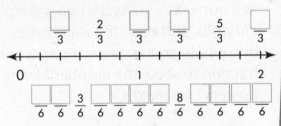

$\frac{\square}{3}$ $\frac{2}{3}$ $\frac{\square}{3}$ $\frac{\square}{3}$ $\frac{5}{3}$ $\frac{\square}{3}$

0 ——— 1 ——— 2

$\frac{\square}{6}$ $\frac{\square}{6}$ $\frac{3}{6}$ $\frac{\square}{6}$ $\frac{\square}{6}$ $\frac{\square}{6}$ $\frac{\square}{6}$ $\frac{8}{6}$ $\frac{\square}{6}$ $\frac{\square}{6}$ $\frac{\square}{6}$ $\frac{\square}{6}$

3. Look at the number line. Write two equivalent fractions for each whole number.

$1 = \dfrac{\square}{3} = \dfrac{\square}{6}$ $2 = \dfrac{\square}{3} = \dfrac{\square}{6}$

☆ Independent Practice ☆

In **4–7**, write two equivalent fractions for each whole number. You can draw number lines to help.

4. $4 = \dfrac{\square}{2} = \dfrac{\square}{1}$ 5. $1 = \dfrac{\square}{4} = \dfrac{\square}{1}$ 6. $2 = \dfrac{\square}{3} = \dfrac{\square}{1}$ 7. $5 = \dfrac{\square}{2} = \dfrac{\square}{1}$

In **8–11**, for each pair of fractions, write the equivalent whole number.

8. $\frac{6}{2} = \frac{3}{1} =$ 9. $\frac{3}{3} = \frac{6}{6} =$ 10. $\frac{8}{4} = \frac{6}{3} =$ 11. $\frac{9}{3} = \frac{12}{4} =$

Problem Solving

12. Henry needs to fix or replace his refrigerator. It will cost $376 to fix it. How much more will it cost to buy a new refrigerator than to fix the current one?

New Refrigerator
$969

13. Critique Reasoning Declan says, "To write an equivalent fraction name for 5, I can write 5 as the denominator and 1 as the numerator." Do you agree with Declan? Explain.

14. Look for Relationships Describe one of the patterns in fractions equivalent to 1 whole.

15. Math and Science There are four stages in a butterfly's life cycle: egg, caterpillar, chrysalis, and butterfly. Dan makes one whole poster for each stage. Use a fraction to show the number of whole posters Dan makes.

16. Karen buys 4 movie tickets for $9 each. She has $12 left over. How much money did Karen have to start?

17. Higher Order Thinking Peggy has 4 whole sandwiches. She cuts each whole into halves. Peggy gives away $\frac{2}{2}$ of the sandwiches. Show the number of halves Peggy has left as a fraction.

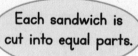

Each sandwich is cut into equal parts.

✓ **Assessment**

18. Complete the equations. Draw lines to match the whole number on the left to the equivalent fractions on the right.

| 4 |
| 1 |
| 2 |
| 6 |

$\frac{6}{1} = \frac{12}{2} = ?$

$\frac{6}{3} = \frac{4}{2} = ?$

$\frac{4}{4} = \frac{1}{1} = ?$

$\frac{8}{2} = \frac{16}{4} = ?$

Help Practice Buddy Tools Games

Another Look!

Whole numbers have equivalent fraction names.

1 whole divided into 1 equal part can be written as $\frac{1}{1}$.

2 wholes each divided into 1 equal part can be written as $\frac{2}{1}$.

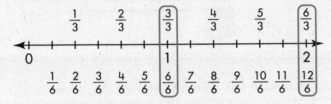

$$\frac{1}{3} \quad \frac{2}{3} \quad \frac{3}{3} \quad \frac{4}{3} \quad \frac{5}{3} \quad \frac{6}{3}$$

$$0 \qquad\qquad 1 \qquad\qquad 2$$

$$\frac{1}{6} \quad \frac{2}{6} \quad \frac{3}{6} \quad \frac{4}{6} \quad \frac{5}{6} \quad \frac{6}{6} \quad \frac{7}{6} \quad \frac{8}{6} \quad \frac{9}{6} \quad \frac{10}{6} \quad \frac{11}{6} \quad \frac{12}{6}$$

You can name fractions as whole numbers and whole numbers as fractions.

This number line shows other equivalent fractions for 1 and 2. You can see how many equal parts make up 1 or 2 wholes.

$$1 = \frac{1}{1} = \frac{3}{3} = \frac{6}{6}$$

$$2 = \frac{2}{1} = \frac{6}{3} = \frac{12}{6}$$

In **1–4**, complete each number line.

1. sixths

$$0 \qquad \frac{2}{6} \qquad \frac{5}{6} \quad 1 \qquad \frac{9}{6} \qquad 2$$

2. thirds

$$0 \qquad 1 \qquad 2 \qquad 3 \qquad 4$$

3. fourths

$$0 \qquad\qquad 1 \qquad\qquad 2$$

4. halves

$$0 \qquad\qquad 1 \qquad\qquad 2 \qquad\qquad 3$$

In **5–8**, write two equivalent fractions for each whole number. You can draw number lines to help.

5. $3 = \frac{\square}{1} = \frac{\square}{3}$

6. $2 = \frac{\square}{1} = \frac{\square}{4}$

7. $8 = \frac{\square}{1} = \frac{\square}{2}$

8. $1 = \frac{\square}{2} = \frac{\square}{3}$

In **9–12**, for each pair of fractions, write the equivalent whole number.

9. $\frac{12}{3} = \frac{4}{1} =$

10. $\frac{18}{3} = \frac{6}{1} =$

11. $\frac{5}{5} = \frac{3}{3} =$

12. $\frac{15}{3} = \frac{5}{1} =$

13. Andy earned $38 on Monday and $34 on Tuesday. How many lucky bamboo plants can he buy with the total money he earned?

Lucky Bamboo Plants $9 each

14. **Critique Reasoning** Julio says, "To turn the whole number 3 into a fraction, I just put 3 under a numerator of 3." Is he correct? Explain.

15. **Look for Relationships** What do you notice about all fractions that are equivalent to 2? Explain and give an example.

16. The kid's meal at Happy Time Diner comes with an apple slice that is $\frac{1}{4}$ of a whole apple. How many kid's meals would need to be ordered to have 3 whole apples?

17. Kevin is selling apples at the farmer's market. He arranges 32 apples into an array with 4 rows. How many columns of apples are there?

18. **Higher Order Thinking** Look at the fraction strip diagram. Write the whole number represented and its equivalent fraction name. Then write a story problem where the same whole number equals the fraction.

1			1			1		
$\frac{1}{3}$	$\frac{1}{3}$	$\frac{1}{3}$	$\frac{1}{3}$	$\frac{1}{3}$	$\frac{1}{3}$	$\frac{1}{3}$	$\frac{1}{3}$	$\frac{1}{3}$

✓ **Assessment**

19. Complete the equations. Draw lines to match the whole number on the left to the equivalent fractions on the right.

3		$\frac{2}{1} = \frac{4}{2} = ?$
5		$\frac{15}{3} = \frac{5}{1} = ?$
1		$\frac{9}{3} = \frac{12}{4} = ?$
2		$\frac{8}{8} = \frac{1}{1} = ?$

Name _____

☆ ☆
Solve & Share

Lindsey and Matt are running in a 1-mile race. They have both run the same distance so far. Write a fraction that shows how far Lindsey could have run. Write a different fraction that shows how far Matt could have run. Construct a math argument to support your answer.

Running Track

Thinking Habits

*Be a good thinker!
These questions can help you.*

- How can I use numbers, objects, drawings, or actions to justify my argument?

- Am I using numbers and symbols correctly?

- Is my explanation clear and complete?

Look Back! **Construct Arguments** Are the two fractions you wrote equivalent? How do you know?

How Can You Construct Arguments?

A

Clara and Ana are making rugs. The rugs will be the same size. Clara has finished $\frac{3}{4}$ of her rug. Ana has finished $\frac{3}{8}$ of her rug. Who has finished more of her rug?

Conjecture: Clara has finished a greater portion of her rug than Ana.

A conjecture is a statement that you think is true. It needs to be proved.

How can I explain why my conjecture is correct?

I need to construct an argument to justify my conjecture.

Here's my thinking...

B **How can I construct an argument?**

I can

- use numbers, objects, drawings, or actions correctly to explain my thinking.

- make sure my explanation is simple, complete, and easy to understand.

C I will use drawings and numbers to explain my thinking.

The number lines represent the same whole. One is divided into fourths. One is divided into eighths.

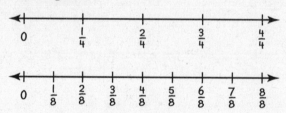

The number lines show that 3 of the fourths is greater than 3 of the eighths.

So, $\frac{3}{4} > \frac{3}{8}$. The conjecture is correct.

Convince Me! **Construct Arguments** Use numbers to construct another math argument to justify the conjecture above. Think about how you can look at the numerator and the denominator.

Name _____

☆ Guided Practice *

Construct Arguments

Paul and Anna are eating burritos. The burritos are the same size. Paul ate $\frac{4}{6}$ of a burrito. Anna ate $\frac{2}{3}$ of a burrito. Conjecture: Paul and Anna ate the same amount.

1. Draw a diagram to help you justify the conjecture.

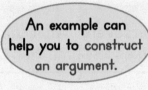
An example can help you to construct an argument.

2. Is the conjecture correct? Construct an argument to justify your answer.

☆ Independent Practice ☆

Construct Arguments

Reyna has a blue ribbon that is 1 yard long and a red ribbon that is 2 yards long. She uses $\frac{1}{2}$ of the red ribbon and $\frac{2}{4}$ of the blue ribbon.

Conjecture: Reyna used the same amount of red and blue ribbon.

3. Draw a diagram to help you justify the conjecture.

4. Is the conjecture correct? Construct an argument to justify your answer.

5. Explain another way you could justify the conjecture.

Problem Solving

Performance Assessment

School Fair

21 students worked at the school fair. Mrs. Gold's students worked at a class booth. The table shows the fraction of 1 hour that her students worked on Monday. Mrs. Gold wants to know all the students who worked less time than Cathy on Monday.

DATA	Student	Tim	Cathy	Jose	Pedro
	Hours Worked	$\frac{1}{4}$	$\frac{2}{4}$	$\frac{2}{6}$	$\frac{3}{4}$

6. **Make Sense and Persevere** What comparisons do you need to make to find out who worked less time than Cathy on Monday?

7. **Be Precise** What is the whole for Cathy's time? Do the times for the other students use the same whole?

8. **Use Appropriate Tools** What tool could you use to solve this problem? Explain how you would use this tool.

> When you construct arguments, you explain why a conjecture is true.

9. **Construct Arguments** Who worked less time than Cathy? Construct a math argument to justify your answer.

Help Practice Tools Games
Buddy

Another Look!

Tonya and Josh have aquariums that are the same size.
Tonya poured enough water to fill $\frac{1}{2}$ of her aquarium.
Josh poured enough water to fill $\frac{3}{6}$ of his aquarium.

Conjecture: Tonya and Josh each poured the same amount
of water.

Tell how you can justify the conjecture.

When you construct
an argument, you can explain
why your work is mathematically
correct.

- I can use numbers, objects, drawings, or actions
  to explain.

- I can make sure my argument is simple, complete, and
  easy to understand.

Construct an argument to justify the conjecture.

Both fractions are for the same whole. The number line shows
that $\frac{1}{2} = \frac{3}{6}$, so Tonya and Josh each poured the same amount
of water.

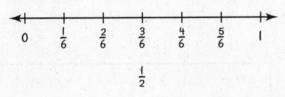

Construct Arguments Mr. Demming jogs for $\frac{13}{8}$ of a mile.
Mrs. Demming jogs for $\frac{13}{6}$ of a mile.

Conjecture: Mrs. Demming jogs farther than Mr. Demming.

1. What are important things to think about when justifying
   a conjecture?

2. Construct an argument to justify the conjecture.

3. Explain another way you could justify the conjecture.

Fruit Smoothie

Liza found a recipe for a fruit smoothie. She wants to know if any ingredients make up an equal amount of the smoothie.

Ingredient	Cups
Vanilla Yogurt	$\frac{6}{8}$
Pineapples	$\frac{1}{4}$
Bananas	$\frac{2}{3}$
Strawberries	$\frac{4}{6}$
Oranges	$\frac{2}{4}$

DATA

4. **Make Sense and Persevere** What comparisons do you need to make to find which ingredients have equal amounts in the smoothie?

5. **Be Precise** What is the whole for the fractions in this problem? Do all the fractions have the same whole?

6. **Model with Math** Use the number lines to represent the fraction of each ingredient. What do equivalent fractions represent?

7. **Construct Arguments** Do any ingredients make up an equal amount of the smoothie? Construct a math argument to explain why or why not.

Diagrams such as number lines can help you to construct an argument.

Find a Match

Work with a partner. Point to a clue.

Read the clue.

Look below the clues to find a match. Write the clue letter in the box next to the match.

Find a match for every clue.

I can ...
multiply and divide within 100.

Clues

A Is equal to 3 × 3	**E** Is equal to 35 ÷ 5	**I** Is equal to 2 × 5
B Is equal to 4 × 4	**F** Is equal to 12 ÷ 4	**J** Is equal to 3 × 10
C Is equal to 9 × 4	**G** Is equal to 5 × 4	**K** Is equal to 9 × 2
D Is equal to 0 ÷ 10	**H** Is equal to 3 × 8	**L** Is equal to 2 × 4

☐ 6 × 6	☐ 3)‾27‾	☐ 6 × 4
☐ 40 ÷ 4	☐ 0 × 9	☐ 3 × 6
☐ 32 ÷ 4	☐ 5 × 6	☐ 4)‾28‾
☐ 10 × 2	☐ 7)‾21‾	☐ 8 × 2

Word List

- denominator
- equivalent fractions
- fraction
- number line
- numerator
- unit fraction

Understand Vocabulary

Write T for *true* or F for *false*.

1. _____ $\frac{1}{6}$ and $\frac{2}{6}$ have the same numerator.

2. _____ $\frac{1}{2}$ and $\frac{4}{8}$ are equivalent fractions.

3. _____ $\frac{3}{8}$ is a unit fraction.

4. _____ A whole number can be written as a fraction.

5. _____ The denominator in $\frac{1}{3}$ and in $\frac{2}{3}$ is the same.

6. _____ A number line always shows fractions.

For each of these terms, give an example and a non-example.

	Example	**Non-example**
7. fraction	_____	_____
8. unit fraction	_____	_____
9. equivalent fractions	_____	_____

Use Vocabulary in Writing

10. Use at least 2 terms from the Word List to explain how to compare $\frac{1}{2}$ and $\frac{1}{3}$.

Name _____

Set A pages 673–678

Two fractions are equivalent if they name the same part of a whole.

What is one fraction that is equivalent to $\frac{6}{8}$?

You can use fraction strips to find equivalent fractions.

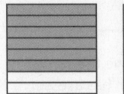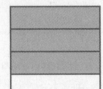

$\frac{6}{8} = \frac{3}{4}$

You can also use area models to see that $\frac{6}{8}$ and $\frac{3}{4}$ are equivalent fractions. The fractions shaded both show the same part of the whole.

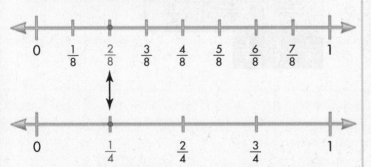

Remember to check that both sets of strips are the same length.

In **1** and **2**, find an equivalent fraction. Use fraction strips and models to help.

1.

$\frac{4}{6} = \boxed{}$

2.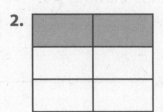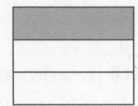

$\frac{2}{6} = \boxed{}$

Set B pages 679–684

Riley says the library is $\frac{2}{8}$ of a mile from their house. Sydney says it is $\frac{1}{4}$ of a mile.

Use a number line to find who is correct.

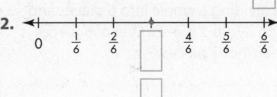

The fractions $\frac{2}{8}$ and $\frac{1}{4}$ are equivalent. They are the same distance from 0 on a number line. Riley and Sydney are both correct.

Remember equivalent fractions have different names, but they represent the same point on a number line.

In **1** and **2**, write two fractions that name the same location on the number line.

1.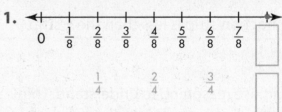

2.

You can use fraction strips to compare fractions with the same denominator.

Compare $\frac{3}{4}$ to $\frac{2}{4}$.

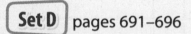

The denominator of each fraction is 4.

Three $\frac{1}{4}$ fraction strips show $\frac{3}{4}$.

Two $\frac{1}{4}$ fraction strips show $\frac{2}{4}$.

The fraction strips showing $\frac{3}{4}$ have 1 more unit fraction than the strips showing $\frac{2}{4}$.

So $\frac{3}{4} > \frac{2}{4}$.

Remember that if fractions have the same denominator, the greater fraction has a greater numerator.

In **1–3**, compare. Write $<$, $>$, or $=$. Use fraction strips to help.

1.

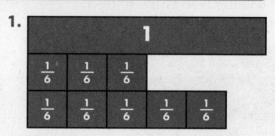

$\frac{3}{6} \bigcirc \frac{5}{6}$

2. $\frac{4}{6} \bigcirc \frac{5}{6}$ 3. $\frac{5}{8} \bigcirc \frac{3}{8}$

You can use fraction strips to compare fractions with the same numerator.

Compare $\frac{1}{6}$ to $\frac{1}{2}$.

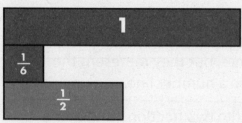

The numerator of each fraction is 1.

The $\frac{1}{6}$ fraction strip is less than the $\frac{1}{2}$ strip.

So $\frac{1}{6} < \frac{1}{2}$.

You can use reasoning to understand. Think about dividing a whole into 6 pieces and dividing it into 2 pieces. One of 6 pieces is less than 1 of 2 pieces.

Remember that if fractions have the same numerator, the greater fraction has a lesser denominator.

In **1–3**, compare. Write $<$, $>$, or $=$. Use fraction strips to help.

1.

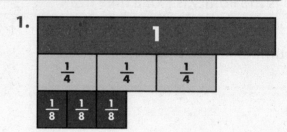

$\frac{3}{4} \bigcirc \frac{3}{8}$

2. $\frac{5}{6} \bigcirc \frac{5}{8}$ 3. $\frac{1}{3} \bigcirc \frac{1}{2}$

Set E | pages 697–702 _____

You can compare fractions using benchmark numbers such as 0, $\frac{1}{2}$, and 1.

Chris and Mary are painting pictures. The pictures are the same size. Chris has painted $\frac{3}{4}$ of his picture. Mary has painted $\frac{3}{8}$ of her picture. Who has painted the greater amount?

$\frac{3}{4}$ is greater than $\frac{1}{2}$.

$\frac{3}{8}$ is less than $\frac{1}{2}$.

Chris has painted the greater amount.

Reteaching
Continued

Remember that you can compare each fraction to a benchmark number to see how they relate to each other.

In **1** and **2**, use benchmark numbers to help solve.

1. Mike had $\frac{2}{6}$ of a candy bar. Sally had $\frac{4}{6}$ of a candy bar. Whose fraction of a candy bar was closer to 1? Closer to 0?

2. Paul compared two bags of rice. One weighs $\frac{4}{6}$ pound, and the other weighs $\frac{4}{8}$ pound. Which bag is heavier?

Set F | pages 703–708 _____

You can use a number line to compare fractions.

Which is greater, $\frac{3}{6}$ or $\frac{4}{6}$?

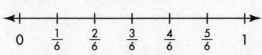

$\frac{4}{6}$ is farther to the right than $\frac{3}{6}$, so $\frac{4}{6}$ is greater.

You can also compare two fractions with the same numerator by drawing two number lines.

Which is greater, $\frac{2}{4}$ or $\frac{2}{3}$?

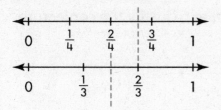

$\frac{2}{3}$ is farther to the right than $\frac{2}{4}$, so $\frac{2}{3}$ is greater.

Remember to draw two number lines that are equal in length when comparing fractions with different denominators.

In **1** and **2**, compare. Write $<$, $>$, or $=$. Use number lines to help.

1. $\frac{2}{6} \bigcirc \frac{3}{6}$

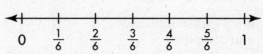

2. $\frac{3}{4} \bigcirc \frac{3}{6}$

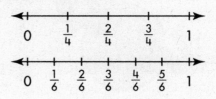

How many thirds are in 2 wholes?

You can use a number line or fraction strips to find a fraction name for 2 using thirds.

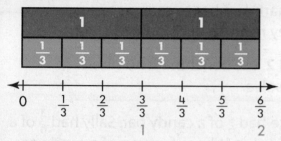

$2 = \frac{6}{3}$

The whole number 2 can also be written as the fraction $\frac{6}{3}$.

Remember that when you write whole numbers as fractions, the numerator can be greater than the denominator.

In **1–4**, write an equivalent fraction for each whole number.

1. 3   **2.** 2

3. 5   **4.** 1

In **5–8**, for each fraction write the equivalent whole number.

5. $\frac{6}{3}$ **6.** $\frac{10}{2}$

7. $\frac{14}{2}$ **8.** $\frac{8}{8}$

Think about these questions to help you **construct arguments.**

Thinking Habits

- How can I use numbers, objects, drawings, or actions to justify my argument?

- Am I using numbers and symbols correctly?

- Is my explanation clear and complete?

Remember that when you construct an argument, you explain why your work is right.

Odell and Tamra paint two walls with the same dimensions. Odell paints $\frac{2}{6}$ of a wall. Tamra paints $\frac{1}{3}$ of the other wall. Conjecture: Odell and Tamra paint the same amount.

1. Draw a diagram to justify the conjecture.

2. Use the diagram to justify the conjecture.

1. Three friends work on a project. Cindy does $\frac{4}{8}$ of the project. Kim does $\frac{3}{8}$ of the project. Sandy does $\frac{1}{8}$ of the project. How much of the project do they complete all together?

2. Serena can compare $\frac{3}{4}$ to $\frac{3}{6}$ without using fraction strips. She says that a whole divided into 6 equal parts will have smaller parts than the same whole divided into 4 equal parts. Three smaller parts must be less than 3 larger parts, so $\frac{3}{6}$ is less than $\frac{3}{4}$. Is Serena correct? Choose the best answer.

   Ⓐ Yes, she is correct.

   Ⓑ No, the wholes do not have to be the same size to compare the fractions.

   Ⓒ No, 4 is less than 6, so $\frac{3}{4}$ is less than $\frac{3}{6}$.

   Ⓓ No, both fractions are equal.

3. Jill finished reading $\frac{2}{3}$ of a book for a summer reading project. Owen read $\frac{2}{8}$ of the same book. Who read more of the book?

   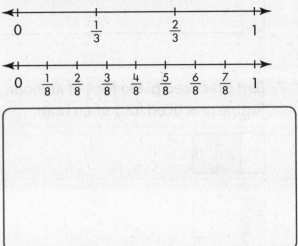

4. There is $\frac{1}{4}$ of a pear in every container of fruit salad. Show the number of pears in 8 containers using a fraction.

5. During the time allowed, Della swam $\frac{3}{6}$ of the length of the pool. Loren swam $\frac{4}{6}$ of it. Write the correct symbol to compare the fractions.

   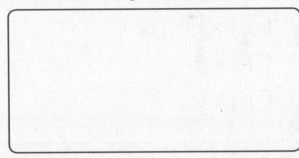

   $\frac{3}{6}$ ◯ $\frac{4}{6}$

6. Mark and Sidney each have a piece of wood that is the same size. Mark paints $\frac{2}{8}$ of his piece of wood. Sidney paints $\frac{5}{8}$ of her piece of wood. Who painted a fraction that is closer to 1 than to 0?

7. Bart practiced piano for $\frac{2}{3}$ of an hour. Ruthie practiced for $\frac{2}{4}$ of an hour.

Which comparisons are true? Choose all that apply.

☐ $\frac{2}{3} < \frac{2}{4}$

☐ $\frac{2}{4} > \frac{2}{3}$

☐ $\frac{2}{3} > \frac{2}{4}$

☐ $\frac{2}{3} = \frac{2}{4}$

☐ $\frac{2}{4} < \frac{2}{3}$

8. Greg colored the fraction model below. Which fractions name the purple part of the model? Choose all that apply.

☐ $\frac{1}{2}$ ☐ $\frac{3}{4}$

☐ $\frac{2}{3}$ ☐ $\frac{4}{6}$

                ☐ $\frac{6}{8}$

9. Two students each bought a school lunch. Yoon ate $\frac{2}{3}$ of her sandwich. Ed ate $\frac{3}{3}$ of his sandwich.

1		
$\frac{1}{3}$	$\frac{1}{3}$	
$\frac{1}{3}$	$\frac{1}{3}$	$\frac{1}{3}$

Which is a true comparison?

Ⓐ $\frac{2}{3} > \frac{3}{3}$

Ⓑ $\frac{3}{3} < \frac{2}{3}$

Ⓒ $\frac{2}{3} < \frac{3}{3}$

Ⓓ $\frac{2}{3} = \frac{3}{3}$

10. Carl and Jen shared some large sandwiches that were the same size and cut into eighths. Carl ate $\frac{7}{8}$ sandwich and Jen ate $\frac{6}{8}$ sandwich. Who ate more? Explain.

Name _____

11. George wants to know if two pieces of wire are the same length. One wire is $\frac{6}{8}$ of a foot. The other is $\frac{3}{4}$ of a foot. Complete the fractions on the number line to show they are the same length.

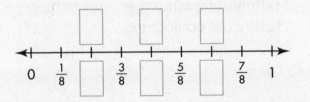

12. Lezlie hiked $\frac{3}{8}$ of a mile on Monday. On Wednesday she hiked $\frac{3}{6}$ of a mile. She hiked $\frac{3}{4}$ of a mile on Friday. Use benchmark numbers to find which day Lezlie hiked the farthest.

13. Jamal spent the day making a painting for his friend. At the end of the day, Jamal finished $\frac{1}{2}$ of a painting. If he is able to finish the same amount of a painting each day, what fraction shows the number of paintings Jamal can make in 4 days?

Ⓐ $\frac{2}{2}$

Ⓑ $\frac{2}{4}$

Ⓒ $\frac{1}{4}$

Ⓓ $\frac{4}{2}$

14. Meagan ate $\frac{3}{4}$ of a cookie. Write an equivalent fraction for the amount of cookie Meagan did not eat.

15. Alejandra brought 2 pies to a potluck dinner. There was $\frac{4}{6}$ of the blueberry pie left and $\frac{5}{6}$ of the apple pie left.

 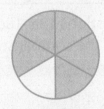

Blueberry   Apple

Choose all of the comparisons that are true.

☐ $\frac{5}{6} < \frac{4}{6}$

☐ $\frac{4}{6} > \frac{5}{6}$

☐ $\frac{4}{6} < \frac{5}{6}$

☐ $\frac{5}{6} > \frac{4}{6}$

☐ $\frac{5}{6} = \frac{4}{6}$

16. Write each fraction in the correct location on a number line. Then circle the equivalent fractions shown on the number lines.

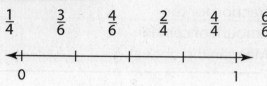

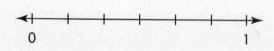

17. Draw lines to match equivalent fractions.

$\frac{1}{2}$		$\frac{4}{4}$
$\frac{3}{3}$		$\frac{4}{2}$
$\frac{4}{6}$		$\frac{2}{3}$
$\frac{6}{3}$		$\frac{4}{8}$

18. For questions 18a–18d, choose *Yes* or *No* to tell if the comparison is true.

18a. $\frac{4}{6} > \frac{4}{8}$ ○ Yes ○ No

18b. $\frac{4}{8} > \frac{4}{4}$ ○ Yes ○ No

18c. $\frac{4}{4} < \frac{4}{6}$ ○ Yes ○ No

18d. $\frac{4}{8} < \frac{4}{6}$ ○ Yes ○ No

19. Eva and Landon had the same math homework. Eva finished $\frac{2}{4}$ of the homework. Landon finished $\frac{4}{8}$ of the homework. Conjecture: Eva and Landon finished the same amount of their homework.

Part A

Complete the number lines to help justify the conjecture.

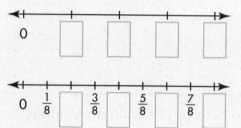

Part B

Use your diagram to justify the conjecture.

20. For each pair of fractions, write the equivalent whole number in the box.

$$\frac{16}{4} = \frac{8}{2} = \boxed{}$$

$$\frac{6}{3} = \frac{4}{2} = \boxed{}$$

$$\frac{8}{8} = \frac{6}{6} = \boxed{}$$

Name _____

Clothing Store
Devin, Jenna, Eli, and Gabby work at a clothing store. On Saturday they each worked the same number of hours.

The **Time Spent at Cash Register** table shows the fraction of time each person spent checking out customers. The **Time Spent on Customer Calls** table shows the fraction of an hour Jenna spent answering phone calls for the store.

Use the **Time Spent at Cash Register** table to answer Questions 1–3.

1. Draw fraction strips to show the fraction of time each person worked at the cash register.

1

Time Spent at Cash Register	
Name	**Fraction of Work Day**
Devin	$\frac{3}{6}$
Jenna	$\frac{2}{6}$
Eli	$\frac{6}{6}$
Gabby	$\frac{5}{6}$

2. Who spent the most time at the cash register?

3. Write a comparison to show the time Gabby spent at the cash register compared to the time Devin spent. Use >, <, or =.

4. Use the **Time Spent on Customer Calls** table to answer the question. On which day did Jenna spend closest to an hour on the phone? Explain how you know.

Time Spent on Customer Calls			
Day	Saturday	Sunday	Monday
Fraction of an Hour	$\frac{3}{6}$	$\frac{3}{5}$	$\frac{3}{4}$

The store sells different colors of men's socks. The **Socks** table shows the fraction for each sock color in the store.

Use the **Socks** table to answer Questions 5 and 6.

Socks	
Color	Fraction
white	$\frac{1}{8}$
black	$\frac{1}{4}$
brown	$\frac{3}{8}$
gray	$\frac{2}{8}$

5. **Part A**

Complete the fractions on the number line. Label the fraction that represents each sock color.

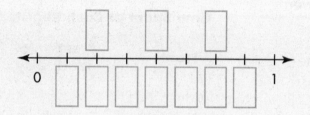

Part B

Does the store have more brown socks or more white socks?

6. Use the number line in 5 Part A to construct an argument to justify the following conjecture: The store has an equal amount of gray socks and black socks.

7. Use the **Miguel's Socks** table to answer the question.

Miguel bought some socks at the clothing store. After he washed them, he counted the number of individual socks he has. Each sock is $\frac{1}{2}$ of a pair. How many pairs of black socks does he have? Write this number as a fraction.

Miguel's Socks	
Color	Number of Socks
black	6
gray	8

Digital Resources

Solve Learn Glossary Practice Buddy

Tools Assessment Help Games

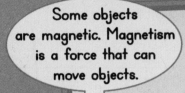

TOPIC 14

Solve Time, Capacity, and Mass Problems

Essential Question: How can time, capacity, and mass be measured and found?

> Some objects are magnetic. Magnetism is a force that can move objects.

> A magnet interacts with certain metals, such as iron. But other materials do not interact with magnets, such as paper.

> Here's a project on magnets.

Math and Science Project: Forces and Interactions

Do Research Use the Internet or other sources to find information about magnets. How are magnets used? What types of magnets are there? Attach different amounts of paper together using a metal paper clip. How can you lift the paper using the magnet? How much paper can the magnet lift?

Journal: Write a Report Include what you found. Also in your report:

- Give examples of magnetic and non-magnetic materials.

- Find the masses of the paper clip and of the paper.

- Write an equation to show how much mass you can lift using the magnet.

Name _____

Review What You Know

A-Z Vocabulary

Choose the best term from the box.
Write it on the blank.

• denominator • numerator
• number line • unit fraction

1. The number above the fraction bar is the _____.

2. The total number of equal parts is the _____.

3. One equal part of a whole can be represented using a _____.

Solving 2-Step Problems

4. Mr. Vernon takes a train for 188 miles. Then he rides a subway for 9 stops. Each stop is 2 miles apart. How far does he travel?

5. Ms. Slate has a box of 320 new light bulbs. She replaces the light bulbs in 50 lamps. Each lamp has 5 sockets. How many new light bulbs does Ms. Slate have left?

Number Lines

Label the missing numbers on the number lines.

6.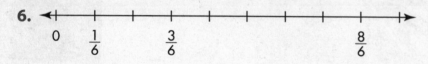

7.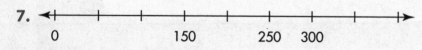

Fractions

8. Rena divides a square into 8 equal parts. What unit fraction should she write as a label for each of the parts?

   (A) $\frac{0}{8}$　　　(B) $\frac{1}{8}$　　　(C) $\frac{8}{8}$　　　(D) $\frac{8}{1}$

9. Write two fractions that are equal to $\frac{1}{2}$.

My Word Cards

Use the examples for each word on the front of the card to help complete the definitions on the back.

A-Z
Glossary

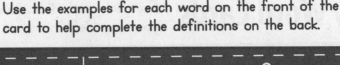

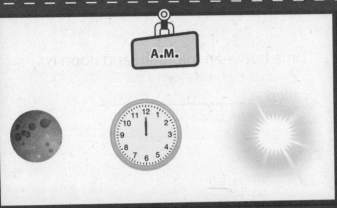

A.M.

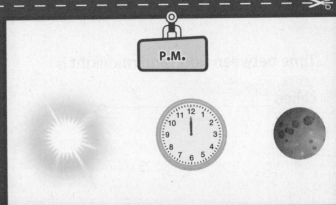

P.M.

elapsed time

Start

End

1 hour of elapsed time

time interval

35 min + ? min = 45 min

35 min + 10 min = 45 min

The time interval is 10 minutes.

Complete each definition. Extend learning by writing your own definitions.

Time between noon and midnight is

called _____.

Time between midnight and noon is

called _____.

A _____ is an amount of time.

The total amount of time that passes from the starting time to the ending

time is called _____.

My Word Cards

Use the examples for each word on the front of the card to help complete the definitions on the back.

capacity (liquid volume)

milliliter (mL)

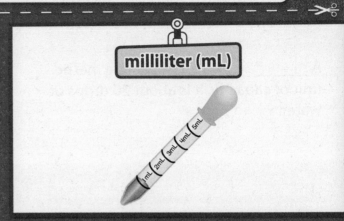

liter (L)

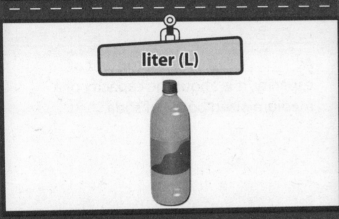

mass

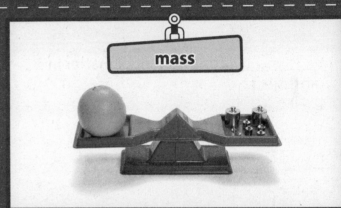

gram (g)

1 gram

kilogram (kg)

1 kilogram

My Word Cards

A _____ is a metric unit of capacity. It is about 20 drops of water.

The amount a container can hold measured in liquid units is called

_____.

_____ is the amount of matter in an object.

A _____ is a metric unit of capacity. It is about the capacity of a medium-sized bottle of soda.

A _____ is a metric unit of mass. It is about the mass of a textbook.

A _____ is a metric unit of mass. It is about the mass of a paper clip.

Name _____

Solve & Share

Xander and his mother are flying from New York to Chicago. Their plane is scheduled to arrive at 8:47. How can you use a clock to show this time? *Explain how you solved the problem.*

I can ...
show and tell time to the minute using clocks.

I can also model with math to solve problems.

Model with math. Show where the minute and hour hands should appear on the clock face at Xander's arrival time.

Look Back! **Be Precise** How many minutes before 9 is Xander's plane scheduled to arrive? To show a time after 8 but before 9, where did you draw the hour hand on the clock face? Be as precise as possible.

How Do You Tell Time to the Nearest Minute?

A

The clock shows the time a train from Memphis is scheduled to arrive at Central Station. What time is the train scheduled to arrive? Write the time in digital form and in two other ways.

Analog clocks are tools that can help you show and tell time to the nearest minute using minute and hour hands.

Digital form uses numbers and symbols to show and tell time. You can also write time using words and numbers.

B **Step 1**

The hour hand is between 12 and 1. The time is after 12:00 and before 1:00.

C **Step 2**

In 5 minutes, the minute hand moves from one number to the next.

Count by 5s from the 12 to the 8.
40 minutes

D **Step 3**

In 1 minute, the minute hand moves from one mark to the next.

Count two more minutes.
The digital time is 12:42. It is 42 minutes past 12 or 18 minutes to 1.

Convince Me! **Model with Math** A train arrives from Atlanta one hour after the Memphis train. Write the arrival time of the Atlanta train in digital form and two other ways. Use a clock face to help.

Name _____

Practice Buddy   Tools   Assessment

Do You Understand?

1. Construct Arguments In the Memphis train example, why is 42 minutes past 12 the same as 18 minutes to 1? Explain.

2. An airplane landed at 3:55. Does the clock show the time the airplane landed? Explain.

Do You Know How?

In **3** and **4**, write the time shown on each clock in two ways.

3.

4.

Independent Practice ☆

In **5–7**, write the time shown on each clock in two ways.

5.

6.

7.

Problem Solving

In **8** and **9**, use the table.

8. **Construct Arguments** Roy says that the scarf and the hat together cost about the same as a blanket and a hat. Is this a reasonable estimate? Explain.

9. What did Jorge buy at the sale if $19 + $19 + $19 + $18 stands for the total cost of his purchase?

Winter Sale		
Blanket		$19
Hat		$12
Scarf		$18

---

10. **Be Precise** Mia left her house at 25 minutes to 3. Draw hands on the clock to show when she left.

11. **Higher Order Thinking** Sandra's party started at 7:00. Her friends Theo and Lily arrive at 10 minutes after 7. Her friend Marcus arrives 35 minutes later. What time did Marcus arrive? Write this time in two other ways.

✓ **Assessment**

12. Clay and his family sit down to eat dinner at the time shown on the clock. Which of the following are other ways to write that time? Choose all that apply.

- ☐ 3:25
- ☐ 5:16
- ☐ 16 minutes after 5
- ☐ 44 minutes before 5
- ☐ 16 minutes before 5

13. Mary Ann called her grandmother. She ended the call at the time shown on the clock. Which of the following are **NOT** other ways to write this time?

- ☐ 14 minutes to 9
- ☐ 3:46
- ☐ 46 minutes after 3
- ☐ 9:19
- ☐ 14 minutes before 4

Help   Practice Buddy   Tools   Games

Another Look!

You can tell time to the minute in different ways. The hour and minute hands of the clock face show the time.

Remember to be precise. Use pictures, words, numbers, and symbols to describe time to the exact hour and minute.

In digital form, this time is written as 10:15.
You can also write the same time as 15 minutes after 10.

In **1–3**, write the time shown on each clock in two ways.

1.

2.

3.

In **4–9**, write the time in digital form. Use clocks to help.

4. 12 minutes to noon

5. 21 minutes after 2

6. 30 minutes past 9

7. 2 minutes after 7

8. 45 minutes to 6

9. 4 o'clock

10. **Be Precise** Tonya's family went to see a movie. The movie started at 4:30 and ended at 6:36. Show the time the movie ended on the clock.

11. **Math and Science** The Hubble Space Telescope has been moving in its orbit for 1 hour. In 37 more minutes it will complete an orbit. How many minutes does it take the Hubble Space Telescope to complete 1 orbit?

12. Ross started walking his dog at 3:15. He finished before 4:00. Use digital form to write a time he could have finished walking his dog.

13. **Higher Order Thinking** Jake rode his bike from 2:30 to 3:30. Then he took a shower. He finished his shower 30 minutes after the bike ride ended. What time was it when he finished his shower? How would you show this time on a clock face?

✓ **Assessment**

14. Jody and her family went to the swimming pool at the time shown on the clock. Which of the following are other ways to write this time? Choose all that apply.

- ☐ 3:13
- ☐ 2:16
- ☐ 16 minutes after 2
- ☐ 44 minutes before 4
- ☐ 13 minutes after 3

15. Phil is reading a magazine. He stops reading at the time shown on the clock. Which of the following are **NOT** other ways to write this time? Choose all that apply.

- ☐ 20 minutes after 3
- ☐ 3:20
- ☐ 7 minutes after 4
- ☐ 4:07
- ☐ 20 minutes after 1

Name _____

Solve

Solve & Share

Denise went to see a movie. The movie started at 1:05 P.M. It ended at 2:35 P.M. How long did the movie last? Explain your reasoning.

I can ...
measure intervals of time in hours and minutes.

I can also reason about math.

Start   End

Use reasoning. Use the clock faces to help you determine the change in time. *Show your work in the space below!*

Look Back! **Reasoning** Without counting hours and minutes, how do you know the movie Denise went to see was less than 2 hours long?

Essential Question **How Can You Find Elapsed Time?**

A

Janey took part in a charity walk. The walk started at 7:10 A.M. It ended at 11:20 A.M. How long did the walk last?

 Start End

Elapsed time is the total amount of time that passes from the starting time to the ending time.

The hours between midnight and noon are A.M. hours. The hours between noon and midnight are P.M. hours.

B **Step 1**

Find the starting time.

C **Step 2**

Count the hours.

1 hour

D **Step 3**

Count the minutes.

The walk lasted 4 hours, 10 minutes.

Convince Me! **Make Sense and Persevere** After the charity walk, Janey talked with friends from 11:25 A.M. to 11:40 A.M. Then lunch was served from 11:45 A.M. until 2:10 P.M. How long did lunch last?

Name _____

Another Example!

You can also use a number line to measure elapsed time.

Janey's charity walk lasted 4 hours, 10 minutes.

The number line shows the number of hours and minutes that elapsed during the walk.

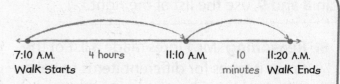

7:10 A.M.   4 hours   11:10 A.M.   10 minutes   11:20 A.M.
Walk Starts   Walk Ends

⭐ Guided Practice *

Do You Understand?

1. Reasoning If a start time is 7:15 A.M. and an end time is 8:05 A.M., why do you not have to count hours to find the elapsed time?

2. A movie started at 2:30 P.M. and ran for 2 hours, 15 minutes. What time did the movie end?

Do You Know How?

3. Draw arrows on the second clock to count the hours from 11:00 A.M. to 5:00 P.M. What is the elapsed time?

Start   **End**

⭐ Independent Practice *

Leveled Practice In **4–7**, find the elapsed or end time.

4. Start Time: 6:30 P.M.   End Time: 9:50 P.M.

Hours from 6:30 P.M. to 9:30 P.M. _____

Minutes from 9:30 P.M. to 9:50 P.M. _____

The elapsed time is __ hours, ___ minutes.

5. Start Time: 10:00 A.M.

End Time: 3:00 P.M.
Elapsed Time:

_____

6. Start Time: 9:15 A.M.

End Time: 10:45 A.M.
Elapsed Time:

_____

7. Start Time: 11:30 A.M.

Elapsed Time: 5 hours, 25 minutes
End Time:

_____

Problem Solving

In **8** and **9**, use the list at the right.

8. **Reasoning** Mr. Flores made a list of the times it takes for different items to bake. Which items will take less than $\frac{1}{2}$ hour to bake?

Item	Baking Time in Minutes
Bread	27
Granola Bars	21
Pasta Dish	48
Vegetables	24

9. Which two items, when you add their baking time together, take less time to bake than the pasta dish?

10. **Reasoning** Sally finds elapsed time using these clock faces. She counts the hours by 1s, but counts the minutes by 5s. Why does she count the minutes by 5s instead of by 1s?

Start

End

11. **Higher Order Thinking** A basketball tournament started at 12:15 P.M. and ended at 4:00 P.M. Did the tournament last more than 4 hours? Explain.

12. **Algebra** A farmer is selling 744 pieces of produce. He has 162 watermelons, 345 ears of sweet corn, and some avocados. Write an equation to find how many avocados the farmer is selling. Let *a* stand for the unknown quantity of avocados.

13. Geo is taking a train from Carlton to Elgin. The train leaves Carlton at 9:25 A.M. and reaches Elgin at 10:55 A.M. How long does the ride last? Use the number line to help.

9:25 A.M.
Train
Leaves

10:25 A.M.

10:55 A.M.
Train
Arrives

Name _____

Another Look!

A children's museum is open from 1:00 P.M. to 6:35 P.M. every day. How long is the museum open?

Step 1

Begin at the starting time.

Step 2

Count the hours.

Step 3

Count the minutes.

There are 5 hours.

There are 35 minutes.

Use a clock face to find elapsed time.

The museum is open 5 hours, 35 minutes.

In **1–6**, find the elapsed or end time. You may use the clock faces or a number line to help.

1. Start Time: 3:30 P.M.
End Time: 7:00 P.M.
Elapsed Time:

_____

2. Start Time: 8:10 A.M.
End Time: 10:55 A.M.
Elapsed Time:

_____

3. Start Time: 3:20 P.M.
End Time: 6:00 P.M.
Elapsed Time:

_____

4. Start Time: 1:20 P.M.
End Time: 2:00 P.M.
Elapsed Time:

_____

5. Start Time: 8:00 A.M.
Elapsed Time: 5 hours, 15 minutes
End Time:

_____

6. Start Time: 7:30 A.M.
Elapsed Time: 2 hours, 20 minutes
End Time:

_____

7. **Algebra** Mindy divides a rectangular piece of fabric into 8 equal-size pieces for two sewing projects. For Project A, she will use $\frac{1}{2}$ of the fabric. For Project B, she will use $\frac{1}{4}$ of the original fabric. Draw a model to show how the fabric was divided, and which pieces will be used. What unit fraction represents one of the pieces? Write an equation to find how much of the fabric will not be used. Let f represent the fraction of leftover fabric.

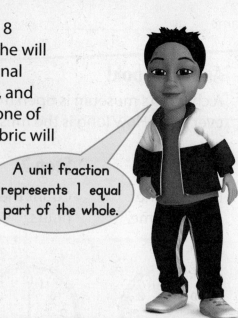

A unit fraction represents 1 equal part of the whole.

8. **Critique Reasoning** Tanner is finding $569 + 274$. His work thus far is shown below. Do you agree with how he added the tens? Finish the problem to find the sum and explain the steps you took.

$$
\begin{array}{r}
\overset{1}{5}69 \\
+274 \\
\hline
3
\end{array}
$$

9. **Make Sense and Persevere**
A movie starts at 2:30 P.M. and ends at 4:15 P.M. After the movie Anne and her friends go for ice cream. They eat ice cream from 4:30 P.M. to 5:00 P.M. How much time elapsed from the start of the movie to the time the friends finished their ice cream?

10. Gary's father dropped him off at soccer practice at 2:45 P.M. Gary's mother picked him up at 5:00 P.M. How long did soccer practice last?

11. **Higher Order Thinking** Raquel attended a volleyball game that began at 9:30 A.M. and ended at 11:45 A.M. She began her lunch at 12:00 P.M., and ended lunch at 1:00 P.M. How much time did Raquel spend at the game and at lunch?

 Assessment

12. A picnic starts at 12:10 P.M. Kevin arrives at 1:40 P.M. The picnic continues until 3 P.M. How much time elapsed between the time the picnic started and Kevin's arrival? Use a number line to help.

12:10 P.M.
Picnic
Starts

1:40 P.M.
Kevin
Arrives

Name _____

Solve & Share

Madison wants to exercise 30 minutes every day. Before school, she only has enough time to exercise for 10 minutes or less. One day, she exercised for 8 minutes before school and 22 minutes after school. This is one way she can exercise for 30 minutes.

Find some other ways she can exercise before school and after school to reach her goal of exercising for 30 minutes each day. **Solve this problem any way you choose. Show your work.**

I can ...
use representations to solve word problems about time.

I can also model with math to solve problems.

Model with math. A number line, bar diagram, or table can be used to show different ways Madison can use her time to exercise 30 minutes each day.

Look Back! **Construct Arguments** Do you think you found all of the ways to solve the problem above? Explain.

How Can You Add or Subtract Time Intervals?

A

Joaquin made a list of the time he should spend on different activities. Joaquin has practiced playing the piano 35 minutes so far. How much longer does he need to practice?

A time interval is an amount of time.

After-School Activities

Play with Ron: 50 min
Practice Piano: 45 min
Homework: 60 min

B

One Way

You can use a bar diagram to represent the problem and show time intervals.

45 minutes

35	?

$35 + ? = 45$
$35 + 10 = 45$

What amount of time do you need to add to 35 minutes to make 45 minutes?

Joaquin has to practice 10 more minutes.

C

Another Way

You can use a number line to represent the problem and show time intervals.

35 minutes

45 minutes

0   10   20   30   40   50

10 minutes

$45 - 35 = ?$
$45 - 35 = 10$

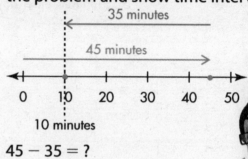

Joaquin has to practice 10 more minutes.

Convince Me! **Model with Math** How much longer will it take Joaquin to finish all of his after-school activities? Show one way to represent and solve.

© Pearson Education, Inc. 3

☆Guided Practice*

Do You Understand?

In **1** and **2**, complete the bar diagram or number line to solve.

1. Rhody plans to ride his bicycle for 55 minutes. So far, he has ridden for 29 minutes. How many more minutes does he have to ride?

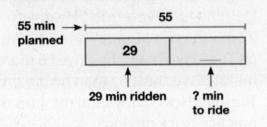

55 min → planned

55

29

29 min ridden | ? min to ride

Do You Know How?

2. Ms. Darren spends the reading period working with two different reading groups. She meets with the first group for 23 minutes and meets with the second group for 17 minutes. How long is the reading period?

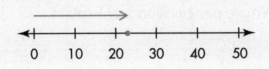

0   10   20   30   40   50

Independent Practice ☆

Leveled Practice In **3–6**, complete or draw a bar diagram or number line to solve.

3. Claire and Owen played video games. The first game lasted 24 minutes. After the first game, Claire and Owen had lunch for 30 minutes. The second game lasted 36 minutes. How many minutes did they play the games?

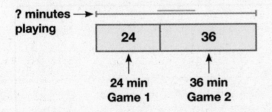

? minutes → playing

24   36

24 min Game 1 | 36 min Game 2

4. Yan jogged for 60 minutes on Friday. Dino jogged 12 fewer minutes than Yan. Both friends swim for 40 minutes each week. How many minutes did Dino jog on Friday?

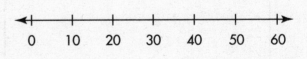

0   10   20   30   40   50   60

5. Mr. Hart's class is putting on a play. The play is divided into two acts. Each act lasts 27 minutes. How many minutes long is the play?

6. A chef wants to bake a meal for 30 minutes. So far, the meal has been baking for 12 minutes. How many more minutes does the meal need to bake?

*For another example, see Set C on page 796.

Topic 14 | Lesson 14-3   **753**

Problem Solving

7. Reasoning Ms. Merrill spends 55 minutes washing all the windows in her two-story house. How much time could she have spent on each floor? Complete the chart to show three different ways.

Time Spent Washing Windows	
1st floor	2nd floor
25 min	

8. Number Sense Harry measures a pencil that is $\frac{4}{2}$ inches. Rhea's pencil is $\frac{6}{2}$ inches. Whose pencil is longer? Explain.

9. Higher Order Thinking Mr. Collins is learning to drive a truck. He drives 22 minutes on Monday and 14 minutes on Tuesday. Finally, he drives 6 more minutes Wednesday than he did on Tuesday. How many total minutes did he practice truck driving?

 Assessment

10. Sonya hikes up Mount Baldy. It takes her 25 minutes to hike to a cliff that is partway up the mountain. After that, she hikes for 17 more minutes. How many total minutes did Sonya spend hiking?

Part A

Draw a number line to show the problem.

Part B

Solve the problem.

11. Meg walks a dog named Shep for 12 minutes. Then, she walks Sparky. Finally, she walks Brownie for 18 minutes. Meg spends 52 minutes walking all three dogs. How much time did Meg spend walking Sparky?

Part A

Draw a bar diagram to show the problem.

Part B

Solve the problem.

Name _____

Another Look!

Jed has 2 homework assignments. He spends 15 minutes doing his math homework. Then, he spends 38 minutes doing his reading homework. How much time does Jed spend doing his homework?

Draw a number line.

First show the number of minutes Jed spends doing his math homework. Then add the number of minutes Jed spends doing his reading homework.

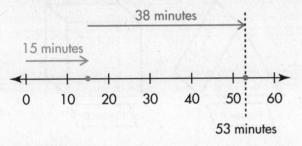

> You can add and subtract time intervals using a number line.

$15 + 38 = ?$

$15 + 38 = 53$. So, Jed spends 53 minutes doing homework.

In **1–4**, complete or draw a bar diagram or number line to solve.

1. A bus travels for 22 minutes from Greensburg to Pleasant Valley. Then it travels 16 minutes from Pleasant Valley to Red Mill. How many minutes does it travel?

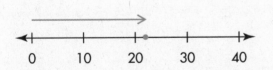

2. Ethan needs to spend 35 minutes cleaning his room. So far, he has been cleaning for 11 minutes. How many more minutes does he need to spend cleaning?

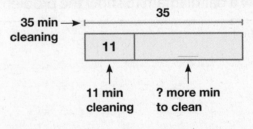

3. James plans on spending 60 minutes each day practicing pitching for baseball. He only has 14 minutes left to practice today. How many minutes has James already practiced today?

4. Margot helps out at a horse farm. She spends 26 minutes one morning brushing a horse. She spends 39 minutes that same day brushing another horse. How many minutes does she brush horses in all?

5. Make Sense and Persevere A barber cuts 3 people's hair in 35 minutes. Each haircut takes at least 10 minutes, and the first haircut takes the most time. List one way the barber could cut 3 people's hair given this information.

6. 🅰️🅩 **Vocabulary** Write a math problem that uses the word *time interval*.

7. Higher Order Thinking Mr. Maxwell spends 34 minutes working in his garden and 25 minutes raking leaves. His son helps him for 10 minutes in the garden and 15 minutes raking leaves. How many minutes does Mr. Maxwell work when his son is **NOT** helping him?

8. Lisa drew the two geometric figures below. Write a statement describing one way the figures are different.

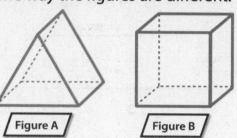

Figure A   **Figure B**

 Assessment

9. Colby's art class is 50 minutes. She spends 21 minutes cutting paper and the rest of the time making a collage. How much time did Colby spend making her collage?

Part A

Draw a bar diagram to show the problem.

Part B

Solve the problem.

10. Dennis spent 39 minutes writing in his journal and 43 minutes talking to a friend. How much time did Dennis spend writing and talking?

Part A

Draw a number line to show the problem.

Part B

Solve the problem.

© Pearson Education, Inc. 3

Name _____

Solve & Share

The water bottle below has a capacity of 1 liter. Estimate the capacity of a large bowl using liters. Use a 1-liter container and a large bowl to solve this problem. **Solve this problem any way you choose.**

I can ...
use standard units to estimate liquid volumes.

I can also be precise in my work.

1 L

When you estimate and measure things, remember to be precise. What unit should you use to estimate the capacity of the large bowl? *Show your work.*

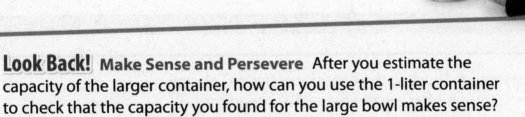

Look Back! **Make Sense and Persevere** After you estimate the capacity of the larger container, how can you use the 1-liter container to check that the capacity you found for the large bowl makes sense?

Essential Question **What Metric Units Are Used to Estimate and Measure Liquid Volume?**

A

What is the capacity of the pail?

A milliliter is about 20 drops from an eyedropper.

Milliliter (mL)

This water bottle holds about 1 liter.

Liter (L)

Capacity (liquid volume) is the amount a container can hold measured in liquid units. Two metric units of capacity are milliliters and liters.

?

B **Step 1**

Choose an appropriate unit and estimate.

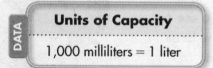
DATA

Units of Capacity

1,000 milliliters = 1 liter

A milliliter is too small. So, use liters. The pail appears to be large enough to hold several liters.

C **Step 2**

Check that the estimate makes sense.

Count how many times you can fill a liter container and empty it into the pail.

The pail holds about 8 liters.

Convince Me! **Reasoning** Suppose the capacity of the pail above is given in milliliters. Is this number greater than or less than the number of liters? Use reasoning about the size of metric units of capacity to explain how you know.

Name _____

Guided Practice

Do You Understand?

1. **Be Precise** Susie made a large pot of soup for her family. The pot Susie used has a capacity of 5 liters. Why could the capacity of the same pot be 5,000 milliliters?

2. **Generalize** Find a container that you predict will hold more than a liter and another that you predict will hold less than a liter. Use liter and milliliter containers to check your predictions by finding the actual capacity of each container.

Do You Know How?

In **3–6**, circle the better estimate for each.

3.

4.

250 mL or 2 L   5 mL or 1 L

5. Bottle of juice   6. Cereal bowl

10 mL or 1 L   300 mL or 3 L

Independent Practice

In **7–14**, circle the better estimate for each.

7.

8.

9.

10.

40 mL or 40 L   15 mL or 1 L   14 mL or 14 L   250 mL or 250 L

11. Teacup   12. Bathtub   13. Bottle cap   14. Teapot

150 mL or 15 L   115 mL or 115 L   3 mL or 3 L   1 L or 10 L

15. Write an estimate for the capacity of a dog bowl. _____

16. Write an estimate for the capacity of a vase. _____

*For another example, see Set D on page 796.

Problem Solving

17. Generalize Which cooler has the greater capacity? Explain your thinking.

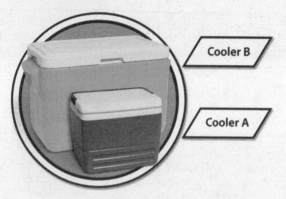

Cooler B

Cooler A

18. List these containers in order from least capacity to greatest capacity. Next to each one, write L or mL to show whether you would measure its capacity using liters or milliliters.

Washing machine   Large pot

Soup spoon   Travel mug

19. Reasoning A basketball team scores 27 points in its first game and 41 points in its second game. After three games, it scored 100 points in all. How many points did the team score in its third game?

20. Higher Order Thinking Becky wants to measure the capacity of her brother's wading pool. She has a 1 L container and a 10 mL container. Which should she use? Explain your reasoning.

21. Generalize A sandgrouse can soak up water in its fluffy feathers. It can carry the water a long way to its chicks. Does a sandgrouse carry 20 milliliters of water or 2 liters of water?

A sandgrouse can soak up enough water to fill a small perfume bottle.

✓ **Assessment**

22. Gary is painting a small storage shed. He estimates that he can do the job with one can of paint. Which of the following is the best estimate of the total volume of a can of paint?

  Ⓐ About 4 mL   Ⓑ About 4 L   Ⓒ About 40 L   Ⓓ About 40 mL

Name _____

Another Look!

Two units of capacity in the metric system are milliliters (mL) and liters (L).

1 liter = 1,000 milliliters

A milliliter is about 20 drops from an eyedropper.

A liter is slightly larger than a quart.

Milliliters are used to measure very small amounts of liquid.

The capacity of this spoon is 5 mL.

Many beverages are sold in 1-liter and 2-liter bottles.

The capacity of this bottle is 2 L.

In **1–12**, circle the better estimate for each.

1.

   350 mL or 35 L

2.

   100 mL or 10 L

3.

   1 mL or 1 L

4.

   2 L or 20 L

5. Wading pool

   1,000 mL or 85 L

6. Fish bowl

   500 mL or 6 L

7. Small water bottle

   500 mL or 5 L

8. Soup ladle

   60 mL or 700 mL

9. Small milk carton

   250 mL or 25 L

10. Soup can

   500 mL or 5 L

11. Sports cooler

   2 L or 20 L

12. Salt shaker

   40 mL or 1 L

13. Write an estimate for the capacity of a glass of juice. _____

14. Write an estimate for the capacity of a pitcher of water. _____

15. (A-Z)**Vocabulary** Explain how a liter is related to a milliliter.

16. Reasoning A gym membership costs $19 each month. If Miss Lacey joins the gym for one year, will she pay more or less than $190? Explain your answer.

In **17** and **18**, use the grid at the right.

17. Model with Math The area of a rectangle is 16 square units. Use the grid to draw what the rectangle could look like. Then shade the area. What are its dimensions?

18. Model with Math Is there another rectangle you could draw on the grid that has an area of 16 square units? If so, what are its dimensions? Draw and shade it on the grid.

---

19. Be Precise Find a container you think might hold about 2 liters of liquid. Use a liter container to measure and find how much it actually holds. Write about what you found.

20. Higher Order Thinking Essie has two identical containers. She fills one with milk and the other with water. If the first container holds about 10 L of milk, how much water does the second container hold? How do you know?

✓ **Assessment**

21. Which container has a capacity that is closest to 1 mL?

Ⓐ 　　Ⓑ 　　Ⓒ 　　Ⓓ

Solve & Share

Use a marked 1-liter beaker to measure the capacity of six other containers. Record your measurements in a chart. Then list them in order from least to greatest volume.

I can ...
use standard units to measure liquid volumes.

I can also be precise in my work.

Be precise. When measuring with a 1-liter beaker, you can measure to the nearest 100 milliliters.

Look Back! Use Appropriate Tools How did you measure the capacity of containers that are less than 1 liter? Is there another way to measure?

Essential Question **How Do You Measure Capacity?**

A

Eric is cleaning his fishbowl and wants to know how much water he needs to refill the fishbowl. How can he find the capacity of the fishbowl?

1 Liter

500 mL

Eric needs to be precise to measure the capacity of the fishbowl.

B

Pour from the filled fishbowl into the 1-liter container. Empty the container and repeat until the fishbowl is empty.

It is helpful to keep a record of measurements made.

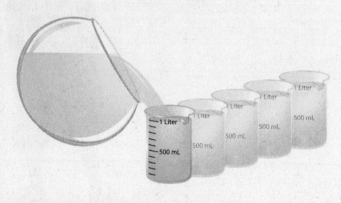

The 1-liter container was filled 5 times.

So, the capacity of the fishbowl is 5 liters.

Convince Me! **Critique Reasoning** Jason says, "I think it is better to find the measurement of the fishbowl using milliliters." Is Jason correct?

Another Example!

When only part of the 1-liter container is filled, use milliliters.

The capacity of the mug is 300 milliliters.

The capacity of the pot is 2 liters 500 milliliters.

☆ Guided Practice *

Do You Understand?

1. **Use Appropriate Tools** Find a container that you think holds less than a liter. Measure the capacity of the container.

2. What is the capacity of 2 mugs like the one in the Another Example shown above?

Do You Know How?

What is the total capacity represented in each picture?

3.

4.

☆ Independent Practice ☆

What is the total capacity represented in each picture?

5.

6.

7.

Problem Solving

8. Lawrence received a gift basket with a 200-milliliter jar of grape jam and a 350-milliliter jar of strawberry jam. His sister used 135 milliliters of the grape jam. How much jam does he have left?

9. Use Appropriate Tools Find a container that you think holds more than a liter. Measure the capacity of the container.

10. Generalize Which of the following measurements is **NOT** reasonable for the capacity of a bathroom sink: 15 liters, 300 milliliters, 10 liters, 9 liters, 12 liters? Explain.

11. How many 2-liter cartons can be filled with 18 liters of juice?

You can draw a picture to show this problem.

12. Higher Order Thinking Emma poured 750 milliliters of gravy into a 1-liter container. If she wants to fill the container, how much more gravy does she need? Explain.

✓ Assessment

13. Use the picture of the water jugs to find the amount of water the team drank during soccer practice.

    Ⓐ 6 liters

    Ⓑ 7 liters

    Ⓒ 9 liters

    Ⓓ 19 liters

Before soccer practice

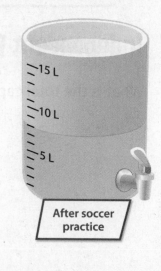

After soccer practice

Help Practice Tools Games
      Buddy

Another Look!

A marked 1-liter container can be used to measure the capacity of other containers.

The capacity of the can is 400 milliliters.

The capacity of the bottle is 2 liters 700 milliliters.

What is the total capacity represented in each picture?

1.

_____

2.

_____

3.

_____

4.

_____

5.

_____

6.

_____

7. Model with Math The capacity of a small bottle of glue is 185 milliliters. How much glue is there in 3 bottles? Use math to represent the problem.

8. Circle the better estimate for the capacity of the container.

2 mL or 2 L

9. Be Precise Tomas filled a cup and then emptied it into the marked liter container. If he drank 8 cups of water during the day, how much water did he drink?

10. Critique Reasoning June had a 500-milliliter carton of milk and drank 350 milliliters. She says that she has more than 200 milliliters of milk left. Is she correct? Explain.

11. Higher Order Thinking Some people use a chart like the one shown to help them decide how many fish they can put in their fish tank.

Harrison has a 40-liter fish tank. How many 4-cm fish can he put in his fish tank?

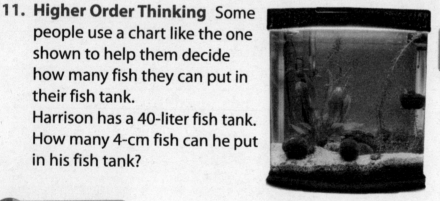

Length of Fish	Water Needed for Each Fish
1 centimeter	2 liters
2 centimeters	4 liters
3 centimeters	6 liters
4 centimeters	8 liters

DATA

✓ **Assessment**

12. Benito made a small pitcher of fruit punch. He mixed together lemonade and cherry juice. Use the picture to find the amount of juice Benito made.

Ⓐ 9 liters

Ⓑ 100 milliliters

Ⓒ 900 milliliters

Ⓓ 2 liters 900 milliliters

Lemonade   Cherry Juice

☆ ☆
Solve & Share

Look at the pictures of the book and olive. List 4 items that should be measured using kilograms and 4 items that should be measured using grams. *Solve this problem any way you choose. Explain your reasoning.*

I can ...
use standard units to estimate the masses of solid objects.

I can also reason about math.

1 gram

1 kilogram   **1,000 grams = 1 kilogram**

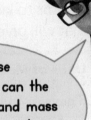

You can use reasoning. How can the mass of a book and mass of an olive help you make your list? *Show your work.*

Look Back! **Use Appropriate Tools** How could you use tools to check that the items in part of your list are reasonable choices for measuring mass with grams? Explain.

Essential Question

How Can You Use Reasoning to Estimate Mass?

A

Stephen and Marissa estimated the mass of an apple. Stephen's estimate is 250 g. Marissa's estimate is 2 kg. Which is the better estimate of the mass of an apple?

Mass is a measure of the amount of matter in an object. Grams and kilograms are two metric units of mass.

1 kilogram (kg)

1 gram (g)

?

B ## Step 1

Use known masses and the table to compare grams to kilograms. Select the unit that will give a better estimate.

DATA

Units of Mass

1,000 grams = 1 kilogram

The apple is smaller than the cantaloupe. A kilogram is too large of a unit to estimate the mass of the apple.

The grape is smaller than the apple. Grams are smaller units that can be used to estimate the mass of the apple.

C ## Step 2

Use a pan balance to find the mass of the apple. Then evaluate Stephen's estimate.

The apple has a mass of 262 grams.

250 grams is close to 262 grams. Stephen's estimate is reasonable.

250 g is a better estimate than 2 kg.

Convince Me! **Critique Reasoning** Zoe says two apples would have a mass greater than a kilogram. Do you agree? Explain.

Name _____

☆ Guided Practice *

Do You Understand?

1. Construct Arguments In Step 2 on page 770, why do you need to find the actual mass of the apple?

2. Use Appropriate Tools Find an object that you think has a mass more than a kilogram and another that has a mass less than a kilogram. Then determine what tools to use to check your estimate.

Do You Know How?

In **3–6**, circle the better estimate for each.

3.

5 g or 5 kg

4.

40 g or 4 kg

5. Sunglasses

16 g or 1 kg

6. Envelope

1 g or 70 g

☆ Independent Practice ☆

Leveled Practice In **7–18**, circle the better estimate for each.

7.

100 g or 10 kg

8.

15 g or 15 kg

9.

4 g or 400 g

10.

200 g or 2 kg

11. Bicycle

2 kg or 12 kg

12. Feather

1 g or 1 kg

13. Horse

5 kg or 550 kg

14. Penny

3 g or 300 g

15. Dining table

350 g or 35 kg

16. Microwave oven

1,500 g or 15 kg

17. Kitten

2 kg or 20 kg

18. Crayon

20 g or 200 g

Problem Solving

19. Use Appropriate Tools Choose the best tool to measure each item described. Write the correct letter of the tool on the blank.

The capacity of a mug _____

The temperature of water _____

The length of a box _____

The mass of a pear _____

The time you finish lunch _____

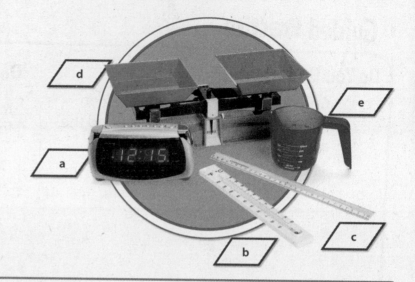

---

20. Number Sense Ethan will subtract a 3-digit number from 920. He says the difference could be a 1-digit number, a 2-digit number, or a 3-digit number. Write three subtraction equations that show each difference. Be sure you start with 920 and subtract a 3-digit number each time.

You can use place value and mental math to solve this problem.

---

21. Math and Science Clay learned that solids have a definite shape. Now he wants to measure some solids, so he measures the mass of a bead. The bead has a mass of 10 grams. He estimates that 10 beads will have a mass of 1 kilogram. Is he correct? Explain.

22. Higher Order Thinking Correct the mistakes in the shopping list below.

Shopping List
2 L of apples
3 kg of milk
5 cm of flour

Assessment

23. Todd is thinking of an animal with a mass greater than 1 kilogram, but less than 20 kilograms. Name two animals that he could be thinking of.

24. Anna has a bar of soap. She estimates its mass before measuring to find the actual mass. Does it make more sense to estimate the mass in grams or in milliliters? Explain.

Name _____

Another Look!

Units of mass include grams (g) and kilograms (kg).

1 kilogram = 1,000 grams

> Mass is a measure of the amount of matter in an object.

A paper clip has a mass of about 1 gram.

A large baseball bat has a mass of about 1 kilogram.

You can estimate the mass of different objects based on the mass of the paper clip and mass of the baseball bat.

In **1–16**, circle the better estimate for each.

1.

150 g or 150 kg

2.

1 g or 100 g

3.

200 g or 2 kg

4.

15 g or 150 g

5. Soccer ball

500 g or 5 kg

6. Tiger

30 kg or 300 kg

7. Dime

2 g or 2 kg

8. Baseball glove

100 g or 1 kg

9. Large dog

400 g or 40 kg

10. Flat screen TV

15 kg or 100 kg

11. Lemon

100 g or 1 kg

12. Cell phone

150 g or 15 kg

13. Boat anchor

40 g or 40 kg

14. Calculator

95 g or 1 kg

15. Sweatshirt

50 g or 300 g

16. Dinner plate

300 g or 3 kg

17. **Use Appropriate Tools** Choose the best tool to measure each item. Write the letter on the blank.

The mass of a peach _____

The capacity of a bowl _____

The time you finish breakfast _____

The length of a crayon _____

18. **Math and Science** A science class estimated the mass of objects that a magnet lifted. The magnet lifted 2 keys and 1 wrench. What was the total estimated mass that the magnet lifted?

Object	Estimated Mass
key	30 g
wrench	350 g

DATA

19. **Model with Math** Stan works for a moving company. There are 36 boxes equally placed on 6 shelves. Draw a picture or bar diagram to find the number of boxes on each shelf.

20. **Higher Order Thinking** Rena knows a dollar coin has a mass of a little less than 10 grams. She guesses 1 kilogram of coins would be worth over a million dollars. Is this reasonable? Explain.

21. Cody is thinking of an object that has a mass greater than 1 gram, but less than 1 kg. Name two objects that he could be thinking of.

✔ **Assessment**

22. Which metric unit should you use to estimate the mass of a cookie? Explain.

Name _____

Solve & Share

Work with a partner to choose 6 objects whose masses can be measured using a pan balance. Estimate the mass of each object. Then use metric weights to find the actual mass for each in grams (g) or kilograms (kg). *Use the table and solve this problem any way you choose. Explain your reasoning.*

I can ...
use grams and kilograms to measure the mass of objects.

I can also look for patterns to solve problems.

Look for relationships. Think about how objects are similar or different to help decide whether grams, kilograms, or both are appropriate units for the mass of each object. *Show your work!*

Object	Estimate	Actual Mass

Look Back! **Construct Arguments** How did you decide which metric unit(s) to use when making your estimates? Explain.

How Do You Measure Mass?

A

A pan balance with gram and kilogram weights can be used to find the mass of an object. What is the mass of a box of chalk?

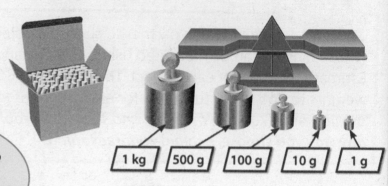

| 1 kg | 500 g | 100 g | 10 g | 1 g |

When measuring mass it is important to be precise. Use grams, kilograms, or both to find an exact measure.

B

Place the box on one pan. Place enough gram and kilogram weights on the other pan so the pans balance.

C

The box balances with one 1-kilogram weight, two 100-gram weights, and four 10-gram weights.

So, the mass of the box is 1 kilogram 240 grams.

Write the larger unit before the smaller unit when recording measurements.

Convince Me! **Be Precise** What metric units would you use to estimate the mass of half of a box of chalk? Explain.

Practice Buddy   Tools   Assessment

☆Guided Practice*

Do You Understand?

1. Reasoning Find an object that you think has a mass greater than a kilogram. Find another object that has a mass less than a kilogram. Use a pan balance with gram and kilogram weights to measure the mass of each object.

2. Construct Arguments If you use a pan balance to measure the mass of a pen, would you use any kilogram weights? Explain.

Do You Know How?

In **3** and **4**, write the total mass represented in each picture.

3.

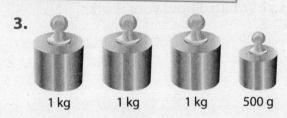

1 kg   1 kg   1 kg   500 g

4.

100 g   100 g   10 g 10 g   1 g 1 g
                  10 g 10 g   1 g 1 g 1 g

Independent Practice ☆

In **5–7**, write the total mass represented in each picture.

5.

100 g   100 g

500 g   100 g   100 g

10 g 10 g 10 g 1 g

6.

1 kg   1 kg   1 kg

1 kg   1 kg   1 kg

7.

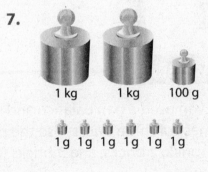

1 kg   1 kg   100 g

1 g 1 g 1 g 1 g 1 g 1 g

Problem Solving

8. Algebra Olivia put 220 grams of nuts in a bag. Then she added more nuts to the bag. The total mass of Olivia's bag of nuts was 850 grams. Use the expression $220 + n = 850$ to find the mass in grams of the nuts Olivia added to her bag. Show your work.

9. A camp counselor bought 8 bags of charcoal. The mass of each bag is 5 kilograms. What is the total mass of the bags of charcoal?

10. Reasoning Sophie used a pan balance to measure the mass of a pineapple. The pans balanced when she used one 500-gram weight and three 100-gram weights. Zach measured the same pineapple but used eight 100-gram weights. Did someone make a mistake? Explain.

11. Higher Order Thinking Lawrence bought some red potatoes with a mass of 410 grams. He also bought white potatoes with a mass of 655 grams. Did he buy more or less than 1 kilogram of potatoes? Explain how you know.

✓ **Assessment**

12. Evan used a pan balance and metric weights to measure the total mass of three bricks. Use the picture and draw lines to connect 1 brick, 2 bricks, and 3 bricks to the correct mass of each.

| 1 brick | | 6 kilograms |

| 2 bricks | | 4 kilograms |

| 3 bricks | | 2 kilograms |

Help Practice Buddy Tools Games

Homework & Practice 14-7
Measure Mass

Another Look!

Tanya estimated the mass of a box of nails to be 2 kilograms. Then she used a pan balance and metric weights to find its actual mass.

You can use reasoning to estimate and measure the mass of an object in grams, kilograms, or both metric units:
1,000 grams = 1 kilogram

The box of nails balanced with one 1-kilogram weight, one 500-gram weight, and four 100-gram weights.

So, the mass of the box of nails is 1 kilogram 900 grams.

In **1–6**, write the total mass represented in each picture.

1.

1 kg   1 kg   500 g   100 g   100 g

2.

500 g   100 g   100 g   10 g   10 g   10 g   10 g

3.

1 kg   1 kg   1 kg

1 kg   1 kg   100 g

4.

1 kg   1 kg   100 g

10 g   10 g   10 g   1 g

5.

100 g   100 g   10 g   10 g

100 g   100 g   10 g   10 g

1 g   1 g   1 g   1 g   1 g   1 g

6.

1 kg   1 kg   1 kg   500 g

7. Ms. Walker has 15 kilograms of clay. She wants to give 3 students an equal amount of the clay. What is the mass of the clay that each student will get?

8. Higher Order Thinking Colby's dog gave birth to 6 puppies. Each puppy in the litter now has a mass of about 3 kilograms. About how much is the mass of the litter of puppies in kilograms? In grams? Remember: 1,000 grams = 1 kilogram.

9. Reasoning Willie has 4 baseball caps. Two of the caps are blue. One of the caps is red and one is green. What fraction of the caps is blue?

10. Make Sense and Persevere Lynn filled each of three bags with 2 kilograms 450 grams of sand. Is the mass of 2 bags greater than or less than 5 kilograms? Explain how you know.

✓ **Assessment**

11. Quincy estimated the mass of each of the following. Then he measured to find the actual mass of each. Draw lines to connect each item with the best estimate of its actual mass.

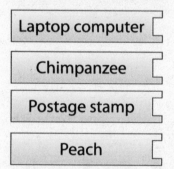

Laptop computer

Chimpanzee

Postage stamp

Peach

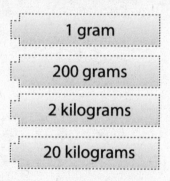

1 gram

200 grams

2 kilograms

20 kilograms

Name _____

Solve & Share

The animals at a pet store eat 80 kilograms of vegetables each day. How many kilograms of vegetables do they eat in one week?

I can ...
use pictures to help solve problems about mass and volume.

I can also model with math to solve problems.

Model with math. Drawing bar diagrams can help you find the needed operations.

80 kilograms

Look Back! **Make Sense and Persevere** Describe the plan you used to solve the problem.

Essential Question **How Do You Use Drawings to Solve Problems?**

A

In a juice factory, one 50-liter container had 28 liters of juice in it. An hour later, it had 45 liters of juice. How many liters of juice were added?

You can use reasoning to figure out the meaning of the numbers. The drawing shows how the amount changed.

28 liters to start   45 liters an hour later

B Draw a picture to show what you know.

45 liters in all

| 28 L | h |

Amount to start with   Amount added

You know the total and one part. Subtract to find how many liters were added.

C

Pictures can help you understand what operation to use.

Subtract to solve the problem.

$45 - 28 = h$

$$\begin{array}{r} 45 \\ -\ 28 \\ \hline 17 \end{array}$$

17 liters of juice were added to the container.

Convince Me! **Make Sense and Persevere** In the example above, another beaker had 33 liters of juice. How many total liters of juice were there in all? How can you solve this problem?

© Pearson Education, Inc. 3

Name _____

☆ Guided Practice ☆

Do You Understand?

1. Suppose 42 liters of juice were evenly divided into 6 batches. Draw a picture to show how many liters of juice are in each batch.

Do You Know How?

2. Alex buys a box of pudding mix and a box of cocoa. The mass of the box of pudding mix is 100 grams. The total mass of the 2 boxes is 550 grams. What is the mass of the box of cocoa?

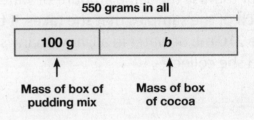

550 grams in all

100 g	b

↑ Mass of box of pudding mix   ↑ Mass of box of cocoa

☆ Independent Practice ☆

Leveled Practice In **3–6**, use drawings to solve.

3. Peter has divided 120 liters of water equally in 3 containers. How many liters has he poured into each container?

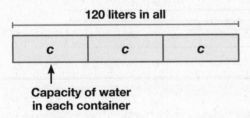

120 liters in all

c	c	c

↑ Capacity of water in each container

4. Adeela pours 235 milliliters of milk in a glass and 497 milliliters of milk in a bottle. How many milliliters of milk did she pour in all? Draw a picture to help solve the problem.

5. Samantha bought 523 grams of grapes. After eating some grapes she had 458 grams. How many grams did she eat?

6. Omar is shipping 3 boxes. Each has a mass of 8 kilograms. What is the total mass of all of the boxes?

Problem Solving

In **7** and **8**, use the table. In **8**, use the bar diagram.

7. Professor Newman has collected a soil sample from the forest preserve in her town. What is the total mass of the 2 minerals in the soil?

8. **Higher Order Thinking** The professor finds that there is the same amount of water in each of the samples that she takes. If there are 210 mL of water in all, how many samples did she collect?

Soil Sample	
Component	**Quantity**
Quartz	141 g
Calcite	96 g
Water	42 mL

DATA

210 mL in all

42 mL | ? batches →

Amount of water
in 1 sample

---

9. Elijah has 2 hours before dinner. He spends the first 37 minutes practicing guitar and next 48 minutes doing his homework. How much time is left until dinner?

10. **Reasoning** Laurie bought a 500 milliliter carton of cream. After using some of the cream, she had 245 milliliters left. How many milliliters of cream did she use?

---

11. **Make Sense and Persevere** Write and solve a problem about the bar diagram.

678 g	
239 g	a

✔ Assessment

12. Eric filled a container to the 18 L mark with juice an hour ago. The juice is now at the 15 L mark. Mark the amount of juice Eric had. Then use the pictures to find how many liters of juice have been poured out.

Amount of juice
one hour ago

Amount of
juice now

Help Practice Buddy Tools Games

Another Look!

You can use different bar diagrams to solve a problem.

Mrs. Jones bought 35 liters of juice for a school picnic. At the picnic each class drank 5 liters of juice. No juice was left over. How many classes were at the picnic?

You can draw a picture of the information given in the problem to solve it.

To find the number of classes, you can divide $35 \div 5$.

$35 \div 5 = 7$ So there were 7 classes at the picnic.

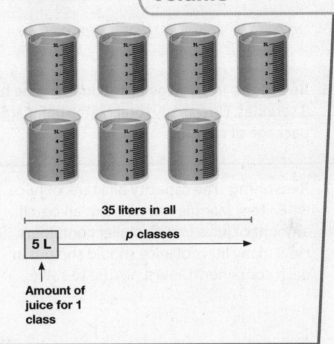

35 liters in all

5 L p classes

↑
Amount of juice for 1 class

In **1** and **2**, draw a picture to help solve the problem.

1. Frank has a mass of 42 kilograms, and Dino has a mass of 39 kilograms. What is their total mass?

2. A small bicycle has a mass of 7 kilograms. The total mass of all the small bicycles at Mike's Bike Shop is 21 kilograms. How many small bicycles does Mike's Bike Shop have?

3. Donna has 6 first aid kits. Each kit is 8 kilograms. What is the total mass of all of Donna's first aid kits?

4. Chloe painted 4 bedrooms in her house. In each room she used 10 liters of paint. How many total liters did she use?

The table at the right shows the mass of fat in grams per serving for certain foods. Use the table for **5** and **6**. Draw a picture to solve.

Total Fat (per serving)	
Food	Amount of Fat (g)
Cheddar Cheese	9
Honey Ham	2
Mixed Nuts	15

DATA

5. What is the sum of the number of grams of total fat per serving for cheddar cheese and mixed nuts?

6. **Be Precise** A package of cheddar cheese has 8 servings. How many total grams of fat are in a package of cheese?

7. **Reasoning** The capacity of a tank of juice is 18 liters. Maggie wants to put an equal amount of juice into 6 smaller containers. How many liters of juice should she put in each container? Draw a picture to solve.

8. **Number Sense** George is thinking of a number less than 10 that has an odd product when multiplied by 5. What could George's number be?

9. **Higher Order Thinking** Tina has 60 grams of popcorn. She wants to give the popcorn to her 3 friends. She says there are 2 ways that she can give her friends the same amount. Is she correct? Explain.

✓ **Assessment**

10. Shawna placed a beaker outside to collect rain. On Monday morning there was 66 mL of rain and 26 mL during the night. On Tuesday night there was 145 mL of rain. Mark the containers to show the amounts of rainfall collected each day. Then find how much more rain was collected on Tuesday than on Monday.

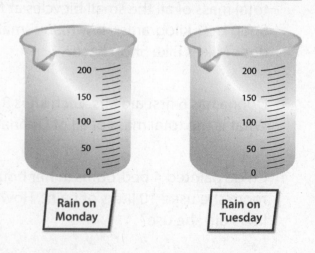

Rain on Monday

Rain on Tuesday

Name _____

Solve & Share

Nina wants to arrive at the community center at 9:30 A.M. for an art class. It takes her 15 minutes to walk to the center, 30 minutes to make and eat breakfast, and 15 minutes to get ready after eating. What time should Nina start making breakfast? Use reasoning to decide.

I can ...
make sense of quantities and relationships in problem situations.

I can also solve time problems.

Arrive at the Community Center

Thinking Habits

Be a good thinker!
These questions can help you.

- What do the numbers and symbols in the problem mean?

- How are the numbers or quantities related?

- How can I represent a word problem using pictures, numbers, or equations?

Look Back! **Reasoning** Does it make sense to use "minutes" as the unit for the answer to this problem? Explain.

Essential Question: How Can You Use Reasoning to Solve Problems?

A

Eric's family wants to arrive at a movie theater at 2:30 P.M. It takes them 30 minutes to eat lunch, 15 minutes to get ready after eating, and 30 minutes to travel to the theater.

What time should the family start eating lunch? Use reasoning to decide.

What do I need to do to solve this problem?

I need to start with the end time. Then I need to use the time lengths given and work backward to find the starting time.

You can draw a picture to help with your reasoning.

Arrive at Theater

B

How can I use reasoning to solve this problem?

I can

- identify the quantities I know.

- draw a number line to show relationships.

- give the answer using the correct unit.

C

Here's my thinking...

I used a number line to show the quantities and my reasoning.

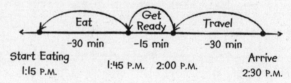

Eat —30 min   Get Ready —15 min   Travel —30 min

Start Eating 1:15 P.M.   1:45 P.M.   2:00 P.M.   Arrive 2:30 P.M.

30 minutes before 2:30 P.M. is 2:00 P.M.
15 minutes before 2:00 P.M. is 1:45 P.M.
30 minutes before 1:45 P.M. is 1:15 P.M.

Eric's family should start eating lunch at 1:15 P.M.

Convince Me! **Reasoning** How can you check that the solution given above makes sense?

Name _____

☆ Guided Practice *

Reasoning

Kevin's doctor appointment is at 10:30 A.M. It takes Kevin 30 minutes to clean his room, 20 minutes to get ready after he cleans, and 20 minutes to walk to the doctor's office. What time should Kevin start cleaning his room? Use reasoning to decide.

Use reasoning to show how quantities in a problem are related.

1. Describe the quantities you know.

2. Solve the problem and explain your reasoning. You can use a picture to help.

Independent Practice ☆

Reasoning

Doreen's favorite television show begins at 5:30 P.M. She will get her hair cut before the show. It takes Doreen 10 minutes to walk to the hair salon and 10 minutes to walk home. Her haircut takes 25 minutes. What time should Doreen leave home so that she will get back in time for her show? Use reasoning to decide.

3. Describe the quantities you know.

4. Solve the problem and explain your reasoning. You can use a picture to help.

5. How did you know whether to use A.M. or P.M. in your answer to 4 above?

For another example, see Set I on page 798.   **Topic 14** | Lesson 14-9   **789**

School Talent Show

Karina is planning a talent show for 28 students. The table below tells how long each act lasts. Karina needs 5 minutes to introduce each act. She also needs to allow a 20-minute break. The break does not need to be introduced. The show must end at 9:00 P.M.

DATA	Acts Before Break	Length in Minutes	Acts After Break	Length in Minutes
	3rd grade dancers	10	5th grade singers	10
	3rd grade singers	10	5th grade magic act	10
	4th grade singers	10	5th grade dancers	10
	4th grade magic act	15	Finale	30

6. **Be Precise** What is the total time needed for all the acts before the break? Explain your thinking.

7. **Critique Reasoning** Sachi says that the 5th grade singers should begin at 7:40 P.M. Phil says that the 5th grade singers should begin at 8:00 P.M. Who is correct?

Use reasoning. Think about the meaning of each of the numbers.

8. **Reasoning** What time should the talent show begin? Explain your reasoning. You can draw a picture to help.

Name _____

Another Look!

Natalie finished listening to music at 4:30 P.M. She had listened to music for 45 minutes. Before that, Natalie spent 15 minutes reading. Before she read, she played soccer for 40 minutes. At what time did Natalie begin playing soccer? Use reasoning to decide.

Tell how you can show the relationships in the problem.

- I can identify the times and show them by drawing a picture.

- I can find the total time needed and work backward.

Solve the problem and explain your reasoning.

Natalie began at 2:50 P.M. I worked backward from 4:30 P.M. and used a number line to show my reasoning.

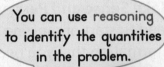

You can use reasoning to identify the quantities in the problem.

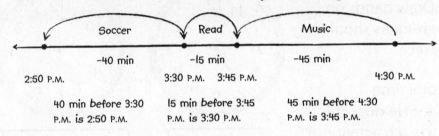

Soccer	Read	Music
−40 min	−15 min	−45 min

2:50 P.M.   3:30 P.M. 3:45 P.M.   4:30 P.M.

40 min *before* 3:30   15 min *before* 3:45   45 min *before* 4:30
P.M. is 2:50 P.M.   P.M. is 3:30 P.M.   P.M. is 3:45 P.M.

Reasoning

Will arrived at his mother's office at 11:00 A.M. It took him 30 minutes to walk from his home to the mall. Will was in the mall for 45 minutes. It took Will 15 minutes to walk from the mall to the office. At what time did Will leave home?

1. Describe the quantities you know.

2. Tell how you can show the relationships in the problem.

3. Solve the problem and explain your reasoning. You can use a picture to help.

Field Day

Jonas is planning Field Day at his school. The table shows the order of activities and how long each activity lasts. It takes 10 minutes to organize each activity before it starts. Students will have lunch at 12:00 P.M. Field Day must end at 2:35 P.M.

DATA	Activity	Length in Minutes
	Tug-of-war	20
	Bean bag toss	15
	Egg relay race	20
	800-yard dash	10

4. **Make Sense and Persevere** What time does Jonas need to start organizing the 800-yard dash? List the information that you need to use and then solve.

5. **Model with Math** The first clock shows the time Field Day must end. Draw hands on the second clock to show when Jonas should start organizing the egg relay race.

Field Day ends

Organize egg relay race

6. **Generalize** Jonas finds the total time to organize and do each activity. He does this by adding the same number to each activity length. What number is this? Explain.

7. **Reasoning** What time should Field Day begin with Jonas organizing the tug-of-war? Explain.

Use reasoning to understand which numbers help you solve the problem.

TOPIC
14

Fluency Practice Activity

Find a partner. Get paper and a pencil. Each partner chooses a different color: light blue or dark blue.

Partner 1 and Partner 2 each point to a black number at the same time. Both partners subtract the lesser number from the greater number.

If the answer is on your color, you get a tally mark. Work until one partner has seven tally marks.

I can ...
subtract within 1,000.

Partner 1

| 790 |
| 382 |
| 180 |
| 327 |
| 705 |

139	283	430	84
228	95	542	235
180	375	173	164
249	547	150	47
572	194	657	462
79	487	689	63

Partner 2

| 243 |
| 610 |
| 555 |
| 133 |
| 869 |

Tally Marks for Partner 1

Tally Marks for Partner 2

A-Z
Glossary

Word List

- A.M.
- capacity
- elapsed time
- gram
- hour
- kilogram
- liter
- mass
- milliliter
- minute
- P.M.
- time interval

Understand Vocabulary

1. Cross out any units below that are **NOT** measurement units of *capacity*.

   gram   milliliter   kilogram   hour   liter

2. Cross out any units below that are **NOT** measurement units of *mass*.

   kilogram   minute   hour   gram   milliliter

3. Cross out any amounts below that are shown in *liters* or *milliliters*.

   5 kg   2 L   80 mL   250 g   12 kg

Choose the right term from the box. Write it in the blank.

4. The hours between midnight and noon are _____ hours.

5. An amount of time is a _____ .

6. The hours between noon and midnight are _____ hours.

7. 1 _____ equals 1,000 grams.

8. The total amount of time that passes from the beginning time to the ending time is called the _____ .

9. 1,000 milliliters equals 1 _____ .

Use Vocabulary in Writing

10. Maggie wants to measure this container. Use at least 3 terms from the Word List to explain how Maggie can measure the container in different ways.

Paint

Set A pages 739–744

What is the time to the nearest minute?

The hour hand is between 10 and 11. The time is after 10:00.

Count by 5s from the 12 to the 5.
5, 10, 15, 20, 25 minutes.

After counting by 5s, count the marks by 1.
5, 10, 15, 20, 25, 26, 27 minutes.

The digital time is 10:27.
It is 27 minutes past 10 or 33 minutes to 11.

Remember that, for minutes, count numbers on the clock by 5s, then count marks by 1.

Reteaching

Write the time shown on each clock in two ways.

1.

2.

Set B pages 745–750

Tomaz starts practicing his viola at 4:25 P.M. He practices until 5:05 P.M. How much time does he practice?

The amount of time is under 1 hour, so count the minutes from the start time to the end time, by 5s.

There are 40 minutes between 4:25 P.M. and 5:05 P.M. So, Tomaz practices for 40 minutes.

Remember that you can use a clock face to find elapsed time.

In **1–3**, find the elapsed time.

1. Basketball practice begins at 6:30 P.M. and lasts until 8:15 P.M. How much time does practice last?

2. Mr. Walters starts preparing breakfast at 6:45 A.M. He finishes at 7:50 A.M. How long does it take for him to prepare breakfast?

3. Jean rides her horse twice a week at Free-and-Bold Stables. One Monday, she goes for a horseback ride. She leaves the barn on her horse at 2:10 P.M., and comes back at 2:50 P.M. How long was her ride?

You can show addition and subtraction of time intervals on a number line.

In the morning, Xavier runs for 19 minutes. In the evening, he runs for 27 minutes. How much time did he spend running in all?

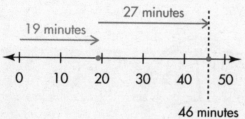

$19 + 27 = ?$

$19 + 27 = 46$ So, Xavier ran 46 minutes.

Remember to decide whether you need to add or subtract.

In **1**, solve by drawing a number line or bar diagram.

1. It takes Don 52 minutes to drive to work. He has already driven for 16 minutes. How many more minutes will it take Don to drive to work?

Estimate the capacity of a pitcher.

A milliliter is too small, so estimate using liters.

Think about what you already know. A liter is about the same size as a large water bottle. A pitcher usually holds more liquid than a water bottle. So, 2 liters seems like a good estimate.

Remember that capacity can be measured using liters and milliliters.

In **1–4**, circle the better estimate.

1.

   1 L or 10 L

2.

   8 mL or 8 L

3. Drinking glass
   5 mL or 500 mL

4. Washing machine
   40 L or 4 L

How much water is in this beaker?

Use the scale to determine how full the beaker is. Think of the scale like a number line. Each mark represents 20 milliliters. The water is 3 marks above 100 mL.

$3 \times 20 = 60$

$100 + 60 = 160$ mL

Remember to use the correct units when measuring capacity.

In **1** and **2**, find the total capacity.

1.

2.

Set F pages 769–774

Estimate the mass of a battery.

A kilogram is too heavy, so estimate using grams.

Think about what you already know. A gram is about the same weight as a grape. A battery weighs about as much as a bunch of grapes. So 30 grams seems like a good estimate.

Remember that mass can be measured using grams and kilograms.

In **1–6**, circle the better estimate for the mass.

1.

    15 g or 15 kg

2.

    500 g or 500 kg

3. One sheep

    800 g or 80 kg

4. Bag of flour

    2 g or 2 kg

5. Notebook computer

    3 g or 3 kg

6. Quarter

    5 g or 500 g

Set G pages 775–780

What is the mass of this bar of soap?

When a pan balance is even, the mass on the left side equals the mass on the right side.

Find the total of the weights on the left side. Use mental math and place value to help add.

$100 + 10 + 5 + 1 + 1 + 1 = 118$

The bar of soap has a mass of 118 grams.

Remember to use the correct units when measuring mass.

In **1** and **2**, find the total mass.

1.

    500 g   100 g   100 g   1 g

2.

    1 kg   1 kg   100 g   100 g   5 g   5 g

There are 7 people on Ed's bowling team. Each owns their own bowling ball. The mass of each bowling ball is 5 kilograms. What is the total mass of the team's bowling balls?

? kg in all

| 5 kg | 5 kg | 5 kg | 5 kg | 5 kg | 5 kg | 5 kg |

$7 \times 5 = \blacksquare$

$7 \times 5 = 35$ The total mass of the the team's bowling balls is 35 kg.

Remember to draw pictures to show the information you know.

In **1** and **2**, use a picture to solve.

1. The water tank in Mary's yard holds 60 liters of water. She used 13 liters to water her plants. How many liters of water remain in the water tank?

2. Eric has 3 dogs that each have a mass of 8 kg. What is the total mass of all of Eric's dogs?

Think about these questions to help you **reason abstractly and quantitatively.**

Thinking Habits

- What do the numbers and symbols in the problem mean?

- How are the numbers or quantities related?

- How can I represent a word problem using pictures, numbers, or equations?

Remember to consider the units in the information you are given.

At 1:00 P.M., Ted will meet a friend in the park. Ted needs 30 minutes to walk to the park. Ted needs 15 minutes to eat lunch and 10 minutes to prepare lunch. When must Ted start to prepare lunch?

1. Describe the quantities you know.

2. How can you show the relationships in this problem?

3. When must Ted start to prepare lunch?

Name _____

1. Draw hands on the clock to show 8:36.

2. Jessica and Cody ran a long distance race during an afternoon. The start times were different so that all the runners did not start at the same time. Who finished faster, and by how many minutes?

Jessica

Start   End

Cody

Start   End

Ⓐ Jessica; 5 minutes faster than Cody

Ⓑ Cody; 5 minutes faster than Jessica

Ⓒ Jessica; 10 minutes faster than Cody

Ⓓ They finished in the same amount of time.

3. A store sells bags of apples. Each bag weighs 2 kg. Draw lines to match each number of bags on the left with the correct total weight on the right.

2 bags		12 kg
6 bags		16 kg
5 bags		4 kg
8 bags		10 kg

4. Name a metric unit that would be best to measure the capacity of a kitchen sink.

5. Mason is looking for a tool to measure the mass of an apple. Which tool should he use?

Ⓐ Pan balance

Ⓑ Ruler

Ⓒ 1-cup container

Ⓓ Clock

6. Dale's school bus picks him up at 7:45 A.M. To get ready for school, Dale needs 15 minutes to eat breakfast, 10 minutes to make lunch, and 10 minutes to get dressed. What time does Dale need to begin getting ready for school? Use reasoning to decide.

Part A

Describe the quantities you know.

Part B

Solve the problem. Explain your reasoning. You can use a picture to help.

7. Mary has a total of 18 liters of water in 6 bottles. If the bottles are equally filled, how much water is in each bottle?

8. Eric played the guitar for 33 minutes on Monday and 19 minutes on Tuesday. How many more minutes did Eric play the guitar on Monday?

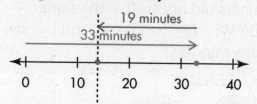

Ⓐ 52 minutes

Ⓑ 33 minutes

Ⓒ 19 minutes

Ⓓ 14 minutes

9. Mr. Griggs writes a shopping list. Look at the measurement units below. Then, complete the shopping list by writing the appropriate measurement units in the blanks.

L   mL   g   kg

3 _____ of apples

1 _____ of milk

100 _____ of sunscreen

100 _____ of salt

Name _____

10. Irene measured the capacity of a large jug using milliliters. Forest measured the same container using liters. How did the measurements compare? Choose all the sentences that are true.

☐ There were more milliliters than liters.

☐ There were more liters than milliliters.

☐ There was an equal number of milliliters and liters.

☐ There were fewer milliliters than liters.

☐ There were fewer liters than milliliters.

11. Jason said the mass of his book is about 1 kilogram. Julie said it is 1 liter. Who is correct? Choose the best answer.

Ⓐ Jason is correct because kilograms are units of mass, and liters are units of capacity.

Ⓑ Julie is correct because liters are metric units.

Ⓒ They are both correct because kilograms and liters are units of mass.

Ⓓ Neither is correct because their estimates are not reasonable.

12. Explain why it would be better to use grams rather than kilograms to measure the mass of a crayon.

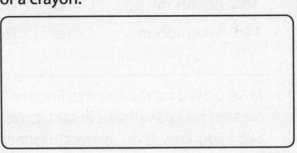

13. It took Wallace 45 minutes to read part of a chapter of his science book. He finished reading the rest of the chapter in 17 minutes. In how much time did Wallace read the chapter?

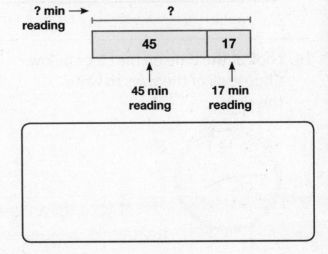

14. Is the capacity of each object best measured in milliliters? Choose Yes or No.

14a. Recycle bin ○ Yes ○ No

14b. Eyedropper ○ Yes ○ No

14c. Aquarium ○ Yes ○ No

14d. Soup spoon ○ Yes ○ No

15. Mike used a pan balance to find the mass of his basketball. He said it was 580 kilograms. Is his answer reasonable? Explain.

16. Look at the time on the clock below. Choose all of the ways to write this time.

☐ 3:46

☐ 14 minutes before 4

☐ 46 minutes after 3

☐ 9 minutes before 4

☐ 4:14

17. Maryann went to the grocery store at 3:10 P.M. She arrived home 1 hour, 15 minutes later. What time did she arrive home?

18. Ricardo used 337 grams of flour to bake in the afternoon. He had already used 284 grams of flour to bake in the morning. How many grams of flour did Ricardo use in all?

19. The lines on the container below show its capacity in milliliters. Joanna filled the container to the 750 mL mark with water. Then she used some of the water. How many milliliters of water did she use?

Name _____

Family Reunion
Anita and her brother Logan make plans for a family reunion.

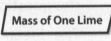
TOPIC
14

Performance
Assessment

1. Use the **Fruit Bought** table to answer the question. Logan estimated the mass of the fruit. He forgot to include the unit of mass. For each item explain if he used a gram or kilogram.

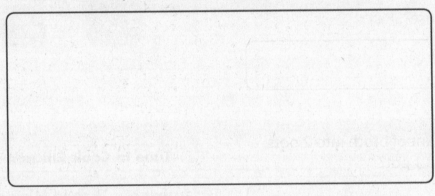

Fruit Bought	
Item	**Estimated Mass**
bag of grapefruit	4
one lemon	90
one watermelon	3

2. Use the **Mass of One Lime** art to answer the questions.

Part A

Each lime has a mass shown at the right. What is the mass of one lime?

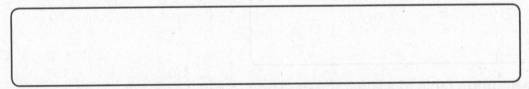

Mass of One Lime

10 g   10 g   10 g

Part B

Logan needs to buy at least 200 grams of limes. He plans to buy 7 limes. Will he buy enough? Use your response to Part A to explain.

3. Use the **Liquids Needed** table to answer the question.

Logan measures the liquids they need. Complete the table to show if Logan should use L or mL to measure each ingredient based on each container.

Ingredient	Container
vinegar	
milk	
water	

Liquids Needed	
Ingredient	**Container**
vinegar	spoon
milk	measuring cup
water	pot

The **Broth Used** art shows the amount of broth that Anita started with and what she had left after she poured it into two different soups.

Broth Used

| Start Amount | End Amount |

4. Use the **Broth Used** art to answer the questions.

Part A

How much broth did Anita use?

Part B

Anita poured an equal amount of broth into 2 pots. How much did she pour into 1 pot?

5. Use the **Time to Cook Chicken** table to answer the question.

Time to Cook Chicken

Activity	Time in Minutes
total time	50
flip	22

The directions give the total cooking time and when Logan has to flip the chicken. How many more minutes does it have to bake after he flips it? Show your work on a number line.

6. Use the **Before Reunion** table to answer the question.

Anita and Logan want to be at the reunion at 1:45 P.M. They need to clean, pack, and drive to the reunion. What time should they start cleaning? Explain.

Before Reunion

Activity	Time in Minutes
clean	20
pack	15
drive	55

Attributes of Two-Dimensional Shapes

Essential Question: How can two-dimensional shapes be described, analyzed, and classified?

Digital Resources

Solve Learn Glossary Practice Buddy

Tools Assessment Help Games

Even though a ball is not moving yet, there are still forces acting on it.

The force of a kick will change the motion of the ball.

I didn't know that! Here's a project on forces and shapes.

Math and Science Project: Forces and Motion

Do Research Use the Internet or other sources to find information about forces and the motion of an object. What does a balanced force mean? What happens when forces are unbalanced?

Journal: Write a Report Include what you found. Also include in your report:

- Examples of balanced and unbalanced forces on objects.

- A drawing that shows force acting on an object and the result.

- A description of shapes in your drawings.

Review What You Know

A-Z Vocabulary

Choose the best term from the box.
Write it on the line.

| • circle | • pentagon |
| • hexagon | • triangle |

1. A shape with exactly 6 sides is called a _____.

2. A shape with exactly 3 sides is called a _____.

3. A shape with exactly 5 sides is called a _____.

Name Shapes

Write the name of each figure.

4.

5.

6.

7.

Shapes

In **8–11** write the number of vertices each figure has.

8.

9.

10.

11.

12. How many faces does a cube have?

   Ⓐ 3   Ⓑ 4   Ⓒ 5   Ⓓ 6

13. How are squares and triangles the same? How are they different?

My Word Cards

Use the examples for each word on the front of the card to help complete the definitions on the back.

---

polygon

polygons   not polygons

---

side

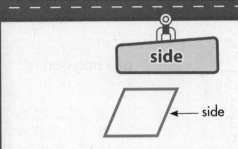

side

---

quadrilateral

Examples of quadrilaterals:

square   rectangle   parallelogram   trapezoid

---

angle

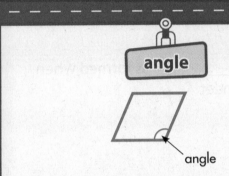

angle

---

vertex

vertex

---

trapezoid

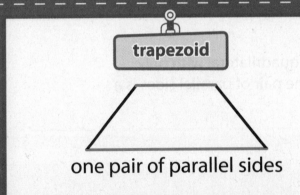

one pair of parallel sides

---

parallel sides

The red sides are parallel sides.

The green sides are not parallel sides.

---

parallelogram

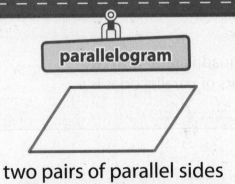

two pairs of parallel sides

Complete each definition. Extend learning by writing your own definitions.

Each _____ of a polygon is straight.

A _____ is a closed figure made up of straight line segments.

An _____ is formed when two sides meet.

A _____ is a polygon with exactly four sides.

A quadrilateral with only one pair of parallel sides is a _____.

A _____ is the point where two sides meet.

A quadrilateral with two pairs of parallel sides is a _____.

_____ of a polygon go in the exact same direction. If the sides cross when you make them longer, they are not parallel.

My Word Cards

Use the examples for each word on the front of the card to help complete the definitions on the back.

rectangle

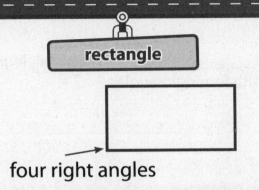

four right angles

right angle

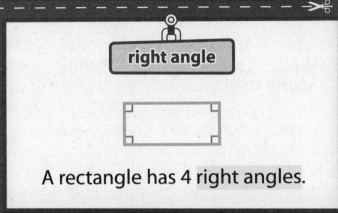

A rectangle has 4 right angles.

rhombus

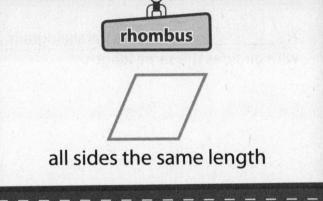

all sides the same length

square

four right angles

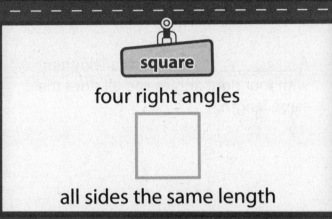

all sides the same length

convex

concave

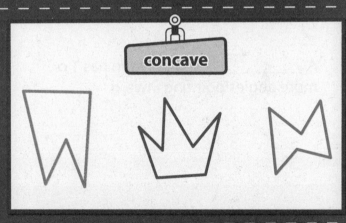

Complete each definition. Extend learning by writing your own definitions.

A _____ forms a square corner.

A _____ is a parallelogram with four right angles.

A _____ is a parallelogram with four right angles and all sides the same length.

A _____ is a parallelogram with all sides the same length.

A _____ polygon has 1 or more angles pointing inward.

All angles in a _____ polygon point outward.

Name _____

☆ ☆
Solve & Share

Look at the shapes below. Name each type of quadrilateral you see below and describe its attributes.

I can ...
identify quadrilaterals and use attributes to describe them.

I can also look for patterns to solve problems.

You can look for relationships. What attributes of the shapes can help you identify each by name?

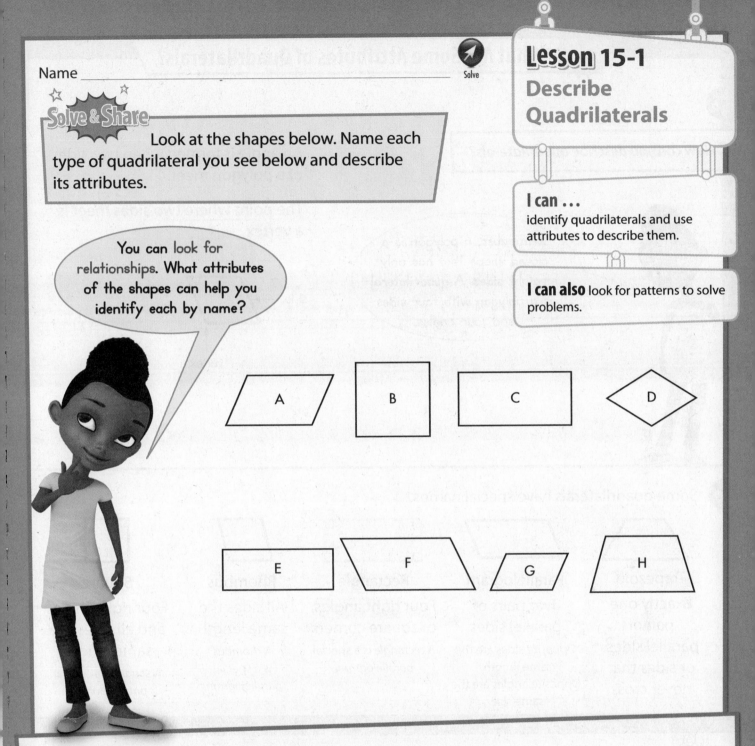

Look Back! **Generalize** Describe how you used what you know about quadrilaterals to identify the shapes.

Essential Question **What Are Some Attributes of Quadrilaterals?**

A

How can you describe quadrilaterals?

Remember, a polygon is a closed shape that has only straight sides. A quadrilateral is a polygon with four sides and four angles.

An angle is formed when two sides of a polygon meet.

The point where two sides meet is a vertex.

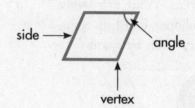

side → angle
vertex

B Some quadrilaterals have special names.

Trapezoid
Exactly one pair of parallel sides, or sides that never cross

Parallelogram
Two pairs of parallel sides
Opposite sides are the same length.
Opposite angles are the same size.

Rectangle
Four right angles, or square corners
A *rectangle* is a special *parallelogram*.

Rhombus
All sides the same length
A *rhombus* is a special *parallelogram*.

Square
Four right angles and all sides the same length
A *square* is a special *parallelogram*.

Convince Me! **Make Sense and Persevere** Draw a quadrilateral that is an example of one of the shapes listed in Box B. Name the shape. Then draw a quadrilateral this is NOT an example of a shape listed in Box B.

Another Example!

These are convex polygons. All angles point outward.

These are concave polygons. One or more angles point inward.

☆ Guided Practice *

Do You Understand?

1. This figure is a rectangle, but it is **NOT** a square. Why?

2. Draw two different quadrilaterals that are not rectangles, squares, or rhombuses.

Do You Know How?

In **3–6**, write as many special names as possible for each quadrilateral.

3.

4.

5.

6.

☆ Independent Practice ☆

In **7–9**, write as many special names as possible for each quadrilateral.

7.

8.

9.

In **10**, name all the possible quadrilaterals that fit the rule.

10. Has 2 pairs of parallel sides _____

Problem Solving

In **11** and **12**, write the name that best describes the quadrilateral. Draw a picture to help.

11. Ⓐ-Ⓩ **Vocabulary** A rectangle with all sides the same length is a _____.

12. Ⓐ-Ⓩ **Vocabulary** A parallelogram with four right angles is a _____.

13. **Look for Relationships** I am a quadrilateral with opposite sides the same length. Which quadrilaterals could I be?

Some problems have more than one correct answer.

14. **Higher Order Thinking** Jae says that the figure on the left is a trapezoid. Carmen says that the figure on the right is a trapezoid. Who is correct? Explain.

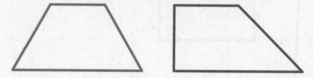

15. Sue bought a book for $12, two maps for $7 each, and a pack of postcards for $4. What was Sue's total cost?

16. **Algebra** Angela drew 9 rhombuses and 6 trapezoids. She wants to find q, the total number of angles in her quadrilaterals. Explain how Angela can find q.

✓ **Assessment**

---

17. Does the name describe the quadrilateral below? Choose Yes or No.

	Yes	No
Convex polygon	○	○
Rhombus	○	○
Square	○	○
Rectangle	○	○

Name _____

Another Look!

Some quadrilaterals have special names because of their sides. Some have special names because of their angles. Here are some examples.

The same polygon can have more than one name.

Parallelogram
Opposite sides are equal and parallel.

Rectangle
Parallelogram with four right angles

Rhombus
Parallelogram with four equal sides

Square
A rhombus with four right angles

Trapezoid
Exactly one pair of parallel sides

In **1–4**, read the description and circle the correct quadrilateral. Write the name.

1. I have 4 right angles and all sides the same length. I am a _____.

2. I have exactly one pair of parallel sides. I am a _____.

3. I have four right angles but only my opposite sides are equal. I am a _____.

4. I have all sides the same length, but I have no right angles. I am a _____.

5. Is a trapezoid also a parallelogram? Explain why or why not.

_____

_____

6. Christine drew the shape shown below. Madison changes Christine's shape so that it has every side equal and every angle equal. What shape does Madison make?

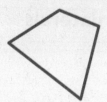

7. **Model with Math** There are 20 slices of bread in a loaf. How many 2-slice sandwiches can you make with 1 loaf? Write a multiplication fact and a division fact you could use to solve this problem.

8. **Math and Science** Mari pushed a box that is a cube. It fell off the table. Does a face of the box have a right angle? Explain how you know.

9. **Be Precise** Mr. Rose asked his students to draw a concave quadrilateral with 4 unequal sides. Draw an example of this kind of quadrilateral.

In **10** and **11**, use the shape at the right.

10. **Higher Order Thinking** Melissa drew the shape at the right. What two quadrilaterals did she use to draw the shape? Draw a line to divide the shape into two quadrilaterals.

11. **Construct Arguments** Suppose Melissa redrew the shape by turning it on its side. Would this change the names of the quadrilaterals she used? Explain.

 Assessment

12. Perry drew a quadrilateral that is convex and has 2 pairs of parallel sides. Could any of these shapes be what he drew? Choose *Yes* or *No*.

○ Yes ○ No

○ Yes ○ No

○ Yes ○ No

Lesson 15-2
Classify Shapes

Solve & Share

Sort the shapes below into two groups. Use colored pencils or crayons to color each group a different color. How did you sort the shapes? How are the shapes in both of your groups alike?

I can ...
classify shapes in several ways based on how they are alike and how they are different.

I can also generalize from examples.

> You can use what you know to generalize. What attributes are the same in the shapes?

Look Back! **Be Precise** Draw a new polygon that could go in your first group. Draw another new polygon that could go in your second group. Color them the same color as the group they belong to.

How Can You Describe Different Groups of Shapes?

A

Ethan made two groups of polygons. How are the groups different? How are the groups alike?

When you classify groups of shapes, you identify the attributes of each and then compare them with other shapes.

Group 1: Rhombuses

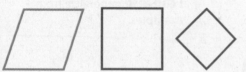

Group 2: Trapezoids

B

Here are some ways the two groups are different.

In Group 1, each polygon has sides that all are the same length.

In Group 2, each polygon has sides that are not all the same length.

In Group 1, each polygon has 2 pairs of parallel sides.

In Group 2, each polygon has only 1 pair of parallel sides.

C

Here are some ways the two groups are alike.

In Group 1 and Group 2, all of the polygons have 4 sides.

In Group 1 and Group 2, all of the polygons have 4 angles.

In Group 1 and Group 2, all of the polygons are quadrilaterals.

Convince Me! **Construct Arguments** Draw a quadrilateral that does not belong to either Group 1 or Group 2. Explain why it does not belong to either group.

☆ Guided Practice *

Do You Understand?

1. **Be Precise** Nellie drew a group of rectangles and a group of trapezoids. How are her groups different?

2. How are rectangles and trapezoids alike?

3. **Generalize** What larger group of polygons do all of Nellie's shapes belong to?

Do You Know How?

In **4–6**, use the groups on page 818.

4. Draw a shape that belongs to Ethan's Group 1.

5. Draw a shape that belongs to Ethan's Group 2.

6. Why is there a square in Group 1?

Independent Practice ☆

In **7–11**, use the groups below.

Group 1   **Group 2**

7. How are the shapes in Group 1 different from the shapes in Group 2?

8. How are the two groups alike?

9. What larger group do all the shapes belong to?

10. Draw a shape that could go in Group 2 but not Group 1.

11. Draw a shape that could go in Group 1 but not Group 2.

Problem Solving

In **12–14**, use the picture at the right.

12. How are the yellow shapes and the blue shapes different? How are they alike?

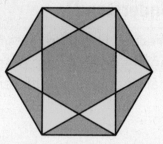

13. Which larger group of polygons do the yellow and blue shapes belong to?

14. Use Structure Does the pink shape belong to the group identified in Exercise 13? Explain your answer.

15. Draw a quadrilateral that is not a rectangle, a rhombus, or a square.

16. Todd bought a jacket for $57 and two maps for $9 each. What was the total cost?

17. Use Appropriate Tools Victoria wants to make two same-sized rhombuses. What tool can she use? Explain.

18. Higher Order Thinking Jessalyn needs to find 3×3, 4×6, and 7×2. She draws area models to solve the problem. What polygon group do her area models all belong to? Explain.

✔ Assessment

19. Draw lines to show which attributes apply to all the shapes in the group.

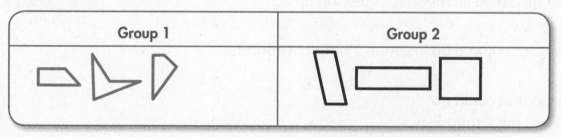

Convex   4 sides   No equal sides   2 pairs parallel sides   4 angles

© Pearson Education, Inc. 3

Another Look!

What attribute do these two shapes have in common?

What is another shape that shares this attribute?

Think about attributes that shapes can have. What attribute do these shapes share?

The rhombus has 2 pairs of parallel sides.
The parallelogram also has 2 pairs of parallel sides.

A rectangle also has 2 pairs of parallel sides.

In **1–3**, use the groups below.

Group 1

Group 2

1. How do the shapes in Group 1 differ from those in Group 2?

2. How are the two groups alike?

3. What group of polygons do all the shapes belong to?

4. Draw a shape that is neither a square nor concave.

5. Draw a shape that is neither a trapezoid nor has a right angle.

6. **Construct Arguments** Frida sorted polygons so Group 1 was only squares. Group 2 was only rectangles, not squares. Frida said all the shapes are parallelograms. Sam said they are all quadrilaterals. Who is right? Why?

7. **Be Precise** Can you draw a square that is **NOT** a rhombus? Explain.

8. **Number Sense** A bike helmet has a mass of 285 grams. Elena says that is about 300 grams. Is her estimate greater than, less than, or equal to the actual mass?

9. **A-Z Vocabulary** Define *parallel sides*. Draw a shape with parallel sides.

10. **Higher Order Thinking** Hope makes 3 groups of shapes. What larger group do the shapes in A and B belong to? What larger group do the shapes in A and C belong to? What larger group do the shapes in B and C belong to?

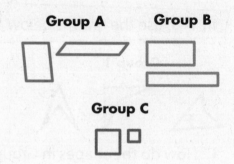

Group A **Group B**

Group C

Assessment

11. Nick sorted the shapes based on the number of sides of a figure. Draw a line from each orange shape to the group it belongs to.

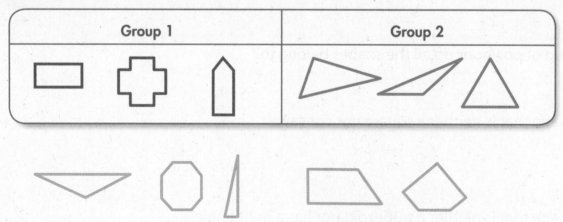

Group 1	Group 2

© Pearson Education, Inc. 3

Name _____

Solve & Share

Describe at least two things that are the same in all or some of these shapes. Describe two things that are different.

I can ...
analyze and compare quadrilaterals and group them by attributes.

I can also look for patterns to solve problems.

You can use structure. Look for common attributes, such as parallel and perpendicular sides.

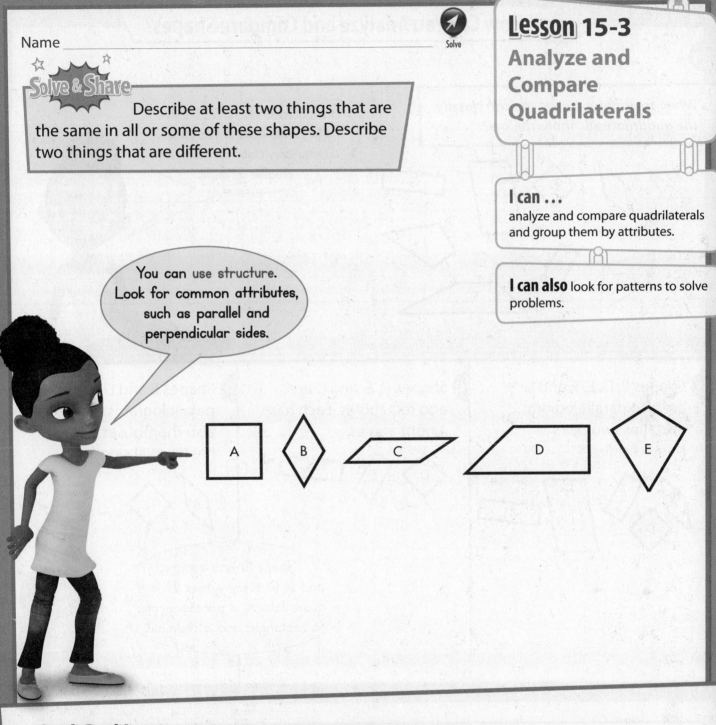

Look Back! **Model with Math** Draw a quadrilateral that is different from all the quadrilaterals above. Tell how it is different.

Essential Question **How Can You Analyze and Compare Shapes?**

A

What are different ways you can classify the quadrilaterals shown below?

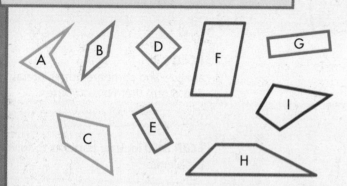

Quadrilaterals have 4 sides. They also have differences, so you can classify them into smaller groups.

B Shapes B, D, E, F, and G are also parallelograms. Each has two pairs of parallel sides.

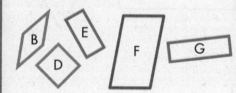

C Shapes D, E, and G are also rectangles. Each has 4 right angles.

D Shapes B and D are parallelograms that are also rhombuses. Each has 4 equal sides.

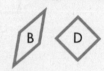

Shape D is a square and is in every group. It is a quadrilateral, a parallelogram, a rectangle, and a rhombus.

Convince Me! **Reasoning** Which of the shapes above can you cover with unit squares and not have any gaps or overlaps? What attributes do the shapes have in common?

☆ Guided Practice *

Do You Understand?

1. Use Structure Which shape on the previous page is a rhombus but not a rectangle? Explain.

2. Reasoning Can you have a square trapezoid? Explain.

Do You Know How?

3. Which shapes on the previous page are not a parallelogram, rectangle, rhombus, or square?

4. What attributes does a square have because it is always a rectangle?

Independent Practice ☆

In **5–9**, list all the polygons shown at the right that fit each description. If there could be no such polygon, tell why.

5. Has at least one set of parallel sides but is not a parallelogram

6. Is a quadrilateral but not a parallelogram or trapezoid

7. Is a square and not a parallelogram

8. Is a rhombus and not a rectangle

9. Is a parallelogram and not a rhombus

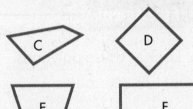
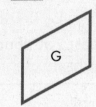

Problem Solving

10. **Use Structure** Cy put blocks 1 and 2 together to make a new shape. How are the blocks he used alike? How are they different?

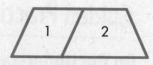

11. **Reasoning** Explain which of the shapes at the right you can cover with unit squares and not have any gaps or overlaps.

12. **Higher Order Thinking** Draw a quadrilateral with no parallel sides. Tell why it isn't a parallelogram or a trapezoid.

Use definitions and drawings to support your answer.

13. Sam needs 25 minutes to get ready and 15 minutes to bike to swim practice. Practice starts at 4:00 P.M. What time should Sam start getting ready?

✓ **Assessment**

14. Look at these polygons.

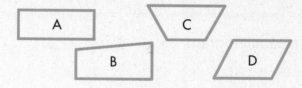

Part A

Name at least 2 attributes that all 4 polygons have.

Part B

Name an attribute that both A and D have that B and C do not.

Name _____

Another Look!

List all the names and attributes of a square.

A square has 4 sides, so it is a quadrilateral. Since it is a quadrilateral, it has 4 angles.

A square has opposite parallel sides, so it is a parallelogram. Since it is a parallelogram, its opposite sides are the same length. Its opposite angles are the same size.

A square has four right angles, so it is a rectangle. Since it is a rectangle, all 4 angles are right angles.

A square has all 4 sides the same length, so it is a rhombus.

You can use structure to analyze and compare the attributes of a square with other polygons.

In **1–6**, list all the polygons shown at the right that fit the description. If no polygon fits the description, tell why.

1. Has parallel sides but is not a trapezoid

2. Has at least one right angle but is not a square

3. Has no sides the same length

4. Is a rectangle but not a parallelogram

5. Is a parallelogram but not a rectangle

6. Is a rectangle with no angles the same size

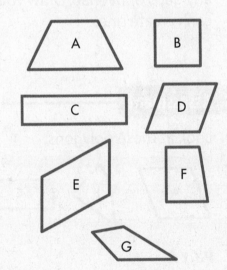

7. **Critique Reasoning** Mary claims that you can cut a parallelogram along its diagonal and get two pieces that are the same size and shape. Larry says that you can't cut all parallelograms this way. Who is correct? Explain your thinking.

8. **Use Structure** How are all the polygons in the mosaic alike and how are they different?

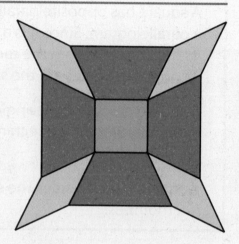

9. **Higher Order Thinking** Can you create a mosaic using the quadrilateral shown? The mosaic should not have any gaps or overlap. Draw your mosaic or tell why you can't create one.

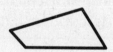

Assessment

10. Look at these polygons.

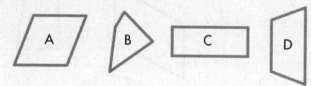

Part A

Name at least 2 attributes that A and C share.

Part B

Tell how B is different from the other 3 polygons.

Name _____

Solve & Share

Draw shapes that match all of these clues. Use math words and numbers correctly to name each shape and explain how your shapes match the clues.

Clue 1: *I am a polygon with 4 sides.*

Clue 2: *I am a polygon with 4 right angles.*

Clue 3: *I am a polygon with 2 sets of parallel sides.*

I can ...
be precise when solving math problems.

I can also identify shapes by their attributes.

Thinking Habits
Be a good thinker!
These questions can help you.

- Am I using numbers, units, and symbols appropriately?
- Am I using the correct definitions?
- Am I calculating accurately?
- Is my answer clear?

Look Back! **Be Precise** How did you use math terms or numbers to make your explanation clear?

How Can You Be Precise When Solving Math Problems?

A

What shapes can you draw for this riddle?

I am a polygon with 4 sides.
Only 2 of my sides are equal.
Only 2 of my sides are parallel.

Be precise means that you use correct math words, numbers, and symbols as you solve problems.

What do I need to do to solve this problem?

I will read the given information and use it to draw shapes that match the description.

B

How can I be precise in solving this problem?

I can

- correctly use the information given.

- use pictures or objects to identify possible answers.

- decide if my answer is clear and appropriate.

C

Here's my thinking...

I know that the shape is a 4-sided polygon with exactly 2 equal sides and 2 parallel sides.

I can draw shapes that match all of the clues. Then I can name each shape.

Trapezoid

Trapezoid

Each of the shapes has 4 sides. 2 of the sides are equal and 2 of the sides are parallel for each trapezoid.

Convince Me! **Be Precise** Draw a shape for this riddle. Name the shape and explain how it matches the clues.

I am a polygon with 4 sides.
None of my angles are right angles.
None of my sides are parallel.

© Pearson Education, Inc. 3

Name _____

Be Precise

Students in Mr. Tesla's class drew pictures of their favorite shapes. Jackie made a polygon with 4 sides. It has 4 right angles but not all of the shape's sides are the same length.

Be precise. Carefully consider and use the information you are given to solve problems.

1. What math words and numbers are important in this problem?

2. Draw and name the type of polygon Jackie made.

3. How can you check to make sure your answer is clear and correct?

☆ Independent Practice ☆

Be Precise

Students in Mrs. Edison's class designed a mural to show what they have learned about quadrilaterals. Ethan made a shape with opposite sides that are the same length.

4. What math words and numbers are important in this problem?

5. Draw a possible polygon Ethan could have made. Is there more than one type of quadrilateral that would correctly match the description? Explain.

6. How can you check to make sure your answer is clear and correct?

*For another example, see Set D on page 838.

Topic 15 | Lesson 15-4   **831**

Problem Solving

Crazy Quilts

Each student in Ms. Beardon's art class is designing a panel for a crazy quilt. Students can use different colors but each panel will be the same. The attributes of the panel design are as shown at the right.

- 4 equal sides
- 2 pairs of parallel sides
- 4 right angles

Draw and name a shape to match this description. Answer Exercises 7–10 to solve the problem.

7. **Make Sense and Persevere** What do you know? What are you asked to do?

8. **Be Precise** What math terms and numbers can help you solve the problem?

9. **Use Appropriate Tools** Choose tools to help you solve this problem. Then draw and name a possible panel design.

Make sure to use correct definitions so your answers can be precise.

10. **Critique Reasoning** Tabby followed Ms. Beardon's directions and made a quilt panel with the shape shown below. Did she follow directions correctly? Explain.

Name _____

Another Look!

Yoshi is thinking of a quadrilateral. It has two sets of parallel sides. All four sides are equal lengths and the shape has no right angles. Look at the array of shapes below. What shape is Yoshi thinking of?

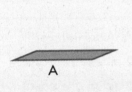
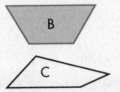

Tell how you can solve the problem with precision.

- I can correctly use the information given.

- I can draw pictures to identify possible answers.

- I can decide if my answer is clear and appropriate.

Be precise as you solve the problem.

All of the shapes are quadrilaterals.
B and C do not have 2 sets of parallel sides. A, D, E and F are parallelograms. A and E do not have 4 equal sides. D and F are rhombuses. F is a square rhombus with 4 right angles. Rhombus D is the only quadrilateral that fits all the clues.

Make sure to be precise when analyzing and comparing Yoshi's shape with those shown in the picture.

Be Precise

Jacobi made a banner in the shape of a polygon that fits the rules at the right. What banner shape could Jacobi have made?

1. What math words and numbers are important in this problem?

- It is a quadrilateral.
- It has two sets of parallel sides.
- Opposite sides are equal lengths.
- Two sides are longer than the other two sides.

2. Draw and name a shape that matches the description of Jacobi's banner.

3. How can you check to make sure your answer is clear and correct?

The Name Game

Pairs of students in Mr. Kuan's class are playing the Name Game. One team member is given a list of attributes and has to draw a shape to match the description. The other team member must then name the shape. The first pair to complete the task wins.

Wilfredo was given a list with the information at the right.

He drew a shape and his partner, Olivia, named it. What shape did Wilfredo draw? Answer Exercises 4–7 to solve the problem.

> • A quadrilateral
> • 2 sides are parallel
> • 2 sides are equal
> • 2 right angles

4. **Make Sense and Persevere** What are you asked to do? What can you do to persevere when solving the problem?

5. **Be Precise** What math terms and numbers can help you solve the problem?

Attend to precision by identifying words and numbers that can help you solve the problem.

6. **Use Structure** What do you know about a quadrilateral? Use what you know to draw and name a shape that matches the information in the list.

7. **Construct Arguments** Is there more than one possible way for Wilfredo to draw the shape? Explain.

Name _____

Shade a path from **START** to **FINISH**. Follow the products and quotients that are even numbers. You can only move up, down, right, or left.

TOPIC 15

Fluency Practice Activity

I can ...
multiply and divide within 100.

Start							
6 × 2	9 ÷ 1	9 × 5	24 ÷ 4	10 × 0	56 ÷ 7	3 × 8	35 ÷ 5
20 ÷ 5	5 × 8	8 × 2	36 ÷ 6	54 ÷ 6	3 × 5	2 × 3	27 ÷ 3
3 × 7	15 ÷ 3	5 × 7	5 ÷ 1	25 ÷ 5	6 ÷ 6	9 × 8	21 ÷ 7
48 ÷ 8	2 × 9	42 ÷ 7	3 × 5	8 ÷ 2	5 × 4	30 ÷ 5	9 × 9
3 × 6	5 × 1	6 × 10	0 ÷ 6	4 × 6	7 × 1	9 × 1	45 ÷ 9
9 × 6	4 × 8	72 ÷ 8	9 × 3	9 ÷ 3	4 × 4	18 ÷ 9	16 ÷ 2
5 × 5	2 × 7	81 ÷ 9	6 ÷ 2	4 × 7	80 ÷ 8	3 × 9	9 × 4
63 ÷ 9	4 × 3	7 × 8	8 × 9	10 ÷ 5	24 ÷ 8	9 × 7	40 ÷ 5

Finish

Topic 15 | Fluency Practice Activity   **835**

TOPIC 15 Vocabulary Review

A-Z
Glossary

Word List
- angle
- concave
- convex
- parallelogram
- parallel sides
- polygon
- quadrilateral
- rectangle
- rhombus
- right angle
- square
- trapezoid

Understand Vocabulary

Circle all the terms that match each description.

1. A quadrilateral

    square   rhombus   trapezoid   polygon

2. A polygon

    angle   quadrilateral   rectangle   concave

3. A polygon with 4 right angles

    square   trapezoid   rhombus   rectangle

4. A parallelogram

    rhombus   parallel sides   rectangle   trapezoid

For each term, draw an example and a non-example.

	Example	Non-example
5. right angle		
6. concave polygon		
7. trapezoid		

Use Vocabulary in Writing

8. Use at least 3 terms from the Word List to explain why a *square* is a *rectangle*.

Name _____

Set A pages 811–816 _____

You can draw quadrilaterals and describe them by their attributes.

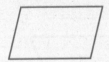

Name: Parallelogram
Attribute: 2 pairs of parallel sides

Name: Quadrilateral
Attributes: Concave, no parallel sides

Name: Rectangle
Attributes: 2 pairs of parallel sides, 4 right angles

Remember that a polygon with four sides is a quadrilateral.

In **1–3**, draw the shapes named or described below and describe their attributes.

1. Trapezoid   2. Rhombus

3. A quadrilateral that is **NOT** a trapezoid, parallelogram, rectangle, rhombus, or square.

Set B pages 817–822 _____

How are the shapes in Groups 1 and 2 different? How are they alike?

Group 1

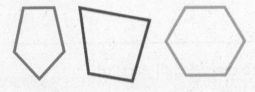

Group 2

The shapes in the groups are different because in Group 1, all shapes are convex. In Group 2, all shapes are concave.

The shapes in both groups are alike because they all have straight lines and are closed. Therefore, they all are polygons.

Remember that all of the shapes in these groups have something in common.

In **1** and **2**, use the groups below.

Group 1

Group 2

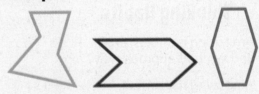

1. How are the shapes in groups 1 and 2 different?

2. How are the shapes in groups 1 and 2 alike?

All of the shapes below have 4 sides, so they are quadrilaterals. Some quadrilaterals can be classified into multiple groups.

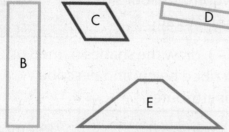

Parallelograms have 2 pairs of parallel sides. Shapes A, B, C, and D are parallelograms.

Rhombuses have 2 pairs of parallel sides and 4 equal sides. Shapes A and C are rhombuses.

Rectangles have 2 pairs of parallel sides and 4 right angles. Shapes A, B, and D are rectangles.

Squares have 4 equal sides and 4 right angles. Shape A is a square.

Trapezoids have 1 pair of parallel sides and no right angles. Shape E is a trapezoid.

Remember that quadrilaterals with different names can have some of the same attributes.

In **1–4**, list all the polygons that fit the given attributes.

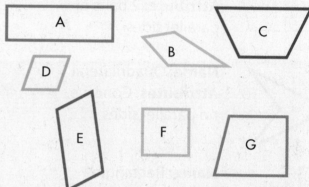

1. Has at least 2 right angles but is not a rectangle

2. Has parallel sides but is not a rectangle

3. Is a quadrilateral with no right angles

4. Has 4 sides the same length but is not a square

Think about these questions to help you **attend to precision.**

Thinking Habits

- Am I using numbers, units, and symbols appropriately?

- Am I using the correct definitions?

- Am I calculating accurately?

- Is my answer clear?

Remember to consider all parts of the question.

Anton drew a quadrilateral with 2 parallel sides and no right angles. No sides are the same length.

1. What quadrilateral did he draw?

2. Is there any other shape that he could have drawn? Explain.

Name _____

1. Sari's friend told her that he drew a quadrilateral with all sides the same length. Sari said the shape must be a square. Is she correct?

   Ⓐ Yes, there is no other shape it could be.

   Ⓑ No, it could also be a triangle.

   Ⓒ No, it could also be a rhombus.

   Ⓓ No, it could also be a trapezoid.

2. Use the words in the box below. Write the names for the shapes in the correct columns.

Quadrilateral	Parallelogram

   rectangle rhombus square trapezoid

3. Name and draw a picture of a concave polygon with 4 sides.

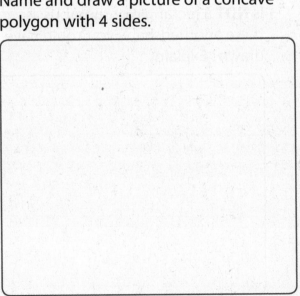

4. Rose drew a parallelogram with 4 right angles. What are the possible shapes it could be?

5. Elliot sorted the shapes below into two groups. He then circled only the shapes that fit a rule for one of the groups. What rule did Elliot use to circle some of the shapes?

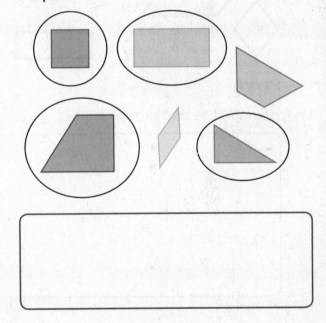

6. Choose all true statements.

   ☐ A trapezoid is a parallelogram.

   ☐ A parallelogram is a quadrilateral.

   ☐ A square is a rhombus.

   ☐ A triangle is a quadrilateral.

   ☐ A square is a rectangle.

7. What two quadrilaterals did Kim use to make the rug design?

8. Look at each group.

Group 1   **Group 2**

Part A

How are the two groups alike?

Part B

How are the two groups different?

9. For Questions 9a–9d, choose Yes or No to tell if a square belongs to the named group.

9a. rectangle ⬡ Yes ⬡ No

9b. rhombus ⬡ Yes ⬡ No

9c. trapezoid ⬡ Yes ⬡ No

9d. parallelogram ⬡ Yes ⬡ No

10. Whose shape has only one set of parallel sides?

Melissa's   Nigel's

Pat's   Rahmi's

11. Name and draw a quadrilateral that is **NOT** a rectangle or rhombus. Is there another shape you could have drawn? Explain.

Name _____

Pet Tags

Amelia and Bryce work at a pet store that sells pet identifcation tags in many shapes. The **Pet Tags** diagram shows the different shapes available.

Use the **Pet Tags** art to answer Questions 1–4.

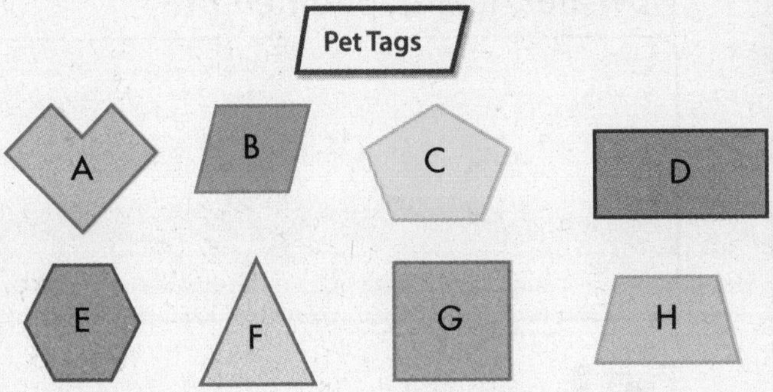

Pet Tags

1. A customer asks Amelia if the store has any pet tags that are concave. How should Amelia respond?

2. Another customer asks Bryce which pet tags have 2 pairs of parallel sides and are quadrilaterals. Which tags have these attributes? Include the common name of each shape.

3. The store owner wants to mark for sale any pet tags that have at least 1 pair of parallel sides and are not rectangles. Which tags should she mark on sale, and what shapes are they?

4. The owner asks Bryce to group the tags to show which ones have at least 1 pair of parallel sides. Complete the table with the pet tag labels.

Parallel Sides	No Parallel Sides

5. Use the **Pet Tags** diagram and the **Tag Sort** table to answer the questions in Part A and Part B.

Amelia sorts some of the pet tags into two different groups.

Tag Sort	
Group 1	**Group 2**
B, G, D, H	A, C, E, F

Part A

How are the groups different?

Part B

How are the groups alike?

Use the **Pet Tags** diagram to answer Questions 6 and 7.

6. A customer says she wants to buy the pet tag that is a rhombus and a rectangle. What tag does she want? Explain.

7. Design a new pet tag that has 2 pairs of parallel sides and 2 pairs of sides the same length, but it is not a rectangle or a rhombus. Explain the shape you drew.

TOPIC 16

Solve Perimeter Problems

Essential Question: How can perimeter be measured and found?

Digital Resources

Solve   Learn   Glossary   Practice Buddy

Tools   Assessment   Help   Games

Animals live in a habitat.

Some animals can only live in certain habitats.

Lots of animals live here! Here's a project on habitats and perimeter.

Math and Science Project: What Lives Here?

Do Research Use the Internet or other sources to research habitats. Include a list of animals that can survive in a certain habitat and some that could not survive there.

Journal: Write a Report Include what you found. Also in your report:

- Draw a picture on grid paper to represent one of the habitats you researched. Label the habitat to show what you might find there. Count the number of square units the habitat measures.

- Find the perimeter of the habitat. Then find another possible perimeter with the same area.

Name _____

Review What You Know

A-Z Vocabulary

Choose the best term from the box.
Write it on the blank.

• area	• square units
• rectangle	• unit square

1. If 14 unit squares cover a figure, the area is 14 _____.

2. You can use square meters or square feet to measure _____.

3. A square with a side length of 1 unit is a _____.

Area of Figures

Find the area for each figure. Use grid paper to help.

4.
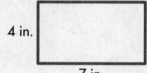
4 in.
7 in.

5.
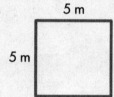
5 m
5 m

6. The area of a rectangle is 32 square centimeters. It is 4 centimeters wide.
   How long is the rectangle?

   Ⓐ   4 centimeters   Ⓑ   8 centimeters   Ⓒ   16 centimeters   Ⓓ   32 centimeters

Area of Irregular Shapes

7. What is the area of the figure at the right? Explain how you
   solved this problem.

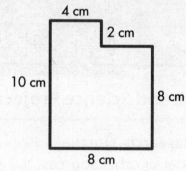
4 cm
2 cm
10 cm
8 cm
8 cm

Dividing Regions into Equal Parts

8. Circle the shapes that show equal parts. Label one of the equal parts using
   a unit fraction.

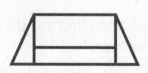

My Word Cards

Use the examples for each word on the front of the card to help complete the definitions on the back.

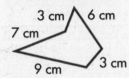

The **perimeter** of this figure is 28 cm.

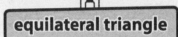

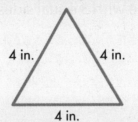

My Word Cards

Complete each definition. Extend learning by writing your own definitions.

An _____
is a triangle with 3 equal sides.

The distance around a figure is called

_____.

Name _____

☆ Solve & Share

Troy made a drawing of his garden. Each square in the grid below has a side length of 1 foot. Find the distance around Troy's garden. Then use grid paper to draw a different garden shape that has the same distance around. **Solve this problem any way you choose.**

I can ...
find the perimeter of different polygons.

I can also be precise in my work.

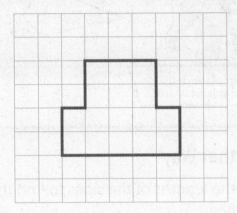

Be precise when finding the total distance. You know the length of each side of the garden. *Show your work in the space below!*

Look Back! **Be Precise** Use words, numbers, and symbols to explain how you found the distance around Troy's garden.

A

Gus wants to put up a fence to make a dog park. He made two different designs. What is the perimeter of each dog park design? Which design should Gus use?

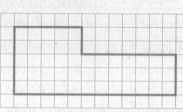
scale: ⊢⊣ = 1 ft

The distance around a figure is its perimeter.

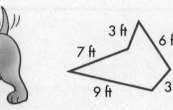
3 ft, 6 ft, 7 ft, 9 ft, 3 ft

The perimeter of the dog park needs to be at least 30 feet.

B **One Way**

You can find the perimeter by counting unit segments.

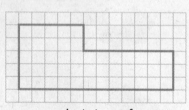

scale: ⊢⊣ = 1 ft

The perimeter is 34 feet.
34 > 30. Gus could use this design.

C **Another Way**

Add the lengths of the sides to find the perimeter.

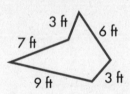
3 ft, 6 ft, 7 ft, 9 ft, 3 ft

$3 + 9 + 7 + 3 + 6 = 28$
The perimeter is 28 feet.
28 < 30. Gus could not use this design.

Convince Me! **Model with Math** Draw a different dog park design that Gus could use. Find the perimeter of your design.

© Pearson Education, Inc. 3

Name _____

Practice Buddy Tools Assessment

Do You Understand?

1. What is the perimeter of the garden shown in the diagram below?

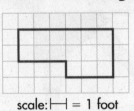

scale: ⊢—⊣ = 1 foot

2. Be Precise In Exercise 1, how do you know what unit to use for the perimeter?

Do You Know How?

In **3** and **4**, find the perimeter.

3.

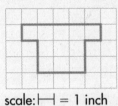

scale: ⊢—⊣ = 1 inch

4.

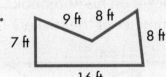
9 ft   8 ft
7 ft   8 ft
       16 ft

Independent Practice ☆

Leveled Practice In **5–7**, find the perimeter of each polygon.

5.

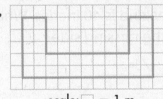

scale: ☐ = 1 m

6.

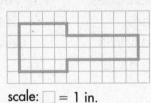

scale: ☐ = 1 in.

7.

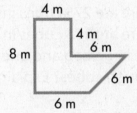
4 m
4 m
8 m   6 m
            6 m
   6 m

8. On the grid below, draw a figure with a perimeter of 20 units.

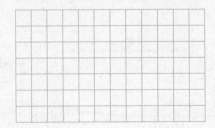

You can draw many different shapes that have the same perimeter.

Problem Solving

9. Model with Math Niko makes beaded necklaces in three different sizes. How many more beads does it take to make 2 medium necklaces than 1 large necklace? Write equations to solve.

Size of Necklace	Number of Beads
Small	68
Medium	129
Large	212

---

10. Jani put this sticker on his notebook. What is the perimeter of the sticker?

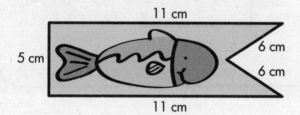

11 cm

5 cm

6 cm

6 cm

11 cm

11. Reasoning What is the perimeter of the cloth patch outline below?

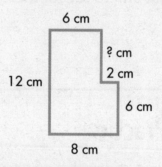

6 cm

? cm

2 cm

12 cm

6 cm

8 cm

---

12. Number Sense Jenny needs 425 cubes. There are 275 cubes in a large bag. There are 175 cubes in a small bag. Will one large bag and one small bag have enough cubes? Explain.

13. Higher Order Thinking The perimeter of this trapezoid is 40 inches. What is the length of the missing side?

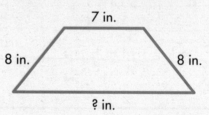

7 in.

8 in.   8 in.

? in.

Assessment

14. Mr. Karas needs to find the perimeter of the patio shown at the right. What is the perimeter of the patio? How can Mr. Karas find the perimeter?

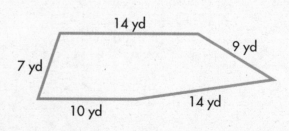

14 yd

9 yd

7 yd

10 yd

14 yd

Another Look!

What is the perimeter of this figure?

Add the lengths of the sides.

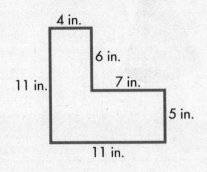

4 in.

6 in.

11 in.

7 in.

5 in.

11 in.

$4 + 6 + 7 + 5 + 11 + 11 = 44$

The perimeter of the figure is 44 inches.

The perimeter of a figure is the distance around it.

Leveled Practice In **1–3**, find the perimeter of each polygon.

1.

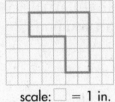

scale: ☐ = 1 in.

2.

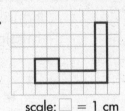

scale: ☐ = 1 cm

3.

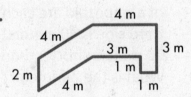

4 m

4 m

3 m

3 m

2 m

1 m

4 m

1 m

1 m

In **4–6**, draw a figure with the given perimeter.

4. 12 units

5. 18 units

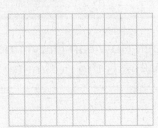

6. 22 units

7. Critique Reasoning Rosa has a garden in the shape of a parallelogram. She says she can find the perimeter of her garden by adding the two sides and doubling the sum. Is Rosa correct? Why or why not?

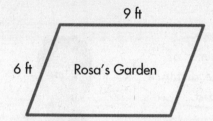

9 ft

6 ft   Rosa's Garden

8. Construct Arguments May bought 12 hats. What solid figure do the hats look like? What attributes help you decide?

9. Vocabulary Explain the difference between perimeter and area.

10. A plane figure has 2 sides that are each 5 inches and 2 sides that are each 3 inches. What is the perimeter of the plane figure?

11. Make Sense and Persevere Two sides of a trapezoid are each 25 meters. The third side is 40 meters. The fourth side is 20 meters shorter than the longest side. What is the perimeter? Explain.

12. Higher Order Thinking Ming drew this figure. Its perimeter is 47 cm. What is the missing length? How can you find it?

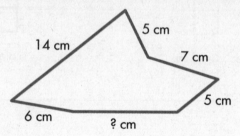

14 cm
5 cm
7 cm
5 cm
6 cm
? cm

✓ **Assessment**

13. Daryl drew this figure on grid paper. How can Daryl find the perimeter of the figure he drew? What is the perimeter of the figure?

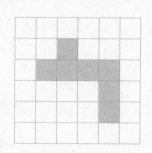

Name _____

Solve

Solve & Share

What is the perimeter of the rectangle below? Show two ways to find the perimeter, other than measuring.

I can ...
find the perimeter of polygons with common shapes.

I can also look for patterns to solve problems.

You can use structure. How could what you know about the attributes of common shapes help you find the perimeter? *Show your work in the space below!*

5 in.

3 in.

Look Back! **Generalize** How could you use addition and multiplication to find the perimeter?

Essential Question **How Can You Find the Perimeters of Common Shapes?**

A

Mr. Coe needs to find the perimeter of two swimming pool designs. One pool shape is a rectangle. The other pool shape is a square. What is the perimeter of each pool?

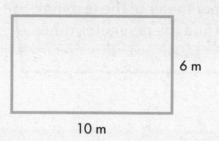

6 m

10 m

9 m

B Find the perimeter of the pool that has a rectangular shape.

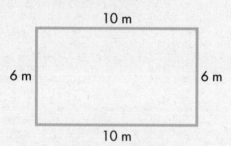

10 m

6 m   6 m

10 m

10 + 6 + 10 + 6 = 32 or
(10 × 2) + (6 × 2) = 32
The perimeter of this pool is 32 meters.

 Remember, opposite sides of a rectangle are the same length.

C Find the perimeter of the pool that has a square shape.

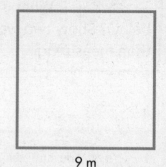 Remember, all four sides of a square are the same length.

9 m

9 m   9 m

9 m

9 + 9 + 9 + 9 = 36 or 4 × 9 = 36
The perimeter of this pool is 36 meters.

Convince Me! **Make Sense and Persevere** Darla drew the parallelogram at the right. Tell how to find the perimeter.

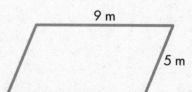

9 m

5 m

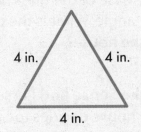

Another Example!

An **equilateral triangle** has 3 sides the same length.

$4 + 4 + 4 = 12$ or $3 \times 4 = 12$.

So, the perimeter of this equilateral triangle is 12 inches.

4 in.   4 in.

4 in.

☆ Guided Practice *

Do You Understand?

1. **Reasoning** How can you use multiplication and addition to find the perimeter of a rectangle with a length of 6 feet and width of 4 feet?

2. **Reasoning** Explain how you can find the perimeter of a square with a side length of 7 cm.

Do You Know How?

For **3** and **4**, find the perimeter.

3. Rectangle

4 ft

8 ft

4. Square

5 cm

Independent Practice ☆

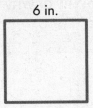

In **5–7**, find the perimeter of each polygon.

5. Square

6 in.

6. Rectangle

12 cm

6 cm

7. Equilateral triangle

6 yd

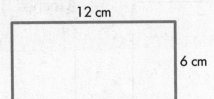

*For another example, see Set A on page 885.

Problem Solving

In **8** and **9**, use the picture at the right.

8. The base of the glass house to the right is a rectangle. What is the perimeter of the base of the house?

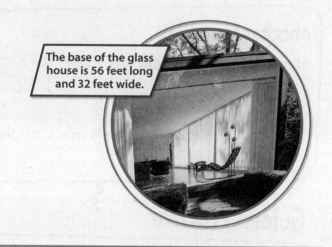

The base of the glass house is 56 feet long and 32 feet wide.

9. Make Sense and Persevere The owner of the house decides to build an extension. The new base is 112 feet long and 64 feet wide. What is the new perimeter?

---

10. Be Precise Identify the number of sides and vertices in the hexagon below.

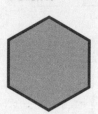

11. Critique Reasoning Mark says he can find the perimeter of a square zoo enclosure by multiplying the length of one side by 4. Is Mark correct? Why or why not?

---

12. Higher Order Thinking Dan drew the trapezoid at the right. The top is 3 inches long. The bottom is twice as long as the top. The length of a side is 5 inches. How can you find the perimeter of the trapezoid? Label the lengths of the sides.

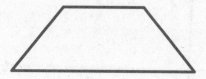

Assessment

13. José draws a rectangle and Mikayla draws a parallelogram. If both shapes have sides that are 6 cm and 15 cm, are their perimeters the same? Explain.

14. Emma says that the total perimeter of two squares with side lengths of 3 inches is the same as the perimeter of a rectangle with a length of 6 inches and width of 3 inches. Is Emma correct? Why or why not?

Help Practice Tools Games
Buddy

Another Look!

Use the attributes of these common shapes to find the missing side lengths. Then find the perimeters.

Rectangle

Two pairs of sides have the same length.

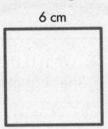

5 in.

4 in.

$4 + 5 + 4 + 5 = 18$ in.
$(4 \times 2) + (5 \times 2) = 18$ in.

Square

All 4 sides have the same length.

6 cm

$6 + 6 + 6 + 6 = 24$ cm
$6 \times 4 = 24$ cm

Equilateral Triangle

All 3 sides have the same length.

5 ft

$5 + 5 + 5 = 15$ ft
$5 \times 3 = 15$ ft

You can use the attributes of polygons to help find perimeters.

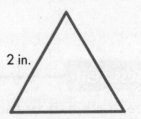

In **1–9**, find the perimeter of each polygon.

1. Square

4 cm

2. Rectangle

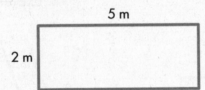

5 m

2 m

3. Equilateral Triangle

3 in.

4. Parallelogram

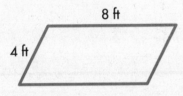

8 ft

4 ft

5. Rectangle

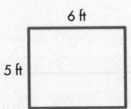

6 ft

5 ft

6. Equilateral Triangle

2 in.

7. Equilateral Triangle

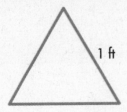

1 ft

8. Square

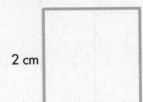

2 cm

9. Rectangle

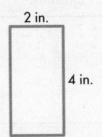

2 in.

4 in.

10. Reasoning The distance around the outside of this maze is the same as the perimeter of a rectangle. The picture shows the lengths of the sides of the rectangle. What is the perimeter of the maze? How did you find the answer?

95 ft

88 ft

11. Algebra Paolo earns $4 for each hour he tutors. He made $28 last week. Write an equation using h to represent the hours he tutored. Then solve the equation.

12. What is the perimeter of a hexagon that has equal sides of 12 centimeters?

13. Math and Science A pond is a habitat for many different kinds of plants and animals. Maria puts this fence around her pond. What is the perimeter of the fence? Show your work.

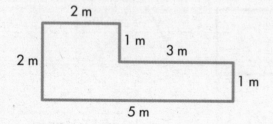

2 m

1 m

3 m

2 m

1 m

5 m

14. Higher Order Thinking Pete put the 5-inch sides of these two trapezoids together to make a hexagon. What was the perimeter of the hexagon Pete made? Explain how you know.

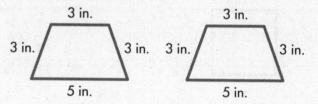

3 in.

3 in.

3 in.

3 in.

3 in.

3 in.

5 in.

5 in.

15. Nina draws a square and Nick draws a pentagon. If all sides of both shapes are each 9 inches long, are their perimeters the same? Explain.

16. Debra says two squares of different sizes can have the same perimeter. Is Debra correct? Why or why not?

Name _____

Solve & Share

Jon has 16 feet of wood that he uses to make a sandbox that has 4 sides. He makes sides with lengths of 6 feet, 5 feet, and 3 feet. What length should he make the fourth side in order to use all 16 feet of the wood? **Solve this problem any way you choose.**

I can ...
find the unknown length of a polygon by using a known perimeter.

I can also reason about math.

Use reasoning to show how the perimeter and given side lengths are related.

5 ft

? ft   3 ft

6 ft

Look Back! **Make Sense and Persevere** Describe the plan you used to solve the problem.

How Can You Find an Unknown Side Length from the Perimeter?

A

Lilia is making a decoration out of straws and cloth, with lace around the outside. How long should she cut the fourth straw to use all of the lace?

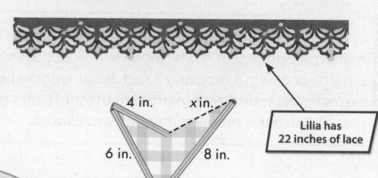

4 in.   x in.

6 in.   8 in.

Lilia has 22 inches of lace

Lilia needs to find the length that will give the shape a perimeter of 22 inches.

B Draw a bar diagram and write an equation.

Let x = the length of the missing side.

The perimeter of the shape is 22 inches.

22			
8	6	4	x

$x + 8 + 6 + 4 = 22$

$x + 18 = 22$

C Solve.

$x + 18 = 22$

Think: What plus 18 equals 22?

$4 + 18 = 22$, so $x = 4$.

So, the fourth side should be 4 inches long.

You can also use subtraction to find $22 - 18 = 4$.

Convince Me! **Look for Relationships** If Lilia had 25 inches of lace, how would the length of the fourth straw change? Explain how to solve.

Name _____

 Practice Buddy   Tools   Assessment

☆ Guided Practice ☆

Do You Understand?

1. Construct Arguments In the problem on page 860, why does $x + 8 + 6 + 4$ equal the perimeter, 22 inches?

2. Model with Math Write an equation you could use to find the length of the missing side of this triangle with a perimeter of 23 cm. Then solve.

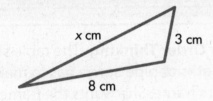

x cm   3 cm   8 cm

Do You Know How?

In **3** and **4**, find the length of the missing side for each polygon so it has the perimeter given.

3. perimeter = 30 cm

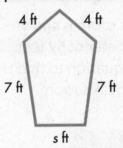

8 cm   x cm   12 cm

4. perimeter = 25 ft

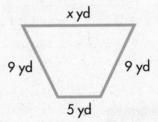

4 ft   4 ft   7 ft   7 ft   s ft

☆ Independent Practice ☆

In **5–10**, find the length of the missing side for each polygon so it has the perimeter given.

5. perimeter = 24 in.

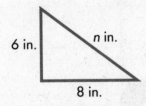

6 in.   n in.   8 in.

6. perimeter = 30 m

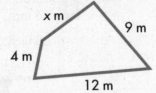

x m   9 m   4 m   12 m

7. perimeter = 37 yd

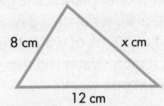

x yd   9 yd   9 yd   5 yd

8. perimeter = 37 cm

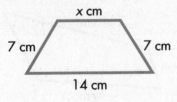

x cm   7 cm   7 cm   14 cm

9. perimeter = 18 ft

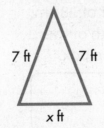

7 ft   7 ft   x ft

10. perimeter = 32 in.

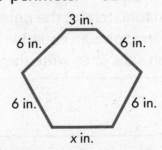

3 in.   6 in.   6 in.   6 in.   6 in.   x in.

Problem Solving

11. **Construct Arguments** These plane figures each have equal sides that are whole numbers. One figure has a perimeter of 25 inches. Which could it be? Explain.

---

12. **Math and Science** Letitia did an experiment to see if giving more or less water was better for her plants. She gave one plant 40 mL of water once a day. She gave another plant 80 mL of water once a day. How much more water did the second plant get in one week?

13. **Make Sense and Persevere** Mason has 18 feet of wood to frame a window. He wants the window to be in the shape of a rectangle 3 feet wide. What should be the length? Tell how you know your answer is correct.

---

14. **Reasoning** Novak's room is shown below. It has a perimeter of 52 feet. Tell how to use an equation to find the missing length in Novak's room.

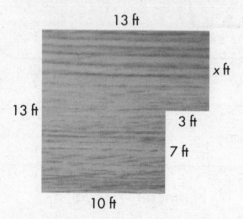

15. **Higher Order Thinking** The table shows the lengths of pipe Sonya has to make a picture frame. She wants the frame to have 5 sides and a perimeter of 40 inches. Draw and label a diagram of a possible picture frame Sonya could make.

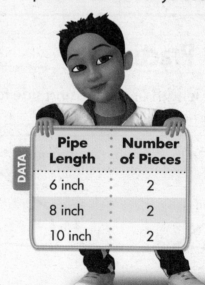

Pipe Length	Number of Pieces
6 inch	2
8 inch	2
10 inch	2

✓ **Assessment**

16. The quadrilateral at the right has a perimeter of 28 cm. Write and solve an equation to find the length of the missing side. Then write the side length in the box.

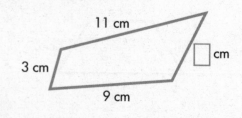

© Pearson Education, Inc. 3

Help Practice Tools Games
      Buddy

Another Look!

When you know the perimeter of a polygon and the lengths of all but one side, you can find the length of the unknown side.

The perimeter of the triangle is 14 meters. Another way to write the perimeter is by adding the lengths of its sides.

$5 + 6 + s =$ perimeter

So, $5 + 6 + s = 14$

$11 + s = 14$

Since $11 + 3 = 14$, $s = 3$ and the length of the unknown side is 3 meters.

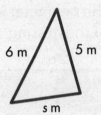

6 m   5 m

s m

In **1–6**, find the length of the missing side for each polygon.

1. perimeter = 29 cm

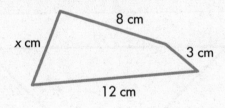

8 cm
x cm
3 cm
12 cm

2. perimeter = 55 ft

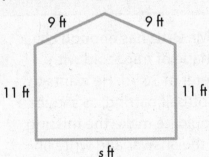

9 ft   9 ft

11 ft   11 ft

s ft

3. perimeter: 30 in.

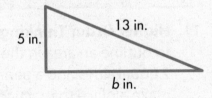

13 in.
5 in.
b in.

4. perimeter = 35 cm

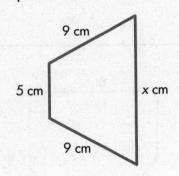

9 cm
5 cm   x cm
9 cm

5. perimeter = 22 ft

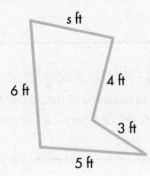

s ft
6 ft
4 ft
3 ft
5 ft

6. perimeter = 48 mm

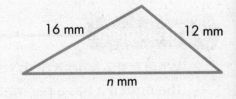

16 mm   12 mm
n mm

---

7. Reasoning A rectangle has a perimeter of 40 cm. One side is 12 cm. What are the lengths of the other 3 sides? Explain your answer.

8. A square has a perimeter of 36 centimeters. What is the length of each side? Explain your answer.

9. Tracy measured the sides of a shape she drew. She forgot to label one side length, but knows the perimeter is 40 cm. What is the length of the missing side?

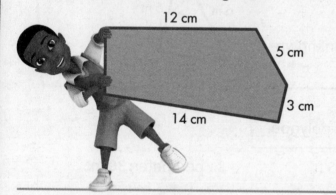

12 cm

5 cm

3 cm

14 cm

10. Model with Math Arturo is putting 18 erasers into equal rows. He says there will be more erasers in 2 equal rows than in 3 equal rows. Is Arturo correct? Explain.

11. Higher Order Thinking Mr. Ortiz has enough chalk to outline an area in the shape of trapezoid with 2 equal sides and a perimeter of 36 yd. He wants to make a place to practice softball batting, as shown on the right. How long should he make the missing sides? Tell how you found the answer and write an equation that could be used to solve the problem.

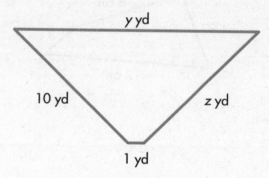

y yd

10 yd

z yd

1 yd

12. What is the length of the missing side for the polygon on the right if it has a perimeter of 30 inches? Write and solve an equation to show your work. Then write the side length in the box.

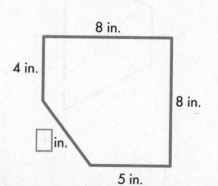

8 in.

4 in.

8 in.

☐ in.

5 in.

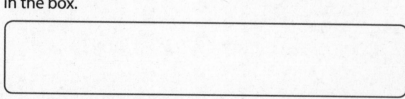

Name _____

Solve

☆ Solve & Share ☆

Draw 2 different rectangles with a perimeter of 10 units. Find the area of each rectangle. Compare the areas. **Solve this problem any way you choose.**

I can ...
understand the relationship of shapes with the same perimeter and different areas.

I can also be precise in my work.

Be precise when drawing and finding the perimeter and area. Think about how perimeter and area are measured and recorded.

Look Back! Construct Arguments Explain why the rectangles have different area.

Essential Question

Can Rectangles Have Different Areas but the Same Perimeter?

A

Beth, Marcia, and Nancy build rectangular pens for their rabbits. Each pen has a perimeter of 12 feet. Which rectangular pen has the greatest area?

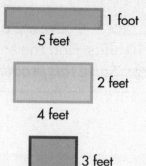

1 foot
5 feet

2 feet
4 feet

3 feet
3 feet

Drawings help you see how the rectangles are similar and different.

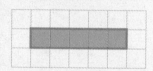

B **Beth's Plan**

Find the perimeter:
$P = 5 + 1 + 5 + 1 = 12$ feet

To find the area multiply the number of rows by the number of square units in each row.

$A = 1 \times 5 = 5$ square feet

Beth's pen has an area of 5 square feet.

C **Nancy's Plan**

Find the perimeter:
$P = 4 + 2 + 4 + 2 = 12$ feet

Find the area:
$A = 2 \times 4 = 8$ square feet

Nancy's pen has an area of 8 square feet.

D **Marcia's Plan**

Find the perimeter:
$P = 3 + 3 + 3 + 3 = 12$ feet

Find the area:
$A = 3 \times 3 = 9$ square feet

Marcia's pen has an area of 9 square feet.

Marcia's pen has the greatest area.

Convince Me! **Generalize** Find possible rectangular pens that have a perimeter of 14 feet. Do they have the same area? What can you generalize from this information?

☆ Guided Practice *

Do You Understand?

1. **Look for Relationships** In the problem on page 866, what do you notice about the area of the rectangles as the shape becomes more like a square?

2. Austin is building a rabbit pen with 25 feet of fence. What are the dimensions of the rectangle he should build to have the greatest possible area?

Do You Know How?

In **3–6**, use grid paper to draw two different rectangles with the given perimeter. Tell the dimensions and area of each rectangle. Circle the one that has the greater area.

3. 16 feet   **4.** 20 centimeters

5. 24 inches   **6.** 40 meters

☆ Independent Practice ☆

In **7–10**, use grid paper to draw two different rectangles with the given perimeter. Tell the dimensions and area of each rectangle. Circle the one that has the greater area.

7. 10 inches   **8.** 22 centimeters   **9.** 26 yards   **10.** 32 feet

Leveled Practice In **11–14**, describe a different rectangle with the same perimeter as the one shown. Then tell which rectangle has the greater area.

11.
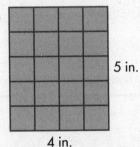
5 in.
4 in.

12.
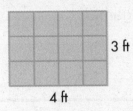
3 ft
4 ft

13.
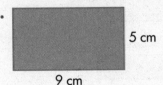
5 cm
9 cm

14.
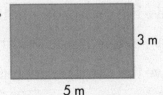
3 m
5 m

Problem Solving

15. Generalize Trish is breaking ground for a rose garden in her back yard. The garden will be a square with a side of 7 meters. What will be the area of the rose garden?

16. Critique Reasoning Karen drew a rectangle with a perimeter of 20 inches. The smaller side measured 3 inches. Karen said the longer side of the rectangle had to be 7 inches. Is she correct?

17. Higher Order Thinking Rectangles X and Y have the same perimeter. Without measuring or multiplying, how can you tell which rectangle has the greater area?

18. Algebra Marcus made the same number of free throws in each of 4 basketball games. Each free throw is worth 1 point. If he made a total of 24 free throws, how many did he make in each game? How many free throw points did he make in each game?

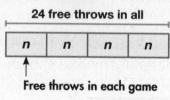

24 free throws in all

Free throws in each game

19. Choose all of the statements that are true about the figures at the right.

☐ They have the same side lengths.

☐ They have different side lengths.

☐ They have the same perimeter.

☐ They have a different area.

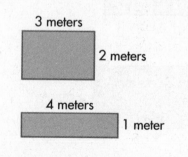

3 meters

2 meters

4 meters

1 meter

Name _____

Another Look!

> Rectangles with different areas can have the same perimeter. Look at the rectangles below.

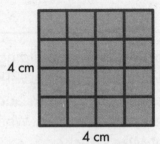

2 cm
6 cm

$A = 2 \times 6$
$A = 12$ sq cm

$P = 6 + 2 + 6 + 2$
$P = 16$ cm

3 cm
5 cm

$A = 3 \times 5$
$A = 15$ sq cm

$P = 5 + 3 + 5 + 3$
$P = 16$ cm

4 cm
4 cm

$A = 4 \times 4$
$A = 16$ sq cm

$P = 4 + 4 + 4 + 4$
$P = 16$ cm

Each of these rectangles has a different area. But they all have the same perimeter.

In **1–4**, use grid paper to draw two different rectangles with the given perimeter. Tell the dimensions and the area of each rectangle. Circle the one that has the greater area.

1. 12 meters

2. 28 inches

3. 20 feet

4. 24 centimeters

Leveled Practice In **5–7**, describe a different rectangle with the same perimeter as the one shown. Then tell which rectangle has the greater area.

5.
4 cm
2 cm

6.
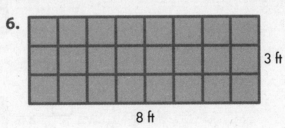
8 ft

3 ft

7.
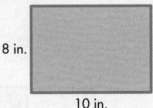
8 in.
10 in.

8. **Make Sense and Persevere** Lamar made a garden in the shape of a rectangle with an area of 36 square feet. Explain how you can find the perimeter of the garden.

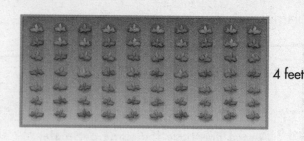

4 feet

9. **Reasoning** Mike is building a deck. The deck will be a rectangle with a longer side length of 20 meters and a shorter side length of 6 meters. What will be the area of Mike's deck?

10. Suppose you arrange 48 counters into rows. The first row has 3 counters. Each row after that has 2 more counters than the row before. How many rows do you need to make to use all 48 counters?

11. **Higher Order Thinking** Jack wants to put a mat on the floor of his tree house. The mat has an area of 72 square feet. His tree house measures 8 feet by 8 feet. Does Jack have enough room in his tree house for the mat? How do you know?

✓ **Assessment**

12. The length of a rectangle is 12 inches and the width is 6 inches. Choose all of the rectangles that have the same perimeter.

☐

9 in.

9 in.

☐

6 in.

6 in.

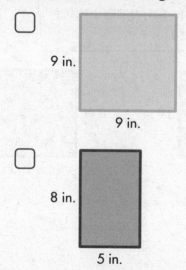

☐

8 in.

5 in.

☐

4 in.

14 in.

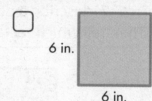

Name _____

Solve & Share

Jessica has 12 square tiles that she wants to use to make rectangles. Find 3 rectangles she can make using all of the squares. Include the area and perimeter of each rectangle. Then compare the areas and perimeters. **Solve this problem any way you choose.**

You can select appropriate tools, such as grid paper or cut-out squares, and use them to help solve the problem.

Lesson 16-5
Same Area, Different Perimeter

I can ...
understand the relationship of shapes with the same area and different perimeters.

I can also choose and use a math tool to solve problems.

Look Back! **Generalize** How does the shape of each of the rectangles affect the perimeter?

A

Can Rectangles Have the Same Areas but Different Perimeters?

16 castle tiles

In a video game, you have 16 castle tiles to make a rectangular castle, and 16 water tiles for a moat. How can you completely surround the castle with water?

16 water tiles

Make rectangles that have an area of 16 square units. Find the perimeter of each rectangle.

The castle tiles represent the area and the water tiles represent the perimeter.

B

Find the area:
$A = 1 \times 16$
= 16 square units

Find the perimeter:
$P = (2 \times 16) + (2 \times 1)$
= 32 + 2
= 34 units

C

Find the area:
$A = 2 \times 8$
= 16 square units

Find the perimeter:
$P = (2 \times 8) + (2 \times 2)$
= 16 + 4
= 20 units

D

Find the area:
$A = 4 \times 4$
= 16 square units

Find the perimeter:
$P = (2 \times 4) + (2 \times 4)$
= 8 + 8
= 16 units

Only the 4 × 4 castle can be surrounded by 16 water tiles.

Convince Me! **Critique Reasoning** Izzie says that if the number of castle tiles increases to 25, it is possible to use exactly 25 water tiles to surround the castle. Do you agree or disagree? Why?

Name _____

⭐ Guided Practice ⭐

Do You Understand?

1. Generalize In the example on page 872, what do you notice about the perimeter of the rectangles as the shape becomes more like a square?

2. Use Structure In Round 2 of the video puzzle game, you have 24 castle tiles. What is the least number of water tiles you will need to surround your castle?

Do You Know How?

In **3–6**, use grid paper to draw two different rectangles with the given area. Tell the dimensions and perimeter of each rectangle, and tell which one has the smaller perimeter.

3. 6 square feet

4. 36 square yards

5. 64 square meters

6. 80 square inches

Independent Practice ⭐

In **7–10**, use grid paper to draw two different rectangles with the given area. Tell the dimensions and perimeter of each rectangle. Circle the one that has the smaller perimeter.

7. 9 square inches

8. 18 square feet

9. 30 square meters

10. 32 square centimeters

Leveled Practice In **11–14**, describe a different rectangle with the same area as the one shown. Then tell which rectangle has the smaller perimeter.

11.
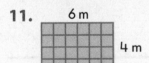
6 m
4 m

12.
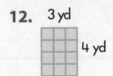
3 yd
4 yd

13.
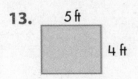
5 ft
4 ft

14.
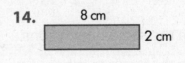
8 cm
2 cm

Problem Solving

15. Make Sense and Persevere Sue bought 2 sweaters for $18 each and mittens for $11. About how much money did she spend? About how much will she get in change if she pays with 3 twenty-dollar bills?

16. Reasoning The perimeter of rectangle *P* is 12 feet. The perimeter of rectangle *A* is 18 feet. Both rectangles have the same area. Find the area and the dimensions of each rectangle.

17. Higher Order Thinking Park School and North School cover the same area. In physical education classes, each student runs one lap around the school. At which school do the students have to run farther? How do you know?

Park School   North School

18. Ms. Fisher is using 64 carpet squares to make a reading area in her classroom. Each square measures 1 foot by 1 foot. She wants to arrange the 64 squares in a rectangular shape with the smallest possible perimeter. What dimensions should she use for her reading area?

19. Look for Relationships Bella is putting down patches of sod to start a new lawn. She has 20 square yards of sod. Give the dimensions of two different rectangular regions that she can cover with the sod. What is the perimeter of each region?

20. Which statement about the rectangles to the right is true?

Ⓐ They have the same dimensions.

Ⓑ They have the same number of rows.

Ⓒ They have the same perimeter.

Ⓓ They have the same area.

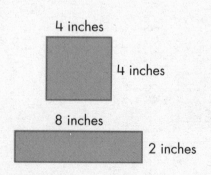

4 inches

4 inches

8 inches

2 inches

Name _____

Another Look!

Phil has 18 square tiles with 1-foot sides. He uses the tiles to make 3 different rectangles. Each rectangle has an area of 18 square feet. What rectangles can he make? What is the perimeter of each rectangle?

You can use grid paper or color tiles to show each rectangle and help find its perimeter.

Rectangle 1

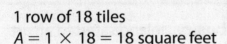

1 row of 18 tiles
$A = 1 \times 18 = 18$ square feet

Find the perimeter:
$P = (2 \times 18) + (2 \times 1)$
$P = 36 + 2 = 38$ feet

Rectangle 2

3 rows of 6 tiles
$A = 3 \times 6 = 18$ square feet

Find the perimeter:
$P = (2 \times 6) + (2 \times 3)$
$P = 12 + 6 = 18$ feet

Rectangle 3

2 rows of 9 tiles
$A = 2 \times 9 = 18$ square feet

Find the perimeter:
$P = (2 \times 9) + (2 \times 2)$
$P = 18 + 4 = 22$ feet

Leveled Practice In **1–4**, describe a different rectangle with the same area as the one shown. Then tell which rectangle has the smaller perimeter.

1.   4 cm

6 cm

2.   6 ft

5 ft

3.   4 m

4 m

4.   10 ft

10 ft

5. **Model with Math** Wes has 20 feet of garden fencing. If he wants the smallest side of his garden to be 3 feet or longer, what possible rectangles can he make?

You can draw a picture to show this problem.

6. Mai drew the design shown below. Each rectangle in the design has the same area. What fraction shows the area of one of the rectangles?

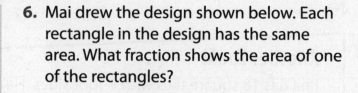

7. **Reasoning** Mari has 39 square feet of patio bricks. Each square brick has sides 1 foot long. What is the greatest perimeter of a rectangle that she can make with the bricks?

8. **A-Z Vocabulary** Jolanda started an art project at 9:00 A.M. and finished it at 9:50 A.M. The _____ for the project was 50 minutes.

9. **Higher Order Thinking** The area of a rectangle is 100 square inches. The perimeter of the rectangle is 40 inches. A second rectangle has the same area but a different perimeter. Is the second rectangle a square? Explain.

✓ **Assessment**

10. The dimensions of a rectangle are 5 inches by 6 inches. Which of the following rectangles has the same area but a different perimeter?

Ⓐ
10 in.
3 in.

Ⓒ
8 in.
4 in.

Ⓑ
5 in.
7 in.

Ⓓ
20 in.
1 in.

Name _____

Solve & Share

Suppose you want to cut a piece of webbing to make a strap to wrap around your math book. Measure the width and height of your book, then use those dimensions to find a possible length for the strap. Be sure to include extra webbing for a buckle. Use reasoning to decide.

Problem Solving

Lesson 16-6
Reasoning

I can ...
understand the relationship between numbers to simplify and solve problems involving perimeter.

I can also solve perimeter problems.

Thinking Habits

Be a good thinker! These questions can help you.

- What do the numbers and symbols in the problem mean?

- How are the numbers or quantities related?

- How can I represent a word problem using pictures, numbers, or equations?

Look Back! **Reasoning** Explain how to solve the problem using a different unit. Does the length you found need to change?

A

Anna is setting up 3 of these tables in a long row for a party. Each person sitting at a table needs a space that is 2 feet wide.

How can Anna find out how many people can be seated at the tables? Use reasoning to decide.

You can draw a picture to help with your reasoning.

What do I need to do to solve this problem?

I need to use the information I know to find the number of people that can sit at 3 tables.

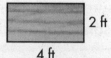

2 ft

4 ft

B **How can I use reasoning to solve this problem?**

I can

- identify the quantities I know.

- draw a picture to show relationships.

- give the answer using the correct unit.

C

Here's my thinking...

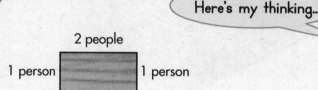

2 people

1 person   1 person

2 people

$2 + 1 + 2 + 1 = 6$. I know 6 people can sit at 1 table.

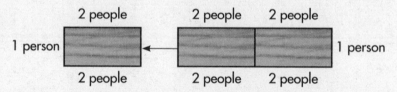

2 people   2 people   2 people

1 person   1 person

2 people   2 people   2 people

For 3 tables, the number of people at the ends stays the same. There are 4 more people at each side.
$6 + 1 + 6 + 1 = 14$. I know 14 people can sit at 3 tables.

Convince Me! **Reasoning** Anna decides to turn the tables sideways. Now they are joined along the longer sides. How does this change the number of people who can be seated? You can use a picture to help.

Name _____

☆ Guided Practice *

Reasoning

Corrine has 3 triangular tables with sides that are the same length. She wants to know how many people she can seat if she puts the tables together side to side in a row. Each person needs a space of 2 feet. How many people can be seated?

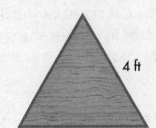

4 ft

1. Describe the quantities given.

2. Solve the problem and explain your reasoning. You can use a picture to help.

☆ Independent Practice ☆

Reasoning

Tito has 3 trapezoid blocks. He wants to find the perimeter of the blocks when he places them together side to side in a row.

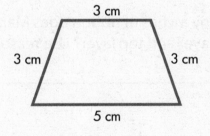

3 cm

3 cm   3 cm

5 cm

3. Describe the quantities given.

Use reasoning by thinking about how the numbers in the problem change.

4. Solve the problem and explain your reasoning. You can use a picture to help.

Problem Solving

A Wedding Cake

The Cakery Bakery makes tiered wedding cakes in various shapes. Maria buys ribbon to decorate three squares of a cake. The ribbon costs 50¢ a foot.

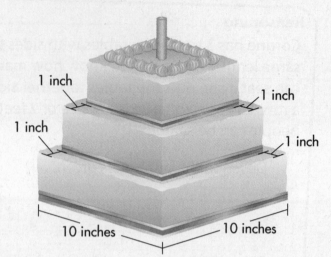

1 inch
1 inch
1 inch
1 inch
10 inches   10 inches

5. **Be Precise** How many inches of ribbon does Maria need for the bottom layer of this cake?

6. **Make Sense and Persevere** How long is a side of the middle layer? Explain how you know your answer makes sense.

7. **Reasoning** How many inches of ribbon does Maria need for the middle layer and top layer? Use reasoning to decide.

Drawing a diagram can help your reasoning when solving a problem.

8. **Critique Reasoning** Maria says that if she buys 100 inches of ribbon she will have enough ribbon for all 3 layers. Grace says Maria needs more than 100 inches of ribbon. Who is correct? Explain.

Help Practice Buddy Tools Games

Another Look!

Marissa and Amy are making a rectangular garden 8 feet long and 6 feet wide. They plan to put a fence around the garden with fence posts 2 feet apart. Each corner has a fence post. How many fence posts will they need? How is the number of posts related to the number of sections?

Tell ways you can show the relationships in the problem.

- I can draw a picture to show relationships.

- I can give the answer using the correct unit.

> Think about the different ways you can use reasoning to solve the problem.

Solve and explain your reasoning.

They need 14 posts. When I draw a picture I see that there are four 2-foot sections on each 8-foot side. So they need 5 posts for each length.

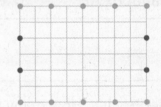

There are three 2-foot sections on each 6-foot side. The corner posts are already shown on the 8-foot side. So I marked 2 posts for each width.

$(5 \times 2) + (2 \times 2) = 14$ posts

The number of sections is equal to the number of posts.
$(4 \times 2) + (3 \times 2) = 14$ sections

Reasoning

A farmer wants to build a straight fence with a post every 7 feet. Each end has a post. For a fence that is 49 feet long, how many posts will the farmer need?

1. Describe the quantities given.

2. Tell how you can show the relationships in the problem.

3. Solve and explain your reasoning.

Field Day

Mitch wants to build a sandbox in his backyard. He needs to decide on a design to use. He will border the sandbox with wood pieces that are 2 feet long. Each wood piece costs $3. Each square foot of sand will cost $2.

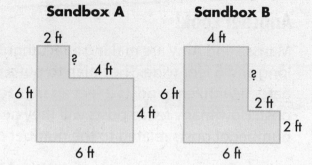

Sandbox A

2 ft
?
4 ft
6 ft
4 ft
6 ft

Sandbox B

4 ft
?
2 ft
6 ft
2 ft
6 ft

4. **Make Sense and Persevere** What are the missing lengths in Sandbox A and Sandbox B?

5. **Be Precise** How many wood pieces does Mitch need for Sandbox A?

6. **Be Precise** How many wood pieces does Mitch need for Sandbox B?

7. **Use Structure** How would the price of buying the wood for Sandbox A compare to the price of wood for Sandbox B? Explain how to solve without computing. Why?

When you use reasoning, remember to check which units should be used.

8. **Reasoning** Which sandbox would cover a greater area? Explain how you know.

Name _____

Work with a partner. Point to a clue. Read the clue.

Look below the clues to find a match. Write the clue letter in the box next to the match.

Find a match for every clue.

I can ...
add and subtract within 1,000.

Clues

A The missing number is 725.

B The missing number is 898.

C The missing number is 580.

D The missing number is 419.

E The missing number is 381.

F The missing number is 83.

G The missing number is 750.

H The missing number is 546.

☐	☐	☐	☐
___ + 219 = 969	529 − 148 = ___	642 + 256 = ___	878 − ___ = 332
☐	☐	☐	☐
850 − ___ = 125	___ + 511 = 930	910 − 827 = ___	399 + 181 = ___

TOPIC 16 · Vocabulary Review

A-Z
Glossary

Word List

- area
- equation
- multiplication
- perimeter
- rectangle
- square
- square unit

Understand Vocabulary

Write T for *true* or F for *false*.

1. _____ To find the *area* of a *square*, you can multiply the side length by 4.

2. _____ *Perimeter* is measured in *square units*.

3. _____ You can use an addition or a *multiplication equation* to find the *area* of a *rectangle*.

4. _____ A *rectangle* with a width of 6 inches and a length of 8 inches has a *perimeter* of 28 inches.

5. _____ A *square* with a side length of 5 meters has an *area* of 20 square meters.

In **6–8**, tell if each equation shows a way to find the *area* or *perimeter* of the shape.

6.
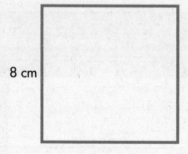

8 cm

$8 \times 4 = ?$

_____

7.
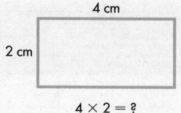

4 cm

2 cm

$4 \times 2 = ?$

_____

8.
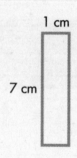

1 cm

7 cm

$7 + 7 + 1 + 1 = ?$

_____

Use Vocabulary in Writing

9. Compare the perimeter and area of each figure. Use at least 2 terms from the Word List in your answer.

Figure A

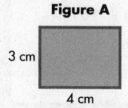

3 cm

4 cm

Figure B

1 cm

6 cm

Set A | pages 847–858

You can find the perimeter by counting unit segments.

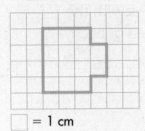

☐ = 1 cm

The perimeter of this shape is 16 centimeters.

You can find the perimeter of a shape by adding the lengths of the sides.

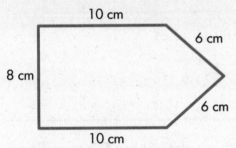

$10 + 10 + 8 + 6 + 6 = 40$

The perimeter of this shape is 40 centimeters.

Remember the distance around a figure is its perimeter.

In **1–3**, find the perimeter of each figure.

1.

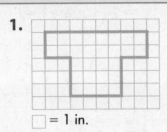

☐ = 1 in.

2.

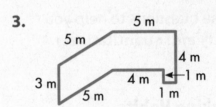

3.

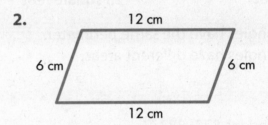

Set B | pages 859–864

If you know the perimeter, you can find the length of a missing side. What is the missing side length of this polygon?

perimeter = 21 yd

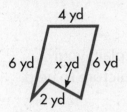

$x + 2 + 6 + 4 + 6 = 21$

$x + 18 = 21$

$3 + 18 = 21$ so $x = 3$

The missing side is 3 yd long.

Remember that to find the missing side length, you need to find the sum of the known sides.

Find the missing side length.

1. perimeter = 35 cm

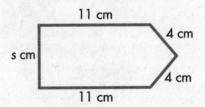

Find the perimeter and area of these rectangles.

8 ft

3 ft

$P = 3 + 8 + 3 + 8$

= 22 feet

$A = 8 \times 3$

= 24 square feet

7 ft

4 ft

$P = 4 + 7 + 4 + 7$

= 22 feet

$A = 7 \times 4$

= 28 square feet

The rectangles have the same perimeter. The rectangles have different areas.

Remember that two rectangles can have the same perimeter but different areas, or the same area but different perimeters.

Draw two different rectangles with the perimeter listed. Find the area of each rectangle.

1. $P = 24$ feet

Draw two different rectangles with the area listed. Find the perimeter of each rectangle.

2. $A = 64$ square inches

Think about these questions to help you **reason abstractly and quantitatively.**

Thinking Habits

- What do the numbers and symbols in the problem mean?

- How are the numbers or quantities related?

- How can I represent a word problem using pictures, numbers, or equations?

Remember to think about how the quantities in the problem are related. You can use a picture to show relationships.

Julian has 5 triangle blocks with sides that are the same length. What is the perimeter of the blocks if Julian places them together side to side?

 2 in.

1. Describe the quantities given.

2. Solve the problem and explain your reasoning. You can use a picture to help.

1. What is the perimeter of a hexagon if all the sides are 6 feet?

2. Robert's tile design is shown below.

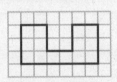

Draw another tile design that has the same area as Robert's design and a different perimeter from Robert's design.

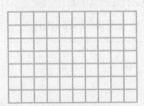

3. Della drew a rectangle with a perimeter of 34 centimeters. She labeled one side 7 centimeters, but she forgot to label the other side. Write a number in the box to show the missing side length.

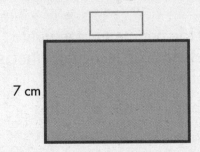

7 cm

4. Mrs. Gee has 24 carpet squares. How should she arrange them so that she has the smallest perimeter?

Ⓐ 12 by 2 rectangle

Ⓑ 1 by 24 rectangle

Ⓒ 8 by 3 rectangle

Ⓓ 4 by 6 rectangle

5. Eugene's garden design is shown below.

Do any of the shapes below have a different area from Eugene's design and the same perimeter as Eugene's design? For questions 5a–5d, choose Yes or No.

5a.  ○ Yes ○ No

5b.  ○ Yes ○ No

5c.  ○ Yes ○ No

5d. 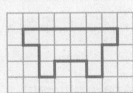 ○ Yes ○ No

6. The perimeter of the polygon is 24 feet. What is the missing side length?

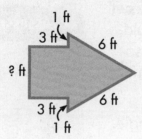

1 ft
3 ft
6 ft
? ft
3 ft
6 ft
1 ft

Ⓐ 4 feet

Ⓑ 5 feet

Ⓒ 6 feet

Ⓓ 7 feet

7. Ms. Kent measures the perimeter of a common shape. One of the sides is 7 cm, and the perimeter is 21 cm. If all of the sides are the same length, what shape does Ms. Kent measure?

8. Choose all of the statements that are true about the figures below.

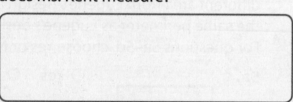

2 cm

4 cm   8 cm

☐ The shapes have different perimeters.

☐ The shapes have the same perimeter.

☐ The shapes have different areas.

☐ The shapes have the same area.

☐ The square has a greater area than the rectangle.

9. Mandy's trapezoid-shaped garden has a perimeter of 42 ft. She knows the length of three sides: 8 ft, 8 ft, and 16 ft. What is the length of the fourth side?

10. Pepper's dog pen is shown below.

6 m

4 m

Part A

Find the perimeter and area of the dog pen.

Part B

Could a square with whole number side lengths have the same perimeter as the dog pen? The same area? Explain.

11. Max found the perimeter of a square with a side length of 24 inches. What is the perimeter?

Ⓐ 24 inches   Ⓒ 80 inches

Ⓑ 48 inches   Ⓓ 96 inches

Name _____

Park Planning

Mrs. Martinez is planning a new park. Three possible designs are shown below. There will be a path along each side of the park.

Design A

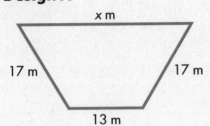

x m

17 m   17 m

13 m

Perimeter = 73 m

Design B

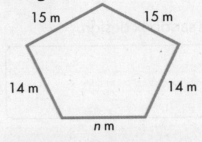

15 m   15 m

14 m   14 m

n m

Perimeter = 75 m

Design C

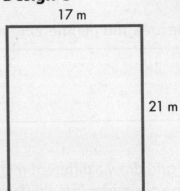

17 m

21 m

Use **Design A**, **Design B**, and **Design C** figures to answer Questions 1–3.

1. For Design A, how long will the path be for the missing side length?

2. For Design B, how long will the path be for the missing side length?

3. Mrs. Martinez chooses the design with the greatest perimeter.

Part A

What is the perimeter of Design C? Explain.

Part B

Which design did Mrs. Martinez choose?

Use the **Sandbox Design** figure to answer Question 4.

4. The park will have a sandbox.
   One design is shown at the right.

   Part A

   Find the area and perimeter of the sandbox design.

   [ ]

   Part B

   On the grid draw a different rectangle sandbox design with
   the same perimeter but a different area. Circle the figure
   that has the greater area.

Use the **South Pond** figure to answer Question 5.

South Pond

5. There will be two ponds in the park.
   Each pond will be a rectangle shape.

   Part A

   Find the area and perimeter of the south pond.

   [ ]

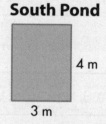

   Part B

   The north pond has the same area but a different perimeter.
   Draw a figure for the north pond.
   Circle the figure that has the greater perimeter.

   North Pond

6. The park will have a sign in the shape of a square.
   One side of the sign will be 2 meters long.
   Explain two ways you can find the perimeter of the sign.

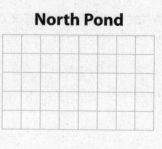

   [ ]

Step Up to Grade 4

Here's a preview of next year. These lessons help you step up to Grade 4.

Lessons

Name _____

Solve & Share

What is the relationship between the value of the first 5 and the value of the second 5 in 5,500? **Solve this problem any way you choose.**

thousands period

ones period

hundred thousands | ten thousands | one thousands | hundreds | tens | ones

I can ...
recognize that a digit in one place has ten times the value of the same digit in the place to its right.

I can also reason about math.

Use reasoning. You can use place value to analyze the relationship between the digits in the problem.

Look Back! **Reasoning** Describe two ways 5,000 and 500 are related.

Essential Question

How Are the Digits in a Multi-Digit Number Related to Each Other?

A

Kiana collected 1,100 bottle caps. What is the relationship between the values of the digit 1 in each place?

A place-value chart can help you examine the relationships between digits in a number.

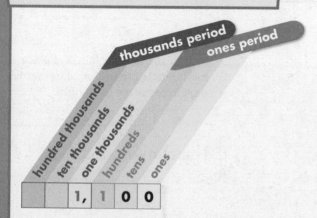

1,100 bottle caps

B 1,100

The first 1 is in the thousands place. Its value is 1,000.

The second 1 is in the hundreds place. Its value is 100.

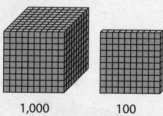

1,000   100

C How is 1,000 related to 100?

10 hundreds   1 hundred

10 hundreds are equal to 1 thousand.

When two digits next to each other in a number are the same, the value of the digit on the left is always ten times as great as the digit on the right.

Convince Me! **Generalize** Is the value of the first 4 ten times as great as the value of the second 4 in 4,043? Explain. What can you generalize about the value of digits that are two places apart in a number?

Another Example!

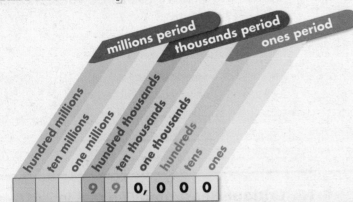

9 9 0, 0 0 0

The first 9 is in the hundred-thousands place. Its value is 900,000.

The second 9 is in the ten-thousands place. Its value is 90,000.

The value of the first 9 is ten times as great as the value of the second 9.

☆ Guided Practice

Do You Understand?

1. **Reasoning** Is the value of the first 7 ten times as great as the value of the second 7 in 7,027? Explain.

2. **Construct Arguments** Is the value of the 8 in 87,503 ten times as great as the value of the 7? Explain.

Do You Know How?

For **3** and **4**, name the values of the given digits in each number. What is the relationship between the values of the given digits?

3. the 5s in 5,500

4. the 2s in 220,400

☆ Independent Practice ☆

For **5–12**, name the values of the given digits in each number.

5. the 8s in 1,884   6. the 4s in 44,391   7. the 9s in 79,951   8. the 2s in 220,000

9. the 5s in 45,035   10. the 4s in 4,448   11. the 2s in 20,723   12. the 7s in 378,708

Problem Solving

13. Construct Arguments What can you say about the 9s in 59,992?

14. Critique Reasoning Mia says in 2,222, all the digits have the same value. Is Mia correct? Explain.

15. Number Sense The Mississippi River flooded in 1927. In the number 1927, is the value of the 9 in the hundreds place ten times the value of the 2 in the tens place? Explain.

16. Critique Reasoning Vin says in 2,616, one 6 is 10 times as great than the other 6. Is he correct? Explain.

17. Describe 2 ways to find the area of the shaded rectangle.

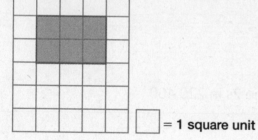

= 1 square unit

18. Higher Order Thinking In 881,588, how is the relationship between the first pair of 8s the same as the relationship between the second pair of 8s?

✔ Assessment

19. Which group of numbers shows the values of the 7s in 57,707?

Ⓐ 70,000; 7,000; 700

Ⓑ 70,000; 700; 70

Ⓒ 7,000; 700; 7

Ⓓ 700; 70; 7

20. In which number is the value of the red digit ten times as great as the value of the green digit?

Ⓐ 886,628

Ⓑ 886,628

Ⓒ 886,628

Ⓓ 886,628

Name _____

☆ ★ ☆
Solve & Share

Find the products for 3 × 4, 3 × 40, 3 × 400, and 3 × 4,000. *Solve these problems using any strategy you choose.*

I can ...
find the products of multiples of 10, 100, and 1,000 using mental math and place-value strategies.

I can also look for patterns to solve problems.

You can look for relationships in the products. How can finding the first product help you find the remaining products? *Show your work in the space above!*

Look Back! **Look for Relationships** What pattern do you notice in the products?

How Can You Multiply by Multiples of 10, 100, and 1,000?

A

Calculate 3 × 50, 3 × 500, and 3 × 5,000 using basic multiplication facts and properties of operations. Then, calculate 6 × 50, 6 × 500, and 6 × 5,000.

The Associative Property of Multiplication states that you can change the grouping of the factors and the product stays the same.

n

B Find 3 × 50, 3 × 500, and 3 × 5,000.

$3 \times 50 = 3 \times (5 \times 10)$
$= (3 \times 5) \times 10$
$= 15 \times 10$
$= 150$

Shortcut rule for 3 × 50:
Multiply 3 × 5 and write 1 zero.
So, 3 × 50 = 150

Shortcut rule for 3 × 500:
Multiply 3 × 5 and write 2 zeros.
3 × 500 = 1,500

Shortcut rule for 3 × 5,000:
Multiply 3 × 5 and write 3 zeros.
3 × 5,000 = 15,000

C Find 6 × 50, 6 × 500, and 6 × 5,000.

Apply the shortcut rules:

6 × 5 = 30
6 × 50 = 300
6 × 500 = 3,000
6 × 5,000 = 30,000

When the product of a basic fact ends in zero, the product will have an extra zero. The extra zero is part of the basic fact that you use.

Convince Me! **Reasoning** How many zeros will be in the product of 5 × 200? Explain.

Tools Assessment

Another Example!

Use place value to calculate 5×50, 5×500, and $5 \times 5,000$.

5×50 is 5 groups of 5 tens or 5×5 tens. 5×5 tens is 25 tens, or 250.

5×500 is 5 groups of 5 hundreds or 5×5 hundreds. 5×5 hundreds is 25 hundreds, or 2,500.

$5 \times 5,000$ is 5 groups of 5 thousands or 5×5 thousands. 5×5 thousands is 25 thousands, or 25,000.

☆ Guided Practice

Do You Understand?

1. **Look for Relationships** Show how you can use the basic fact $4 \times 5 = 20$ to determine the product of 4×500.

2. Bob said $5 \times 800 = 400$. Explain his error.

Do You Know How?

For **3–5**, use strategies you learned to help multiply.

3. $7 \times 3 =$ _____

   $7 \times 30 =$ _____

   $7 \times 300 =$ _____

   $7 \times 3,000 =$ _____

4. 6×60

5. 6×300

☆ Independent Practice ☆

Leveled Practice For **6–11**, find each product.

You can use place-value strategies to calculate each product.

6. $9 \times 40 =$ _____

   $9 \times 400 =$ _____

   $9 \times 4,000 =$ _____

7. $2 \times 90 =$ _____

   $2 \times 900 =$ _____

   $2 \times 9,000 =$ _____

8. $7 \times 80 =$ _____

   $7 \times 800 =$ _____

   $7 \times 8,000 =$ _____

9. $3 \times 3,000$

10. 800×6

11. 2×70

Problem Solving

12. Math and Science The Amazon River is about 5 times the length of the Rhine River. If the Rhine River is about 800 miles long, about many miles long is the Amazon River? Write and solve an equation.

13. Model with Math Sophia, Emma, and Jacob are trying to raise $300 for a local shelter. Sophia raised $50. Emma raised $140. How much money does Jacob need to raise in order to reach their goal?

$300		
$50	$140	?

For **14** and **15**, use the table at the right.

14. There are 7 boys and 2 adults in Ethan's scout troup. How much did the troop pay for tickets to the amusement park?

15. Higher Order Thinking Mason visited Happyland with her dad and a friend. They bought tickets for Plan C. How much money did they save on the two children's tickets for Plan C instead of buying separate tickets for Plan A and Plan B?

Happyland Ticket Prices

Plans	Adult	Child
Plan A Waterpark	$50	$40
Plan B Amusement Park	$40	$30
Plan C Combined A + B	$80	$60

Assessment

16. Isabella says 7 × 900 is greater than 9 × 7,000. Noah says 7 × 900 is less than 9 × 7,000.

Part A

Without calculating the answer, explain how to use place-value strategies or the Associative Property to find which is greater.

Part B

Without calculating the answer, explain how to use relationships or basic facts to find which is less.

Name _____

Step Up to Grade 4

Lesson 3
Mental Math: Multiply Multiples of 10

Solve & Share

The principal of a school needs to order supplies for 20 new classrooms. Each classroom needs the following items: 20 desks, 30 chairs, and 40 pencils. How many of each item does the principal need to order? *Solve these problems using any strategy you choose.*

You can use structure. What basic facts can you use to help solve these problems? How are they related? *Show your work in the space below!*

I can ...
use place-value strategies or patterns to multiply by multiples of 10.

I can also look for patterns to solve problems.

Look Back! **Look for Relationships** Look at the factors and products. What patterns do you notice?

Essential Question **How Can You Multiply by Multiples of 10?**

A

The number of visitors of each age group for the Sunny Day Amusement Park are shown below. How many adults under 65 visit the park in 20 days? How many children visit the park in 30 days? How many adults 65 and over visit the park in 50 days?

You can use a pattern to multiply by a multiple of 10.

Adults under 65: **60**

Adults 65 and over: **40**

Children: **80**

Number of visitors each day

B **Adults under 65 in 20 days**

Find $20 \times 60 = a$.

To multiply 20×60, use a pattern.

$2 \times 6 = 12$
$20 \times 6 = 120$
$20 \times 60 = 1,200$

$a = 1,200$

1,200 adults under 65 visit the park in 20 days.

C **Children in 30 days**

Find $30 \times 80 = c$.

The number of zeros in the product is the total number of zeros in both factors.

$30 \times 80 = 2,400$

↑ 1 zero   ↑ 1 zero   ↑ 2 zeros

$c = 2,400$

2,400 children visit the park in 30 days.

D **Adults 65 and over in 50 days**

Find $50 \times 40 = a$.

If the product of a basic fact ends in zero, include that zero in the count.

$5 \times 4 = 20$
$50 \times 40 = 2,000$

$a = 2,000$

2,000 adults 65 and over visit the park in 50 days.

Convince Me! **Look for Relationships** Write the missing numbers for each of the following. Explain.

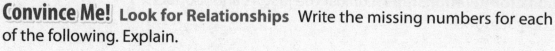

_____ $\times 7 = 280$ _____ $\times 40 = 1,600$ _____ $\times 50 = 3,000$

Another Example!

Find 30 × 80. The product has the same number of zeros as in both factors.

$$30 × 80 = 3 × 10 × 8 × 10$$
$$= (3 × 8) × (10 × 10)$$
$$= 24 × 100$$
$$= 2,400$$

You can use the Commutative and Associative Properties of Multiplication to see why the patterns with zeros work!

☆ Guided Practice

Do You Understand?

1. **Reasoning** Find 50 × 80. How many zeros are in the product?

2. Fewer people go the park in September than March. There are 30 days in September. If 50 people visit the park each day in September, how many people visit for the whole month?

Do You Know How?

For **3–8**, use basic facts and place-value strategies to find each product.

3. 10 × 90   4. 40 × 10

5. 80 × 10   6. 50 × 90

7. 60 × 40   8. 70 × 70

Independent Practice ☆

For **9–16**, use basic facts and place-value strategies to find each product.

9. 10 × 50   10. 40 × 20   11. 70 × 30   12. 20 × 90

13. 40 × 80   14. 30 × 60   15. 30 × 20   16. 90 × 80

For **17–22**, find the missing factor.

17. 10 × _____ = 100   18. _____ × 20 = 1,400   19. _____ × 70 = 3,500

20. 30 × _____ = 1,500   21. _____ × 80 = 5,600   22. 50 × _____ = 3,000

Problem Solving

23. Reasoning The product of two factors is 3,200. If one of the factors is 40, what is the other factor? Explain.

24. Algebra There are 30 players on each high school football team. Explain how you can find the total number of players if there are 10 teams. Write and solve an equation.

25. Alan leaves the water running while brushing his teeth. He uses 2 gallons of water. He then uses 10 gallons of water to wash clothes. How many more quarts of water did Alan use while washing his clothes than brushing his teeth?

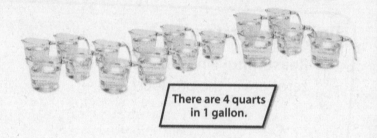

There are 4 quarts in 1 gallon.

26. Look for Relationships Emily walked 60 minutes each day for 80 days. Show how you can use basic facts to find how many minutes Emily walked.

27. Higher Order Thinking Explain why the product of 50 and 20 has three zeros when 50 and 20 each have one zero.

Assessment

28. Mr. Cantor travels 20 weeks a year for work. He is home the other 32 weeks. There are 7 days in 1 week. Which of the following expressions can Mr. Cantor use to mentally find the number of days he is home?

- (A) $(7 \times 2) + (3 \times 10)$
- (B) 7×100
- (C) $(7 \times 30) + (7 \times 10)$
- (D) $(7 \times 30) + (7 \times 2)$

29. Mrs. Cantor travels 22 weeks a year for work. She is home the other 30 weeks. There are 7 days in a week. Which of the following basic facts can Mrs. Cantor use to help find the number of days she is home?

- (A) 2×7
- (B) 3×7
- (C) $22 + 7$
- (D) $30 + 7$

Name _____

☆ ⭐ ☆
Solve & Share

There are 10 teams in a baseball league. Each team has 25 players. How many players are in the league? *Solve this problem using any strategy you choose.*

I can ...
use models and properties of operations to help multiply.

I can also choose and use a math tool to solve problems.

You can use appropriate tools. Place-value blocks or grid paper can help you visualize the problem. *Show your work in the space above!*

Look Back! **Reasoning** How do the digits in a number being multiplied by 10 compare to the digits in the product? Explain.

A

How Can You Use an Array or an Area Model to Multiply?

Essential Question

Max's Moving Company has boxes for packing books. If each box holds 24 books, how many books would fit into 20 boxes?

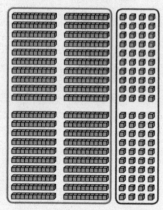

Making an array with place-value blocks or using an area model helps to visualize the partial products.

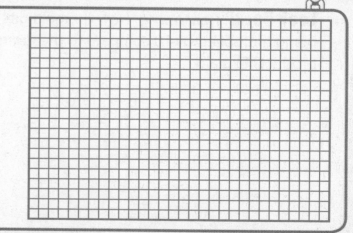

24 Books

B Use place-value blocks to make an array.

Find $20 \times 24 = b$.

$$\begin{array}{r} 400 \\ + \ 80 \\ \hline 480 \end{array}$$ ← Partial Products

$20 \times 24 = 480$

$b = 480$

480 books will fit into 20 boxes.

400   80

C Draw an area model.

Find $20 \times 24 = b$.

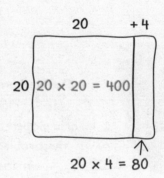

20   + 4

20 | 20 × 20 = 400

↑
20 × 4 = 80

$$\begin{array}{r} 400 \\ + \ 80 \\ \hline 480 \end{array}$$ ← Partial Products

$20 \times 24 = 480$

$b = 480$

480 books will fit into 20 boxes.

Convince Me! Model with Math Use the grid to show an array for 20×27. What is the product?

---

906   **Step Up** | Lesson 4

© Pearson Education, Inc. 3

Name _____

☆ Guided Practice

Do You Understand?

1. **Model with Math** Draw an area model to show 20 × 22. Then find the product.

Do You Know How?

2. The place-value block array shows 10 × 14. Find the product.

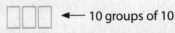 ← 10 groups of 10

+ ← 10 groups of 4

← Add the partial products.

☆ Independent Practice ☆

For **3–12**, use place-value blocks, area models, or arrays to find each product.

3. 10 × 25

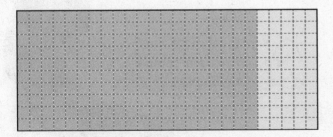

4. 10 × 12

You can use a sheet of grid paper to draw arrays or area models.

5. 20 × 31   6. 20 × 46   7. 30 × 25   8. 40 × 34

9. 10 × 63   10. 50 × 16   11. 70 × 21   12. 80 × 46

Problem Solving

13. Algebra In the last 3 months of the year, an electronics store sold 908 cell phones. How many cell phones did the store sell in December? Write and solve an equation.

Cell Phone Sales

Month	Number Sold
October	319
November	257

DATA

14. The store sold 34 power cords. Each power cord sells for $30. What was the total cost of the cords?

---

15. Model with Math During a basketball game, 55 cups of lemonade were sold. Each cup holds 20 fluid ounces. How many total fluid ounces of lemonade were sold?

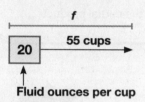

f

20   55 cups

Fluid ounces per cup

16. Higher Order Thinking There are 58 third graders at a school. Each third grader writes 4 book reports. Show how to use the Distributive Property to find the number of book reports written.

✓ **Assessment**

17. William sold 17 magazine subscriptions for $40 each. Abigail sold 28 subscriptions for $30 each. Use arrays or area models to explain who raised more money.

Representations can help you write a complete explanation.

Name _____

Solve & Share

Suppose you are making gift baskets of fruit. You have 14 apples, and you plan to put 4 apples in each basket. How many baskets can you fill? Will there be any apples left over? If so, how many? *Solve this problem using any strategy you choose.*

Solve

You can draw a picture to model with math. *Show your work in the space below!*

I can ...
apply what I know about dividing items into equal groups to solve problems.

I can also model with math to solve problems.

Look Back! **Model with Math** How many apples are in the baskets? Write a multiplication sentence to represent the number of apples.

After Dividing, What Do You Do With the Remainder?

A

When you divide with whole numbers any whole number that remains after the division is complete is called the **remainder**.

Ned has 27 soccer cards in an album. He can put 6 cards on each page. He knows that 27 ÷ 6 = 4 with 3 left over, because 6 × 4 + 3 = 27.

Use an R to write a remainder: 27 ÷ 6 = 4 R3

How do you use the remainder to answer questions?

> The remainder must be less than the divisor.

B

How many pages can Ned fill?

To answer this question, find how many groups of 6 there are. The remainder can be ignored.

27 ÷ 6 = 4 R3

Ned can fill 4 pages.

C

How many pages will Ned work on?

To answer this question, find how many groups are filled or started. Add 1 to the quotient, and ignore the remainder.

27 ÷ 6 = 4 R3

Ned will work on 5 pages.

D

How many cards will Ned put on the fifth page?

The answer to this question is the remainder.

27 ÷ 6 = 4 R3

Ned will put 3 cards on the fifth page.

Convince Me! **Make Sense and Persevere** The calculation to the right is incorrect. What error was made? What is the correct answer? Draw a picture to help.

45 ÷ 6 = 6 R9

Another Example!

Use counters to find 20 ÷ 3. Write the quotient including the remainder.

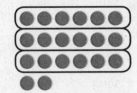

3 equal groups of 6 with 2 left over
20 ÷ 3 = 6 R2, because
3 × 6 + 2 = 20.

☆ Guided Practice

Do You Understand?

1. **Reasoning** When a divisor is 4, can the remainder be 6? Explain.

2. Mia is packing 27 sweaters into boxes. Each box will hold 4 sweaters. How many boxes will she fill? How many boxes will she need? Explain.

Do You Know How?

For **3–6**, find the number of groups and the number left over. Draw an array if needed.

3. 14 ÷ 5 = _____ with _____ left over

4. 7 ÷ 3 = _____ with _____ left over

5. 18 ÷ 7 = _____ with _____ left over

6. 29 ÷ 3 = _____ with _____ left over

☆ Independent Practice ☆

For **7–10**, find the number of groups and the number left over.

7. 15 ÷ 2 = _____ with _____ left over

8. 28 ÷ 6 = _____ with _____ left over

9. 52 ÷ 5 = _____ with _____ left over

10. 34 ÷ 7 = _____ with _____ left over

For **11–13**, interpret each remainder.

11. 9 football cards, 4 cards on each page

    How many pages can Alex complete?

12. 19 baseball cards, 6 cards on each page

    How many cards are on the 3rd page?

13. 42 stickers, 8 stickers on each page

    How many pages will have some stickers?

Problem Solving

In **14–15**, use the table at the right.

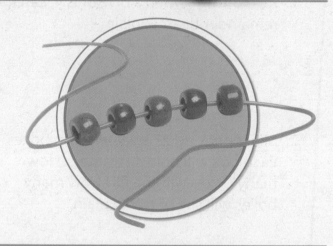

Ticket Exchange	
Prize	Number of Tickets
Yo-yo	8
Ring	9
Marble	7
Sticker	4

14. Madison has 50 prize tickets. How many rings can she get?

15. Liam chose 4 yo-yos and 7 marbles. How many tickets did he use?

16. Jayden makes necklaces like the one in the picture at the right. She has 14 blue beads and 9 red beads. How many necklaces can she make? How many of each color bead will be left over?

17. Critique Reasoning Michael calculated $29 \div 7 = 3 \text{ R}8$. Is his answer correct? If not, what is the correct answer? Explain.

18. Higher Order Thinking Write a problem that requires adding 1 to the quotient when interpreting the remainder.

✓ **Assessment**

19. There are 33 children at a park. They want to make teams with 8 children on each team. Five of the children go home. How many complete teams can they make? Explain.

You can draw an array to help solve the problem.

Name _____

Solve

Solve & Share

Kyle and Jillian are working on a sports banner. They painted $\frac{3}{8}$ of the banner green and $\frac{4}{8}$ purple. How much of the banner have they painted? *Solve this problem any way you choose.*

You can use appropriate tools. You can use drawings, area models, or fraction strips to solve this problem. *Show your work in the space below!*

I can ...
use tools such as fraction strips or area models to add fractions.

I can also choose and use a math tool to solve problems.

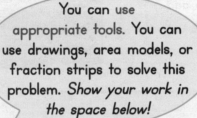

Look Back! **Use Appropriate Tools** Kyle says $\frac{1}{8} + \frac{1}{8} + \frac{1}{8} = \frac{3}{8}$. Jillian says $\frac{1}{8} + \frac{1}{8} + \frac{1}{8} = \frac{3}{24}$. Use fraction strips to decide who is correct.

How Can You Use Tools to Add Fractions?

A

Ten canoeing teams are racing downriver. Five teams have silver canoes and two teams have brown canoes. What fraction of the canoes are either silver or brown?

You can use tools such as fraction strips to add two or more fractions.

B

Find $\frac{5}{10} + \frac{2}{10}$. Use five $\frac{1}{10}$ fraction strips to show $\frac{5}{10}$ and two $\frac{1}{10}$ strips to show $\frac{2}{10}$.

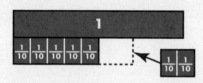

Five $\frac{1}{10}$ strips joined with two $\frac{1}{10}$ strips are seven $\frac{1}{10}$ strips.

Add the numerators. Then write the sum over the like denominator.

$$\frac{5}{10} + \frac{2}{10} = \frac{7}{10}$$

C

Find $\frac{5}{10} + \frac{2}{10}$. Mark five $\frac{1}{10}$ segments to show $\frac{5}{10}$ and two $\frac{1}{10}$ segments to show $\frac{2}{10}$.

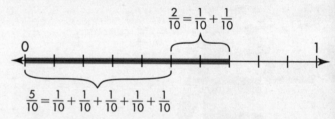

$$\frac{2}{10} = \frac{1}{10} + \frac{1}{10}$$

$$\frac{5}{10} = \frac{1}{10} + \frac{1}{10} + \frac{1}{10} + \frac{1}{10} + \frac{1}{10}$$

Adding $\frac{5}{10}$ and $\frac{2}{10}$ means joining five $\frac{1}{10}$ segments and two $\frac{1}{10}$ segments.

$\frac{7}{10}$ of the canoes are either silver or brown.

Convince Me! **Make Sense and Persevere** What two fractions would you add to find the fraction of the canoes that are either green or brown? What is the sum? How do you know your sum is correct?

Name_____

☆ Guided Practice

Do You Understand?

1. Reasoning In the problem on the previous page, why aren't the purple $\frac{1}{10}$ strips the same length as the red strip?

2. What two fractions are being added below? What is the sum?

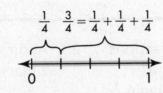

Do You Know How?

For **3–4**, find each sum.

3. $\frac{2}{5} + \frac{2}{5}$

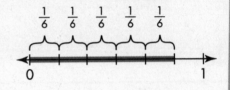

4. $\frac{1}{6} + \frac{4}{6}$

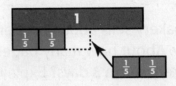

Independent Practice ☆

Leveled Practice For **5–16**, find each sum. Use fraction strips or other tools.

5. $\frac{3}{12} + \frac{6}{12}$

6. $\frac{4}{10} + \frac{4}{10}$

7. $\frac{2}{12} + \frac{6}{12}$

8. $\frac{3}{6} + \frac{2}{6} + \frac{1}{6}$

9. $\frac{1}{4} + \frac{3}{4}$

10. $\frac{2}{3} + \frac{1}{3}$

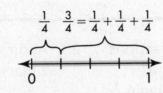  

11. $\frac{4}{8} + \frac{1}{8}$

12. $\frac{1}{12} + \frac{3}{12}$

13. $\frac{4}{10} + \frac{3}{10}$

14. $\frac{1}{8} + \frac{6}{8}$

15. $\frac{2}{6} + \frac{3}{6}$

16. $\frac{1}{10} + \frac{2}{10} + \frac{4}{10}$

Problem Solving

17. Number Sense Using four different numerators, write an equation in which four fractions, when added, have a sum of 1.

18. Model with Math A rope is divided into 10 equal parts. Draw a picture to show $\frac{3}{10} + \frac{5}{10} = \frac{8}{10}$.

19. A bakery sells about 5 dozen bagels per day. About how many bagels does the bakery sell in 3 days? Explain.

There are 12 bagels in one dozen.

20. What addition problem is shown by the fraction strips below?

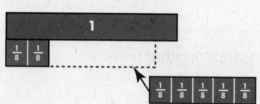

21. Higher Order Thinking Elizabeth ran $\frac{2}{10}$ of the distance from school to home. She walked $\frac{3}{10}$ more of the distance and then skipped $\frac{1}{10}$ more of the distance. What fraction of the distance home does Elizabeth still have to go?

Look back to see if you answered the question that was asked.

✔ **Assessment**

22. Chloe said, "I am thinking of two fractions that when added have a sum of one." Which fractions could Chloe have been thinking about?

Ⓐ $\frac{1}{2}$ and $\frac{2}{2}$

Ⓑ $\frac{1}{6}$ and $\frac{2}{6}$

Ⓒ $\frac{3}{8}$ and $\frac{5}{8}$

Ⓓ $\frac{3}{5}$ and $\frac{4}{5}$

23. Andrew has 6 red hats, 4 blue hats, and 2 black hats. Which statement is true?

Ⓐ $\frac{2}{12}$ of the hats are either red or black.

Ⓑ $\frac{4}{12}$ of the hats are either red or black.

Ⓒ $\frac{1}{2}$ of the hats are either red or black.

Ⓓ $\frac{8}{12}$ of the hats are either red or black.

Name _____

Solve & Share

Karyn has $\frac{11}{8}$ pounds of chili to put into three bowls. The amount of chili in each bowl does not have to be the same. How much chili could Karyn put into each bowl? **Solve this problem any way you choose.**

Step Up to Grade 4

Lesson 7
Decompose Fractions

I can ...
use fraction strips, area models, or drawings to decompose fractions.

I can also model with math to solve problems.

How can you model the amount of chili Karyn puts in each bowl? *Show your work in the space below!*

Look Back! **Use Appropriate Tools** Use a drawing or fractions strips to help write equivalent fractions for the amount of chili in one of the bowls.

How Can You Represent a Fraction in a Variety of Ways?

A

Charlene wants to leave $\frac{1}{6}$ of her garden empty. What are some different ways Charlene can plant the rest of her garden?

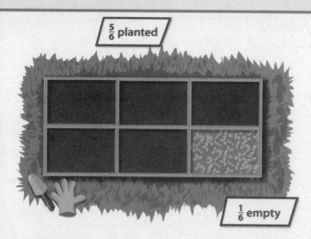

$\frac{5}{6}$ planted

$\frac{1}{6}$ empty

Decompose means to break into parts. Compose means to combine parts. The fraction of the garden that Charlene will plant can be decomposed in more than one way.

B **One Way**

Charlene could plant four $\frac{1}{6}$ sections with blue flowers and one $\frac{1}{6}$ section with red peppers.

$\frac{5}{6}$ is $\frac{4}{6}$ and $\frac{1}{6}$.

$$\frac{5}{6} = \frac{4}{6} + \frac{1}{6}$$

C **Another Way**

Charlene could plant one $\frac{1}{6}$ section with green beans, one $\frac{1}{6}$ section with yellow squash, one $\frac{1}{6}$ section with red peppers, and two $\frac{1}{6}$ sections with blue flowers.

$\frac{5}{6}$ is $\frac{1}{6}$ and $\frac{1}{6}$ and $\frac{1}{6}$ and $\frac{2}{6}$.

$$\frac{5}{6} = \frac{1}{6} + \frac{1}{6} + \frac{1}{6} + \frac{2}{6}$$

Convince Me! **Use Appropriate Tools** Draw pictures or use fraction strips to show why these equations are true.

$\frac{5}{6} = \frac{3}{6} + \frac{2}{6}$ $\frac{5}{6} = \frac{1}{6} + \frac{2}{6} + \frac{2}{6}$

Another Example! How can you decompose $3\frac{1}{8}$?

$3\frac{1}{8}$ is 1 whole + 1 whole + 1 whole + $\frac{1}{8}$.

Each whole can also be shown as eight equal parts.

$3\frac{1}{8} = 1 + 1 + 1 + \frac{1}{8}$

$3\frac{1}{8} = \frac{8}{8} + \frac{8}{8} + \frac{8}{8} + \frac{1}{8}$

A mixed number has a whole number part and a fraction part.

Guided Practice

Do You Understand?

1. **Model with Math** Draw a model to show one way to decompose $\frac{6}{8}$.

2. Sam said the sum of $\frac{2}{8} + \frac{3}{8} + \frac{4}{8}$ is the same as the sum of $\frac{1}{8} + \frac{4}{8} + \frac{4}{8}$. Is she correct? Explain.

Do You Know How?

For **3–4**, decompose each fraction or mixed number in two different ways. Use drawings or fraction strips as needed.

3. $\frac{3}{6} = \frac{\square}{\square} + \frac{\square}{\square}$ $\frac{3}{6} = \frac{\square}{\square} + \frac{\square}{\square} + \frac{\square}{\square}$

4. $1\frac{1}{5} = \frac{\square}{\square} + \frac{\square}{\square}$ $1\frac{1}{5} = \frac{\square}{\square} + \frac{\square}{\square}$

Independent Practice

Leveled Practice For **5–10**, decompose each fraction or mixed number in two different ways. Use drawings or fraction strips as needed.

5. $\frac{4}{10} = \frac{\square}{\square} + \frac{\square}{\square}$ $\frac{4}{10} = \frac{\square}{\square} + \frac{\square}{\square} + \frac{\square}{\square}$

6. $\frac{3}{7} = \frac{\square}{\square} + \frac{\square}{\square}$ $\frac{3}{7} = \frac{\square}{\square} + \frac{\square}{\square} + \frac{\square}{\square}$

7. $1\frac{3}{4} = \frac{\square}{\square} + \frac{\square}{\square}$ $1\frac{3}{4} = \frac{\square}{\square} + \frac{\square}{\square} + \frac{\square}{\square}$

8. $3\frac{1}{2} = \frac{\square}{\square} + \frac{\square}{\square}$ $3\frac{1}{2} = \frac{\square}{\square} + \frac{\square}{\square} + \frac{\square}{\square}$

9. $\frac{7}{8} =$ $\frac{7}{8} =$

10. $2\frac{1}{3} =$ $2\frac{1}{3} =$

Problem Solving

11. Mathew ate $\frac{3}{10}$ of a bag of popcorn. He shared the rest with Addison. List three ways they could have shared the remaining popcorn.

12. Model with Math Draw an area model to show $\frac{3}{8} + \frac{2}{8} + \frac{2}{8} = \frac{7}{8}$.

13. In a class of 16 students, 12 students are girls. Write two equivalent fractions that tell which part of the class is girls.

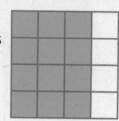

The area model shows 16 sections. Each section is $\frac{1}{16}$ of the class.

14. There were 56 girls and 71 boys at a school play. Each ticket to the play costs $8. How much were all the tickets to the performance?

15. Higher Order Thinking Jason wrote $1\frac{1}{2}$ as the sum of three fractions. None of the fractions had a denominator of 2. What fractions might Jason have used?

✔ Assessment

16. A teacher distributes a stack of paper to 3 groups. Each group received a different amount of paper. Select all the ways the teacher can distribute the paper by decomposing $1\frac{2}{8}$ inches. Use fraction strips if needed.

$1\frac{2}{8}$ inches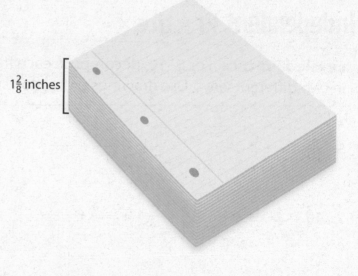

☐ $1 + \frac{1}{8} + \frac{1}{8}$

☐ $\frac{3}{8} + \frac{4}{8} + \frac{5}{8}$

☐ $\frac{1}{8} + \frac{1}{8} + \frac{1}{8} + \frac{1}{8} + \frac{1}{8} + \frac{1}{8} + \frac{1}{8} + \frac{1}{8}$

☐ $\frac{2}{8} + \frac{3}{8} + \frac{5}{8}$

☐ $1 + \frac{3}{6}$

Name _____

☆ ☆
Solve & Share

A right angle forms a square corner, like the one shown below. Draw two angles that are open less than the right angle. *Solve this problem any way you choose.*

I can ...
recognize and draw lines, rays, and angles with different names.

I can also reason about math.

You can use reasoning. The closer the sides of an angle, the smaller the angle measure. *Show your work in the space below!*

Look Back! **Reasoning** Draw an angle that is open more than a right angle.

Essential Question: **What Are Some Common Geometric Terms?**

A

Point, line, line segment, ray, right angle, acute angle, obtuse angle, and straight angle are common geometric terms.

Lines and parts of lines are named for their points. A ray is named with its endpoint first.

Geometric Term	Example	Label	What You Say
A point is an exact location in space.	•Z	Point Z	Point Z
A line is a straight path of points that goes on and on in opposite directions.	←•—•→ A B	$\overleftrightarrow{AB}$	Line AB
A line segment is a part of a line with two endpoints.	•—• G R	$\overline{GR}$	Line Segment GR
A ray is a part of a line that has one endpoint and continues on forever in one direction.	•—•→ N O	$\overrightarrow{NO}$	Ray NO

B An angle is formed by two rays that have the same endpoint.

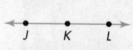

Angles are named with 3 letters. The shared endpoint of the rays is the center letter. The other letters represent points from each ray.

  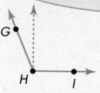

∠ABC is a right angle. A right angle forms a square corner.

∠DEF is an acute angle. An acute angle is open less than a right angle.

∠GHI is an obtuse angle. An obtuse angle is open more than a right angle but less than a straight angle.

∠JKL is a straight angle. A straight angle forms a straight line.

Convince Me! **Look for Relationships** Complete each figure to show the given angle.

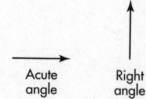

Obtuse angle   Straight angle   Acute angle   Right angle

Guided Practice

Do You Understand?

1. Be Precise What geometric term describes a part of a line that has two endpoints? Draw an example.

2. What geometric term describes part of a line that has only one endpoint? Draw an example.

3. Which geometric term describes an angle that forms a square corner? Draw an example.

Do You Know How?

For **4–7**, use geometric terms to describe what is shown.

4.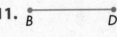

5.

6.

7.

Independent Practice

For **8–11**, use geometric terms to describe what is shown.

8.

9.

10.

11.

For **12–14**, use the diagram at the right.

12. Name 2 right angles.

13. Name four rays.

14. Name four line segments.

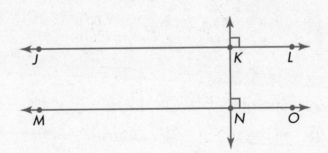

Problem Solving

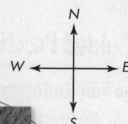

For **15–17**, use the map of Nevada. Write the geometric term that best fits each description. Draw an example.

15. Be Precise The route between 2 cities.

16. The cities

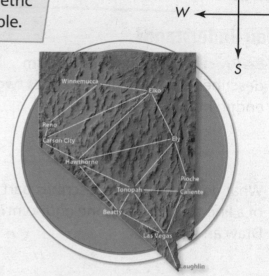

17. Where the north and east borders meet

---

18. **A-Z** **Vocabulary** Write a definition for *obtuse angle*. Draw an obtuse angle. Give 3 examples of obtuse angles in the classroom.

19. Higher Order Thinking Jarrett says he can make a right angle with an acute angle and an obtuse angle that have a common ray. Is Jarrett correct? Draw a picture and explain.

✓ Assessment

20. Which geometric term describes ∠*HJL*?

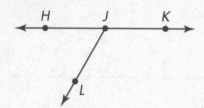

  Ⓐ Straight   Ⓒ Right

  Ⓑ Acute   Ⓓ Obtuse

21. Lou drew 2 rays that share an endpoint. Which of the following is Lou's drawing?

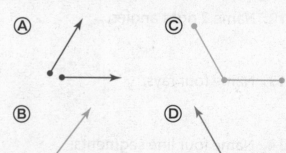

© Pearson Education, Inc. 3

Name _____

Solve & Share

If a clock shows it is 3 o'clock, how could you describe the smaller angle made by the two hands of the clock? **Solve this problem any way you choose.**

Solve

You can make sense of the problem by using what you know about acute, right, and obtuse angles. *Show your work in the space below!*

I can ...
use what I know about fractions to measure angles.

I can also make sense of problems.

Look Back! **Reasoning** What two fractions do the hands divide the clock into?

Essential Question **What is the Unit Used to Measure Angles?**

A

An angle is measured with units called degrees. An angle that turns through $\frac{1}{360}$ of a circle is called a unit angle . How can you determine the angle measure of a right angle and of angles that turn through $\frac{1}{6}$ and $\frac{2}{6}$ of a circle?

An angle that measures 1° is a unit angle or one-degree angle.

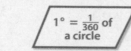

$1° = \frac{1}{360}$ of a circle

B Divide to find the angle measure of a right angle.

Right angles divide a circle into 4 equal parts.

$360° \div 4 = 90°$

The angle measure of a right angle is 90°.

C Multiply to find the measure of an angle that turns through $\frac{1}{6}$ of a circle.

Multiply by $\frac{1}{6}$ to calculate the angle measure.

$\frac{1}{6} \times 360° = \frac{360°}{6}$ or 60°

The angle measure is 60°.

D Add to find the measure of an angle that turns through $\frac{2}{6}$ of a circle.

$\frac{1}{6} = 60°$ $\frac{2}{6} = ?$

Remember that $\frac{2}{6} = \frac{1}{6} + \frac{1}{6}$. So you can add to calculate the measure of $\frac{2}{6}$ of a circle.

$60° + 60° = 120°$

The angle measure of $\frac{2}{6}$ of a circle is 120°.

Convince Me! **Critique Reasoning** Susan thinks the measure of angle *B* is greater than the measure of angle *A*. Do you agree? Explain.

Another Example!

Find the fraction of a circle that an angle with a measure of 45° turns through.

A 45° angle turns through $\frac{45}{360}$ of a circle.

$45° \times 8 = 360°$, so 45° is $\frac{1}{8}$ of 360°.

One 45° angle is $\frac{1}{8}$ of a circle.

$45° = \frac{1}{8}$ of a 360° circle

☆ Guided Practice

Do You Understand?

1. What fraction of the circle does a 90° angle turn through?

2. **Model with Math** Maya cuts a pie into 3 equal pieces. What is the angle measure of each piece? Write and solve an equation.

Do You Know How?

3. A circle is divided into 9 equal parts. What is the angle measure of one of those parts?

4. The angle turns through $\frac{1}{8}$ of the circle. What is the measure of this angle?

Independent Practice ☆

For **5–8**, find the measure of each angle.

5. The angle turns through $\frac{1}{10}$ of the circle.

6. The angle turns through $\frac{2}{5}$ of the circle.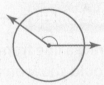

7. The angle turns through $\frac{1}{5}$ of the circle.

8. The angle turns through $\frac{3}{8}$ of the circle.

Problem Solving

9. **Reasoning** Use the clock to find the measure of the smaller angle formed by the hands at each time.

   a. 9:00

   b. 8:00

   c. 5:00

10. **Algebra** Natalie wrote an equation to find an angle measure. What do the unknowns a and b represent in Natalie's equation? $360° \div a = b$

11. **Math and Science** A mirror can be used to reflect a beam of light at an angle. What fraction of a circle would the angle shown turn through?

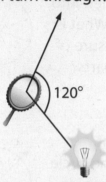

120°

12. David paid $421 for three plane tickets. One ticket cost $159. Another ticket cost $138. How much did the other ticket cost?

$421		
?	138	159

13. **Make Sense and Persevere** A pizza was cut into equal parts. Three pieces of the pizza were eaten. The 5 pieces that remained created an angle that measured 225°. What was the angle measure of one piece of pizza?

14. **Higher Order Thinking** Alexis cut a round cake into 12 equal pieces. 5 of the pieces were eaten. What is the angle measure of the cake that was left?

✓ **Assessment**

15. Draw a line from the time to the smaller angle the time would show on a clock. Use the clock to help.

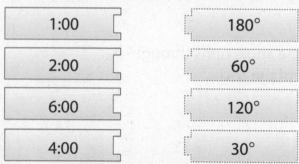

| 1:00 |
| 2:00 |
| 6:00 |
| 4:00 |

| 180° |
| 60° |
| 120° |
| 30° |

Solve

Lesson 10
Lines

Solve & Share

The number line below is an example of a line. A line goes on forever in a straight path in two directions. Draw the following pairs of lines: two lines that will never cross, two lines that cross at one point, two lines that cross at two points. If you cannot draw the lines, tell why.

I can ...
draw and identify perpendicular, parallel, and intersecting lines.

I can also be precise in my work.

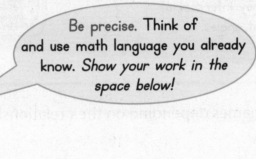

Be precise. Think of and use math language you already know. *Show your work in the space below!*

Look Back! **Be Precise** Terry said, "The lines shown intersect at three points." Is Terry correct? Explain.

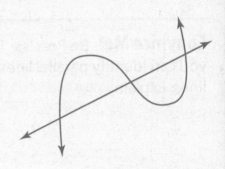

Essential Question **How Can You Describe Pairs of Lines?**

A

A line is a straight path of points that goes on and on in opposite directions. A pair of lines can be described as parallel, perpendicular, or intersecting.

Railroad tie

The railroad tracks in the picture are parallel because they never meet. The railroad ties are perpendicular to the railroad tracks because they intersect at right angles.

Railroad track

B Pairs of lines are given special names depending on their relationship.

Parallel lines
never intersect.

Intersecting lines
pass through the
same point.

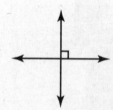

Perpendicular lines
are lines that form
right angles.

Convince Me! **Be Precise** Find examples in your classroom where you can identify parallel lines, intersecting lines, and perpendicular lines. Explain.

Tools Assessment

☆Guided Practice

Do You Understand?

1. **Be Precise** What geometric term could you use to describe the bottom edges that cross and make square corners in an aquarium?

2. What pair of lines looks like the blades of an open pair of scissors? Why?

Do You Know How?

For **3–6**, use the diagram.

3. Name four points.

4. Name four lines.

5. Name two pairs of parallel lines.

6. Name two pairs of perpendicular lines.

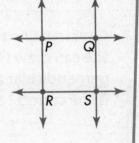

Independent Practice ☆

For **7–15**, use the best geometric terms to describe what is shown.

7.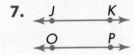

8.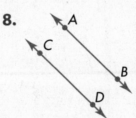

9.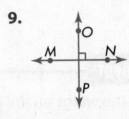

10. •Y

11.

12.

13.

14.

15.

Problem Solving

16. Construct Arguments Josh names this line $\overleftrightarrow{AC}$. Ava names the line $\overleftrightarrow{AB}$. Who is correct? Explain.

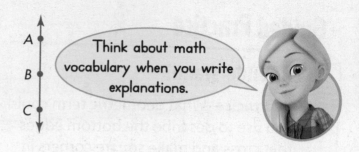

Think about math vocabulary when you write explanations.

17. Construct Arguments Josie says she can draw two lines that are both perpendicular and parallel to each other? Is she correct? Explain.

18. Model with Math Draw three lines so two of the lines intersect and the third line is perpendicular to one of the lines. The lines should meet at exactly one point. Label the lines with points.

19. Higher Order Thinking If all perpendicular lines are also intersecting lines, are all intersecting lines also perpendicular? Use the picture at the right to explain.

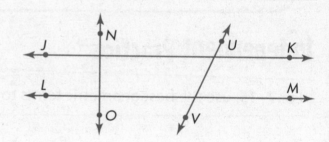

✓ Assessment

20. Look at the wings on the plane. Which geometric term would you use to describe them?

   Ⓐ Perpendicular lines

   Ⓑ Parallel lines

   Ⓒ Intersecting lines

   Ⓓ Plane

Glossary

A

A.M. The time between midnight and noon.

acute angle An angle that is open less than a right angle.

addends Numbers added together to give a sum.
Example: $2 + 7 = 9$

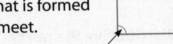

Addend   Addend

angle A figure that is formed where two sides meet.

angle measure The degrees of an angle.

area The number of unit squares needed to cover a region.

array A way of displaying objects in equal rows and columns.

Associative (Grouping) Property of Addition The grouping of addends can be changed and the sum will be the same.

Associative (Grouping) Property of Multiplication The grouping of factors can be changed and the product will be the same.

B

benchmark fraction A commonly used fraction such as $\frac{1}{4}, \frac{1}{3}, \frac{1}{2}, \frac{2}{3}$, and $\frac{3}{4}$.

C

capacity (liquid volume) The amount a container can hold measured in liquid units.

centimeter (cm) A metric unit of length.

column An arrangement of objects or numbers, one above another.

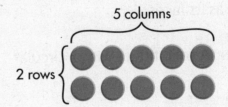

5 columns

2 rows

Commutative (Order) Property of Addition Numbers can be added in any order and the sum will be the same.

Commutative (Order) Property of Multiplication Numbers can be multiplied in any order and the product will be the same.

compare To decide if one number is greater than or less than another number.

compatible numbers Numbers that are easy to add, subtract, multiply, or divide mentally.

compensation Choosing numbers close to the numbers in a problem to make computation easier and then adjusting the answer for the numbers chosen.

compose To combine different parts.

conjecture A statement that is believed to be true, but it has not been proven.

cone A solid figure with a circle as its base and a curved surface that meets at a point.

cube A solid figure with 6 same-size squares as its faces.

cylinder A solid figure with 2 circular bases.

data Pieces of information.

decompose Breaking a number into parts.
Example: $\frac{2}{5}$ can be broken into $\frac{1}{5} + \frac{1}{5}$.

degrees (°) A unit of measure for angles.

denominator The number below the fraction bar in a fraction, which shows the total number of equal parts.

difference The answer when subtracting one number from another.

digits The symbols 0, 1, 2, 3, 4, 5, 6, 7, 8, and 9 used to write numbers.

Distributive Property A multiplication fact can be broken apart into the sum of two other multiplication facts.
Example: $5 \times 4 = (2 \times 4) + (3 \times 4)$

dividend The number to be divided.
Example: $63 \div 9 = 7$
↑
Dividend

division An operation that tells how many equal groups there are or how many are in each group.

divisor The number by which another number is divided.
Example: $63 \div 9 = 7$

Divisor

dollar sign A symbol ($) used to indicate money.

E

edge A line segment where 2 faces meet in a solid figure.

eighth One of 8 equal parts of a whole.

elapsed time The total amount of time that passes from the starting time to the ending time.

equal (equality) When the two sides of an equation have the same value.

equal groups Groups that have the same number of items.

equation A number sentence that uses an equal sign (=) to show that the value on its left side is the same as the value on its right side.

equilateral triangle A triangle with all sides the same length.

equivalent fractions Fractions that name the same part of a whole or the same location on a number line.

estimate To give an approximate number or answer.

even number A whole number that can be divided by 2 with none left over.

expanded form A number written as the sum of the values of its digits.
Example: $476 = 400 + 70 + 6$

F

face A flat surface of a solid that cannot roll.

fact family A group of related facts using the same numbers.

factors Numbers that are multiplied together to give a product.
Example: $7 \times 3 = 21$

Factor   Factor

foot (ft) A customary unit of length. 1 foot equals 12 inches.

fourth One of 4 equal parts of a whole.

fraction A symbol, such as $\frac{1}{2}$, used to name a part of a whole, a part of a set, or a location on a number line.

frequency table A table used to show the number of times something occurs.

gram (g) A metric unit of mass, the amount of matter in an object.

half (halves) One of 2 equal parts of a whole.

half hour A unit of time equal to 30 minutes.

hexagon A polygon with 6 sides.

hour A unit of time equal to 60 minutes.

Identity (Zero) Property of Addition The sum of any number and zero is that same number.

Identity (One) Property of Multiplication The product of any number and 1 is that number.

inch (in.) A customary unit of length.

intersecting lines Lines that cross at one point.

inverse operations Two operations that undo each other.

key The explanation for what each symbol represents in a pictograph.

kilogram (kg) A metric unit of mass, the amount of matter in an object. One kilogram equals 1,000 grams.

kilometer (km) A metric unit of length. One kilometer equals 1,000 meters.

line A straight path of points that is endless in both directions.

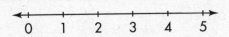

line plot A way to organize data on a number line.

line segment A part of a line that has 2 endpoints.

liter (L) A metric unit of capacity. One liter equals 1,000 milliliters.

mass A measure of the amount of matter in an object.

meter (m) A metric unit of length. One meter equals 100 centimeters.

mile (mi) A customary unit of length. One mile equals 5,280 feet.

milliliter (mL) A metric unit of capacity.

millimeter (mm) A metric unit of length. 1,000 millimeters = 1 meter.

minute A unit of time equal to 60 seconds.

mixed number A number with a whole number part and a fraction part. *Example:* $2\frac{3}{4}$

multiple The product of a given whole number and any non-zero whole number. *Example:* 4, 8, 12, and 16 are multiples of 4.

multiplication An operation that gives the total number when you join equal groups.

nearest fourth inch A measurement that ends with a $\frac{1}{4}$, $\frac{2}{4}$, $\frac{3}{4}$, or full inch.

nearest half inch A measurement that ends with a $\frac{1}{2}$ or full inch.

not equal When two sides of a number sentence do not have the same value.

number line A line that shows numbers in order using a scale. *Example:*

numerator The number above the fraction bar in a fraction, which shows how many equal parts are described.

obtuse angle An angle that is open more than a right angle.

octagon A polygon with 8 sides.

odd number A whole number that cannot be divided by 2 with none left over.

open number line A number line which only displays the numbers being computed.

order To arrange numbers from least to greatest or from greatest to least.

ounce (oz) A customary unit of weight.

P.M. The time between noon and midnight.

parallel lines Lines that never cross each other.

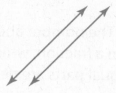

parallel sides Sides of a polygon that go in the exact same direction; if the sides cross when they are made longer, they are not parallel.

parallelogram A quadrilateral with 2 pairs of parallel sides.

pentagon A polygon with 5 sides.

perimeter The distance around a figure.

perpendicular lines Two intersecting lines that form right angles.

pint (pt) A customary unit of capacity. One pint equals 2 cups.

place value The value given to the place a digit has in a number.
Example: In 946, the place value of the digit 9 is *hundreds*.

point An exact position often marked by a dot.

polygon A closed figure made up of straight line segments.

pound (lb) A customary unit of weight. One pound equals 16 ounces.

product The answer to a multiplication problem.

quadrilateral A polygon with 4 sides.

quart (qt) A customary unit of capacity. One quart equals 2 pints.

quarter hour A unit of time equal to 15 minutes.

quotient The answer to a division problem.

ray A part of a line that has one endpoint and continues endlessly in one direction.

rectangle A parallelogram with 4 right angles.

rectangular prism A solid figure with 6 rectangular faces.

regroup (regrouping) To name a whole number in a different way.
Example: 28 = 1 ten 18 ones

remainder The number that is left over after dividing.
Example: 31 ÷ 7 = 4 R3
↑
Remainder

rhombus A parallelogram with all sides the same length.

right angle An angle that forms a square corner.

round To replace a number with a number that tells about how much or how many to the nearest ten, hundred, thousand, and so on.
Example: 42 rounded to the nearest 10 is 40.

row An arrangement of objects or numbers, one to the side of another.

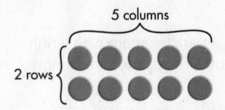

5 columns

2 rows

scale The numbers that show the units used on a graph.

scaled bar graph a graph that uses bars to show data.

scaled picture graph a graph that uses pictures to show data.

second A unit of time. 60 seconds equal 1 minute.

side A line segment forming part of a polygon.

sixth One of 6 equal parts of a whole.

solid figure A figure that has length, width, and height.

sphere A solid figure in the shape of a ball.

square A parallelogram with 4 right angles and all sides the same length.

square unit A measure of area.

standard form A way to write a number showing only its digits.
Example: 845

straight angle An angle that forms a straight line.

sum The answer to an addition problem.

survey To collect information by asking a number of people the same question and recording their answers.

tally mark A mark used to record data on a tally chart.
Example: 𝍅 = 5

third One of 3 equal parts of a whole.

time interval An amount of time.

trapezoid A quadrilateral with only one pair of parallel sides.

triangle A polygon with 3 sides.

triangular prism A solid figure with two triangular faces.

unit angle An angle with a measurement of 1 degree.

unit fraction A fraction representing one part of a whole that has been divided into equal parts; it always has a numerator of 1.

unit square a square with sides 1 unit long, used to measure area.

unknown A symbol that stands for a number in an equation.

vertex of a polygon The point where two sides of a polygon meet.

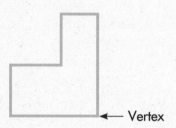

← Vertex

week A unit of time equal to 7 days.

weight A measure of how heavy an object is.

word form A number written in words. *Example:* 325 = three hundred twenty-five

yard (yd) A customary unit of length. One yard equals 3 feet or 36 inches.

Zero Property of Multiplication The product of any number and zero is zero.

enVisionmath 2.0
SCOTT FORESMAN · ADDISON WESLEY

Photographs

Every effort has been made to secure permission and provide appropriate credit for photographic material. The publisher deeply regrets any omission and pledges to correct errors called to its attention in subsequent editions.

Unless otherwise acknowledged, all photographs are the property of Pearson Education, Inc.

Photo locators denoted as follows: Top (T), Center (C), Bottom (B), Left (L), Right (R), Background (Bkgd)

F34 Eric Isselée/Fotolia; **001** Gemenacom/Shutterstock; **008** Pearson Education; **028** Corbis; **032** Pearson Education; **034** Pearson Education; **03?** Pearson Education; **057** Jacek Chabraszewski/F?; **068** Pearson Education; **070** Pearson Educa?? ?74L Pearson Education; **074R** Pearson Educa?? ?74T Pearson Education; **092** Pearson Edu??n; **105** pk7comcastnet/Fotolia; **122** Pears? ?ducation; **130** Pearson Education; **134** Pearson F?ucation; **165** Christopher Dodge/Shutterstoc?? ?76L Pearson Education; **176R** Pearson Educ?.ion; **176T** Pearson Education; **182** Pearson Educa?.on; **184** Pearson Education; **188B** Pearson Ed??ation; **188T** Pearson Education; **200** Pearson Education; **208** Pearson Education; **297** Marques/Shutterstock; **355** Barbara Helgason/Fotolia; **401** Erni/Shutterstock; **418** Pearson Education; **430** Pearson Education; **436** Corbis; **454** Pearson Education; **456** Rabbit75_fot/Fotolia; **471** Arnold John Labrentz/ShutterStock; **488** KennStilger47/Shutterstock; **494B** imagebroker/Alamy; **494TL** hotshotsworldwide/Fotolia; **494TR** imagebroker/Alamy; **496B** Pearson Education; **496T** John Luke/Index open; **508** David R. Frazier Photolibrary/Alamy; **535** Sam D'Cruz/Fotolia; **542** Palou/Fotolia; **571** Nancy Gill/ShutterStock; **582** Pearson Education; **588** Pearson Education; **605** B.G. Smith/Shutterstock; **669** Cathy Keifer/ShutterStock;

733 Pearson Education; **742B** Getty Images; **742C** Pearson Education; **742T** Getty Images; **758B** Pearson Education; **758C** Pearson Education; **758T** Pearson Education; **759BL** Pearson Education; **759BR** Pearson Education; **759CL** Pearson Education; **759CR** Pearson Education; **759TL** photolibrary/Photos to go; **759TR** Simple Stock Shot; **760BR** Simple Stock Shot; **760T** Pearson Education; **768** Jenoe/Foto?a; **770B** Pearson Education; **770T** Pearson Educati?n; **771BL** Jupiter Images; **771BR** Pearson Educat?.n; **771CL** Getty Images; **771CR** Pearson Edu??ion; **771TR** Stockdisc/Punch Stock; **772** Pea??? ?ducation; **805** Amy Myers/Shutterstock; **84?** ?otocreo Bednarek/Fotolia; **856** Jupiterimages?.hinkStock; **912** Pearson Education; **916** Olek? ?gitov/ShutterStock; **932** Photos to go.